Strategic Purchasing and Supply Chain Management

Second Edition

MALCOLM SAUNDERS

THE
CHARTERED INSTITUTE OF
PURCHASING & SUPPLY

Prentice Hall
FINANCIAL TIMES

An imprint of Pearson Education
Harlow, England • London • New York • Boston • San Francisco • Toronto
Sydney • Tokyo • Singapore • Hong Kong • Seoul • Taipei • New Delhi
Cape Town • Madrid • Mexico City • Amsterdam • Munich • Paris • Milan

To my wife, Thelma,
and to Caroline and Graham

Pearson Education Limited
Edinburgh Gate
Harlow
Essex CM20 2JE
England

and Associated Companies throughout the world

Visit us on the World Wide Web at:
http://www.pearsoneduc.com

First published in Great Britain in 1994
Second edition published 1997

© Malcolm Saunders 1997

The right of Malcolm Saunders to be identified as Author
of this Work has been asserted by him in accordance
with the Copyright, Designs and Patents Act 1988.

ISBN 0 273 62382 6

British Library Cataloguing in Publication Data
A CIP catalogue record for this book can be obtained from the British Library

10
07 06 05 04 03

Typeset by M Rules
Printed and bound in Great Britain by Bell and Bain Ltd, Glasgow

CONTENTS

management in the context of business and corporate strategy •
Summary • Notes and references

PREFACE

Introduction

During the three years since the first edition of this book was published, there has been a continuing interest in the way in which organisations should and do manage the flow of supplies which are required by themselves and, where appropriate, by their customers. This interest has been manifested in developments both in practice and in ideas which have been published and made available in the public domain. The authors of these publications come from many different areas – not just those identified specifically with the field of purchasing and supply. Authors from other business and management fields and also across the spectrum of academic disciplines in both the areas of social sciences and technology/engineering have commented on supply issues, studied for many different purposes. Within this rapidly-expanding body of knowledge, particular attention has been given to *strategically managing* the flow of supplies – the theme of this book. Accounts relating to this theme have added to our understanding from both a theoretical and a practical point of view, and are relevant, hopefully, to both students and practitioners.

The structure of the first edition appears to have been satisfactory in encompassing the diversity of ideas regarding the strategic management of purchasing and supply. Therefore, no major restructuring, in terms of the themes of the Parts and chapters, was thought to be necessary. Many readers of the first edition have commented kindly that this first book to tackle the subject area from a strategic point of view successfully filled a gap in the literature. It provided a basis for forming perspectives of the subject to guide strategic actions at levels of both the total supply requirements of the organisation and also of individual items or of groups of similar commodities.

However, a second edition is necessary, to reflect recent developments. Thus, within the original basic framework, additions and amendments have been made. These will be identified in more detail later in this Preface. Before doing so, it will be helpful to look at some of the significant themes which have been identified and developed in the literature since the first edition of this book was published in 1994. Some of these topics simply add emphasis, and further comments and insights, on issues that were mentioned in the previous edition.

Purchasing and supply issues

1 Ideas about the strategic management of supplies, embracing both theoretical and practical treatments, have continued to develop. There have been discussions about the enhancement of the function from, historically, a perspective that was more operationally oriented to one in which there is a need to manage supply affairs strategically as well. A strategic perspective shifts

the emphasis away from procedures and techniques associated with basic purchasing and supply transactions and places more emphasis on managing the supply of 'external resources'. The objective might be to improve the capability of the organisation to satisfy the needs of its own customers and, at the same time, meet its own financial goals.

2 The importance of managing supplies strategically is viewed from both the business and the corporate point of view and the ways that the management of supplies can impact on the performance of the organisation as a whole have been further elaborated. In the case of firms in the private sector, this contribution, perceived in terms of such criteria as quality, delivery, cost and flexibility, is advocated as making an impact on the competitive capability of the firm to meet customer requirements and match, if not beat, their competitors. In the public sector, demands placed upon organisations to perform more effectively and efficiently have also fed through to the need to improve the management of processes involved in the acquisition and provision of goods and services, both for internal consumption and for 'clients' and 'customers'. Notions about 'adding value' and 'removal of waste' are held to have applications in both sectors and additions have been made to the list of ideas on how these goals might be achieved.

3 It follows that the planning and control of purchasing and supply activities need to be linked to processes connected to the strategic management of the organisation as a whole. Ideas continue to evolve concerning strategic management at functional, business unit and corporate levels.

4 These developments add to the scope and status of the function and require staff of a higher calibre, in terms of knowledge and skills, who can think and act at a strategic level and communicate with personnel in other functions and at high levels in the management structure.

5 While the previous points focus on purchasing and supply and its position within the organisation of which it is a constituent part, other developments in thinking apply to the external interfaces and relationships with the wider business environment. The positioning of the organisation and the relationships it has with others, especially as customers or suppliers, are topics which have occupied much space in recent publications. An important trend in this respect has been the advocacy of more holistic views about supply systems which extend beyond the direct interfaces that an individual organisation has with others. There has been debate on policy guidelines for ways through which the interests of the firm and the 'extended enterprise' or 'lean enterprise'[1] can be pursued. The fashion for 'outsourcing', of both goods and services, which seems to be apparent in the 1990s in both private and public sector organisations, is increasing further the importance of external sources of supply and adding to the interdependent nature of businesses. The destiny of an individual organisation is only in part dependent on the values and costs generated internally. It is also determined by the effectiveness and efficiency of other organisations involved in the supply system.

6 Many authors have considered the issue of types of relationships with external suppliers. It seems clear that there is no 'one right way' and there is a

need to develop a portfolio of approaches which combine different amounts of *competitive pressure*, on the one hand, and elements of *co-operation* or *collaboration*, on the other.

7 Considerations of collaboration and relationships with other organisations have raised questions about whether legal contracts can be relied on as the best way to co-ordinate flows of supplies. Do other less formal approaches allow a more fluid approach to the dynamic development of arrangements? Public sector changes and private sector interest in adopting or adapting Japanese approaches have led to investigations and re-evaluations of these issues.

8 While these developments in thinking have contributed to greater under-standing of what practitioners are doing and what they might consider as possibilities, they have also contributed to a problem that has been associated with purchasing and supply for many years. There have been difficulties in identifying the scope of the field (in terms of the range of activities to be included) and the labels which should be used to delineate the area. These labels have mostly tended to be concerned with organisational structures and the division of activities into different groupings – hence the use of terms such as purchasing, purchasing and supply, materials management and logistics management. Neologisms, such as supply chain management, supplier management, supply base management and network sourcing, have been introduced into both everyday speech and publications, each apparently representing some innovation in approach and method. Other terms, such as value streams, value chains or systems, supply chains, supply networks, extended enterprise and virtual corporations, have also come in. These terms tend to lack commonly accepted definitions and the problem of ambiguity is compounded by the fact that users do not always make clear the meaning they attach to these terms, and sometimes use them inconsistently. Understanding is thereby diminished rather than enhanced, and confusion, rather than clarity, clouds communications. (In the first edition of this book the terms purchasing and supply management and purchasing and supply chain management were used more or less interchangeably, and, in general, the problem of terminology was not given adequate attention. An attempt to remedy this has been made in this edition – *see* Appendix to Chapter 1.) A contributing factor to this general problem is the need to take into account the context in which purchasing and supply issues are located.

Contextual issues

1 A problem that has become more apparent in recent debates about supplies issues is that, while it is useful to develop ideas for general application, it is also necessary to pay attention to particular contexts in which they are to be applied. There is perhaps scope for an intermediate position, between treating each situation as unique, requiring its own unique solutions, and regarding all situations as identical, to which universally applicable approaches can be implemented. Thus, what might be appropriate for the

automotive industry in controlling the flow of parts for production might not be suitable for other types of supplies or in other industries or sectors of the economy.

2 Changes in ideas about purchasing and supply matters need to be appreciated against a backcloth of changing ideas about management and organisation as they affect both the private and the public sector. The implications of these changes for specialist functions have become clearer as programmes to improve performance have been implemented. These include such features as reducing layers in the hierarchical pyramid, introducing cross-functional teams, pushing responsibility for decision making and for introducing ideas for improvement to lower levels and changing the boundaries of organisations through outsourcing. Initiatives associated with 'New Management' in the public sector (at least in the United Kingdom), have introduced a more commercial orientation as a counterbalance to previous bureaucratic and professional approaches. Methods, such as market testing, purchasing within internal markets and agency forms of control, and the accent on value for money and quality of service, have brought a degree of convergence in managerial approaches adopted in public and private sector organisations.

3 Except for people who are starting up new businesses or new business units on a 'greenfield' site, different organisations start from different positions, which have emerged from past actions and events. Programmes for change, though guided by visions of directions of development for the future, must, nevertheless, take account of history and an organisation's current position. Ideas in the literature are frequently presented in a vacuum, both temporally and contextually.

Implications for strategic purchasing and supply management

The boundaries between functions or departments inside organisations and those between firms competing in both supply and customer markets have become somewhat blurred. Acceptance of this view means that it is harder to define clearly the roles and responsibilities of specialists and 'professionals' as they become involved in cross-functional organisational units and cross-organisational groups or 'quasi-organisations', as well as in project or multi-functional teams. It also raises questions of how far the specialist function delegates operational tasks (in particular) to others and how far it leads other functional representatives in teams in the strategic management of supplies. (This is a problem not only for purchasing and supply, but also for other functions.) In a changing organisational environment, in which the barriers between the functions are being lowered and more attention is being focused on cross-functional processes, the role of specialist departments is more open to question.

Paradoxically, there is a view that the more important purchasing and supply issues are seen to be, the less they can be managed solely within a tightly demarcated department. Purchasing and supply matters become a wider corporate concern and it is argued that others need to be involved in managing them. Therefore, personnel from other areas of an organisation may need to be conversant with progressive ideas about the management of supplies. Specialists may, thus, become involved in increasing the awareness of other personnel about 'best practice' and in shaping the ways through which they might participate.

The views of purchasing and supply that are emerging indicate that there are problems involving not only traditional procedures and techniques (in a rational, technical and economic sense). Increasingly, supply problems are being perceived as involving interpersonal relationships. The social nature of supply processes can, therefore, involve questions of how to build shared understanding and commitments to agreements of possible ways of proceeding. In addition, issues such as power, mutual interest and trust may arise in attempts to establish effective arrangements.

Changes in the second edition

The changes made to this book, for the second edition, are as follows:

1 Sections have been added:
   - To analyse more deeply problems of 'making sense' of purchasing and supply. The Appendix to Chapter 1 examines the range of terms and 'models' and provides a guide to assessing these and constructing a framework to suit individual purposes. Some readers may wish to return to this Appendix after reading other parts of the book, as it introduces some points that are discussed in more detail in later chapters.
   - To extend the consideration of decision-making theories, to consider perspectives based on different levels of complexity – *see* Chapter 3.
2 Improvements have been made to the layout of material and diagrams have been added to help readers find their way through the structure of the book.
3 Throughout, comments are made about recently published works which have added to theoretical and empirical knowledge.
4 The Notes and References at the ends of chapters incorporate the more recent publications mentioned in the text and the Further Reading list has been extended accordingly.
5 A guide to the topics covered by the Case studies which make up Chapter 12 has been added at the beginning of the chapter. In addition, suggested questions for consideration are included at the end of each case.
6 Additional emphasis has been placed on some topics, such as:
   - Information systems (in Chapter 5)
   - Strategies with regard to the provision of logistics services (in Chapter 7)
   - Core competence and capabilities in business strategy (in Chapter 3)
   - Human resources aspects in manufacturing systems (in Chapter 4)

Concluding comments

The field of strategic thinking and strategic management, both for businesses as a whole and for specialist functions, including purchasing and supply is continuing to pass through a period of transition in which ideas are still evolving. As suggested in the first edition of this book, the changes may be seen later as more of a revolution in ways of conducting business – a paradigmatic change – than as incremental modifications within an established framework. Readers might like to form their own views as they read this book. It is not intended to be a simple 'how to do it' type of book with checklists of actions. Strategic thinking requires a more sophisticated assessment of actual situations and of a wide repertoire of action possibilities before any possible actions can be formulated and agreed upon.

Malcolm Saunders
Coventry Business School
Coventry University

NOTES AND REFERENCES

1 The term 'lean enterprise' can be found, for example, in Womack, J.P. and Jones, D.T., 'From Lean Production to Lean Enterprise', *Harvard Business Review*, March–April 1994, pp. 93–103. The terms 'extended enterprise' and 'lean enterprise' are used to denote a group of companies in a supply chain which are responsible, collectively, for making a product and its main constituent elements. Aspects of 'lean' production and 'lean' supply are discussed further in Chapter 1 and Chapter 2.

PLAN OF THE BOOK

CHAPTER 1
Introduction

PART ONE

Environmental change and strategic requirements

CHAPTER 2 Changes in environmental conditions and their impact on business	CHAPTER 3 Approaches to strategic management
CHAPTER 4 From corporate strategy to purchasing and supply chain management strategy	CHAPTER 5 The content of supply chain management strategies

---

PART TWO

The implications of purchasing and supply chain management strategies

CHAPTER 6 Strategic management of quality	CHAPTER 7 Strategic management of material flow	CHAPTER 8 Strategic management of costs and added value
CHAPTER 9 Strategic management of supplier relationships		CHAPTER 10 Strategic management of human resources in the supply chain
CHAPTER 11 Conclusions		CHAPTER 12 Case studies

CHAPTER 1

Introduction

Purchasing and supply can no longer be treated as a second-order function. The way forward lies with integrated materials management, pulling together suppliers, production and distribution. In the years ahead, those who have not got their purchasing and supply operations right will not be competitive.

This quotation has not been taken from somebody inside the purchasing profession who feels that the function is being treated as a Cinderella activity and is not being given the prominence it deserves. It is extracted from a booklet published by the Department for Enterprise (Department of Trade and Industry), and is one of the 'Managing into the '90s' programmes as part of the Enterprise Initiative campaign.[1]

'Purchasing and supply', together with 'design', 'quality' and 'production', was an area singled out as needing publicity to foster the adoption of strategic approaches in order to improve overall competitiveness of industry. The booklet is illustrative, therefore, of the need to design and implement strategic approaches in purchasing and supply management. Although it is aimed at the private sector, the same message can be adapted to meet the needs of improving efficiency and effectiveness in public sector organisations as well.

The same booklet lists eight key questions and it is worth listing them, as they help to lead into the subject matter of this book. They are aimed particularly at practitioners in the field, both inside and outside the function:

1 Are you underrating the importance of purchasing and supply to your business?
2 How good is your purchasing and supply operation?
3 Do you have a strategic approach to purchasing and supply?
4 Have you allocated purchasing and supply the resources they need for their strategic role?
5 Are your relationships with suppliers co-operative rather than adversarial?
6 Do purchasing and supply integrate with other disciplines?
7 Can you improve your purchasing effectiveness?
8 How can you move towards a more strategic and integrated approach to purchasing and supply?

THE TERM 'PURCHASING AND SUPPLY' IN THIS BOOK

What ideas about the content have been triggered off in the minds of readers by the title of this book, 'Strategic Purchasing and Supply Chain Management'? Do they match the intentions of the author? The choice of words to form the title of a book is a difficult matter and its effect can be quite significant. The title is the first thing likely to catch the eye of potential buyers and readers and it can help to shape expectations as to whether the book is likely to be relevant and useful. The phrase created, therefore, needs to capture and describe the content of the book as accurately and as succinctly as possible. One of the purposes of this Introduction is to analyse and describe the book's content in more detail, by giving an outline of the overall structure and of the topics in each chapter. Clearly, other promotional material and additional information on the book's cover may have assisted already in giving a clearer indication of what to expect.

The phrase in the title that can lead to different interpretations is 'purchasing and supply', as it can be used as a label to cover different groups or lists of activities. Argument and confusion over both terms and content has arisen and has caused much heated conflict. Purchasing, procurement, stores management and stock control, materials management, logistics management, physical distribution management, and supply chain management are other terms that might have been considered. Much time has been taken up in debating these issues by both writers and practitioners, and the lack of common agreement has held back the formation of a united image which can be communicated to those in other business functions. There may be many definitions of the word 'marketing', but at least there is unanimity in using the label. The positive outcome of the discussions of the appropriateness of particular labels is that the debates have enriched understanding of both particular activities and also the possibilities of their combination within more integrated control mechanisms. Naturally, the development and implementation of strategies for purchasing and supply management will need to include decisions that delineate the area to be encompassed by them. For the moment, it is as well to note two points.

The first point is to draw a distinction between activities and departments or functions. Activities are tasks that have to be undertaken in an organisation, irrespective of any particular departmental grouping. A department or function is a structure that may have been created and labelled to provide a way of identifying, grouping and allocating responsibilities to personnel for carrying out those activities. A broad view of the range of activities involved in managing the flow of products, materials and services is adopted in this book. The advantages and disadvantages of different organisational arrangements for co-ordinating them will be investigated as well.

Second, this catholic view of the field, to be encompassed by the phrase 'purchasing and supply', seems to be in line with the philosophy of the Chartered Institute of Purchasing and Supply. Different types of organisation or business can be involved in purchasing and supply activities, but not necessarily in all the same ones, and they may have created different organisational arrangements to cope with them. The view that there is no single right way suitable for all of them is one that can be strongly defended. However, an important feature of current thinking is recognition of the interdependency of many of these activities and the need to consider the impact of decisions and actions in one point of the supply chain both on other activities elsewhere and on the performance of the supply chain as a whole. Matters concerning both the structural division of tasks and mechanisms of integration are strategic issues which receive further attention in later parts of the book.

In conducting its work on developing Standards of Competence for purchasing, the Purchasing and Supply Lead Body developed a 'Functional Map of the Purchasing and Supply Chain'.[2]

The key purpose suggested for the purchasing and supply chain is:

> Provide the interface between customer and supplier in order to plan, obtain, store and distribute as necessary, supplies of materials, goods and services to enable the organisation to satisfy its external and internal customers. (page 30)

The definition continues by listing major functions, as follows:

1 Contribute to the formulation, communication and implementation of policies, strategies and plans.
2 Contribute to the establishment and improvement of purchasing related systems.
3 Establish and maintain a database of purchasing and stores information.
4 Establish and develop sources of supply.
5 Acquire supplies.
6 Provide goods and materials to internal and external customers through storage, movement, distribution and transport.
7 Monitor and control the purchasing, supply, storage, distribution and transport chain.
8 Contribute to effective working.

This map, produced by the Lead Body, provides a useful picture of the activities that will generally be the basis for strategic consideration in this book. Incidentally, it might also be added that all of the eight points above were broken down into further subdivisions, showing purposes decomposed into finer levels of detail.

It may be noted that there is no reference to production planning and control in the above picture, an area of activity that is often included in materials management or logistics management definitions. However, when purchasing and supply management is being discussed in relation to manufacturing firms, production planning and control issues will be brought into the perspective.

The Appendix at the end of this Chapter considers problems of meaning in more detail.

OBJECTIVES OF THIS CHAPTER

Now that the parameters of the functional area have been established as a basis for directing discourse throughout the book, attention will be switched to specific objectives to be covered in this introductory chapter. (In each of the subsequent chapters, also, an outline of its key objectives to be pursued is given.)

1 To identify the varying nature of purchasing and supply management in different types of organisation
2 To introduce the main themes in purchasing and supply management that form the basis of strategic planning and analysis considerations
3 To reassess the significance of purchasing and supply management with regard to the parent organisations in which it might reside
4 To consider purchasing and supply as a 'learning process'
5 To provide an outline of the rest of the book

THE VARYING NATURE OF PURCHASING AND SUPPLY MANAGEMENT

Earlier discussion has borrowed a generic definition of the purchasing and supply chain from the Purchasing and Supply Lead Body. However, practitioners are often quick to point out that not all organisations operate in the same way and can be different 'animals'. It is necessary to reflect on these differences as a means of understanding different viewpoints which can arise partly as a result of experiences gained in different types of supply chain. The heat can often be taken out of fierce arguments when these differences are recognised. However, just as there are dangers in treating every situation as the same, there are equally faults in treating every situation as being totally different and requiring its own prescriptions. There is a middle ground of tailoring strategies to the salient contingent features in each case. The question then arises as to what are the main characteristics that might allow differentiated perspectives to be constructed. Though not necessarily exhaustive, the following will be put forward as candidates for consideration:

1 Primary function of the organisation and its impact on types of resource needs and their relative importance.
2 Size.
3 Complexity in relation to product and geographical spread.
4 Ownership type – public or private sector.
5 'Market' or 'non-market' mode of operation.

However, before turning to the first item, it is helpful to construct a table that lists different types of resource needs (*see* Table 1.1). Each type of need generates different problem characteristics and demands some differences in knowledge, skills, procedures, information requirements and techniques. Strategic management of the function needs to take note of them.

Other characteristics, such as degree of risk, degree of uncertainty or relative expenditure, may need to be evaluated when developing strategic supply plans for individual items or groups of items. The idea of managing a portfolio of different types of products and services, each requiring different approaches, emerges from this point.

Table 1.1 Characteristics of resource needs

Type of resource	Type of expenditure	Terminal point of supply chain	Life of product
Inputs to production	Revenue	External customer	Short – used quickly
Capital equipment	Capital	Internal	Long
Consumables/MRO	Revenue	Internal	Short – used quickly
Goods for resale	Revenue	External customer	Short – sold quickly
Services	Revenue	Internal	Cannot be stored

Primary functions of different types of organisation

Four different types of organisation are depicted, based on differences in their primary function:

1 Primary sector – extractive organisations
2 Secondary sector – manufacturing organisations
3 Tertiary sector – wholesale or retail organisations
4 Tertiary sector – service providers

Extractive organisations

The main task of such organisations is that of extracting a product or material, which already exists in a state of nature, such as the mining of ores or the extraction of crude oil.

The key resource requirements, which will be the main preoccupation of purchasing and supply, are likely to be those of capital equipment and consumables or maintenance, repair and operating (MRO) supplies.

Manufacturing organisations

The key function in this category of organisations is to process, shape, form, transform, convert, fabricate or assemble materials, parts, components and subassemblies into finished or intermediate products for sale to external customers. It is tempting to treat this category as being homogeneous based on this simple definition. However, experience and theory suggests that there are subdivisions, though there are different classifications upon which these might be based, and that these should be reflected in the formation of corporate strategy, as well as supporting manufacturing and purchasing and supply strategies.

Process types

One frequently mentioned scheme is that discussed by Terry Hill.[3] Five different process types are:

1 Project
2 Jobbing unit or one-off
3 Batch
4 Line
5 Continuous processing

Such a scheme takes into account variations in the volume, continuity and variety of products being manufactured. Different patterns, based upon these characteristics, can also be expected to influence the nature of purchasing and supply work and the requirements of the upstream supply chain in feeding the necessary material inputs into the manufacturing stage.

Factory layouts

From a material control point of view and from the point of view of the interface with purchasing and supply, it is useful to consider another way in which manufacturing contexts might vary. The main principles, which have been identified as guides to the design of factory layouts, are embodied in the following four approaches:

1 Fixed position – all resources, including workers, machinery and equipment and materials, are brought to the fixed location where the product is to be built.
2 Functional or process layout – the factory is divided up into separate areas or work centres, each of which specialises in a type of process.
3 Line or flow process – materials pass in a fixed sequence through a series of processes, sometimes dedicated to particular products.
4 Cellular manufacturing or group technology – separate work centres are established, each with a self-sufficient group of workers and equipment to make specialised 'families' of parts or products.

Factory layouts can affect the performance of the following factors:

1 Level of inventory and work in process
2 Frequency and complexity of materials handling activities
3 Individual task and total job cycle times
4 Scope of the factory, in terms of product range, volume and flexibility
5 Level of skills and degree of specialisation of the shopfloor workforce
6 Approaches to supervision and levels of responsibility and accountability
7 Feasibility of individual versus group or team working processes
8 Degree of scheduling difficulty
9 Extent of variations in volume and variety of materials

Although this typology has originated to reflect differences in manufacturing environments, the 'models' can be related to operating environments in service industries.

Planning/ordering modes

However, especially following the development and application of integrated planning and control systems in manufacturing, an alternative scheme has emerged, based upon the extent to which operations and material requirements are based upon actual customer orders, as opposed to market forecasts.[4] In other words, to what extent can activities be based on actual customer demand rather than anticipated demand? Planning on the basis of the latter means having to cope with the uncertainties and consequences traditionally experienced when forecasting sales. Clearly, errors in forecasts can lead to either overstocked or shortage situations in the supply chain, both of which cause extra costs. The ideal is to be able to plan and conduct all activities within the customer's order leadtime. Of course, market conditions and leadtimes of operations will not often permit this. A typology based on this consideration creates the following types:

1 Make for stock (production plans are based on forecasts of requirements needed to replenish finished goods stocks and stocks in the distribution pipeline to meet sales as they arise).
2 Assemble from stock to order (final assembly is based on actual sales orders, using parts made against forecast requirements).
3 Make to order from purchases based on forecasts of needs (production of parts and final assembly operations are based on actual orders).
4 Purchase materials to order and make to order.
5 Design, purchase and make to order.

The mode depends on the leadtimes of the various steps in the production and supply process in relation to the leadtime of the customer orders. A strategic approach may be taken, of course, to shorten the times of the steps and increase the amount of the supply chain that can be controlled by actual customer requirements. In this way the level of uncertainty can be reduced.

Having dealt with the analysis of different types of manufacturing situation, attention can be turned to the main resource requirements to be managed by purchasing and supply in manufacturing firms. The main focus for purchasing and supply management will be the control of the flow of production materials to support the production operations and the distribution of the finished products to the external customers. Though patterns of flow will vary, it is likely that as much as 70 per cent of purchasing expenditure will be spent on this category in a typical manufacturing firm. It is not surprising, therefore, that personnel with this background tend to form perceptions of purchasing and supply management which tend to take for granted the characteristics of these supply chains. Indeed, it can be said that in many discussions about purchasing and supply issues, there is a tendency to assume this type of context, although such an assumption is implicit rather than explicit in many accounts. Purchase and supply of other categories of resources, such as consumables, services and even capital equipment, are treated almost as an afterthought or at least not given the same degree of priority. These should not be neglected, however, as wrong decisions can lead to harmful and costly consequences.

Tertiary sector – wholesale or retail organisations

Other terms, such as merchant or distributor, might also be used to label firms in this classification. The main function is that of buying and stocking goods for resale and it is these tangible products which are sold on to customers. The point is that these goods flow through a supply chain from external suppliers to external customers and it is the demands of the latter that need to be satisfied. 'What you buy, you sell' is a phrase that encapsulates the idea. The difference, compared with a manufacturing supply chain, is that there is no internal transformation process which converts material inputs into completed products. The primary focus for purchasing and supply in wholesale or retail firms will be aimed at 'goods for resale', as the main resource category and capital equipment and consumables categories will be less significant.

Tertiary sector – service organisations

A variety of different examples can illustrate this category, but the distinguishing feature is that the 'product' received by customers is largely intangible by nature. Central and local government units, educational institutions, financial institutions, the National Health Service and the armed forces fall into this category. Purchasing and supply activities will tend to entail the supply of capital equipment and consumable supplies, although the provision of some services may also be supported by the supply of tangible products to the customer, such as documents, for example.

To conclude this analysis of the varying resource needs of different types of organisation, it can be seen that personnel involved with purchasing and supply activities can be located in supply chains which demonstrate different characteristics and which may need different strategic treatment as a result.

Size

The size of the organisation, measured in terms of either capital employed, or number of employees, or value of sales or level of purchasing expenditure, is likely to affect the position of the purchasing and supply function. In larger organisations, there are more opportunities to employ a larger number of personnel in the function and to develop a wider range of specialist expertise. The role of the function inside the organisation may thus occupy a more prominent position and lend itself to more highly developed strategies. Similarly, purchasing and supply personnel may have more power and influence in relation to other players in markets and supply chains. Large organisations may be able to exercise a more dominating role in structuring and shaping practices to be adopted in such chains. The position now enjoyed by key national retailing chains, for example, grants them the ability to impose their strategies on manufacturers and transport and distribution companies. Purchasing and supply strategies need to be based on careful assessment of the potential effects that might result from their application.

While large size may enhance the power and influence of the purchasing and supply function, small and medium sized firms should not neglect the development of effective and efficient supply strategies and the use of appropriately skilled personnel. What counts may not be absolute size *per se*, but size of purchase relative to individual suppliers and the market as a whole.

Complexity in relation to product and geographical spread

A further dimension that contributes to different demands for purchasing and supply chain management is that of varying complexity, which in this context is designated as referring to both product range and spread of geographical locations. Thus the simplest situation would be that of a firm operating on one site and with a single product range. The purchasing and supply chain management task would, therefore, consist of controlling the supply of resources to this one location. As the product range becomes more numerous, so input requirements will become more diversified and, as the number of operating sites increase, so the supply arrangements have to cope with different geographical locations. Problems of organising and controlling more complex patterns of supply grow more difficult, therefore, and strategic issues, in relation to centralisation and decentralisation, integration of information systems and national and international supply arrangements, for instance, come into the picture.

Public and private sectors

Form of ownership has often been taken as a significant aspect which differentiates organisations. Indeed, for some people, the division between public and private sectors creates two quite different worlds, which require quite different approaches to purchasing and supply management. Public ownership imposes obligations with regard to public accountability, which lead to prescribed methods of purchasing and prescribed policies towards the treatment of suppliers. National legal requirements and government policies with regard to competitive tendering procedures, supplemented by directives of the European Community and by regulations arising from the GATT (General Agreement on Tariffs and Trade), are obvious examples that seem to lend substance to the separation of the two worlds. However, others argue that the differences have been exaggerated and that both public and private sector purchasing and supply management can also share some common concerns and techniques. The need to obtain value for money in purchasing is just one example. The boundaries, in any case, are becoming more blurred as European Community directives restrict the freedom of some companies, namely the utility companies, in the gas, water and energy industries by the imposition of similar tendering rules.

'Market' or 'non-market' mode of the operation

A feature that is sometimes introduced into the public sector – private sector debate concerns the basic mode of operation and the key financial implication associated with it. Organisations operating in markets sell their goods and services to customers and their financial performance can be gauged in terms of profit or loss. On the other hand, organisations operating in a non-market mode provide goods or services without receiving payment from the direct recipients.[5] Funding for supplies is allocated ultimately from taxation for public sector organisations and from donations in the case of charities. Clearly, profit is a concept which is not applicable in the non-market mode. Efficiency has to be expressed in terms of the level of service provided in relation to the level of expenditure incurred. However, purchasing and supply management can contribute to the overall performance in both market and non-market organisations by controlling the use of resources effectively and efficiently – supplying the right things at the lowest cost.

It follows from this analysis that some public sector organisations, the public corporations, operate in the market sector as they do sell products to their customers and profitability can be used as at least one of the yardsticks of performance.

A range of factors have now been introduced which can help to distinguish between different contextual circumstances in which the function of purchasing and supply management can be found. Recognition of these can increase sensitivity to the fact that people can generate different viewpoints about its nature because their perceptions are based upon different vantage points. The next objective in this chapter, to which attention can now be turned, is that of identifying the strategic themes that will be addressed in the book.

STRATEGIC THEMES IN PURCHASING AND SUPPLY MANAGEMENT

It may be helpful to identify the main themes that will enter into discussions of purchasing and supply management strategy in the main parts of the book. Identification helps to explain why strategic purchasing and supply chain management has become an important issue for organisations as a whole and for the function itself. The list of themes is presented in Fig 1.1 and each one is then introduced in turn.

Changing environmental conditions

It is intended to use this heading to embrace both general business conditions and also other factors such as ecological and 'green' interests, technology and innovation, and changing economic and political circumstances.

```
 1  Changing environmental conditions
 2  General strategic issues
 3  Integration of functional, business and corporate strategies
 4  Managing change and changing ideas of management
 5  The role of purchasing and supply management
 6  Competitive and co-operative strategies
 7  Sourcing strategies
 8  Organisation of the function
 9  Human resource issues
10  Application of information technology
```

Fig 1.1 Strategic themes

Political and economic changes

Starting with the political and economic changes, four major developments will be briefly highlighted. First, there have been startling political events which have brought about the collapse of the communist world, bringing to an end the cold war, but leaving instability in some of the parts of that world. New investment and trading opportunities have been opened up, but uncertainty and a degree of risk may be associated with them.

A second area of change concerns policies of the British Conservative government towards the restructuring and reform of the public sector. Restructuring has involved the return to the private sector of many of the former public corporations. New ways of managing operations in the National Health Service, through the introduction of the 'internal market' and the split between 'purchasers' and 'providers', have introduced a new set of relationships relevant to discussions of purchasing and supply management strategy. The same is true of policies emphasising compulsory competitive tendering and market testing approaches for the provision of services.

Third, the development of the European Union, still in a state of transition, has already had a significant impact on trading and business conditions, although, of course, it may have an even more fundamental impact on the political structure of Europe. Organisations have had to add a European dimension to their corporate strategies and there are also numerous implications for purchasing and supply management strategies.

A fourth evolving development has wider global implications. This is the growth and development of the Pacific Rim, or South East Asian countries, led in particular by Japan. So far, this factor has had a more dramatic impact on business practice and trading outcomes than the collapse of the communist world. The standards of performance and the marketing and investment ambitions and successes of the Japanese have altered the balance of economic power. Significant inroads have been made into European and American economies, and, just as importantly, many traditional business ideas employed in these areas of former economic dominance have been challenged to the core. Though the national and business cultures of these countries may demonstrate some significant features, the questions arise as to how far business practices can or should be imported into the West. Evidence suggests that what has been referred to as 'Japanisation' is possible and that new methods can be introduced and performance standards can be raised in Europe and America, the two other main trading blocs in the world.[6]

Technological change and product innovation

Technological change has been both a cause and an effect of changing business conditions. It can be conceived as including many elements, such as changes to product designs, production processes, information systems, materials handling and transport media. Strategies in purchasing and supply management can play a valuable part in supporting and encouraging the adoption of such innovations, which may be essential if improved standards of performance are to be reached. Nevertheless, analysts emphasise the importance of not neglecting the human and managerial dimensions, if new technology is to be introduced successfully. Investment in 'hardware' alone is insufficient. Implications and opportunities with regard to working practices and managerial planning and control systems need to be considered if the full potential of technological change is to be harvested.

Business conditions

National and international markets have become more competitive as a result of the developments on both European and wider global fronts. The dynamic nature of these markets has led to the need for continuous change in business practices in order to keep pace with or overtake world leaders. The search for competitive advantage and world class standards has brought all traditional business practices under the microscope, and fundamental changes have been introduced already into many companies. Customers have become more demanding in terms of the standards of product quality and delivery service which they now expect, while still looking for cost and price reductions. The future success of businesses is also seen to be dependent on the pursuit of continuous improvement. Purchasing and supply management needs to develop strategies appropriate for these rapidly changing situations. The function can be proactive and become an agent of change and be a force in innovation processes. At the very least, it needs to develop effective responses to the changes occurring in the environment with which it comes into contact. For a firm to reach world class standards in serving its own customers, it is vital to achieve world class standards in controlling its network of suppliers.

Ecological and 'green' issues

Concern for the environment, in the sense of ecology and 'green' products, is growing in importance and, increasingly, has to be taken into account in both corporate and functional strategies. Legal and political pressures, customer demands, the prospect of profitable business opportunities and standards of corporate responsibility are all forces contributing to this growing concern. Purchasing and supply arrangements can be either harmful or beneficial in relation to their impact on the environment. Relevant aspects include the ingredients of the products being designed and purchased, the packaging materials being used, the production processes required, the natural resources being exploited, as well as problems associated with the creation and disposal of waste. Impetus in Europe, which is both increasing awareness of and adding legal obligations in relation to environmental issues, has been stimulated by the European Union and by major international conferences.

General strategic issues

Given the dynamic nature and number of factors relating to environmental and business conditions which have been mentioned in even the above brief survey, it is not surprising that there have been developments in ideas of how to create and implement corporate and business strategies. Generally it has been argued that short-term, tactical responses are inadequate in coping with and helping to influence the changes taking place. There may be problems of confronting risk and uncertainty, but it is essential to attempt to control the long-term direction of businesses and to enhance their flexibility of response to pertinent factors beyond their control. The difficult problem is perhaps to cope with immediate short-term pressures and at the same time give attention to long-term developments. Ideas concerning strategic planning processes, the content of such strategies and problems of implementation have proliferated. A key point among these ideas is that concern for strategic management is seen increasingly as one that should involve functional line managers and not be just the task for a somewhat remote specialist corporate planning department.

Corporate issues

After the introduction and then subsequent disappointment with initial ideas of corporate planning approaches, much of the early conceptual development in strategic thinking concentrated on the problems of diversified, conglomerate companies and led to techniques of what has come to be known as portfolio analysis. This approach addresses the question primarily of what businesses the company should be involved in and helps to guide decisions with regard to the buying, selling and closing down of individual businesses. However, as world competition became more acute, priorities started to shift towards strategies needed to make an individual business successful. The pursuit of diversification as a route to corporate success declined as many firms decided to concentrate on trying to defend and make viable their core businesses.

Business issues

Thus, the search for factors that give a business a sustainable competitive advantage in the market-place and the observations of those who experienced Japanese business practices have helped to create a stream of new techniques and philosophies. The idea of a business as part of a value chain, positioned between suppliers and customers, and the emergence of notions such as total quality management (TQM) and just in time (JIT), have transformed both assessments of what might be possible and the action plans implemented by companies themselves. A valuable outcome of this expansion of ideas is that perspectives of supply chain management have been both sharpened and given much wider recognition. Views of the role that purchasing and supply management can play have been expanded and will need to be examined in more detail in due course.

Integration of functional, business and corporate strategies

The attention focused on individual business strategies has also led to wider acceptance of the need for such business strategies to reflect and be in harmony with the strategies of the main functions in the business. Marketing and finance were seen as being highly relevant in corporate portfolio analysis techniques and these functions are similarly believed to be able to make a significant and essential contribution at the business level. However, production and operations management has by now gained more publicity and advocates have promoted the need to build manufacturing and operations strategies into strategic approaches. Progress has been made in rectifying this omission from strategic planning processes and in developing more sophisticated approaches in structuring content to give strategic direction to the development of manufacturing and operations capabilities.

While leading voices in the purchasing and supply profession have advanced frequently their claims for wider recognition of a strategic role for purchasing, the message has not been taken up to the extent that it possibly deserves. Occasional fears of world-wide shortages of key commodities or sudden surges in their prices on the commodity exchanges have raised the profile of purchasing only intermittently. Also, periods of high interest rates and price inflation did from time to time accentuate corporate concern for purchasing and supply affairs. However, the more turbulent and changing business environment of the 1980s and 1990s and the aggressive exploitation of different business practices by Japanese companies and others trying to emulate them have increased the number and strength of the spotlights turned on purchasing and supply management. The climate is, therefore, more favourable than it has ever been for the development and implementation of a strategic approach for purchasing and supply management. 'The Revolution in Purchase', referred to in an article by

Russell Syson, is already happening.[7] If those inside the profession and those still aspiring to gain entrance fail to meet this challenge then others from other functions might take over leadership. Production and operations management literature often takes purchasing and supply management affairs under its umbrella.

An important goal in the development of strategic purchasing and supply management is to link strategies into those at both business and corporate levels, as well as making them harmonious with other functional strategies. It is dangerous and it may be ultimately detrimental to the fortunes of the business if functional strategies are developed in isolation. Ways of achieving close integration and of harvesting the synergies of doing so will need to be explored. Opportunities for co-ordination of strategies at the corporate level in multi-product companies also need to be investigated. The scope for this will grow as the commonality of supply requirements and the interdependency of operations increase between the different parts of the company.

Managing change and changing ideas of management

Styles of management

Some people might view the introduction of such ideas as TQM and JIT as simply the latest management fads or fashions, and like fashions in retailing, their popularity might be expected to decline and be replaced sooner or later. Others, however, challenge this evaluation and see their emergence as leading to a fundamental change in attitudes, styles of management, methods of organisation, and ways of harnessing and developing human resources. In other words, they suggest that a revolution in management theory and practice is taking place. In this viewpoint, the revolution rejects much of what might be referred to as the classical management tradition, as represented by the ideas of management writers, such as Frederick Taylor, and as implemented by practitioners, such as Henry Ford I, for instance. The ideas replacing it encourage a more supportive style of management, and employees are seen in a more positive light, in the sense of being able to become a major force in developing improved ways of working. They are seen to be able to develop and apply expertise and take on a wider range of jobs than is the case in a Tayloristic approach. In the latter, management experts devise methods and give instructions to be carried out by the workforce, a separation between those who think and those who do things.

This is a key debate, which is ongoing, and it is one that does have major implications in purchasing and supply management. In the first place, the purchasing and supply function cannot be immune from the wider corporate context of management style and culture and those in managerial and supervisory positions in the function have to adopt and put into practice an approach of some kind. Furthermore, in so far as buyers are able to influence their suppliers' operations, they can exert significant pressure on the styles and work practices adopted in suppliers' organisations.

Structures of organisations

A further outcome of the new approach is the flattening of managerial hierarchies, as levels in the structure of organisations are removed. Responsibility is pushed down to the lowest levels that seem to be feasible. More emphasis is placed upon teamwork and horizontal relationships associated with processes which cut across departmental boundaries, and indeed across interorganisational boundaries. Material supply chains are illustrative of such horizontal interdependencies between activities. Thus, multi-functional teams are appearing, which may include purchasing and supply personnel, as well as design, process and production engineers and others, to manage design, production and distribution operations. Representatives of both customer and supplier organisations may also be treated as members of such teams.

Change topics

Managing change as a phrase can embody many different elements which require changing, and among these are changes in product designs, process equipment and information technology. Manufacturing and operations systems can be envisaged as having both 'structural' (hard features, such as equipment, warehouses, and factory capacity and location) and 'infrastructural' (soft features, such as job designs and work practices, control systems, methods of pay and organisational structures) aspects. The search for improvements in performance have brought about many changes in these areas and the lesson seems to be that an integrated strategic approach is a prerequisite of success and that fragmented, piecemeal approaches are doomed to lead to disappointment and failure.

'Lean' production

A notable research study, carried out by an international team of researchers, looked at the comparative performance of the major car assemblers in the world-wide automotive industry.[8] It concluded that the result of adopting the structural and infrastructural changes associated with TQM and JIT is a new type of production model, a new way of organising production. It has become known as the 'lean' production model and is seen as a successor to the 'mass' production model, as typified by the high-volume car assembly line, as developed by Henry Ford I. The practices covered by the umbrella terms of TQM and JIT are essentially those operated by the best of the Japanese companies. The main goal of being 'lean' is to obtain the same output from half the resources used by older methods – half the number of workers, half the number of design engineers and half the level of inventory, for example. At the same time, higher levels of quality, more frequent new model launches and more varied product variations were found to be achievable. The western principle of high-volume output of standardised products to obtain the advantages of economies of scale seemed to come under fire at a time when customer demand for more varied product designs was growing.

Public sector

The discussion regarding change and changing ideas of management has so far tended to assume both a private and manufacturing sector background, possibly because it is this sector that has caused the most concern in recent decades. It has been the most exposed sector with regard to international competition and has suffered greatly as a result of outmoded practices, though that is not to say that there have not been other contributing factors. This has been the case especially, but not only, in the United Kingdom. However, the winds of change have also hit both the services sector and non-market operations in the public sector. Different managerial practices and different forms of accountability are making inroads in these spheres as well. The search to become 'leaner' is thought to be just as appropriate and meaningful as an aim as in manufacturing companies. Once again, there are issues that also have an effect on purchasing and supply management in these non-manufacturing organisations. 'Lean' supply performance, to complement and support 'lean' operations, is a desirable goal.[9]

The role of purchasing and supply management

A theme that has already started to emerge from the discussions so far, but now needs to be emphasised in its own right, is that of the role of purchasing and supply. A fundamental strategic issue in whatever type of organisation it is located in is the kind of role that should be written for it. A more detailed account of the various models proposed will be investigated in other parts of the book. It is sufficient for current purposes to simply contrast two quite different perceptions.

At one end of the spectrum is an image of the purchasing and supply function which characterises it as involving mainly clerical, order-placing activities and in which personnel tend to adopt only a short-term, hand-to-mouth approach, merely reacting to contingencies as they arise. Movement towards the other end of the spectrum opens up possibilities in which a strategic, long-term approach is developed in shaping the direction of sourcing and supply plans, and immediate requirements are controlled in the light of these. Such a proactive image also emphasises the strategic importance of performance in purchasing and supply management for organisations as a whole. It takes a broad systemic or holistic view of supply chains or pipelines and suggests that it can exercise significant influence in relation to the creation of product value at various stages along the chain. Indeed, in many cases suppliers add more value to the final product in their operations than is added in the final stage of the company apparently making it. The purchasing strategies of more powerful companies can influence the structure of the supply chain as well as the behaviour of other participants in the chain. Finally, pursuit of improvements in methods and of reductions in the waste of resources throughout the supply chain can contribute to 'leaner' supply performance and increased value for the final customer.

Competitive and co-operative strategies

Having raised the question of what kind of role is wanted for purchasing and supply management, an additional question needs attention. What strategies should be used to manage suppliers and to establish arrangements for the supply of goods and services? Traditional purchasing practices have been built on basic theories of market competition. The process of obtaining competitive quotations or tenders, together with the use of forceful negotiating tactics, was seen to be the route to follow in order to obtain the best price for what was required.

The alternative to buying supplies through market transactions from independent suppliers was seen to be that of vertical integration. In other words, facilities for producing and supplying the goods or service would be brought under direct ownership of the firm and controlled by the management hierarchy. The strategic choice, in this traditional picture, therefore, is between the two options of 'make' or 'buy'.

However, as knowledge of Japanese practices increased so it became apparent that different policies were used to manage the flow of supplies and to control the interface between buyers and sellers. Close collaboration between customers and suppliers on a long-term basis and the cultivation of co-operative relationships appeared as another sourcing approach. Such a framework relies less on legal conditions of contract and more on mutual trust and mutual recognition of shared interests for successful implementation of arrangements. Furthermore, collaboration enables both sides to work together to foster improvements over time and to enhance performance in all aspects of supply. In other words it is a vehicle that stimulates innovation. This third sourcing policy is seen to fall in the middle between competitive market exchanges and direct internal managerial control. The topic of 'partnership' or 'co-makership' arrangements and the search for the right balance between competitive and co-operative approaches form a central part in a consideration of strategic purchasing and supply management.

Sourcing strategies

Closely linked to the basic question of relationships with suppliers are the supporting strategies designed to achieve control of performance with regard to basic requirements of quality, delivery, cost and service. Early supplier involvement, supplier development, supplier assessment, supplier certification and measurement of performance come into the picture, as do inventory policies and strategies with regard to transportation of supplies. Policy guidelines for topics such as purchasing research, single versus multi-sourcing, intra-company purchasing, reciprocal trade, international purchasing and purchasing ethics are also relevant.

Organisation of the function

One topic for the strategic planning process is the design of an organisation structure for the purchasing and supply function and the establishment of mechanisms to enhance co-operation and integration, both within the function and with other functions. Organisational structure plays a strong part in allocating responsibilities and specifying relationships between personnel. It will, therefore, influence the way in which strategies will be implemented. One issue concerns the grouping and linking of specialist activities horizontally along the internal supply chain. Perhaps crucial to the image and role of the function is the location of the function in the vertical plane and the position of the functional head in the overall hierarchy. However, some organisations may use matrix and project management approaches. Questions of organisational structure also carry implications with regard to political and power relationships as well as career paths of staff.

Human resource issues

From the point of view of the strategic management of the function, staffing aspects should not be neglected, and some might say that these are critical with regard to the successful implementation of selected strategies. The knowledge and skills of staff contribute most to the capability of the function in managing supply affairs. Aspects of recruitment, staff development and training and staff reward schemes, as well as management style, all contribute to the culture of the function, the underpinning attitudes and values, which strongly influence behaviour and performance. As the role of the function expands, so the expertise of the staff needs to grow accordingly. 'Learning' has become a vital ingredient of managing change and this topic will be dealt with in more depth after the last theme has been brought into the picture. One other human resource issue to highlight is the growing emphasis on not only technical and cognitive skills but also interpersonal skills, such as ability to operate in teams, to provide appropriate forms of support and leadership and to establish effective relationships with suppliers. Newer strategies place particular emphasis on the need to deploy these skills.

Application of information technology (IT)

Personnel in purchasing and supply management are in a sense information processors. They receive, analyse, make decisions and distribute information in order to manage the flow of goods and services in the supply chain. Developments in the fields of both telecommunications and computer technologies have found many applications in supply chains. Indeed, the introduction of IT can transform jobs and the way in which they are carried out. Strategies with regard to IT thus need to be considered as an integral part of strategic thinking for purchasing and supply management. Many companies have already introduced integrated planning and control systems inside their organisations which include connections with purchasing and supply activities. However, as a boundary-spanning function, communication with other organisations is an essential requirement of purchasing and supply management. Scope for adopting IT approaches in this external role is increasing through techniques that have come to be known as 'electronic data interchange' – with EDI as the accepted acronym.

THE SIGNIFICANCE OF PURCHASING AND SUPPLY MANAGEMENT

Earlier expositions of purchasing and supply management tended to emphasise the contribution of the function to profitability and cashflow. Purchasing expenditure was seen to be a key portion of the total costs of manufacture. Purchasing, therefore, offers opportunities for significant 'leverage' on profitability and any reduction in the cost of bought items could be seen to go straight to the 'bottom line'. Commitments to suppliers through purchase ordering patterns could be seen to have an effect on outward flows of cash and the build-up of future liabilities. With regard to inventory management, companies realised that levels of stock investment represented both a demand for capital to finance them and resulted in a cost of tying up money in this form of investment. Other costs of storing and caring for goods were seen to add to the costs of ownership. Materials handling and transport and distribution activities generated other costs which were influenced by the performance of personnel in purchasing and supply management. However, accounting systems tended not to give a clear total picture of all these. While these apparently 'simple truths' about the financial significance of purchasing and supply management seem to be obvious, they were not always sufficient to gain the support of top management. In many companies far more resources were aimed at controlling direct labour costs than direct material costs, in spite of the fact that the latter were usually higher (*see* Fig 1.2).

The argument with regard to the financial contribution of purchasing and supply management to corporate performance is nevertheless still an important one. Indeed, it has become stronger as many manufacturing companies have increased their bought out content and have reduced their direct labour costs as a result of strategic responses to changing business conditions. For non-manufacturing firms and in organisations operating in a non-market mode, similar arguments with regard to the impact of the costs of purchasing and supply activities on the financial posture of organisation have been advanced. Low purchase prices and low logistics costs have helped the major retail chains to build up strong positions in consumer markets and they have played a key part in the implementation of low-cost, low-price, high-volume strategies, for instance.

Thus, perceptions of the strategic role for purchasing and supply management and of the overall significance of the function to the organisation will continue to retain this financial aspect. However, emerging ideas regarding an expanding role for the function are also adding other concerns. Instead of a focus on

---

1 Leverage on 'costs', 'profits' and 'cashflow' by means of:
   - prices paid for goods and services;
   - investment in stocks;
   - holding goods in stores;
   - materials handling costs;
   - transport costs;
   - administration costs.
2 'Contribution' to the creation and acquisition of 'value' for internal and external 'customers' by means of:
   - involvement in product design processes (goods and services);
   - advice regarding operations processes to produce and deliver goods and services;
   - contribution to meeting delivery times and quantity targets at salient points in the supply chain.

Note: 'Total costs of acquisition' or 'Total costs of ownership' give a more comprehensive view of 'costs', rather than focusing on one element in isolation (see Chapter 8).

Fig 1.2 The significance of purchasing and supply

contributions of each subdivision of purchasing and supply management a more holistic perspective is adopted, which emphasises the contribution of managing the whole supply chain. Managing the added value at each stage, as well as reducing wasteful activities (non-value-added activities), contributes to the meeting or exceeding of customer expectations in the end product market-place. Expectations of different customers might vary with regard to priorities in relation to quality, delivery, price, flexibility of service, etc., and it is the task of purchasing and supply management and the organisation as a whole to be sensitive to them. Success for the business is seen to be helped, therefore, by meeting customer requirements and, at the same time, contributing to the financial goals of the organisation. The need for continuously improving supply chain performance is also seen to be vital, especially if most of the added value is created by upstream suppliers.

PURCHASING AND SUPPLY AS A 'LEARNING' PROCESS

Images or metaphors have always played a part in developing ideas about matters under discussion or investigation. In organisational literature, for example, terms like 'mechanistic' or 'organic' have been borrowed from the natural sciences in order to bring out more clearly the contrasting features of two different models. Another metaphor that has gained credence is 'the learning organisation'. It has emerged as having value at a time when the need for managing change is being recognised as a necessity for coping with changing business conditions. Learning is an integral part of the process in both understanding and analysing often complex situations, as well as searching for potential solutions. Innovation, by definition, means doing something in a new way and a new way has to be discovered and learnt. The outcome of learning is, therefore, knowledge and experience of new methods and approaches. Knowledge and capability, rather than capital or natural resources, are seen by some to be the main source of competitive advantage and to retain that advantage processes that cultivate learning are necessary. In the last analysis, however, learning can only be achieved by people, though they can make their output of knowledge available to the organisation as a whole and the fruits of it can be harvested from the decisions that are guided by it. Has this idea of 'the learning organisation' any relevance to purchasing and supply management? This is a question that will now be addressed.

Learning theories

In a sense purchasing and supply management always has involved the possibility of learning – learning about suppliers, about new products and materials and about market conditions, for instance. The concept of purchasing research and its implementation in organisations is an example of formalising the process. However, there have been differences in practice with regard to the extent to which it has been adopted either in specialist units or by line buyers. It can therefore be argued that learning is a basic activity, but there may be new ways of both speeding up and improving the effectiveness of learning. The use of multi-functional sourcing teams and simultaneous engineering approaches may produce benefits in this way, as can techniques of value analysis and value engineering. (Simultaneous engineering is an approach to product design and development, which attempts to pool the expertise of design engineers, process engineers, production engineers and the ideas of others, including purchasing, marketing, suppliers and customers to enhance the new product development process in terms of quality, cost and time.) A proactive approach to purchasing puts a premium, therefore, on the use of learning processes.

Learning, however, can also take place at a more fundamental business level. It can involve challenging basic ideas, which are often taken for granted in normal business behaviour. Assumptions, which enter into ways of perceiving situations and of assessing the value of possible courses of action, frequently remain implicit and are not examined or challenged. In an era of more dynamic and turbulent conditions, it is these basic foundations in mental frameworks or frames of reference which need to be brought into conscious thought and compared with alternatives. Following the famous work of Thomas Kuhn,[10] ideas about progress in developing scientific knowledge have been reappraised. Instead of a steady accumulation of new theories which are able to both embrace and expand the range of phenomena that can be covered, the idea was proposed that science proceeded by means of occasional revolutions and the emergence of new paradigms. Newtonian theories in physics, it is suggested, are not directly comparable with those of Einstein because they embody different concepts. The foundations of the traditionally accepted philosophy of the objective truth of knowledge have been seriously eroded by Kuhn's ideas.

The relevance of this development in the philosophy of science to other fields is that it suggests that theories may have a less permanent validity than previously thought. New theories, which either are seen to be better or seem to be able to cope with new problems and factors not encompassed by the old, may arise and compete with the old. They may be found to be more relevant and useful in solving problems under investigation. If the Kuhnian viewpoint is followed it is possible to argue that the business world in Europe and America is currently undergoing such a revolution in ideas. New theories of how to manage and organise firms, different conceptions of the potential contribution of employees and different ways of managing relationships between suppliers and buyers have come forward for attention. At the very root of these debates are basic attitudes and values towards people and business. It is argued that firms may need to undergo a fundamental cultural change in order to compete and survive – to introduce a total quality culture, for instance. Rover, partly benefiting from its links with Honda, might be seen as a company that has undergone or is still undergoing just such a transformation.

Within purchasing and supply management literature, the debate between older traditional ideas and the newer approaches, apparently borrowed from Japan, can be readily discovered. Reference was made earlier to the idea of a 'revolution in purchase'.[11] From the point of view of strategic thinking, it is important to be able to stand back from operations and be able to reflect and consider the range of 'mindsets' that are available and that can suggest different courses of action. The ability of people to do this and indeed their degree of preference for reflective activity does vary. It is useful to pursue this point further by examining some of the theories of learning processes that have been put forward. In the current context it is worth thinking of learning as a process, instead of thinking of knowledge as such, the product of the process.

The first and perhaps most well-known theory is Kolb's experiential learning theory.[12] The core of this theory is the so-called learning cycle, in which there are four stages (*see* Fig 1.3):

1 Concrete experience
2 Observation and reflection
3 Generalisation and abstract conceptualisation
4 Active experimentation

Stages 1 and 3 are the ones which can start the learning process. Learning can begin with an experience that stimulates the individual to think about it and generate ideas, or the person can develop or pick up an idea that can be put into practice, from which a concrete experience can be gained, thus allowing further movement through the successive stages. Observation and reflection of experiences gained by visitors to Japan gradually allowed the West to build up insights into Japanese practices, which have then been tried out and the results assessed. Ironically, it was discovered that some of these practices were based upon observations of some American business methods and the lessons that had

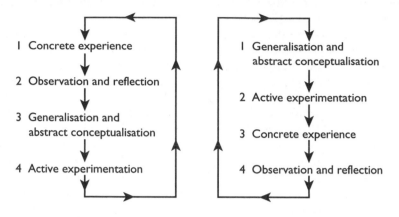

Fig 1.3 Learning processes

been learnt from American lecturers and consultants, such as Edwards Deming, whose views had fallen on deaf ears in America at the time. Books and other literature, conference presentations and suggestions from colleagues might all help a learner at stage 3 to expand the range of ideas that might be tried out. Case studies and simulation exercises might also supplement actual with synthetic learning experiences. Aircraft simulators, for example, are invaluable for training pilots.

However, experiences may not necessarily lead to any new learning if they are not analysed and may simply lead to repetitive, habitual behaviour. The underlying assumptions and theoretical components in the course of action remain invisible and ideas subconsciously directing the individual's approach cannot be transferred easily to anyone else. Though such habits may work in the conditions in which they were first used, they may be inappropriate if the initial conditions undergo a major change.

While Kolb's views are helpful with regard to the relationship between conceptualisation and action, they do not explore the depth of understanding associated with the assimilation of knowledge. Bloom has produced a taxonomy of learning and this is helpful in identifying different cognitive skills.[13] There are six levels in this scheme:

1 **Knowledge** – being able to define, repeat, record, list, recall, name and relate, etc.
2 **Comprehension** – being able to translate, restate, discuss, describe, recognise, explain, express, identify, locate, review and tell, etc.
3 **Application** – being able to interpret, apply, employ, use, demonstrate, practise, illustrate and operate, etc.
4 **Analysis** – being able to distinguish, analyse, differentiate, appraise, compare, contrast, criticise, debate, question, relate, examine and categorise, etc.
5 **Synthesis** – being able to compose, plan, design, formulate, assemble, construct, create, organise, arrange and prepare, etc.

6 **Evaluation** – being able to judge, appraise, rate, assess, revise and estimate, etc.

The point about this scheme is that movement from level 1 to level 6 represents an increase in the level of sophistication of cognitive ability. From the perspective of strategic thinking, higher demands will be made of the skills associated with analysis, synthesis and evaluation. At an operational and tactical level, knowledge, comprehension and application may be more heavily utilised. There are implications with this framework, therefore, for the ability to learn, but also from the point of view of attributes in relation to personnel issues with regard to staffing, training and education.

A further study, by Biggs, differentiates between 'surface' and 'deep' learning.[14] The former concerns the learning of the bare essentials, often by rote, with a view to simple reproduction, but without searching for meaning and understanding and without developing the more sophisticated levels of analysis, synthesis and evaluation in the Bloom model. It is the latter that take on greater importance when analysing situations in terms of relevant factors and the relationships between them, or developing, through synthesis, a picture of the wider system and its functioning as a whole as a result of the interdependency of its parts. An example in purchasing and supply management is the ability to understand each stage of activity in a supply chain, as one side of the coin, but also to be able to appreciate how the stages interrelate and to consider the performance of the chain as a whole.

An omission from the picture of learning, so far, is concern for the psychological and emotional aspects of learning. To what extent are people motivated to learn and to what extent do they gain satisfaction from doing so? Learning in isolation requires significant self-discipline and motivation in individuals. But the right social climate in the place of work may help to act as a stimulus to learning. Clearly, there is scope for managerial styles and policies with regard to reward and support which can help to cultivate a climate that encourages learning.

Before leaving this account of learning theory it is pertinent to set the book's intended objectives on strategic purchasing and supply management into their learning context. It is not attempting simply to transfer a body of knowledge as if it were an inert commodity to be regurgitated in an exam and then promptly forgotten. Some current or former students reading this sentence might unfortunately recognise this pattern of behaviour. It is hoped that the ideas in the book will serve a more useful purpose. The hope is that it provides an opportunity for readers to broaden awareness and understanding of possible courses of action in strategic purchasing and supply management that might be considered, tried and evaluated and further extended and tailored to specific situations in which they have to operate. Knowledge in the printed book may not give complete descriptions and solutions for automatic implementation, but it may be able to point out the questions that could be asked and a set of concepts to help form the framework of a picture. In addition, it may suggest a more varied repertoire of action possibilities. The sharing of ideas and reports of experiences can save too many people from trying to 'reinvent the wheel'. In short, it is hoped that ideas in the book can help to stimulate active learning processes.

Foundations of knowledge about purchasing and supply activities

Before leaving the topic of learning processes, it is useful to take stock of the knowledge about purchasing and supply activities and to analyse the foundations on which it is built. The first thing which might be remarked upon is the wide range of sources and disciplines from which ideas have been drawn. However, before identifying and assessing them, another more general issue needs to be raised with regard to the basic nature of the knowledge that is being diffused. This issue is concerned with the distinction between 'descriptive' and 'normative' or 'prescriptive' approaches. Some readers, of course, may well be familiar with this already.

Descriptive approaches

A descriptive approach is primarily designed to describe things and situations 'as they are' in the world that is being perceived and constructed in the piece of writing. Thus, an investigator or consultant, for example, might carry out a study and report what has been found to be the existing circumstances. An account or case study, say, might portray the current state of affairs with regard to the management of purchasing and supply activities and might describe the structural approach currently being adopted in an organisation. The most powerful description is one that embodies an explanation of relationships between the factors that are being observed, especially if these are quantified. Many who support this scientific ideal have attempted to transfer the approach into studies of the social world, which can be said to also include business affairs. Whether the mental objects to be looked for in the social world have the same degree of separation from the observer, as when considering natural phenomena in the physical world, is a debatable issue, but not a matter to be taken further in this book.

Conceptual frameworks come into play to direct the attention of the investigator and structure the account of what is looked for and seen. In the same way, a practitioner needs to make sense of the situation that has to be dealt with before potential solutions to problems can be generated. In so far as choice exists in selecting factors to be studied, an element of subjectivity can enter into the description. People from different backgrounds may see things differently and may focus on different priorities. It is worth remembering this point when considering the practical problem of operating in multi-functional teams. Confusion and misunderstandings can be reduced if people are more open about the meanings they embody in their own interpretations of situations.

Normative or prescriptive approaches

A normative or prescriptive approach is logically different and is more concerned with making recommendations of what to do or of what should be done. Principles and techniques of how to negotiate or how to place a purchase order may fall into such a mould. Indeed, much of the content of the business literature and of training courses and conferences tends to emphasise this approach. Rules, procedures and policy guidelines in business take on the same character. However, though there are approved ways of driving a car which instructors will try to ensure their pupils will adopt, it does not mean that drivers continue to use them all after they have successfully passed a driving test. Therefore, a descriptive account may show a difference in practice from what should be done.

So far the analysis of the difference between descriptive and normative approaches suggests that authors of presentations simply choose one or the other. In practice, aspects of both might be interwoven together. The promotion of a particular method or technique for adoption tends to make some assumptions about the nature of a situation in which it might be used. Its validity as a practical recommendation depends on these assumptions being realistic and met in the practical world. Likewise, descriptive accounts often contain evaluations and either explicit or implicit normative recommendations. Currently, techniques discovered and described as 'best practice' carry a suggestion that they should be adopted by others. In some cases, though, the conditions in which they are successful may not have been clarified and implementation in the wrong setting may lead to disappointment. A further danger is that descriptive, theoretical descriptions, which purport to explain behaviour in the world of experiences, may never have been subjected successfully to empirical testing.

Purchasing and supply literature

After this digression into methodological issues, attention will now be turned to identifying the main sources of ideas that are relevant to the world of purchasing and supply management. The best starting point is to talk about the purchasing and supply literature itself. The main textbooks tend to be mainly prescriptive in emphasis,[15] though accounts of examples of techniques being used in practice may add a descriptive flavour. Within them, one or more chapters may deal with strategic aspects of purchasing and supply management. Certainly, these books have played and will continue to play a very valuable role in training and developing practitioners and in cultivating a professional approach to purchasing and supply management. A growing range of journals relating directly to supply chain activities adds further information and knowledge to the public domain.[16] Articles relating to strategic treatment of the subject have made a valuable contribution to the development and application of a strategic approach and specific references will be given later when they are considered in more detail.

Other sources

This body of specialist literature, books and journals is not isolated from other areas, for it borrows concepts and theories from other disciplines, such as economics, law and quantitative studies. In addition, it is also constructed out of building blocks taken from accounting, marketing, personnel and production/operations management, as well as the more general subject of management and organisation. This eclectic nature of purchasing and supply knowledge will already have been noted by many readers. However, as new ideas arise in these sources, it is important that the value and implications of them are appraised and drawn into the purchasing and supply literature. Ideas, such as 'activity based costing', 'cellular manufacturing' and 'value chains' are all relevant, for instance. Developments in personnel or human resource management, with regard to 'cultural change' and 'empowerment', have repercussions in relation to managing the purchasing and supply function. In today's more dynamic era, innovative ideas are emerging everywhere and need to be considered.

There has also been a growing interest in purchasing and supply activities in other subject areas and this interest has led in particular to a rich flow of essentially descriptive studies. First, industrial marketing has established a research tradition in both America and Europe, which has made a significant contribution to understanding industrial buying practices.[17] Perhaps of greater value are the studies that have adopted an interactive framework that looks at the interactions of buyers and sellers.[18] There are normative benefits for purchasing and supply management, even though the main purpose might be to improve industrial marketing.

A second stream of studies is concerned primarily with Japanese business practices and comparisons with western methods. This concern has been partly to discover what methods and techniques have made Japanese businesses inside Japan so successful in building a platform from which to export and conquer markets in other parts of the world. The studies have partly focused on the attempts to emulate and adapt such techniques in other countries, either in Japanese transplants or in indigenous firms. Japanese purchasing and supply or subcontracting practices were highlighted as having made a major contribution to the superior competitive capability of their companies. As these practices were adopted in the West, the view began to emerge that the 'partnership' arrangements between buyers and sellers had become a major catalyst of change. Powerful buyers, through their supply chain strategies, were seen to influence the structure of industries in terms of size of companies and their location. Furthermore, in so far as arrangements encourage the adoption of Japanese working practices, there are implications with regard to personnel policies, trade union attitudes and policies and the climate of industrial relations. Thus, while at one time there may only have been a small pocket of literature with regard to purchasing and supply management, there has suddenly been a deluge of books and journal articles that make reference to purchasing and supply practices.[19]

The current climate of change and its pervasive effect on business conditions, and its demands on the actions required by firms to cope and survive, presents a challenging time for practitioners. However, it is a challenging, indeed stimulating, time from an intellectual point of view as well. Strategic thinking requires a vision of the way forward and the search for innovative ways, and thus there is a link between the practical and the intellectual challenges. Such a thought may be reinforced by a concluding comment to this discussion about learning. It is sometimes said that the most important, enduring skill that can be developed today is the ability 'to learn how to learn'. People need to assess the value and applicability of new approaches and be prepared to jettison old ones when their utility appears to have reached their 'sell-by date'. As the role of purchasing and supply management expands, learning skills and an open-minded outlook can be listed in the abilities and dispositions required by personnel associated with the function.

OUTLINE OF THE BOOK

The remainder of the book is divided into two main parts. Part One concentrates on the analysis of changing environmental conditions and their impact on strategic requirements of organisations. Chapter 2 looks in detail at the factors in the environment and assesses their impact on organisations in both the public and private sectors. Chapter 3 evaluates the developments in strategic management thinking in general and their lessons and implications for purchasing and supply management. Chapter 4 considers how strategic approaches in purchasing and supply management can be integrated with corporate, business and other functional strategies. The final chapter in Part One, Chapter 5, investigates more closely the content of strategies for purchasing and supply management.

Part Two switches the emphasis to the implementation of purchasing and supply management strategies in relation to particular goals. Thus, Chapter 6 considers aspects of managing the quality of goods and services in supply chains. Chapter 7 switches attention to strategic approaches concerned with the control of the flow of materials and services in pursuing objectives of quantity and time. The management of costs and prices is the subject of Chapter 8, and concern for the creation of value and the elimination of waste in supply chains will also be addressed. Strategies relating to buyer and seller relationships, by means of which plans for managing supply chains are formulated and implemented, are examined in Chapter 9. Human resource issues with regard to purchasing and supply management become the focus of attention in Chapter 10. Chapter 11 provides some concluding points with regard to the development of a strategic approach to purchasing and supply management.

SUMMARY

Aspects relating to the five basic objectives set for this introductory chapter have been covered:

1 The varying nature of purchasing and supply management
2 The main relevant strategic themes
3 The strategic significance of purchasing and supply management
4 Purchasing and supply as a learning process
5 An outline of the book.

The need for strategic thinking

The emerging conclusion to be carried into the remainder of the book is that there is a need for people to think strategically about purchasing and supply management. To give strategic direction to the function, those who are in a position of influence should develop a wide breadth of vision and understanding. This is essential to guide the development of and give direction to the strategies that are appropriate in coping with the dynamic conditions, which are becoming now the norm rather than the exception. The vision also needs to encompass a systemic view of a network of supply chains and its constituent parts. Communication and sharing of such visions and strategies then become a prerequisite of successful implementation. However, an underlying message of more general concern is that strategic planning processes in organisations should not neglect the inclusion of purchasing and supply management strategies.

The nature of changing environmental conditions enhances the need for all organisations to treat purchasing and supply as an important strategic function. It can have a significant effect on the ability of organisations to satisfy the needs of their relevant stakeholders, be they private investors and financial institutions, customers or clients, suppliers, governments, councils or electorates. Schemes that identify stages which mark the development of the function towards this strategic perspective have been depicted by various authors and these receive attention in Part One.

Two levels

At one level, strategies relate to the management of the function of purchasing and supply and its constituent subdivisions as a whole. These direct the activities of the function and also become an input into higher levels of business and corporate strategy. At another level, however, strategies relate to the management of particular supply chains for particular goods or services. This task might be called commodity management. At this level, it is not only managers and supervisors who need to develop strategic approaches. Other staff associated with the development and implementation of strategies to ensure that the supply of particular resource requirements of the organisation are catered for also need to adopt a strategic perspective. A connection between the two levels will be the employment of appropriate analytical frameworks to establish what might be called a portfolio approach. The purpose of such analyses is to distinguish different categories of supply problems and to link different strategies and priorities to each class. Not all supply requirements have the same degree of importance attached to them and varied approaches need to be tailored accordingly.

It can also be appreciated that the successful implementation of a strategic purchasing and supply management approach involves the following related elements. First are human factors. These include the adoption of appropriate attitudes, perspectives, skills and philosophies by all those who are associated with activities in the supply chain. Interpersonal relationships, both internally and externally, play an important part in the development of effective and efficient arrangements. Second, departmental structures and other organisational mechanisms have to be established and the choice, from a range of possible models, can affect the behaviour of those involved and the extent to which the integrated control of activities can be achieved. However, the structuring of information systems can also be a key factor in managing supply chains. The development of a coherent approach to the management of these elements is at the heart of a strategic perspective of purchasing and supply management.

NOTES AND REFERENCES

1 The quotation and questions that follow have been taken from the booklet, *Managing into the '90s*, first published in 1989 by the DTI, with an introduction by Lord Young of Graffham, then the Secretary of State. Subsequently, other useful booklets have been published and reissued from time to time on particular aspects of purchasing and supply. They are:
DTI. *Purchasing: A Competitive Business* (1991).
DTI. *Building a Purchasing Strategy* (1991).
DTI. *Logistics and Supply Chain Management* (1991).
DTI. *Managing Your Purchasing Operation* (1991).
DTI. *Getting the Best from Your Suppliers* (1991).
DTI. *Better Value for Money from Purchasing* (1991).
This series has been republished as:
DTI. *Logistics and Supply Chain Management* (1995).
DTI. *Supplying the Challenge* (1995).
DTI. *Efficiency and Value in Purchasing and Supply* (1995).
DTI. *Getting the Best from your Partners* (1995).
2 The description of the 'Functional Map of the Purchasing and Supply Chain' was set out, for example, in Information Pack No. 2 (1992). The Purchasing and Supply Lead Body was established by the Employment Department Training Agency (subsequently renamed as the Training, Enterprise and Education Directorate – TEED). Further reference to standards of competence for purchasing, part of the national standards programme leading to National Vocational Qualifications, is made in Chapter 10.
3 This topic is covered in several publications by Terry Hill:
Hill, T. *Production/Operations Management*, 2nd Edition, Prentice-Hall (1991).
Hill, T. *Manufacturing Strategy*, 2nd Edition, Macmillan (1993).
Hill, T. *The Essence of Operations Management*, Prentice-Hall (1993).
4 Nevem Working Group. *Performance Indicators in Logistics*, IFS Publications UK (1989), Chapter 2.
5 The distinction between market and non-market operations was made by Robert Bacon and Walter Eltis when analysing the British economy:
Bacon, R. and Eltis, W. *Britain's Economic Problems: Too Few Producers*, 2nd Edition, Macmillan (1978).

6 Oliver, N. and Wilkinson, B. *The Japanization of British Industry*, 2nd Edition, Blackwell (1992).

7 Syson, R. 'The Revolution in Purchase', *Purchasing and Supply Management*, September 1989, pp. 16–21.

8 Womack, J.P., Jones, D.T. and Roos, D. *The Machine that Changed the World: The Triumph of Lean Production*, Rawson Associates: Macmillan (1990). This book provides an account of the research and findings of the International Motor Vehicle Program (IMVP) team based at the Massachusetts Institute of Technology.

9 Lamming, R. *Beyond Partnership: Strategies for Innovation and Lean Supply*, Prentice-Hall (1993).

Other books which provide information about Japanese practices with regard to buyer-supplier relations are:

Trevor, T. and Christie, I. *Manufacturers and Suppliers in Britain & Japan*, Policy Studies Institute (1988).

Morris, J. and Imrie, R. *Transforming Buyer-Supplier Relations*, Macmillan (1992).

10 Kuhn, T.S. *The Structure of Scientific Revolutions*, 2nd Edition, University of Chicago Press (1970).

11 *See* Syson (1989), mentioned in note 7 above.

12 Kolb, D.A. *Experiential Learning*, Prentice-Hall (1984).

13 Bloom, B.S. (editor). *Taxonomy of Educational Objectives: Cognitive Domain*, David McKay (1956).

14 Biggs, J.B. 'Individual and Group Differences in Study Processes', *British Journal of Educational Psychology*, 48, 1978, pp. 266–79.

15 Baily, P. and Farmer, D. *Purchasing, Principles and Management*, 7th Edition, Pitman Publishing (1994).

Dobler, D.W., Burt, D.N. and Lee, L. *Purchasing and Materials Management*, 5th Edition, McGraw-Hill (1990).

Heinritz, S., Farrell, P.V., Giunipero, L. and Kolchin, M. *Purchasing: Principles and Applications*, Prentice-Hall (1991).

Since the first edition was prepared other relevant books have been published. These include accounts of research into many of the newer practices discussed in this book and they also provide international comparisons. They include:

Baily, P., Farmer, D., Jessop, D. and Jones, D. *Purchasing, Principles and Management*, 7th Edition, Pitman Publishing (1994).

Burt, D.N. and Doyle, M.F. *The American Keiretsu: A Strategic Weapon for Global Competitiveness*, Business One: Irwin (1993).

Hines, P. *Creating World Class Suppliers: Unlocking Mutual Competitive Advantage*, Financial Times/Pitman Publishing (1994).

Lamming, R. and Cox, A. (editors). *Strategic Procurement in the 1990s: Concepts and Cases*, Earlsgate Press (1994).

MacBeth, D.K. and Ferguson, N. *Partnership Sourcing: An Integrated Supply Chain Approach*, Financial Times/Pitman Publishing (1994).

Nishiguchi, T. *Strategic Industrial Sourcing: The Japanese Advantage*, Oxford University Press (1993).

Sako, M. *Prices, Quality and Trust*, Cambridge University Press (1992).

Thoburn, J.T. and Takashima, M. *Industrial Subcontracting in the UK and Japan*, Avebury (1992).

Wells, P. and Rawlinson, M. *The New European Automobile Industry*, St Martin's Press (1994).

16 The following are some of the useful journals relevant to purchasing and supply management:
Purchasing and Supply Management
Purchasing
International Journal of Purchasing and Materials Management
International Journal of Physical Distribution and Logistics Management (formerly Materials Management)
International Journal of Operations and Production Management
BPICS Control
Production and Inventory Management
European Journal of Purchasing and Supply Management

17 Robinson, P.J. and Faris, C.W. *Industrial Buying and Creative Marketing*, Allyn and Bacon (1967).
Webster, Jnr., F.E. and Wind, Y. *Organisational Buying Behaviour*, Prentice-Hall (1972).
Brand, G.T. *Industrial Buying Decisions*, Cassell (1972).
Hill, R.W. and Hillier, T.J. *Organisational Buying Behaviour*, Macmillan (1977).

18 Ford, D. (editor). *Understanding Business Markets: Interaction, Relationships and Networks*, Academic Press (1990). This book provides a useful collection of articles, based upon the interactive approach.
The pioneering work of the International Marketing and Purchasing (IMP) Group is reported in:
Hakansson, H. (editor). *International Marketing and Purchasing of Industrial Goods: An Interaction Approach*, John Wiley (1982).
Another book which relates to the interaction approach is the work of another group, the Industrial Buyer Behaviour (IBB) Group, reported in:
Parkinson, S.T. and Baker, M.J., with Moller, K. *Organisational Buying Behaviour*, Macmillan (1986).

19 Thomas, R. and Oliver, N. 'Component Supplier Patterns in the UK Motor Industry', *International Journal of Management Science*, Vol. 19, No. 6, 1991, pp. 609–16.
Turnbull, P. 'The Japanization of Production and Industrial Relations at Lucas Electrical', *Industrial Relations Journal*, Vol. 17, No. 3, 1986, pp. 193–206.
Wood, S. (editor). *The Transformation of Work*, Unwin Hyman (1989).
Thoburn, J.T. and Takashima, M. 'Improving British Industrial Performance: Lessons from Japanese Subcontracting', *National Westminster Bank Quarterly Review*, February (1993).
National Economic Development Council (NEDC). *The Experience of Nissan Suppliers: Lessons for the United Kingdom Engineering Industry*, NEDC (1991).

APPENDIX: MAKING SENSE OF PURCHASING AND SUPPLY

A major problem, in relation to business practice and the extensive literature about purchasing and supply matters, is the lack of agreement on:

1 the range of activities to be encompassed by the subject; and
2 the appropriate terms to be used to describe the domain.

It can be argued that the lack of any agreed framework results in a wide diversity of perceptions about the nature of the field. This can lead to serious misunderstandings in communications, or, perhaps worse, can contribute to fierce conflicts and political battles between individuals. Such problems affect not only practitioners, but also writers, educators and members and officers of professional bodies.

Conflict might appear to be dangerous, therefore. On the other hand, ideas about the subject and the range of possibilities for application by practitioners can contribute to the dynamic development of new opportunities and successful achievements in terms of performance. However, a degree of sensitivity and a degree of toleration in comprehending other points of view are called for, perhaps, if such a healthy and constructive outcome is to be obtained from such debates.

This Appendix aims to tackle the problems identified above and to help readers to make sense of the nature of the field and its possibilities. While some practitioners or writers might have their own views on these matters, individuals encountering these matters still have to be actively involved in receiving and interpreting them. In doing so, they will rarely form identical impressions, because of differences in prior knowledge and experiences, as well as because of failings associated with the process of communication itself. An evolutionary approach to the development of ideas will be adopted as a method of analysing the problems of meanings already alluded to.

The topic of this Appendix should not be seen as an arid debate amongst academics and writers. Basic frameworks of concepts, associated with the two issues, shape the 'view of the world' that people adopt and which guides their ability to comprehend opportunities for action that might be available to them.

The subject matter of the Appendix, will be discussed under the following headings:

● Some causes of difficulty in establishing common meanings
● The traditional model of purchasing and its context
● Trends in the evolution of ideas about the context of the function
● Directions of change in the expansion of ideas about purchasing
● Implications and benefits of current developments

Some causes of difficulty in establishing common meanings

The first difficulty arises from the fact that a variety of viewpoints develop because of the different purposes and contexts which help to shape perceptions. Thus, practitioners are likely to be influenced by the context in which they are located – the type of organisation, its activities and its history, with regard to the development and structure of its specialist functions. Within particular organisations, shared perceptions, based on commonly accepted vocabularies which become the basis of regular communications, might be quite strongly established and be part of the local culture of that organisation. However, there might be a much wider divergence of viewpoints between practitioners who come from quite different organisational backgrounds. The varied contexts, associated, say, with such diverse fields as manufacturing, retailing and service organisations, might result in practitioners from each having different pictures of the possibilities. (*See* the section in Chapter 1 entitled 'The varying nature of purchasing and supply management' for analysis of a range of factors that might cause contextual differences.)

Writers and academics, however, are likely to be more concerned with developing ideas of a more generic nature and, in doing so, may minimise or ignore the impact of differences in particular contexts. Students, especially those who are not attached to an organisation, may also be interested in increasing their awareness and understanding of ideas which are purported to have general applicability. Persons linked to professional bodies may share similar concerns in identifying groups who appear to have common interests and a shared body of knowledge, techniques and skills. The overall impact of this first difficulty is that, even when the same words are used, different constructions or meanings may be placed upon them. Dictionaries may help to standardise meanings, but usage of words often tends to defy such attempts.

A second, related, difficulty, which is more fundamental, arises from considerations of the very basis of knowledge and the nature of the world in which people operate. When considering what the purchasing and supply function is, it is possible to approach the question in a number of different ways. One approach might be to construct a view that is based upon what people do in a specialist department or unit within the structure of a particular organisation. Another route is to consider the function in terms of a range of activities encompassed by the phrase 'purchasing and supply'. Though there may be considerable overlap, some purchasing activities in a particular organisation may not be carried out by the specialist department. The word 'function' is, thus, open to ambiguity. From a strategic point of view, two opposing ways of managing and organising the relevant activities emerge from this conclusion. One is to centralise all the activities denoted as belonging to the idea of purchasing and supply within the remit of a specialist department. The second policy might allow people in other departments to take on at least some of the activities, though they might apply policies and procedures devised by the specialist department.

Within the body of knowledge associated with the specialist area covered by this book, different purposes can be detected, although the differences may sometimes at first be obscured. Prescriptive approaches set out ideas for practitioners to adopt and implement in their own contexts. In setting goals to be followed and procedures and techniques to be utilised in pursuing them, the reader is offered ideals to aspire to. However, in so far as the presenters of these prescriptions base their recommendations on their observations or impressions of practice, an implied descriptive approach may underpin their accounts. Other writers, however, start out primarily with the purpose of describing and explaining practice. Some may focus on the behaviour and actions of people, while others cover what the function sets out to achieve in terms of objectives and contributions to the wider organisation. The latter functional descriptions tend to treat the function as an independent entity, and to reify it or give it human qualities. Such comments lead on to questions of an ontological and epistemological nature which focus on the existence of the phenomena under investigation and the ways through which knowledge about them can be established. Such questions become important in assessing the nature of some of the newer terms appearing in the purchasing and supply literature – 'supply chains', for example.

A strong tradition in business studies, either explicitly or implicitly, has been to emulate the assumptions of the mainstream social science disciplines, which in turn reflect what are thought to be the basic foundations of knowledge in the natural sciences. Within this paradigm, phenomena are seen to exist in the real world and be open to observation and to be amenable to being explored objectively and theoretically in terms of their relations to other phenomena. Part of the field of purchasing and supply might be said to have a tangible and physical base and, thus, be appropriate for this mode of research and description. In relation to manufactured goods, physical constraints arising from the nature of the materials being processed, the weight, quantity, distance and time factors associated with their transportation and other tasks, such as storing and inspecting them, are clearly open to objective observations.

While many social scientists seek out factors in the social world which can be accounted for objectively by independent human investigators, doubts have arisen as to whether such an enterprise is possible. The phenomena are not tangible and not as easily accessible to the senses. The main problem is that the observer or investigator is involved in interpreting or establishing the meanings of terms being used by those under investigation and whose behaviour is being studied. Of course, another side to purchasing and supply work is that concerned with the interpersonal and social aspects of the activities, and it brings out problems of meanings associated with terms that are used in communications.

Another school of thought within the social sciences adopts the view that there is greater subjectivity in explanations of the social world, including the business world. People are involved in constructing their viewpoints through processes which involve choices of words and interpretations of them. However, it is claimed that they often take conceptual frameworks for granted and do not automatically question them. Though providing guidance to conduct, such 'mindsets' can also act as a straitjacket, in the sense that they prevent other perceptions from being formed. On the other hand, it is possible for people to choose to reflect and consider whether there are alternative ways of seeing things, and different constructions might then be brought into play. There is an element of creativity and learning, therefore, in how situations are perceived and opportunities for problem solving developed.

Within the argument developed in the previous paragraph, language and the meaning of words play an important role. During periods of change, basic conceptual frameworks, which formerly were taken for granted, are more likely to be questioned. In response, some minor modifications could be introduced or, on occasion, even more radical and substantial changes may need to be made to the way in which situations and possibilities are perceived. As basic frameworks are consciously appraised and evaluated, the artificial nature (in the sense of human creation) of such structures may become more apparent. Other structures can be built up as part of a learning process. However, as new patterns of thinking become established and shared, these might take on a more independent existence, as a new orthodox version, and a strong guiding force in the construction of a 'world view' in the minds of individuals.

Major improvement initiatives, which organisations have implemented in recent years, have posed fundamental challenges to previously accepted ways of managing people and organisations. These initiatives are typified by programmes such as total quality management (TQM),[1] just-in-time (JIT),[2] lean production (LP)[3] and world class manufacturing (WCM)[4] in the manufacturing sector and efficient consumer response (ECR)[5] and quick response (QR)[6] in the retailing sector. 'New management' has been introduced into the public sector in the United Kingdom. (Please note that further references to these programmes will be made in the next chapter and in Part Two.)

Visions which have stimulated the introduction of these programmes tend to have as a driving force a similar set of goals, which include raising the level of quality, better delivery performance, reduced costs and improved financial performance, as well as enhanced and more flexible levels of service for customers. However, as we have pointed out, interpretations of these terms vary, giving rise to differences in details and priorities in individual implementation programmes. In particular, a major point of variation is the extent to which traditional methods of management and organisation have been challenged and altered. These programmes have contributed to changes of views about the contextual background to the purchasing and supply function, and have also been influential in leading towards alterations in ways of thinking about purchasing and supply matters themselves.

We now turn to the traditional model of purchasing – a model which tries to depict some of the pivotal characteristics making up the basic outlook of this area of activity, when envisaged as a specialist field in its own right. We then trace the development of ideas which have presented alternative perspectives and analyse the salient features of these.

The traditional model of purchasing and its context

The pivotal features of what is referred to here for convenience as the traditional model, emerged at a time when the advantages of specialisation and the development and application of relevant skills and knowledge were being advocated. The features are summarised in Fig 1A.1. The basis for a profession was established and career prospects within this function were promoted. A normative or prescriptive body of knowledge captured and underpinned such developments. The immediate context for purchasing is seen to be the firm or organisation of which it is a part, and so ideas about the management of the purchasing function tend to reflect orthodox doctrine about the management and control of this wider unit. For companies in the private sector, the dominant features of this approach stem from the responsibilities and objectives which are derived from the legal framework which applies to this particular form of business unit. Ideas, which support both specialisation of efforts and the control and co-ordination of activities in pursuit of company goals, are taken from the classical and scientific management traditions. These stress the use of rational planning and objective decision-making approaches in the pursuit of both efficiency and effectiveness. The role of experts and managers in deciding what should be done tends to be separated from those carrying out

---

1 Purchasing as a specialist department
   – in its own right; or
   – as a sub-unit within another department.
2 Purchasing responsible for placing orders with suppliers.
3 Policies and procedures to guide enquiry/competitive bidding processes and order placing or contract management activities, including expediting or progressing tasks.
4 Objectives are summed up by the phrase: 'the right quality, in the right quantity, at the right time, from the right supplier, at the right price and to the right place'. Price, however, often features strongly in decision making and in the evaluation of performance.
5 Individual transactions, involving the exchange of goods and services, usually in return for money, form the basis of the purchasing task, though some contracting to cover repeat requirements does occur.
6 The purchasing department is seen as fitting into a hierarchical organisational structure. This context is characterised by classical management and scientific management principles, ideas reflected in what now may be called 'Taylorism'.
7 Relationships with suppliers are largely competitive or adversarial in nature, as far as both indirect, 'arm's length' paperwork mechanisms and more direct, negotiating processes are concerned.
8 Especially before the advent of computer systems, administrative and paperwork procedures take up a significant percentage of time.

Fig 1A.1 Features of the traditional model of purchasing

tasks in the lower levels of the organisation. Such a perspective tends to be allied with economic thinking, which takes, as its ideal, the model of perfect competition. Arising from such a perspective, the role of the company is to compete in markets for both the supply of input factors and the sale of outputs, whether in the form of goods or services. The metaphor of the market-place, thus, provided the wider context in which firms are seen to operate and purchasing, as a specialist function might, thus, be given responsibility to operate at the interface with suppliers in such markets.

The function of stores and stock control, encompassing both the management of goods in warehouses and the control of stock levels and their replenishment, could be subjected to similar analysis to that in Fig 1A.1, as could other areas which are seen as separate specialisms, such as transport and distribution and production control. Developments in these areas, as they relate to purchasing, will be examined later.

Trends in the evolution of ideas about the context of the function

Before exploring the developments in the progression from the traditional model of purchasing, it is useful, first, to take into account recent alternative viewpoints of its context. These include ideas about the nature of organisations, the management of them and their relationship to the wider context of the economic system. Again, the main points can be presented in summary form, as indicated in Fig 1A.2. In general, it might be argued that these changes lead to a more flexible, responsive organisation able to develop innovative responses to requirements. These trends arise as responses to external forces to become more efficient and effective, as outlined elsewhere in Chapter 1.

Directions of change in the expansion of ideas about purchasing

We can now trace developments in the expansion of ideas about the purchasing function and other closely linked specialist activities. Although changes have, in part, arisen from contextual factors, as organisations have undergone major transformations, some influential ideas have been generated within the function. Those within the function have also contributed to wider changes. Where collaborative arrangements have been established between buying and selling companies, it might be said that these have replaced methods associated with exchange transactions in atomistic markets. Industrial purchasing and also industrial marketing and selling practices are conducted on a radically different basis and different mindsets need to be adopted. The main points in the development of purchasing thinking are presented in summary form in Fig 1A.3.

Experiences of operating within specialist purchasing departments have revealed that a wide array of activities in relation to the flow of goods, both

1   Changes in organisational structures, especially of larger organisations:
   - de-layering, i.e. reducing the number of levels in hierarchies;
   - attention given to cross-functional processes which serve customers;
   - development of mechanisms to encourage co-ordination of work on a multi-functional basis;
   - delegation of responsibility to the lowest levels considered feasible, to encourage initiative and innovation by those directly involved in the tasks;
   - less emphasis on vertical channels of communication and more attention given to horizontal directions;
   - modifications in managerial and supervisory styles to give attention to a facilitating role;
   - changes to incentive and staffing systems to support the other developments.

2   Changes in organisational approaches in relation to the wider context:
   - closer attention to what activities should be carried out within the boundaries of ownership and to what should be left to suppliers or customers to carry out – to give more focus to developing 'core competences' and only doing what the firm can do competitively in relation to others. Such make-or-buy studies and market testing approaches have led to more outsourcing of jobs, involved with the production of both goods and services and the vertical disintegration of many larger, more complex companies;
   - while some changes result from the use of competitive methods, other changes arise out of the recognition that improvements in arrangements for the supply of goods and services might be achieved by closer co-operative working methods between suppliers and customers, which emulate the fostering of collaboration between functions internally;
   - taken together the preceding two points permit organisations to consider working closely with key suppliers and customers and creating integrated production and supply networks which transcend organisational boundaries as depicted in terms of legal ownership of assets and groupings of employers and employees.

Fig 1A.2   Trends in the evolution of ideas about the context of the function

inside and outside the immediate sphere of control, were interlinked. The interdependent nature of features of, for example, the harmonisation of administrative procedures, records and vocabularies, as well as the conjuncture of responsibilities at the interfaces, were recognised. Above all, it was realised that factors and considerations outside the immediate remit of a particular specialist department might be affected by actions and decisions being contemplated. How are potential conflicts of interest to be overcome, when performance measures might encourage narrow departmental goals to be followed at the expense of the interests of an organisation as a whole? In other

1   Trends towards the integration of supply activities within individual organisations, as revealed by the following possibilities:
   – the adoption of organisational structures which group a wider array of activities under the unified control of a single manager (see Fig 1A.4);
   – the diffusion, to those involved in supply issues, of a philosophy which is built on an awareness and an understanding of the wider considerations;
   – the introduction of other integrating mechanisms, such as cross-functional units, aligned to horizontal processes, and multi-functional teams, such as project-based teams, joint committees, working parties and task forces;
   – the development of integrated information systems, which establish joint planning and control systems and shared databases – computer-based approaches especially may offer such potential.

2   The emergence of perceptions of the interdependent nature of supply issues, which transcend ownership-based organisational boundaries.

   This wider systemic nature of supplies activities, as captured by such phrases as 'supply chains', value systems', 'networks' and 'extended enterprises' opens up possibilities that are less visible or not even conceivable within narrower conceptual frameworks. The main implications are as follows:
   – the development of strategies for the role and positioning of an organisation in the wider entity and of the configuration of its shape and structure;
   – the widening of frameworks for decision making, to include objectives and factors relevant to the sequence of activities in the chains or networks of material flow;
   – the consideration of collaborative arrangements – such as joint planning and control systems – which might give rise to decisions made by inter-organisational groups of personnel, who might be considered as belonging to 'quasi-organisations'.

   (*Note*: The terms 'supply chain management' or 'network sourcing' might be used to cover the approaches outlined above.)

3   Developments in strategic planning processes in relation to supplies matters, shifting the emphasis away from shorter-term transactions.

Fig 1A.3 Directions of change in the expansion of ideas about purchasing

words, a wider systemic perspective supports moves to foster interdepartmental co-operation and closer co-ordination of activities in order to pursue the objectives of what might be conceived as a more inclusive system.

One of the proposed solutions stresses the need to set up more integrated units within an organisation's structure, though units that were formerly separate might be retained as sub-functions within the revised arrangement. Any conflicts of interest can be settled in terms of the responsibilities and of the performance of the broader structure as a whole. A number of possibilities are identified in Fig 1A.4.

Among the possible structures are the following:

1 **Purchasing and supply**, combining 'purchasing' and 'stores and stock control'.

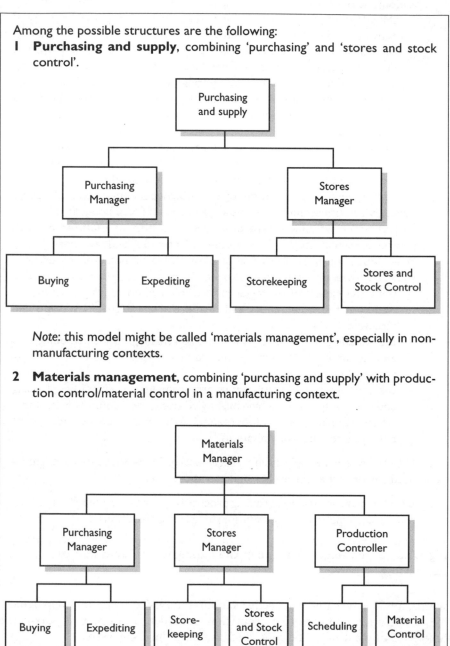

Note: this model might be called 'materials management', especially in non-manufacturing contexts.

2 **Materials management**, combining 'purchasing and supply' with production control/material control in a manufacturing context.

Fig 1A.4 Integrated structures

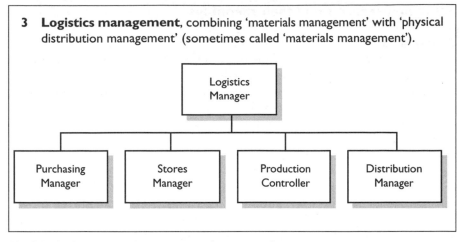

3 **Logistics management**, combining 'materials management' with 'physical distribution management' (sometimes called 'materials management').

Fig 1A.4 Integrated structures (*continued*)

There is no doubt that the perception which places the purchasing function and its parent organisation within a holistic framework built around ideas of the 'supply chain' or 'supply network', instead of within more conventional boundaries of 'markets' or 'industries', has opened up new roles for firms and novel strategic visions with regard to the operational possibilities and the range of techniques that might be implemented. There is no doubt that observations of Japanese approaches have had a part to play, though the lessons that have been learnt have led, in many cases, to their adaptation to western business environments, rather than simple step-by-step adoption process.

Changes in perception have affected not only the purchasing side, but also views of the marketing function and they have contributed to notions of 'relationship marketing'.

However, this Appendix focuses on a discussion of some of the key terms which have helped to structure thinking about this wider perspective and highlights their value. The status of these terms has been the subject of much discussion, but for the moment the analysis will assume that they are metaphors which have a pragmatic or heuristic value, even if they are not 'entities' capable of 'objective' definition. In so far as common perspectives, based on such terms, are shared between a group of people, they can help to generate programmes of activity that might not otherwise have been envisaged. In time, the concepts become taken for granted in constructions of 'views of the world' and may take on the appearance of independent factors. These interpretations frequently differ or are ambiguous, giving rise to some confusion, but also bringing benefits by expanding the full implications of the concepts and by making use of them in different circumstances.

Some newer terms and their meanings

Supply chain

One of the more widely used of the newer terms, this attempts to capture the idea of a sequence of interdependent tasks.[7]

The scope of the perspectives based on this term can vary, depending on the position and purpose of the person involved. It might be restricted to activities carried out within the confines of the boundaries of a firm, as defined in conventional legal terms. There may be internal chains within a single site, but, in more complex organisations, there may be chains linking operations between geographically separate operations (possibly on a global basis). Externally, there are chains in the flow of goods from original sources of raw materials through to the final customer. Firms located within a chain can, therefore, mix the 'chain' metaphor with a 'rivers' metaphor and refer to 'upstream' and 'downstream' sides. The idea of a 'supply pipeline' is similar.

Pictures based on these conceptions open up different ways of managing the flow of supplies and can stimulate the search to improve performance. Techniques for understanding the structures and assessing performance, such as flowcharts, are used to 'map' supply chains. The total impact of leadtimes and individual cycle times can be understood more clearly, for example, as a step towards reducing times.

Porter[8] uses the term 'value chain' to stress that each activity in the chain can be evaluated in terms of how it adds value and incurs costs. Although Porter limits the term 'value chain' to internal flows, he introduces the term 'value system' to cover the linkages between firms. Others have coined the term 'value stream' to address the wider system.[9]

Supply chain management

This phrase is concerned with processes and techniques brought into play to manage the flow of supplies through such chains. It is not normally conceived of as an organisational structure, along the lines of those identified in Fig 1A.4. However, it is not entirely clear whether it applies to a particular approach which emphasises 'progressive', collaborative arrangements, or whether it can embody a portfolio of different approaches for different situations. There seems to be some merit in adopting the latter view. While 'partnership' policies have been strongly advocated, as will be seen in Chapter 9, the view that a range of different types of relationships should be utilised is gaining support, as illustrated by Cox et al.[10]

Extended enterprise, lean enterprise and virtual organisation

These terms are similar, in the sense that they share a view that the destiny of particular firms is not tied solely to what they do themselves, internally, but is also affected by the collective performance of all the main contributing firms within connected supply chains.

Network

An extension of the supply chain concept is that of a supply network, to encompass the realisation that suppliers usually do not provide exclusive services to one customer only. Rather, they are involved in trading regularly with other key customers. Also, there may be scope for collaboration, for example between suppliers who serve the requirements of a particular customer, but who do not trade directly with each other. One mechanism is the supplier association.[11]

The phrase 'production networks' is sometimes used as a synonym for 'extended enterprise'.

An implication of the supply network is that the boundaries of different 'extended enterprises' might overlap, as particular suppliers are 'nodes' within different enterprises. Patterns of relationships may, therefore, be more complex.

Implications and benefits of current developments

There is no doubt that the emergence of new ways of thinking about supply matters has increased the need for strategic management of this field. In addition, a more varied range of possibilities has become available. Much of the remainder of the book is concerned with examining these in greater depth.

While the proliferation of terms and the apparent lack of agreement about their nature and their meaning might appear to be detrimental, nevertheless, they are an indication of the richness of the range of possibilities. Sensitivity to these issues is needed, however. Indeed, negotiation might be needed to establish agreed frameworks of ideas so that common perceptions can be arrived at. It is also difficult for individual people to use language consistently. In the context of this book terms such as 'purchasing' and 'purchasing and supply' will often be used to imply a broad picture of the range of activities and issues that might need to be taken into account in frameworks for decision making, as opposed to narrower definitions.

'Purchasing' was used as a starting point from which to explore the evolution of ideas arising from the growing recognition of the scope for managing interdependent chains and networks. However, it must be stated that similar developments in thinking have started in other specialisms, such as production or operations management. The image of the manufacture and supply of goods and services as a series of interdependent processes or activities, which are seen to cut across the boundaries of both specialist departments and individual organisations, is a powerful one. It gives rise to initiatives to improve performance on a more holistic basis and it reveals the limitations of some traditional decision models which adopt a 'closed' approach based on only a small number of variables. This point is referred to again in Chapter 3.

NOTES AND REFERENCES

1 *See*, for example, the following books on TQM related especially to purchasing:
Cali, J.F. *TQM for Purchasing Management*, McGraw-Hill (1993).
Hutchins, G. *Purchasing Strategies for Total Quality*, Business One: Irwin (1992).

2 In relation to purchasing, a useful reference is:
  Ansari, A. and Modaress, B. *Just-in-Time Purchasing*, The Free Press (1990).

3 *See*:
  Jones, D.T. 'Beyond the Toyota Production System: the Era of Lean Production,'
  Manufacturing Strategy – Process and Content (editor C.A. Voss), Chapman and
  Hall (1992), pp. 189–210.
  Womack, J.P. and Jones, D.T. 'From Lean Production to the Lean Enterprise',
  Harvard Business Review, March–April 1994, pp. 93–103.
  Womack, J.P., Jones, D.T. and Roos, D. *The Machine that Changed the World: The
  Triumph of Lean Production*, Rawson (1990).

4 For an account of 'World class manufacturing', *see*: DTI. *Aiming for World Class
  Manufacturing* (1991).

5 *See*: Buzzell, R.D. and Ortmeyer, G. 'Channel Partnerships Streamline Distribution',
  Sloan Management Review, Spring 1995, pp. 85–97.

6 *See*: Fernie, J. 'Quick Response: An International Perspective' *International Journal
  of Physical Distribution and Logistics Management*, Vol. 24, No. 6, 1994, pp.
  38–46.

7 *See*:
  Burnes, B. and New, S. 'Understanding Supply Chain Improvement' *European
  Journal of Purchasing and Supply Management*, Vol. 2, No. 1, 1996, pp. 21–30.
  New, S. and Mitropoulos, I. 'Strategic Networks: morphology, epistemology and
  praxis' *International Journal of Operations and Production Management*, Vol. 15,
  No. 11, 1996, pp. 52–61.

8 *See*:
  Porter, M.E. *Competitive Advantage: Creating and Sustaining Superior
  Performance*, The Free Press (1985).

9 *See* note 3 above.

10 *See*:
  Cox, A. 'Relational Competence and Strategic Procurement Management' *European
  Journal of Purchasing and Supply Management*, Vol. 2, No. 1, 1996, pp. 57–70.
  Cox, C., Hughes, J. and Ralf, M. 'Influencing the Strategic Agenda' *Purchasing and
  Supply Management*, September 1996, pp. 36–41.

11 *See* the following:
  For ideas on network sourcing and supplier associations, *see*:
  Hines, P. *Creating World Class Suppliers: Unlocking Mutual Competitive
  Advantage*, Financial Times/Pitman Publishing (1994).
  On innovations and networks *see*:
  Biemans, W.G. *Managing Innovation Within Networks*, Routledge (1992).
  Gadde, L.E. and Hakansson, H. *Professional Purchasing*, Routledge (1993).

PART ONE

Environmental change and strategic requirements

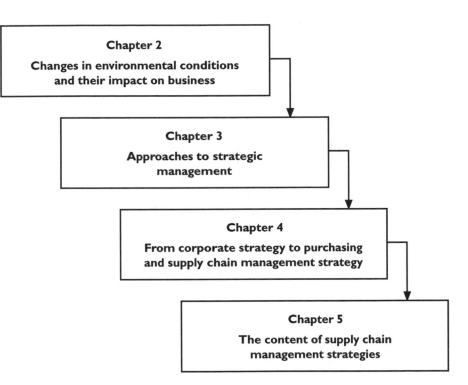

Chapter 2

Changes in environmental conditions
and their impact on business

Chapter 3

Approaches to strategic
management

Chapter 4

From corporate strategy to purchasing
and supply chain management strategy

Chapter 5

The content of supply chain
management strategies

INTRODUCTION

The world economy is arguably in a state of transition, in which the previously accepted 'best practice' conditions for industrial performance are changing and – with them – the whole structure of economic society.[1]

This quotation by John Bessant suggests that the context in which businesses and organisations now have to operate is undergoing major radical changes, which require radical responses by those businesses and organisations themselves. In other words, it is necessary for their leaders to develop not only appropriate short-term measures to pursue their goals in changing conditions but also strategies which can have a much more fundamental and long-term effect on the future direction and prospects of their businesses and organisations. At the same time, strategies for the functional areas, including purchasing and supply management, need to be created and linked in to the overall strategic approach being adopted.

The main task of Part One, therefore, is to consider, first, the nature and conditions of the environment and their implications for corporate and business strategy (Chapter 2). Then, approaches to strategic management will be considered and, also, their links to functional strategies (Chapter 3). In particular, aspects of how to integrate strategic purchasing and supply management into this overall picture will be discussed (Chapter 4). The content of the strategies for this particular function will be covered in the last section of Part One (Chapter 5). The model depicted in Fig 2.1 displays the relationships that guide Part One.

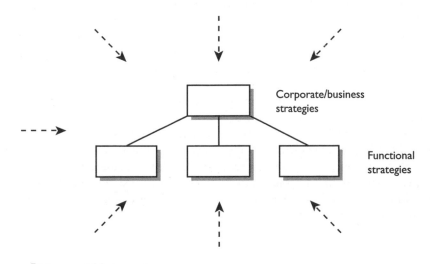

Fig 2.1 Environmental factors and the strategic approach

The underlying approach implies that, in so far as a conscious and deliberate attempt to formulate and apply strategy is possible, the process will involve the following main tasks. The scheme below, as portrayed in a popular text by Johnson and Scholes,[2] is representative of this 'rational' approach:

1 Strategic analysis of:
   - the environment;
   - expectations, objectives and power;
   - resources.
2 Strategic choice:
   - generation of options;
   - evaluation of options;
   - selection of strategy.
3 Strategy implementation:
   - resource planning;
   - organisation structure;
   - people and systems.

Although it is important to take into account 'process' and 'content' in relation to strategy, the 'context', with regard to both time and current situation and circumstances must also be considered. 'Situation' encompasses both the 'external' (*see* Chapter 2) and the 'internal' (*see* Chapter 4) environments. The context, the perceived starting conditions, in other words, acts as a constraint on what is feasible in terms of practical implementation programmes.

Philip Drucker, doyen of management writers, also suggests, in his book *The New Realities*, that the world is changing in a discontinuous fashion.[3] In his view, these changes affect all aspects of society, from government and politics to the economy and business, and operate on a global scale. People might disagree with the details of his analysis and his thoughts about the 'next century', but there is a warning about the dangers of underestimating the extent to which both the world and our ideas about the world are changing. Maintenance of the *status quo* and a more gradual, evolutionary pattern of change might seem to be more attractive to some and many might feel more comfortable with it, but discontinuous change seems to be occurring. Charles Handy, in *The Age of Unreason*, puts forward this viewpoint.[4] However, he also argues that the future is not inevitable and that it can be influenced, if people know what they want to do about it. This reinforces the view that businesses and organisations need to develop strategies to fit the environment, but that they may need to think of things in a new way and employ 'creative upside down thinking'.[5] Chapter 2 will attempt to trace in more detail the nature of these changes that are taking place and will also look at some of the changing ideas through which they can be interpreted.

NOTES AND REFERENCES

1 Bessant, J. *Managing Advanced Technology*, NCC Blackwell (1991), p. 9.
2 Johnson, G. and Scholes, K. *Exploring Corporate Strategy: Text and Cases*, 3rd Edition, Prentice-Hall (1993).
3 Drucker, P. *The New Realities*, Mandarin (1990).
4 Handy, C. *The Age of Unreason*, 2nd Edition, Century Business (1992).
5 *See* Handy, p. 19 (note 4 above) for a discussion of this point.

CHAPTER 2

Changes in environmental conditions and their impact on business

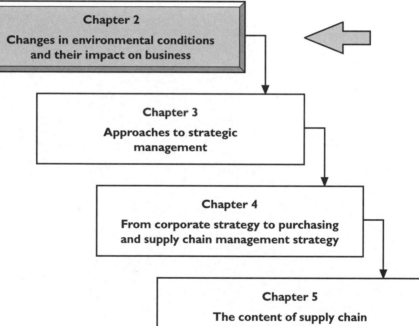

OBJECTIVES OF THIS CHAPTER

The main objectives to be covered in this chapter are:

1 To identify the main environmental factors that affect the formulation and implementation of corporate, business and functional strategies, including purchasing and supply strategies
2 To identify the changing nature of competition in national and international markets and changing priorities in the demands facing firms
3 To investigate and assess the impact of changing environmental conditions on the structure, methods and styles of management in meeting demands placed upon firms
4 To examine constraints and demands for improved performance in the public sector, with particular emphasis on non-market operations
5 To highlight the main implications of environmental conditions for strategic purchasing and supply management

THE NATURE OF CHANGE

The introduction to Part One drew attention to several analysts who have portrayed the nature of change in a dramatic, apocalyptic way. It is always tempting to adopt such a stance and to use the approaching turn of the century and the start of a new millennium as a stepping-off point for picturing a new age. It may be asked whether it is simply a convenient ploy to dress up change in a startling way to try and capture the imagination of potential readers. However, to see it as just a way of packaging and promoting ideas to capture attention would seem to ignore the points of evidence with which their ideas have been supported.

Nevertheless, if the views that have been advanced do seem to be too fanciful for some readers there is still some value in being exposed to them. There is, if nothing else, a warning about being too complacent and a reminder that there are dangers of failing to examine taken for granted perspectives of business activities and business conditions, which may no longer be valid or relevant. Consider for a moment the following two snapshot views of the United Kingdom.

View 1

1 United Kingdom industrial production is greater than that of Germany.
2 UK exports of manufactured goods exceed the combined total of France, Germany and Japan.
3 Coal is the main indigenous source of energy for heat and power. Steel and shipbuilding are important industries.
4 The pattern of trade involves net imports of food and raw materials and net exports of manufactured goods.
5 The main markets are in Commonwealth countries and in North America.

6 Japanese goods are cheap and of low quality.
7 International relations are dominated by the 'cold war' between the USSR and the West and the division in Europe is marked by the 'iron curtain'.

View 2

1 A fall by three-and-a-half million in the number employed in manufacturing compared with View 1 and the growth of the service sector to a prominent position.
2 The United Kingdom is now a net importer of manufactured goods and has continuing trade deficits.
3 Average rates of inflation and unemployment are generally greater than in View 1.
4 Coal, shipbuilding and steel industries are in relative decline (terminal?).
5 There are significant imports of goods from Japan.
6 Japanese investment has arrived in the United Kingdom, in particular in the automotive and electronic industries.
7 The United Kingdom is a member of a still evolving European Community.
8 Markets in Europe are vital for United Kingdom trade.
9 The 'iron curtain' and communist USSR no longer exist – the cold war has ended and the former empire of the USSR has fragmented into some independent republics.
10 Japan and Pacific Rim countries are now a significant trading bloc in world markets.
11 Shops in the United Kingdom display a wide range of rapidly changing consumer products.
12 There is now a prominent role for IT and for advanced manufacturing technology (AMT) in business.

A comparison of these two views suggests that there have been many major changes, even on the surface, over a period of only half a lifetime of someone born in the Second World War. However, a more detailed analysis and explanation of the changed picture can reveal just as significant a change in underlying business methods and ideas. To some this simply represents the decline of the manufacturing sector in the United Kingdom and is simply the result of the 'British disease', the proliferation of industrial disputes and restrictive working practices. However, characteristics such as trade deficits, imports of Japanese products and the introduction of Japanese transplants have also affected the economy and supremacy of even the United States. In developing an understanding of the problems and conditions faced by firms in the United Kingdom, it will be necessary to consider not only particular weaknesses in the United Kingdom, but also more general issues which pose a threat to North America and Europe in general. As well as goods, though, innovative ideas of how to manage businesses and of how to relate to suppliers and customers are also being imported from Japan. These are having a major effect on methods of operations and on the way in which businesses are being managed. Purchasing and supply management, of course, has played a significant part in the changing pattern of trade and the sourcing of goods from other parts of the world. As a function, it has also been affected by the importation of new ideas, as was indicated in the previous chapter.

ENVIRONMENTAL FACTORS

Bearing in mind the general background that has been depicted, of both national and wider world economies being in a state of transition, it is useful to consider a more formal model as a means of guiding an analysis of the environment, which a firm or its purchasing and supply function may wish to undertake. Key generic factors will be identified to help shape perceptions. They form a framework or skeleton (*see* Fig 2.2), which can direct more detailed investigations of the special circumstances that are salient for a particular organisation. Each firm or individual has to put the flesh on the bones, as it were, by collecting and analysing relevant data. Some examples will be given to help illustrate specific issues.

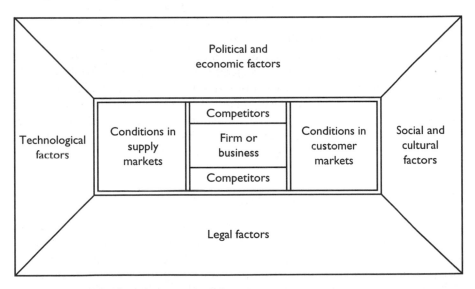

Fig 2.2 Model of environmental factors

The core of the model is the focal firm or organisation for which the analysis is being conducted. Also included inside the outer ring are three other boxes to indicate that the factors of the general external environment impact on the activities on both the upstream (suppliers) and downstream (customers) sides of the total supply chain, as well as on competitors in the same industry. The state of relationships between these factors and the focal firm are also relevant. The general factors in the outer ring will be discussed first.

Macro-economic and political factors

Breadth of perspective

The problem for the analyst is to decide which levels or tiers from the following list are pertinent to the study for a particular firm:

1 Local government and local economic factors
2 Regional government and regional economic factors
3 National government and national economic factors
4 Supra-national government and regional (in a broader sense of the word than in item 2) economic factors
5 International agreements

The relative power and influence of each tier may vary from country to country. Clearly, in the case of European countries the European Union and its constitution can affect operations of businesses within one country and between those in different member states, as well as between those in member states and others in non-member states. As far as the United Kingdom is concerned, and other member states, the impact of European Union policy and regulations emanating from Brussels is extensive with regard to business affairs. The creation of the single market and the flood of directives to bring about common and simplified trading conditions will be picked up in more detail when purchasing strategies are dealt with later on in the book. It is sufficient for the moment simply to mention that the development of rules for the free movement of goods between member countries, the development of common technical standards and the application of tendering rules are particularly relevant. Also, for those firms that deal in food products, the Common Agricultural Policy (CAP) is a major factor to be taken into account.

Regional and international trading arrangements

The strategies of firms inside the European Union naturally have to reflect consideration of the pertinent EU policies and regulations. However, the existence of trade barriers to those outside may affect the strategies of external firms. The operation of quota arrangements, which restrict imports of motor vehicles and protect the production of vehicles within member states, for instance, has been one of the significant reasons why Japanese car assembly companies have opted to pursue a policy of investment in manufacturing facilities inside the EU.

The rate of progress in the development of the European Union has been uneven and it has been marked by frequent controversies and crises. The extent to which rules and regulations have been adopted and enforced within member states has also varied. How quickly the EU will continue to develop and how fast the economies of member states converge, allowing the introduction of full monetary union, are difficult questions to answer at present. While exchange rate uncertainties exist, it is more difficult to conclude contracts between parties in different countries, because of the risk involved.

Other international agreements between countries, such as the General Agreement on Tariffs and Trade (GATT), can also be significant with regard to such trading factors as tariffs, quotas and other practices which might act as a barrier to free trade, such as public sector tendering. From time to time, under the umbrella of the GATT facility, changes are negotiated to further extend free trade conditions, though it can take several years to achieve such a 'round' of agreements, as illustrated by the tortuous negotiations of the so-called Uruguay Round, from which the World Trade Organisation (WTO) has emerged. In the absence of the GATT, there would be a stronger possibility of world trade degenerating into more rigidly divided and separated regional trading blocs.

Perhaps the most surprising and sudden change in international affairs in the second half of the twentieth century has been the breakdown of the communist world and the fragmentation of the former USSR into separate individual republics or the confederation of independent republics. The relative stability of the balance of power between the USA and the USSR (achieved under the threat of nuclear warfare and at the cost of high defence expenditure) has been replaced by some instability as a result of the surfacing of dormant ethnic differences and hostilities. Nevertheless the newly emerging conditions in eastern Europe are opening up new trading and investment opportunities. More open trading conditions are already affecting the price and availability of goods in the West, such as coal. The merger between former East and West Germany is but one of the developments that may increase European unity and lead to further expansion of the European Union itself. However, the ending of the cold war has contributed to a reappraisal of national defence policies by countries and the cutting of defence expenditures and a change of priorities with regard to weapons requirements. Changes in defence procurement policies have thus had an effect on the level and nature of demand for products from defence industries and their supply chains.

The final problem to be introduced for the analyst, with regard to political and economic factors, is to decide which countries should be brought into the framework for investigation. Selection should be guided by the relevance and potential influence of a country on key supply or customer markets, or on competitors of the focal firm. The level of opportunities and threats can change as a result of economic and political developments in countries. Changes in wage rates, levels of employment, distribution of income and governmental fiscal and monetary policies are just some of the factors that may need to be monitored. Changes in the constitutional structure of countries and in the fortunes of political parties gaining access to power may also have an impact on prospects. As both the number of countries and the level of world trade increases, so the problems of maintaining adequate reconnaissance of developments can become more complex.

Socio-cultural factors

As well as having a relationship with the prospects of firms, political and economic factors will also interrelate with social conditions. In turn, socio-cultural factors and developing trends in social conditions will have a relevance for the strategic developments of firms. For current purposes, two main aspects will be highlighted. First, the impact of socio-cultural factors on the nature of consumer and other customers' demands for goods and services will be considered. This discussion will be followed by a brief look at the impact of socio-cultural issues on employment and human relations strategies.

Impact on demand

The function most concerned with building up expertise and knowledge about customer demand is obviously that of marketing, but it is important that those concerned with supply are conversant with the relevant conditions and changes in them. Changing customer tastes for goods and services and changes in habits, with regard to shopping and points of product and service delivery, can impact on supply strategies. Changes in advanced industrial nations, such as a rise in average levels of affluence, have fuelled demand for a much more varied range of products and services than was the case when consumers had only sufficient resources, at best, to concentrate on basic requirements of food, housing and clothing. Increased mobility, as a result of the continuing growth in the use of cars, has permitted a shift of emphasis away from town and city centre shopping to out of town sites. Retailers and their suppliers have had to become more adept at meeting these changing expectations.

There are, of course, variations in the distribution of consumer spending power. Variation in levels of income, often associated with different occupations, opens up prospects of market segmentation.[1] A market may be perceived to be subdivided into relatively homogeneous groups based on this factor, and each one may then be served by a tailored marketing mix with regard to product, price and promotional approaches. As society has become more diversified, other bases for segmentation may be found to be more appropriate. Different patterns of family structures, changing life-styles and other demographic characteristics, product usage patterns, geographical location, attitudes and psychographic features are just some of the other possible bases for segmentation. Industrial markets may also offer opportunities for the detection of appropriate ways of subdividing markets as a basis of developing differentiated marketing strategies. From both a marketing and a corporate viewpoint, a strategic choice arises with regard to which segments of the market are to be targeted. It will be argued later that manufacturing and purchasing and supply matters also have a bearing on the ability of a firm to meet the needs of customers in the different segments and that these should be taken into account when making strategic decisions.

Effect on HRM issues

The second concern with the nature of the social and cultural fabric of society is its impact on employment markets and human relations policies of firms. Levels of education and skill development, the degree of flexibility with regard to patterns of work, levels of unemployment and comparative wage and salary structures are all relevant factors. They impact on the ability of a firm to recruit and retain human resources and help to determine appropriate reward structures for firms. Socio-cultural conditions help to shape human factors, which play an integral part in the processes of introducing technological change and changes in other business methods. Both the content of strategies and their implementation should incorporate concern for these issues. Indeed, they may be the most critical with regard to whether projects are a success or a failure.

Technological factors

The most visible sign of technological change to consumers is that of changes built into the array of products and services offered in the market-place. The field of consumer electronics products, such as televisions and hi-fi equipment, is a good example, in which designs may be changed as often as twice a year. The pace of change is increasing and product design life cycles are shortening, as a result of both 'market pull' and 'technological push'. Product policies of firms, in other words, may reflect both new and changing customer needs and new product possibilities, which are being developed by research and development processes in the firm. In the case of new products, marketing policies may help to fashion customer tastes and create demand. There is a danger, of course, that too much attention to technological factors and too little to the needs of the market may lead to products failing to be viable because of a lack of demand. An analysis of changes in the design of products that reach the final customer will usually reveal that the innovative features are not just those added by the final producer's manufacturing operations. Many are embedded in the parts and materials which have been produced by the upstream supply side of the supply chain.

A further manifestation of technological change, which may be connected, though it does not have to be, with new product launches, is that of manufacturing or process techniques.[2] The introduction of robotics, for example, has dramatically altered the scope of processes with regard to performance characteristics, such as speed, consistent quality and cost, in such operations as car body assembly work. The introduction of automated teller machines in the world of banking has transformed both money transfer processes and the relationship of clients and the bank. It has also affected greatly the jobs of bank workers. The latter example demonstrates that new technology has to be considered in relation to its impact on staff and workers as part of an integrated strategy. Simply investing large sums of money in new technology may lead to disappointing results if carried out without considering these other aspects sufficiently. Consider the following quotation:

. . . successful exploitation of technological opportunity depends not only on the technical system but on the match between that and the social and institutional framework.[3]

Advances in technology have also opened up new opportunities in the field of storage, transport and distribution; and exploitation of these innovations has contributed to improved performance in supply operations. Several examples help to reinforce this point. Combinations of mechanisation and automation have led to the use of automated warehousing techniques. Shipping, road and air transport have all adapted to the use of containers as a way of speeding up and reducing the costs of materials handling. The use of computers and bar-coding has created the ability to track and control the movements of goods and parcels more effectively. Thus, opportunities for improved supply chain performance in this field need to be carefully monitored.

As well as directly affecting the physical aspects of business (products, processes and equipment), changes in technology have also transformed administrative and office operations. Applications of information technology have led to widespread use of computer-aided design (CAD) and computer-aided engineering (CAE) techniques in developing product designs. Thus, drawings and design data can be stored and transmitted via computer systems. Similarly, computer-aided production management (CAPM) and the use of IT in purchasing and supply management have also had major effects on the way in which work is conducted and decisions made and on the level of performance achieved by operations. Some progress has been made in linking some of these so-called 'islands of automation' in pursuit of the idea of computer integrated manufacturing (CIM).

Technological change, through its various manifestations which have now been outlined, impacts on the development of business conditions and creates new opportunities for suppliers, producers and customers. Personnel in purchasing and supply management can influence the extent to which their organisations take advantage of them. A failure to recognise and exploit such innovations may jeopardise the future of their organisations. While day-to-day operations are affected by new technology, a strategic perspective is important in introducing it.

Legal factors

To complete the account of the environmental factors in the model, attention will now turn to the identification of the main legal aspects that affect both the way in which commercial affairs should be conducted and also the way in which organisations should be managed. As far as the United Kingdom is concerned, its Parliament is the source of legislation, which can impose duties and obligations on firms, as well as providing a framework within which commercial transactions should be conducted. It also enacts and empowers the requirements emerging from the machinery of the European Community. Current legislation, and any proposed changes to it, clearly have to be taken into account in the development of strategies for organisations in general and purchasing and supply management in particular. The main areas of concern can be identified, though it is not intended to analyse any of them in detail in this book:

1 Company law and other laws governing the operation of public sector organisations
2 Commercial and consumer law governing ways of conducting commercial transactions and competition
3 Health and safety legislation
4 Employment and industrial relations
5 Law of carriage and transport

'Green' issues and environmental protection

Concern is growing throughout the world for 'green' issues and environmental protection and it is an aspect of particular importance for both corporate and purchasing and supply management strategies. Conservation of resources, pollution of the air, water and land through the operations of firms and the removal and disposal of waste products are items on an agenda for attention. However, it is a topic that does not fit neatly into the framework of analysis. It is no less important than the others as a result of this difficulty. Indeed it transcends the four categories of the model. There is growing political interest in the topic and there are legal measures through which obligations and duties may be imposed on companies. It is also a matter of social concern, which may manifest itself through customer preferences for the types of goods and services that people are prepared to buy. Finally, there are major implications from the point of view of technological change and the design of products, plant and equipment.

The model used to guide the identification of the relevant environmental factors for businesses and the development of strategies tends simply to generate a list of the key ones. It does not focus, however, on the reasons why changes are occurring, nor does it explain the nature of the relationships that might exist between suppliers and the producer and between the producer and customers. Furthermore, it does not account for the nature of competition and levels of performance in the industry. The next section will attempt to remedy these deficiencies.

THE CHANGING NATURE OF COMPETITION AND DEMANDS ON FIRMS

A starting point to build up an understanding of the changing nature of competition and the demands placed on firms is to analyse the performance of firms in the economy of the United Kingdom. It will become apparent later that issues within this country are not necessarily different from those faced by other countries in Europe and America.[4] There has been no shortage of attempts to examine the problems of the economy in the United Kingdom since the end of the Second World War.[5] Many proposals to solve them have also been prescribed, based on the diagnoses which have been made.[6] Initially, concern for the relatively weak performance of the United Kingdom's economy was based on comparisons with the USA and other European countries. However, new standards of performance came into the reckoning, especially in the late 1970s and in the 1980s, as the Japanese economy marched ahead. Japanese companies not only conquered markets in Europe and America with their products, but also began to invest in productive facilities in those continents and to enter into alliances with other European and American companies.

The nature of discussions started to change as a result of this transformation of global competition. Studies began to declare that similar problems and demands confronted companies in other countries, as well as in the United Kingdom. At the same time, the nature of the problems and explanations of them, as well as proposed remedies, have changed. The value to be gained from looking at these general analyses is that an agenda of the significant issues and appropriate strategies for overcoming them can be compiled. Items on this agenda are directly relevant to corporate, business and functional strategies – including purchasing and supply management strategies amongst the latter. Indeed, concern for the latter area has been accentuated by commentators and has raised the profile of purchasing and supply management issues.

To explore these problems further, attention will be turned first to the manufacturing sector, an area that suffered most severely in the early 1980s. There are several indicators that point to the relative decline of manufacturing (in some years the decline was absolute and there was a drop in total output). These include the output of the sector declining as a percentage of the economy as a whole, a decline of the percentage of world trade and the fall in the level of employment. Other signs of poor performance are a low return on capital, low levels of investment in new plant and in research, as well as high levels of stock and work in progress. Low rates of increase in productivity by international standards is also seen as another sign of weakness. Perceptions of the problems were sharpened by the harsh economic conditions then prevailing, and the battle for survival left no room for complacency. It can be argued that conditions of adversity can not only make it easier to introduce changes, but also allow serious consideration for more revolutionary solutions. Many companies have introduced radical changes as a result, but some did not survive long enough to contemplate what was needed. So, what were seen to be the causes of the problems faced by firms in the manufacturing sector?

General arguments for the relative decline in manufacturing

Certain general arguments regarding the relative decline in manufacturing will be presented first. These include:

1 De-industrialisation
2 Catching up by other countries
3 Cultural aspects
4 Lack of competitiveness

De-industrialisation

There is a view that the decline of manufacturing is a stage in the development of advanced economies and that the service sector becomes the dominant sector as growing affluence builds up demand for outputs from it. In the United Kingdom there appeared to be some support for the idea that manufacturing no longer mattered, as long as activities and the creation of wealth grew elsewhere. Similar trends have been occurring in other countries. However, for a country like the United Kingdom the realisation that there are strong reasons for attempting to retain a significant manufacturing capability gained strength. In order to continue to import the range of goods and services, foreign earnings had to come from the export of goods. Capacity for foreign earnings to expand sufficiently from the services sector was deemed to be infeasible. An additional point put forward is that, compared to services, there are greater prospects of productivity growth in the manufacturing sector, and, therefore, it is beneficial to the growth of the economy as a whole. A fact not always recognised is that the manufacturing sector is not separate from the services sector as it is an important consumer of service products. Thus, there have been various initiatives to stem the decline and to revive the fortunes of the manufacturing sector.[7]

Catching up by others

Another argument is that other countries were bound to catch up the country that had led the way as the 'workshop of the world'. The main problem with this point is that others had not only caught up, but overtaken the United Kingdom. The latter has demonstrated generally slower rates of growth and lower rates of increase in productivity by comparison.

Cultural aspects

A view related specifically to industrial performance in the United Kingdom puts the main weight on the predominant culture of the country, which is seen by some to be anti-industrial.[8] Educational systems did not support the values of industry and the brightest output of the traditional universities scorned going into manufacturing, preferring to create careers in the civil and diplomatic services. Alternatively, a career in finance in the City of London or in the media is to be preferred to 'getting dirty hands' in industry. Success in industry is not something that is given recognition in society. While this thesis may play a part, it is doubtful whether all the problems can be explained by it.

Lack of competitiveness in the manufacturing sector

A final general argument is that firms in the United Kingdom lacked the capability to compete in world markets and even in the domestic market, where they were unable to ward off the invasion of foreign producers. Shipbuilding, motor cycles and televisions are some examples to illustrate this point. Lack of competitiveness was seen to embrace not only price, but, perhaps more significantly, other dimensions such as quality and delivery performance. 'British is best' is an epithet that had lost its validity, if it ever had enjoyed it. Lack of competitiveness is a key point that will now be analysed in more depth.

Causes of the lack of competitiveness

It is possible to suggest that there are two main lines of argument with regard to the possible contributing factors to the lack of industrial competitiveness. On the one hand, factors with regard to government economic policy may have created a context in which it was difficult for manufacturing firms to perform well. Following this line of argument, the finger of blame might be pointed at specific measures with regard to taxation, investment allowances, interest rates, exchange rate policy and regional policy, for example. Perhaps more importantly, the overall thrust of fiscal and monetary approaches leading to instability – swinging from 'stop' to 'go' phases – may have been a more serious problem. The overall effect of these 'stop-go' cycles is that it is difficult for firms to plan investments for steady growth. However, there is little that individual firms can do about government policy, other than develop their competence in lobbying politicians. The other groups of factors contributing to weaknesses bring the factors closer to home – factors within the firm, over which there is some control.

Weaknesses in firms

Analysts have drawn up a long list of contenders that may be relevant as explanations of poor performance. No one point is sufficient on its own, but rather all have had some part to play at times, though not all together in any one firm. The list consists of, at least, the following:

1 Inept management, because of a lack of education and training.
2 Management slow to innovate and exploit inventions.
3 A lack of research and development – except in defence industries, where returns were low.
4 Management attitudes that perpetuate the division of 'them' and 'us'.
5 Lack of investment in new technology.
6 Restrictive work practices, defended and perpetuated by trade unions, including opposition to new technology.
7 Disruptions caused by strikes.

8 'Short-termism', which meant that managers had to concentrate on delivering good results in the short term to satisfy the stock market.

9 A lack of capital because of the lack of support and understanding amongst financiers.

10 Companies in other countries, especially in Japan, had improved faster in terms of producing better quality products, at lower cost and in shorter periods of time. These companies had also become more successful in managing the development of new products.

The decade of the 1980s became a period of transition as the manufacturing sector attempted to find solutions to its problems, and the process of transition is by no means complete. Different industries and different companies have progressed at varying rates. The leading industries have been those of electronics and automobiles. New ideas had been sought in earlier decades and many of these had been imported from the USA. However, analysts who visited Japan from the late 1970s onwards came back with findings that triggered off a more fundamental reappraisal of both business practice and theory.[9] This reappraisal seemed to have relevance for western business practice in general and not just for the United Kingdom. The search for 'competitive advantage' and attempts to achieve 'world class manufacturing standards' became the goals of firms on both sides of the Atlantic. These concerns will be examined shortly in more detail, and the implications for purchasing and supply management will be examined. However, before doing so, it is necessary to say something about competitiveness in the service sector.

Problems in the service sector

As recession returned to the United Kingdom at the end of the 1980s, following a period of revival in the middle of the decade, hopes for a period of continuing growth were severely dented. Some progress had been made in improving the prospects of manufacturing, but doubts about the efficiency and effectiveness of the service sector began to grow as the recession began to bite here as well. Concern for improved performance was partly coloured by ideas transplanted from the manufacturing sector and partly stimulated by other forces for change, such as changing technology in banking and retailing. The government had also been concerned with levels of public expenditure and had raised doubts with regard to both the levels of effectiveness and efficiency being achieved by public sector organisations. Thus, these other parts of the economy were not immune to the fundamental reappraisals of methods of managing and organising businesses taking place in the manufacturing sector. Indeed, some had taken a lead in introducing changes, for example the retailing sector.

CHANGING IDEAS OF MANAGEMENT AND ORGANISATION AS A RESPONSE TO CHANGING ENVIRONMENTAL CONDITIONS

Both economists and management writers have contributed to the reappraisal of business practices and to the formation of proposals to improve performance. In doing so, questions have been raised with regard to the relevance, validity and value of what might be regarded as accepted conventions within both streams. Basic ideas about how to manage the internal affairs of firms and about the relationships between firms have been challenged, therefore. The following quotation, from Morris and Imrie, underlines the nature of the changes that have been taking place:

> The transformation of industrial organisation in Britain has been profound and dramatic since the early 1980s, given the development of new manufacturing systems, new styles of industrial relations, and the adaptation of new frameworks for product development, systems engineering, and marketing . . . a key component is the realignment of buyer-seller relations and the adoption of new supply practices by segments of British industry.[10]

Michael Best has argued that the West was slow to explain post-war Japanese economic performance, because initially there was no framework of ideas to explain it.[11] When this had been developed, he argued, the solutions to problems arising from the analysis required managers to adopt a new paradigm – a new set of concepts to restructure businesses and to manage production. He has put forward a critique of traditional theory and has highlighted what he sees as the main points of the 'new competition'. His work belongs to what is referred to as the institutional approach. An account will be given of some of his key ideas, but first it is necessary to identify the main building blocks of traditional thinking.

Perspective from institutional economics

Traditional economic theory had tended to focus on the behaviour of markets and prices in the model of perfect competition, and had tended to give little attention to differences in management practice as a source of variation in performance. It is essentially a static model and emphasises profit maximisation, price competition and cost minimisation. Little scope is left for managerial choice and selection of different strategies. Economic theory had also left only two basic choices with regard to co-ordination and control of the chain of different stages of production. The first is to use the market mechanism to organise the exchange of goods and services between independent firms. The alternative would be for a firm to own the assets of different stages itself and to become vertically integrated, thereby extending the umbrella of the managerial hierarchy as a means of exercising direct control.

A research study, reported by Robert Hayes and Kim Clark, also drew attention to the significance of managerial policies in the explanation of different levels of productivity and cast doubt on the validity and utility of economic explanations.[12] Economic studies tend to look at variables, such as industry structure, size and technology, as causes of variation and relegate managerial and social factors to the status of a 'residual factor' of minor importance. However, under the category of managerial policies, they studied the impact of variables under the headings of equipment policies, waste and work-in-process inventory policies, workforce policies and policies affecting confusion in the factory (actions that disrupt the stability of the factory – fluctuations in volume, number of products produced, schedule changes, engineering change orders, introduction of new equipment). Finally, in this study one conclusion reached was that a dynamic perspective is needed, in which 'learning' is an important contributor to change.

To return to the 'new competition' views of Best, a dynamic perspective, which stresses the importance of continuous improvement, is one that he supports as well. Innovation in product, process and organisation should be the basis of the search for strategic advantage, in line with the theories of the economist, Joseph Schumpeter. The firm is depicted as being entrepreneurial in nature, and competition is as much in terms of new commodities, new technology and new sources of supply as of price competition. Strategic choice involves firms in 'choosing the terrain on which to compete'.[13] Firms are seen as social institutions with unique cultures, not just factors of production, and shared ideas, beliefs and norms are important in the development of teamwork and a resource to be cultivated. Teamwork is held to be important in achieving co-operation and co-ordination within the firm.

This revised view of the firm seemed to be able to accommodate the practices observed in Japan, such as just in time approaches to the elimination of waste, more effective management of new product development, the reduction of changeover and set-up times and more flexible work practices. The western principle of high volume, standardised production to achieve 'economies of scale' was challenged by the notion of 'economies of scope' – the ability to make a wider variety of products without suffering the penalty of high unit costs. However, another significant contributing factor was seen to be the interfirm relationships between buyers and sellers.

Instead of the 'arm's length', competitive practices of the market and reliance on the 'invisible hand' to bring about adjustments, a consultative, co-operative approach is seen as an alternative way of achieving co-ordination across the supply chain. Thus, 'partnerships', established on a long-term basis offer a way of employing the expertise of suppliers in supporting innovative strategies. There are benefits to be gained from the joint problem solving and joint actions of mutually interdependent firms in coping with technological change. Collaborative relationships can also be used to focus efforts on cost and price reductions. Thus, this partnership model represents a third type of mechanism and involves a less permanent arrangement compared to full vertical integration. It may offer a more productive outcome than the full competitive market model.

The 'new competition' model embodies different views about styles of management and attitudes towards workers compared with traditional western management views, as depicted in the concept of 'Taylorism'. This conflict is portrayed in the following quotation, by Konosuke Matsushita:

> We will win and you will lose. You cannot do anything about it because your failure is an internal disease. Your companies are based on Taylor's principles. Worse, your heads are Taylorised too. You firmly believe that sound management means executives on the one side and workers on the other, on the one side men who think and on the other side men who can only work. For you, management is the art of smoothly transferring the executives' ideas to the workers' hands.[14]

This statement perhaps underestimates the capacity of firms and people for change. Many of the ideas about Japanese business methods have been introduced and adapted to fit into firms in Europe and North America. Firms like Rover, through its alliance with Honda, and others, which have developed capabilities to become acceptable suppliers to Japanese transplant companies, have shown that it is possible to transform themselves. Former European companies, which have been taken into Japanese ownership, have also demonstrated the capability of introducing Japanese practices, while retaining the same workforce. A part of Dunlop's tyre making operation was bought out by a former franchisee, Sumitomo Industries, and it now thrives as SP Tyres. Nevertheless, while some of the leading companies have adapted their approaches in line with Japanese best practice, there are doubts as to whether Japanese practices have been widely adopted in industries other than the motor industry.[15]

Contrasting perspectives of management and organisation

It is possible to construct two models which capture the essential characteristics of the old and the new images of management and organisation – labelled here as the traditional model and the business process model.

The traditional model

The main characteristics of this model, implicit in traditional approaches to management of businesses as a whole and to management of particular functions, are as follows:

1 It stresses the hierarchical nature of and the vertical relationships of the organisation.
2 It adopts a reductionist approach and breaks down problems into separate closed ones, each to be solved individually.
3 Importance, because of item 2, is attached to specialist functions, each with its own goals and clear demarcation lines.
4 Emphasis is given to the goal of efficiency and top-down control.
5 Minimal attention is given to external links and interorganisational relationships.
6 Profit and the interests of shareholders are seen as the main corporate concerns.

7 Separation of knowledge and expertise from those who do the work on the shop-floor.

The business process model

On the other hand, the business process model gives emphasis to the following features:

1 It recognises the need to cope with a more turbulent and complex environment, in which there are multiple stakeholders – shareholders, customers, suppliers and employees.
2 The need to be effective and achieve competitive advantage in the market to attract and retain customers is stressed.
3 Emphasis is given to horizontal relationships, both internally and with other organisations, with particular attention being given to supply chains.
4 Use is made of multi-functional teams which adopt a broader, more holistic outlook on problems.
5 Problem solving approaches adopt a systemic perspective and emphasise the need for integration, often using information technology to achieve it.
6 Organisational structures have flatter hierarchies and blur both organisational and functional boundaries.
7 Development of skills and expertise and their application at the lowest levels in the organisation is part of the approach, which shows also a particular concern for pursuing continuous improvement.
8 As well as encouraging more participation by workers in improvement activities, work is allocated on a more flexible basis.

Roger Wolfe, for example, discusses some aspects of process management and the challenge it represents for managers.[16] If the discussion so far has concentrated on the more theoretical aspects of how organisations may need to respond in order to succeed in the changing environment, then attention to what has been called the 'lean production' model will switch the emphasis to more descriptive and empirical aspects. This model has been constructed by the IMVP study of the world automotive industry, which was referred to in Chapter 1.[17]

The 'lean' approach

John Krafcik contrasts the 'lean' approach to the older style which he calls the 'buffered' approach. The latter is characterised by large stocks of inventory, large repair areas and narrowly specialised workers. The Japanese 'lean' system, by contrast, has small stocks of inventory, its repair areas are smaller and workers are multi-skilled and work in teams. The 'buffered' system is described as offering low risk, safe conditions, but with low prospects of high rewards. Conversely, the 'lean' appears to offer more risk, but opportunities for much higher gain. The latter relies on things being right first time, as there is no built-in buffer or protection to cover mistakes and uncertainties. Thus, the importance of managing affairs well, in order to minimise the possibility of the more highly dependent system breaking down, has to be stressed.[18]

Daniel Jones, in his account, puts forward five principles that were found to characterise lean production organisations. They are as follows:

1 The maximum number of tasks and responsibilities are transferred to those actually adding value to the product on the line.
2 There is an effective system for immediately detecting defects and problems and tracing them to their root cause to make sure they do not recur.
3 There is a comprehensive information system so everyone can respond quickly to any problems and to understand the overall situation of the plant.
4 None of this is possible unless the workforce is organised into work teams, that need to be trained to do all the jobs in their area . . .
5 Such a high level of involvement in proactively solving problems cannot work without a strong reciprocal sense of obligation between the firm and its employees.[19]

To see this model in its historical context, the IMVP research team has compared it to the earlier, familiar models of craft production and mass production used at different stages in the automotive industry. At first the industry consisted of a larger number of small car producers and they relied upon the use of skilled craftsmen to tailor parts to make each car on a custom-built basis. Subsequently performance was transformed by the introduction of mass production as developed, in particular, by Henry Ford I. The adoption of assembly line techniques, the use of interchangeable parts and the application of the principle of specialisation taken to an extreme in the design of jobs, for instance, allowed the mass production approach to dramatically lower the unit cost of production. The combination of high-volume, low-cost, low-priced output allowed a mass market to be opened up, though initially little variation in product design was permitted.

The emergence of the lean production model represents another major transformation, according to the thesis of the IMVP research team. The lean production approach has been found to give a significantly superior level of performance compared with the mass production model. It is called 'lean', because 'it uses less of everything – half the time and effort to design the product and half the human effort and tooling to make it, with half the defects and less than half the inventories. As a result, the lean production system can offer the customer twice the number of products, that only need to be built in half the normal volume per model'.[20]

In essence, the standards being set by the lean production model encapsulate the challenge now confronting industry in Europe and America. Even in Japan, not all car makers had achieved them. A point emphasised by Daniel Jones is that all activities, manufacturing, product design and development, component supply and distribution, are capable of this two-to-one difference in performance. Aspects of managing the supply chain in terms of methods, relationships and performance are, therefore, an integral part of the lean approach. The implications for strategic purchasing and supply management are, thus, of major importance.

The approach, based on the 'lean model', has been elaborated further in subsequent work by Womack and Jones.[21] In addition, it has been extended to cover groups of firms, linked by collaborative arrangements in the supply chain to form the 'lean enterprise'. Opportunities to generate a competitive advantage arise, according to their thesis, by improving the performance of this wider unit of analysis. Kay[22] has also commented on the importance of establishing 'distinctive capability' in the 'external architecture' (i.e. relationships with suppliers) of organisations. However, according to Cusumano,[23] for example, there may be limits to the extent to which 'leanness' can or should be achieved. Problems may arise when there is a static or declining level of output and there are fears about the level of 'work intensification' that the workforce may have to endure.

Another study, also related to the automotive industry, is worth bringing into the picture at this point.[24] It focused on the design and development process and it too pointed to the superior performance of the best Japanese car assembly companies. A significant feature in this is the involvement and contribution of suppliers in helping to reduce both leadtime and product costs. The following quotation reinforces the strategic importance of supplier relationships in the engineering process:

> There is a growing recognition in the auto industry (and in other industries as well) that a network of capable suppliers integrated into the engineering process has significant advantages. The implication is that the critical managerial problem in product development is not only securing effective collaboration within the firm, but in managing the supplier network to achieve integration of the engineering effort.[25]

It has been demonstrated in this section of the chapter that developments, in both national and world markets, have indicated the need to achieve much higher standards of performance. Furthermore, radically new techniques and methods of management and organisation may be needed for firms to be able to achieve them. It is now appropriate to switch attention to the public sector and to examine the forces for change and their impact on organisations in this sphere.

CHANGES IN THE PUBLIC SECTOR

The Conservative Party, which held the reins of government in the UK throughout the 1980s, had a period of power in which it could and did introduce a series of radical changes with regard to public sector organisations. It may be suggested that it was motivated by two considerations. In the first place, it wished to 'roll back the frontiers' of the state, as a matter of principle. It was also concerned with the level of public expenditure. On the one hand, some of its members were persuaded by the thesis of Bacon and Eltis, that the non-market sector was taking too many resources from the wealth-creating market sector.[26] Others were concerned about the way in which public sector organisations used the resources that were given them and felt that 'value for money' was not being obtained. Concern for the latter, as well as a commitment to the discipline of the market, seems to have influenced the policy initiatives that have been taken and that have had a significant effect on the structure of the public sector and the methods of management and control of the operations in public sector organisations. Once again, there will be implications in analysing these developments for strategic purchasing and supply management. Peninah Thomson has produced a perceptive and convenient analysis of these changes in public sector management.[27]

Themes in public sector changes

For present purposes only some of the themes and characteristics identified by Peninah Thomson will be highlighted, and these will be discussed in relation to particular reforms and initiatives. However, Colin Lyne[28] has provided a good account of the full implications of the changes for local government (with particular reference to procurement aspects), with regard to the acquisition of both support services within the local authorities and public services for their 'customers'. Walsh[29] has investigated the 'enabling nature' of the public sector, as shaped by recent reforms in the United Kingdom, as well as a much greater reliance, for the main mechanisms, on contracts (with external providers) and 'quasi-contracts' (with internal providers). Walsh has also drawn attention to the limitations of such contract management operations and has suggested that longer-term collaborative arrangements may have a part to play in the effective and efficient provision of services.

Privatisation

Privatisation of the state-owned monopolies is part of an ongoing programme and essentially involves those organisations that were in the market sector, with water, gas, electricity and telecommunications being illustrative examples. Nevertheless, as privatised monopolies they are subject to the surveillance of regulatory bodies which have been set up by Parliament. Such utilities are also covered by the directives of the European Community with regard to tendering regulations.

Delegation of managerial responsibility

Examples of this theme in operation can be seen in the reforms of the National Health Service and Local Management of Schools, in which responsibility has been pushed down to lower levels adjacent to the points of delivery of the service.

Competition

This is an area of special interest with regard to purchasing and supply management and there are two particular approaches that are pertinent:

1 **Competitive tendering.** Initiatives to extend compulsory competitive tendering and market testing, to cover the acquisition of services which had traditionally been provided in-house, raise several issues. They create new roles and also pose a threat to traditional employment and supervisory practices. Competition for the provision of services is extended to include private contractors and it also treats the internal 'direct service organisation' as a contractor as well, and it is seen to be separated from the 'client' for whom the service is provided. There is a growth in the use of tendering and contracting skills and expertise, therefore, in these developments.[30]

2 **The internal market.** The reforms of the National Health Service are partly based on the idea of introducing a clearer separation between those who provide the services and those who purchase them. One intention behind this new relationship is to try to bring the provision of services more in line with the needs of customers – ultimately the patients. At the same time, the introduction of purchasing and contracting procedures is designed to introduce competition and to exercise more effective control over the use of resources through the pricing mechanism of contracts. Thus, specialists in the District Health Authorities and doctors in practices which have been granted Fundholder status (responsibility for their own budgets) are taking on the purchasing role.[31]

A relevant strategic issue that emerges from the implementation of these competitive policies is the extent to which they are compatible or incompatible with the ideas of partnership and collaborative relationships between buyers and sellers, which are being pursued in the private sector.[32] This issue is discussed in more detail in subsequent chapters in discussions of the development and implementation of purchasing and supply management strategies. The 'internal market' is looked on as a mechanism to apply pressure for greater effectiveness in meeting the needs of patients. It is also a way of increasing efficiency and accountability in the use of limited resources at a time when demographic trends are contributing to a growth of demand on a year-by-year basis. The possibility of outsourcing services, as a result of competitive tendering, is a similar problem to 'make or buy' in manufacturing and raises questions in relation to structuring and control of supply chains.

Service quality

Policy initiatives with regard to service quality are in parallel with interests in the private sector in so far as there is increased emphasis on the quality of service outputs and the interests of customers or recipients of services. It represents a swing away from 'product-determined' service provision. This focus on customer service is demonstrated through the drafting of 'Charters' for the various organisations in the public sector (similar to the Citizens Charter) and the insertion of quality standards in contracts governing the provision of services.

Managerial approach

As well as allowing market and quasi-market forces to penetrate the management and control of the provision of services there is another development of major significance. The various reforms and measures signal a swing away from processes of administration to processes of management, which implies a number of changes in approach. There is more emphasis on leadership and a strategic role for chief executives and on the evaluation of processes and procedures, as well as calls for tighter financial control and performance monitoring. The management of cultural change, as organisations undergo fundamental reform and reorganisation, becomes a significant activity. In essence, the result is 'a move away from enforcement of defined processes and rules to the exercise of discretion'.[33]

In summary, therefore, the public sector has not been insulated from forces of change which have confronted the private sector. The introduction and management of changes has been just as evident in this part of the economy as well. Concern for value for money and the needs of customers are goals which can be shared with organisations in the private sector. Also, the encouragement of managerial approaches and the new relationships and procedures associated with tendering and contracting for specified services help to narrow the differences between the two sectors. Similar skills and expertise are applicable in both.

IMPLICATIONS FOR PURCHASING AND SUPPLY MANAGEMENT

The final objective of this chapter is to draw out the main points for strategic purchasing and supply management from the analysis of changes in the environment and of the problems facing organisations. These can be presented briefly and will serve the purpose of directing thoughts in the development of strategies for purchasing and supply management in Chapters 4 and 5.

1 Organisations, in both private and public sectors, are having to achieve higher standards of performance in terms of creating value for money in producing goods and services.
2 Environmental conditions are undergoing more rapid rates of change and organisations are having to undergo fundamental changes in both management approach and organisational structure in order to cope.
3 New ideas with regard to management and organisational approaches are helping to guide the strategic changes being introduced into organisations.
4 The relevance of purchasing and supply management and the need to manage supply chains have been identified as having a significant effect on the ability of firms to adapt to requirements.

5 The balance and mix of co-operative and competitive approaches in managing supply chains are aspects which need to be evaluated in the selection of purchasing and supply management strategies.

SUMMARY

In 1992, Toyota, the Japanese company that has been held up as the model of so much 'good practice' in making it a leader in the global automotive industry, began to produce the first cars from the assembly line of its new factory in the United Kingdom, at Burnaston in Derbyshire. It is following in the footsteps of other Japanese transplants in building up production facilities in this country. To some, this trend represents a threat, particularly immediate competitors, which may find its industry has too much capacity in relation to expected market demand. To others, however, such developments represent opportunities for the country. The arguments underpinning this second assessment are several.

In the first place, investment in new facilities creates employment opportunities and makes a contribution to the output of the economy. Also, the balance of trade position is helped because the new domestic output can reduce imports in meeting home demand. This output might, in addition, generate foreign earnings if some of it is destined for sale in foreign markets. There are other less direct benefits, which are also important, which stem from the standards being set. Potential suppliers can take advantage of opportunities to learn and to be involved in collaborative relationships with Japanese customers, which provide a framework within which to develop improvement programmes. The examples of the successful application of such new approaches are a clear demonstration that they can work in this country and that they can be taken up by the indigenous workforce. Finally, even direct competitors can be stimulated to make reform efforts, in order to improve their chances against others which lag further behind. In other words, there is visible evidence close at hand from which lessons can be learnt.[34]

The alternative viewpoint is that there is a threat to the economy, as ownership of industry falls into the hands of foreigners. Thus, the Japanese invasion is seen by some as a threat to Europe. They are reacting in the same way as those who saw danger in the economic invasion of Europe by American companies in the 1960s.[35] However, to resist the introduction of new approaches and to perpetuate the continuation of less effective and less efficient processes could spell danger in the long run. To some extent, protective barriers, in the form of quotas on car imports, for instance, have kept European countries from the full force of competition from imported products and may have slowed down the pace of change.

The introduction to Part One used a quotation to indicate that industry is in a state of transition. Some companies have already changed or are already going through a period of major readjustments, others have not yet started. It is a particularly challenging time for strategic thinking for both businesses and specialist functions. Pursuit of 'lean' performance in operations is becoming a necessity, in both public and private sectors, and purchasing and supply management is one of the areas that can play a major part in winning the race. John Bessant, when discussing the management of technological change, also points to the importance of interfirm linkages in successfully managing change processes.[36] He also makes reference to a view that says that the newly emerging forms of organisation are an indication that a major transformation in the way of organising and managing businesses is in progress. It is suggested that this fits the 'long wave' theory, first proposed by the Russian economist, Kondratiev. The new paradigm, to follow that of mass production and mass consumption, is sometimes called the post-Fordist model. Historians in the next century will be able to judge eventually if it is correct to view current changes in such revolutionary terms.

NOTES AND REFERENCES

1 For a discussion of the principles and strategies associated with market segmentation, *see*, for example:
   Adcock, D., Bradfield, R., Halborg, A. and Ross, C. *Marketing: Principles and Practice*, Pitman Publishing (1995), Chapter 7.
   Baker, M.J. *Marketing Strategy and Management*, Macmillan Press (1992).
2 The following books analyse the topic of technological change and discuss aspects of managing such change processes:
   Bessant, J. *Advanced Manufacturing Technology Management*, Pitman Publishing (1991).
   Harrison, M. *Advanced Manufacturing Technology Management*, Pitman Publishing (1990).
3 Bessant, J. *Advanced Manufacturing Technology Management*, (*see* Note 2), p. xi.
4 Abernathy, W.J., Clark, K.B. and Kantrow, A.M. 'The New Industrial Competition', *Harvard Business Review*, September–October 1981.
   Concern for a deepening sense of malaise in the USA was expressed in:
   Hayes, R.H. and Wheelwright, S.C. *Restoring Our Competitive Edge: Competing through Manufacturing*, John Wiley (1984), Chapter 1.
5 Many commentators have traced the problems of declining performance, both in the economy as a whole and in manufacturing, back to the previous century. *See*, for example, a brief survey of earlier studies and a reference to Prince Albert, the Great Exhibition at Crystal Palace in 1851 and the growing competitive challenge from overseas, in:
   Francis, A. 'The Process of National Industrial Regeneration and Competitiveness', *Strategic Management Journal*, Vol. 13, 1992, pp. 61–78. This same article provides, more importantly, many useful insights into present day difficulties and compares findings from both economists and management writers.
6 A famous example at the time was the study carried out by the Brookings Institution and which was reported in:
   Caves, R.E. and associates. *Britain's Economic Prospects*, George Allen and Unwin (1968).
7 The Confederation of British Industry (CBI), for example, produced a report 'Competing with the World's Best' and set up a National Manufacturing Council to help promote improvements in manufacturing firms.

8 Wiener, M. *English Culture and the Decline of the Industrial Spirit,* Harmondsworth (1981).

9 Examples of authors and consultants who did much to give early publicity to ideas about Japanese methods are:
Schonberger, R.J. *Japanese Techniques: Nine Hidden Lessons in Simplicity*, Free Press (1982).
Hayes, R.H and Wheelwright, S.C. *Restoring Our Competitive Edge: Competing through Manufacturing*, John Wiley (1984).
Hall, R.W. *Zero Inventories*, Dow-Jones Irwin (1986).

10 This quotation is taken from:
Morris, J. and Imrie, R. *Transforming Buyer-Supplier Relations*, Macmillan (1992), p. 17.

11 Best, M.H. *The New Competition: Institutions of Industrial Restructuring*, Polity Press (1990).

12 Hayes, R.H. and Clark, K.B.. 'Explaining Observed Productivity Differentials Between Plants: Implications for Operations', *Interfaces*, Vol. 15, No. 6, 1985, pp. 3–14.

13 Best, M.H. *The New Competition: Institution of Industrial Restructuring*, Polity Press (1990), p. 11.

14 This quotation, by Konosuke Matsushita in 1988, is printed in:
Best, M.H. *The New Competition: Institution of Industrial Restructuring*, Polity Press (1990), p. 1.

15 This comment is based upon a finding in a report by S. Miles of Industrial Relations Services and reported in *Procurement Weekly*, 23 July 1993.

16 Wolfe, R. 'Managing and Redesigning Business Processes to Achieve Dramatic Performance Improvements', *European Business Journal*, Vol. 3, No. 4, 1991.

17 *See*, in particular:
Womack, J.P., Jones, D.T. and Roos, D. *The Machine that Changed the World: The Triumph of Lean Production*, Rawson Associates, Macmillan (1990).
See also the publications listed in Note 21.
However, the following articles give particular attention to the analysis of the characteristics of 'lean production' and its perceived benefits:
Krafcik, J.F. 'Triumph of the Lean Production System', *Sloan Management Review*, Fall 1988, pp. 41–52.
Krafcik, J.F. 'A New Diet For Manufacturing', *Technology Review*, Vol. 92, Part 1, 1989, pp. 28–36.
Jones, D.T. 'Beyond the Toyota Production System: the Era of Lean Production', *Manufacturing Strategy – Process and Content* (editor C.A. Voss) Chapman & Hall (1992), pp. 189–210.

18 *See* the articles by Krafcik, J.F. (1988) and (1989), as identified in note 17 above, for a detailed discussion of 'lean' and 'buffered' systems.

19 These principles are quoted from Jones, D.T. (1992), as mentioned in note 17 above.

20 This quotation is from p. 191 of Jones, D.T. (1992), as mentioned in note 17 above.

21 *See* the recent publications by Womack and Jones listed below:
Womack, J.P. and Jones, D.T. 'From Lean Production to the Lean Enterprise', *Harvard Business Review*, March–April, 1994, pp. 93–103.
Womack, J.P. and Jones, D.T. *Lean Thinking: Banish Waste and Create Wealth in Your Corporation*, Simon & Schuster (1996a).
Womack, J.P. and Jones, D.T. 'Beyond Toyota: How to Root out Waste and Pursue Perfection', *Harvard Business Review*, September–October, 1996, pp. 148–58 (1996b).

22 Kay, J. *Foundations of Corporate Success*, Oxford University Press (1993).

23 Cusumano, M.A. 'The Limits of "Lean"', *Sloan Management Review*, Summer 1994, pp. 27–32.

24 For an account of research findings into supplier involvement in product development, as part of a wider study of product development processes carried out by a team at Harvard University, *see*:
Clark, K.B. 'Project Scope and Project Performance: The Effect of Parts Strategy and Supplier Involvement on Product Development', *Management Science*, Vol. 35, No. 10, October 1989, pp. 1247–63.

25 This quotation is from p. 1261 of Clark, K.B. (1989), mentioned in note 24 above.

26 Reference was made to the work of Bacon and Eltis in the discussion in Chapter 1 of the difference between the market and non-market sectors of the economy. *See*:
Bacon, R. and Eltis, W. *Britain's Economic Problems: Too Few Producers*, 2nd Edition, Macmillan (1978), for the presentation of their main thesis.

27 Thomson, P. 'Public Sector Management in a Period of Radical Change: 1979–1992', *Public Money & Management*, July–September 1992.

28 Lyne, C. 'Strategic Procurement In The New Local Government', *European Journal of Purchasing and Supply Management*, Vol. 2, No. 1, 1996, pp. 1–6.

29 Walsh, J. *Public Services and Market Mechanisms: Competition, Contracting and The New Public Management*, Macmillan (1995).

30 *See* the Local Government Act 1988, which enforced the policy of Compulsory Competitive Tendering (CCT) for certain services. The policy of the UK government since has been to extend the coverage of competitive tendering procedures and to introduce market testing into the civil service.

31 *See* the National Health Service and Community Care Act 1990, which established the separation of purchasers and providers.

32 Two papers at the 2nd Conference of the Purchasing and Supply Educational Research Group, held at the University of Bath set out ideas about this issue. They are:
Furlong, P., Lamont, F. and Cox, A. 'Competition or Partnership: CCT and EC Public Procurement Rules in The Single Market', Conference Paper at PSERG 2nd Conference (1993).
Erridge, A. 'Competitive and Partnership Models and Public Procurement', Conference Paper at PSERG 2nd Conference (1993).

33 This quotation is taken from p. 35 of Thomson, P. (1992), as mentioned in note 27 above.

34 The value of Japanese influence is discussed, for example, by:
Rhys, G. 'The Motor Industry and the Balance of Payments', *The Royal Bank of Scotland Review* (1990), pp. 11–25.
Eltis, W. and Fraser, D. 'The Contribution of Japanese Success to Britain and to Europe', *National Westminster Quarterly Review*, November 1992, pp. 2–19.

35 For an analysis of the American challenge and proposed remedies, *see*:
Servan-Schreiber, J. *The American Challenge*, Pelican (1969).

36 Bessant, J. *Advanced Manufacturing Technology Management*, Pitman Publishing (1991), Chapter 1, for an account of the Fifth Wave and the Long Wave theory.

CHAPTER 3

Approaches to strategic management

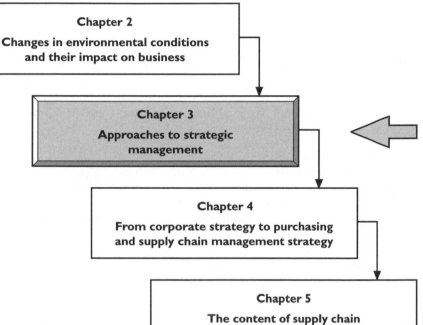

INTRODUCTION

> You can't change a company like Rover overnight. It is only now that Rover is reaping dividends from the strategies established in the mid- to late-1980s.

This statement was printed in 1993, and Professor Bhattacharyya, Professor of Manufacturing Systems at the University of Warwick, was thus quoted when commenting on the overhauling of the economics of the company.[1] This quotation provides a helpful introduction to this chapter, which is concerned with the nature of strategy and strategic management. It identifies two aspects of strategy. First, it relates the relevance of strategy to the management of change. It also refers to the long-term nature of it, one of the dimensions of strategy. Rover had had to undergo a period of renewal and a change of direction, as low-cost world-class competition had left it with inferior products and an inefficient organisational structure and an inability to compete in volume car markets. The strategy involved becoming a higher-quality, lower-volume, niche market producer.

The underlying message is that as environments change, new challenges and threats arise, which require companies to respond. Dietger Hahn,[2] writing about German companies, suggests that the following are the major developments anticipated in the 1990s:

- increasing globalisation
- intensified competition
- higher prices of raw materials
- shorter product life cycles
- difficulties in covering expenditures for research and development during commercialisation
- a need to increase flexibility within the whole company
- the implementation of new forms of interindustry and international co-operation.

There are many questions that can be asked about the nature of strategic management. What is meant by the concept of strategy? How can firms manage the process of strategy formulation? What successful strategies have companies used? How should strategies be implemented? The purpose of this chapter will be to address these questions, and others, in order to gain insights into strategic management processes. However, while it might be interesting to do this as a subject on its own, the main concern will be to establish ideas that will provide a context within which to locate functional strategies, especially purchasing and supply management strategies. Also, it is possible to glean some hints as to how to create and implement strategic thinking with regard to activities in the functional areas.

OBJECTIVES OF THIS CHAPTER

1 To analyse the concept of strategy and the nature of strategic management
2 To identify and discuss the main strands of thinking about strategic management

3 To consider problems of implementation and the management of change processes
4 To analyse the treatment of purchasing and supply management and supply chain issues in the approaches to strategic management

THE CONCEPT OF STRATEGY AND THE NATURE OF STRATEGIC MANAGEMENT

The problem is to decide where to start with the subject of strategy. There are many questions of interest, as mentioned earlier, but there are also different basic approaches, as well as a large body of literature, which is 'vast, diverse and since 1980, has been growing at an astonishing rate', according to Henry Mintzberg.[3] The evolutionary path followed by the literature has been partly a response to the emergence of new problems and issues in a changing environment. Also, different perspectives of strategy can be constructed because of the different types of organisation that exist. There is, thus, a contingent nature to the growth of the literature and to the perceptions people might form about the value and relevance of the ideas which are being promulgated.

Proliferation of terms

There are many different terms which attempt to define the field, such as corporate strategy, business strategy, business policy, strategic management and corporate or strategic planning. As is often the case in these situations, the different terms can be defined differently by the various authors or users. It is also worth mentioning that consultancy firms have also contributed to the development of both theory and practice. J.I. Moore, however, suggests that all address the same issue:

> the determination of how an organization, in its entirety, can best be directed in a changing world.[4]

Michael Porter, one of the most influential voices in the field, suggests that 'the reason why firms succeed or fail is perhaps the central question in strategy'.[5] Answers to this question clearly can then become a guide to what firms should do. There is a connection, therefore, between the essentially normative approach of those proposing principles of strategic management and those primarily concerned with empirical research. Practitioners, of course, would like to be able to find recipes for success, recipes which have been shown to contribute to superior profitability.

The main term used in this chapter will be that of 'strategic management'. In order to lead towards an explanation of why this has been selected, the meaning of 'strategy' will first be examined.

The meaning of 'strategy'

Strategy is the direction and scope of an organisation over the long term: ideally, which matches its resources to its changing environment, and in particular its markets, customers or clients so as to meet stakeholder expectations.[6]

This quotation captures a number of key characteristics of strategic decisions.

---

1 They relate to the 'scope' of the organisation in terms of the types of goods or services and of the geographical boundaries that will provide a focus for its activities.

2 They will attempt to match these activities to the organisation's environment.

3 They will strive to match these activities to its resource capabilities.

4 Strategic decisions have major resource implications.

5 Strategic decisions affect operational decisions – 'set off waves of lesser decisions'.

6 Such decisions will be affected by the 'values and expectations of those in power in and around the organisation'.

7 Strategic decisions are likely to influence the direction of the organisation in the long term.

Note: Quotations in points 5 and 6 are from Johnson, G. and Scholes, K., *Exploring Corporate Strategy: Text and Cases*, 3rd Edition, Prentice-Hall (1993), p. 9.

Fig 3.1 Characteristics of strategic decisions

An analysis of the characteristics, listed in Fig 3.1, suggests that some of them are to do with the purpose or content of strategic decisions and others are concerned with a comparison between 'strategic' and other types of decisions. Following this latter line of thought can bring out a comparison with 'tactical' decisions, a distinction that has historical origins in military thinking.

Grant, for example, states that 'strategy is the overall plan for deploying resources to establish a favourable position' and 'a tactic is a scheme for a specific action'.[7] He also claims that strategic decisions 'are important', 'involve a significant commitment of resources' and 'are not easily reversible'. Tricker, also, refers to the longer-term nature and broader horizons of strategic thinking.[8] Definitions of strategic decisions based upon these characteristics allow the use of the word 'strategic' and the concept of strategy to be applied to functional areas of businesses and not just the business as a whole. This point underlines the validity of using the word 'strategic' in the title of this book, 'Strategic Purchasing and Supply Chain Management'.

On the other hand, some definitions of the concept of strategy which concentrate on content and purpose would only be applicable to businesses as a whole. Thus, Hax sees strategy as embodying six points.

I Strategy as a coherent, unifying and integrative pattern of decisions.
2 Strategy as a means of establishing an organisation's purpose in terms of its long-term objectives, action programmes, and resource allocation priorities.
3 Strategy as a definition of a firm's competitive domain.
4 Strategy as a response to external opportunities and threats and to internal strengths and weaknesses as a means of achieving competitive advantage.
5 Strategy as a logical system for differentiating managerial tasks at corporate, business and functional levels.
6 Strategy as a definition of the economic and non-economic contribution the firm intends to make to its stakeholders.

Fig 3.2   Hax's six points

Two comments can be made about the list created by Hax, shown in Fig 3.2.[9] First, the idea, now widely accepted, of strategies at different levels (corporate, business and functional), is included. The locus for strategic decision making can vary, therefore. But, it might be said that corporate strategy, involving the organisation as a whole, as opposed to specific business or functional units should be the concern of the top management team and board of directors. Second, this same point leads into the notion that strategy involves concern for the structure of the organisation, the division of tasks and the allocation of responsibilities.

As well as 'content', in terms of types of strategy to be adopted to achieve the identified goals, a further aspect of strategy, which is brought out in the terminology used by Hax, is the feature of 'process'. However, the process of strategy can involve not only steps in the formation or formulation of strategies, but also stages or steps involved in implementing selected strategies. To conclude this investigation of the meaning of 'strategy', it can be seen that it involves 'concept', 'content' and 'process'. Analytically, they might be seen as separate components, but in practice they are closely interrelated.

The nature of managing strategically

Now that the meaning of 'strategy' and 'strategic' has been discussed, it is possible to bring 'management' briefly into the picture. It is not thought to be necessary to make a detailed analysis of the concept of management in this book and it will be sufficient just to emphasise a number of aspects. As a process, management involves the functions of planning and control. Thus, it involves the drawing up of strategic plans and the supervision of their implementation. The control element involves the monitoring and measurement of performance. Finally, styles of leadership are relevant to the implementation phase, as well as having implications for the degree of participation in the formulation of strategies. Hahn has provided both a summary and a discussion of what he sees as being the main tasks and responsibilities of strategic management.[10] The main tasks are described as:

1 Determining the corporate philosophy.
2 Defining the corporate objectives and goals.
3 Formulating business strategies, functional strategies and regional strategies (the latter refers to geographical areas to be covered).
4 Planning the company's organisation structure and its legal forms.
5 Planning the management system and process, including management development, information system and management pay and incentives.
6 The process of implementation and supervision.
7 The design of the desired corporate culture.

Schendel and Hofer provide a useful overview when they say that:

> Strategic management is a process that deals with the entrepreneurial work of the organization, with organizational renewal and growth, and more particularly, with developing and utilizing the strategy which is to guide the organization's operations.[11]

This discussion of the various interpretations and definitions of strategy has shown that there are differences of opinion. Any definition is based upon a conscious selection of items to be included, but it also omits others. To some extent definitions change with the passage of time and as ideas progress in response to the circumstances in which they are applied. The steps in the evolution of the main approaches will be addressed, but before doing so another reason for the differences will be looked at. This reason is to do with the purpose and underlying methodological position of the person proposing the definition. It is important to be aware of the underpinning assumptions, even though they are usually implicit rather than explicit.

Methodological issues

The analysis of methodological issues will first consider the mainstream normative approach with regard to strategic management, which is based fundamentally on a rational model of decision making. A critique of this will follow, taking into account behavioural limitations on the extent to which it can be put into practice.

The rational model

All the accounts that have been given of the nature of strategy and of strategic management tend to adopt a particular perspective and share a number of underlying assumptions. They tend to have a normative or prescriptive bias and they are thoughts intended to help shape the ideas and actions of practitioners. They also tend to emphasise the rational and analytical nature of the task. It is implied that decision makers can study their environment and that they can identify and evaluate the consequences of courses of action. Having done so, they can choose a particular course of action or strategy in the light of clearly formulated criteria in relation to their objectives. It might be noticed that there are similar assumptions in the model of perfect competition, as it is presented in most basic textbooks of economics. Various techniques, often with a quantitative foundation, can further assist in this rational approach. However, it is necessary to consider some of the problems that arise from the adoption of these assumptions of rational behaviour in the model. These difficulties arise with regard to the characteristics both of the decision maker as a human being and also of the social context in which the decision maker is located. (Gore, Murray and Richardson discuss these issues within the context of strategic decision makers.[12])

Limitations of the rational model

The limitations of the decision maker as a human being will be addressed first. Relevant to both economics and business is the work of Simon.[13] He argued that human rationality was limited and could not match up to the 'omniscient man' of classical economics. In practice, human beings would not be able to have complete knowledge of all the possible course of action or of all the consequences. With regard to the latter, decision makers only have a limited perception of all the possible effects. While computers can extend the power of the human brain, there are also limitations with regard to computational abilities.

There are difficulties in anticipating the future and evaluating the impact of these uncertainties. In addition, the selection of goals to be pursued can represent a problem, especially as there can be many situations in which multiple goals need to be pursued and relative priorities come into consideration. In such circumstances, Simon doubted whether optimising behaviour was possible and proposed the concept of 'satisficing' behaviour as a more realistic practice. The question of the selection of goals is a matter of judgement and involves issues of values and preferences. It is not a matter of fact. Thus, at best, decision makers may attempt to be 'intendedly rational'. Nevertheless, this limited or 'bounded' rationality is a long way from being 'irrational' – the opposite end of the spectrum from the classical view. Another point which Simon makes is that at higher levels of decision making, situations are 'unprogrammed' or 'unroutinised'. The range of factors to be taken into account, their interconnections and the goals to be pursued are less well known, compared to the more clearly structured, often repetitive situations of a simpler, short-term kind (*see* Fig 3.3). Strategic decision-making situations are more inclined to match the features of the 'unroutinised' picture. Eisenhardt and Zbaracki have written an article reviewing some of the more recent literature about rationality and bounded rationality in strategic decision making.[14]

Routine/programmed decisions ⟵————————————————⟶ Unroutinised/unprogrammed decisions

Fig 3.3 Routine and unroutinised factors

Glaister and Thwaites raise the problem of perception in the context of strategy formation.[15] Firms and their personnel have to develop specific frameworks of analysis to deal with their unique situations and this involves selection and subjective judgement. A way of seeing is also a way of not seeing! Neutral observation is perhaps impossible, because conceptual frameworks direct attention to what is seen. They act as filters or a 'pair of spectacles'. Likewise implicit or explicit theories can influence explanations of what has been observed. Such perceptions may not fit 'objective reality' and key aspects may be left out of the problem picture and jeopardise the efficacy of any courses of action. They do not, however, suggest how a picture of 'objective reality' can be established, though they do make the helpful suggestion that all those involved should interact, and through discussion broaden understanding and reduce or eliminate any perceptual bias which might arise because of differences in experiences and responsibilities. As far as decision making is concerned, the environment exists as perceived.

In purchasing, a similar problem of perception arises in negotiations. The behaviour of negotiators, and the offers they are prepared to make or accept, will be affected by the way in which they perceive the situation. In the same way, the value of products and services that buyers or customers receive depends ultimately on their evaluations and the perceived features on which those evaluations are based. The decision to purchase or not will be dependent on such perceptions. It doesn't matter what the supplier or producer thinks!

A point that arises out of the discussion of the problem of perception is that usually strategic management involves more than one person, with regard to both the formation and implementation stages of strategy. This immediately brings social factors and relationships into the picture, with the possibility of different people having different views and preferences with regard, for instance, to the values and goals to be pursued. It therefore raises the possibility that political processes and the distribution and leverage of power will affect the strategic decision making processes. In the world of practice, both the process of constructing pictures of the world to be managed and the tasks of developing and implementing strategies will be influenced by social and political factors.

Behavioural alternatives

Cyert and March, building on the basic ideas of Simon, who might be called the 'father of the behavioural theory of decision making', developed ideas at the firm level and proposed a behavioural theory of the firm as an alternative to the classical rational economic model.[16] In this theory, recognition was given to the existence of coalitions and political processes. It recognises that complex problems and possible conflicts are simplified by the division of work into separate functions, with each giving attention to limited sets of problems and goals. It might be noted that more recent thinking, which develops wider systemic views of interdependent activities, bring to the surface the weaknesses of these 'quasi-resolution of conflict' practices which Cyert and March portrayed. They also suggested that there was 'uncertainty avoidance', by concentrating on the application of decision rules that emphasise short-term reaction to short-term feedback from the environment. This appears to be a dangerous tactic. Burying heads in the sand like ostriches may lead to the failure to perceive the emergence of fundamentally new issues requiring strategic changes of direction. 'Problemistic search' was another proposition of the theory, which suggested that search for alternatives is stimulated by the perception of difficulties. Search efforts may cease as soon as a satisfactory solution has been found. The fourth factor that Cyert and March built into their theory of the firm was that of 'organisational learning'. Organisations accumulate knowledge as they learn from experience. Yoram Wind applied this behavioural theory to the study of decision making in the area of industrial purchasing decision-making behaviour.[17]

Thus, descriptive studies, concerned with actual behaviour of participants in particular situations, will usually give greater recognition to the behavioural limitations that arise from both the cognitive limitations of people and also the pressures of social and political forces. Those with a preference for action, rather than for theorising and reflecting about possibilities, might have reservations about some of the prescriptions of 'good practice'. Yet it can be argued that everyone should strive to be as rational as possible and to minimise the harmful effects of these other factors. As well as developing cognitive skills for strategic decision-making purposes, however, the normative implication is that the application of interpersonal skills of communication and persuasion are relevant too. Furthermore, personnel can strive to increase the amount of deliberate, conscious effort devoted to the construction of the conceptual framework and the search for information as a basis for strategic planning. The extent to which minds are open or closed to new possibilities will vary, and may be influenced by the personalities and predispositions of the people involved.

'Intended' versus 'realised' strategy

Another influential voice which provides a further critique about the rational/ analytical approach to strategic decision making is that of Henry Mintzberg.[18] In so far as a strategy is a plan, an 'intended' course of action, part of what actually happens, the 'realised' strategy may thus be the result of 'deliberate' strategy, that part of 'intended' strategy that was implemented. However, some parts of the plan may not happen, 'unrealised' strategy in Mintzberg's terms. Finally, what happens might also be the result of 'unintended' actions. These he calls 'emergent' strategies. Thus, an observer attempting to discern what strategies exist in firms should allow for the fact that 'realised' strategies may be the result of both 'deliberate' and 'emergent' strategies. A point arising from these distinctions and the gap between intended and realised strategies is that attention needs to be paid to the phase of implementation and the interpretations made by those involved.

Decision making in purchasing and supply

To conclude this account of the various theories of decision making, it is useful to draw out some pointers to approaches used in the purchasing and supply function. Three different approaches will be outlined:

- rule based
- 'closed' quantitative models
- complex problem environments

Rule based

As a guide for decision situations that are perceived to be well known (i.e. in which the characteristics of anticipated problems can be described) rules to govern procedures can be prepared in advance. The problem solver is required to select and follow appropriate rules for particular situations which have been identified.

'Closed' quantitative models

Particular situations may be investigated and 'modelled' to allow quantitative (possibly scientific) solutions to be determined. In such models the goal or objective to be pursued is taken as 'given.' Such models propose mechanisms for optimising achievement of the target objective, taking into account factors that are thought to be relevant and which are built into the model. A classic example in purchasing and supply is the economic order quantity (EOQ) equation. Among the limitations of this approach are, first, that conditions met by the person applying the model may not match the assumptions built into the model by its architect. Second, models ignore opportunities and interactions with other factors regarded as being outside the model.

Complex problem environments

The emergence of current progressive approaches in supply chain management means that frameworks for decision making can encompass a much wider array of factors and goals, whose causal interactions may be more uncertain and ambiguous. Although attempts which use computer simulation techniques are being used, it can still be difficult to capture the full complexities of the problems. Less formal techniques, which make use of inputs from groups of people and which rely less on quantitative analysis, are used to devise arrangements and programmes of action. Some might argue that there is much greater scope for creativity of thought and intuition in such processes than in those that are rule based.

THE STRATEGIC MANAGEMENT APPROACH

Earlier in the chapter the strategic management approach was outlined, and some of the methodological issues have now been identified and discussed. It is now appropriate to return to it and to examine its content and stages of development. It can be seen as belonging to the rational/analytical school, as Stacey classifies it.[19] It represents what he calls the conventional wisdom, as represented in the main popular texts.[20] There are differences in detail and emphasis, but the broad approach of these texts is a common one. Analysis of the situation, choice of strategic options and implementation of chosen strategies form the kernel of their accounts. (See the introduction to Part One for the outline of the basic scheme adopted by Johnson and Scholes.) Stacey suggests that most textbooks on strategic management:

> focus heavily on techniques and procedures for long-term planning, on the need for visions and missions, on the importance and the means of securing strongly shared cultures, on the equation of success with consensus, consistency, uniformity and order. (page xix)

It is helpful to identify the main ideas and techniques within this strategic management tradition by tracing them in relation to the approximate historical sequence in which they emerged. Ansoff and McDonnell have argued that the pattern of evolution and application of ideas can be linked to the need to cope with the increasing changeability of the environment and its increasing unpredictability.[21] They state:

> As the turbulence levels changed, management developed systematic approaches to handling the increasing unpredictability, novelty and complexity. As the future became more complex, novel and less foreseeable, systems became correspondingly more sophisticated, each complementing and enlarging upon the earlier ones. (page 12)

Three main stages will be adopted as a convenient framework within which to examine these developments. It is worth bringing in a word of caution about this scheme. There is always a danger of oversimplifying the presentation and creating an opportunity for disagreements about the selection of the stages. It is partly based on the scheme that Taylor produced,[22] though with some modifications and an enlargement of his third stage. Nevertheless, it does have some pragmatic advantage in trying to develop ideas in a logical way. The three stages are as follows:

1 Long-range planning
2 Strategic planning
3 Strategic management

Figure 3.4 provides a summary of these three approaches.

Long-range planning

This first stage represents the emergence of strategic thinking as a special topic of interest and extends from the mid-1950s to approximately the mid-1970s. It emerged from the position of firms being largely controlled by budgetary planning and control processes, though with an emphasis on one-year periods. Smaller companies may still have operated with less formal

1 **Long-range planning**
   - financial planning and budgets
   - Ansoff's Growth Vector matrix
2 **Strategic planning**
   - analytical approaches
      scenarios
      SWOT analysis
   - evaluating options
      portfolios (growth share matrices) e.g. BCG, GE, AD Little etc.
      experience curves
      product life cycles
   - organisational structures
      divisions and/or holding companies
3 **Strategic management topics**
   - levels of strategy
      corporate/business/functions
   - industry and competitive analysis (Porter)
      five forces model
      generic strategies
      value chains and value systems
   - resource-based approaches
      core capabilities/competences
   - prescriptions of excellence
      7-S Framework, etc.
   - improvement programmes
      just-in-time, total quality management, benchmarking, business
      process re-engineering, etc.
   - collaborative/co-operative approaches
   - alliances, partnerships, joint ventures, networks

Fig 3.4 Summary of major approaches to corporate/business strategy

approaches with leadership in the hands of single entrepreneurs or just a small group. In the latter type of firm, strategy might at best have existed in the minds of the top leader or of a small nucleus of managers. As such firms expanded, many perceived the need for a more formal approach to replace the more informal decision processes of a small close-knit group. A tightening of the financial grip on operations was a way of achieving it.

The period identified with this first stage was one in which relatively stable growth was achieved. Thus, firms wished to plan for growth and to help them make their investment decisions, it was seen to be necessary to anticipate further ahead than one year. Thus, budgets were prepared for longer periods, five-year budgets, for example. Forecasting techniques were introduced to help in the process of predicting revenues, costs, cashflows and profits. Often, however, such forecasts were simple extrapolations from past data and were not based upon a detailed understanding of the environment. Capital investment appraisal techniques were brought in to evaluate the viability of expansion plans. Some of the larger firms introduced special planning departments as a way of implementing the approach.

Ansoff's Growth Vector matrix

A further development linked to the desire for growth was a concern for marketing and a more formal analysis of the possible directions that growth might take. Growth might be achieved organically or by merger/takeover. Ansoff proposed the Growth Vector matrix, which allowed the scope of products and product-markets to be analysed.[23] Four strategies emerged from this approach:

1 **Market penetration.** The task of this strategy is to increase sales and market share in existing products in existing markets, a continuation of the current approach.
2 **Product development.** This strategy is founded on developing new products to serve existing markets.
3 **Market development.** In this approach development work is focused on opening up new markets for present products.
4 **Diversification.** In this original presentation, the fourth strategy was the most innovative, as it involved both new products and new markets. The previous three had a common thread in either product technology or marketing skills, or both. Further analysis of the diversification route was based on the degree to which the technology related to the new products and the extent to which the type of customers differed.

In the revised 1987 edition, Ansoff added a third dimension, a geographical dimension, to the original matrix.[24] It is understandable, given the recognition of the increased globalisation of markets, that this new factor should be introduced to enrich the earlier attempt to analyse corporate scope. It is also possible to observe Ansoff's interest in the need for companies to define their businesses, as well as identifying the interest of companies in diversification as a direction of growth.

Two other directions of growth had been recognised. The first, vertical integration, involves expansion into a different stage of operation in the chain of supply, other than the existing one. This can be either backwards, to an earlier stage on the supply side, or forwards towards the final market, into either another manufacturing stage or a distribution activity. Horizontal, on the other hand, means extending the scope of operations at the same stage or level in the supply chain.

Although strategy is seen to be concerned with the management of the business as a whole, the observation may be made that there is already a significant input into strategic thinking from the subjects of marketing and management accounting. Nevertheless, as environments became more changeable and less predictable, disenchantment with the overoptimism and unreliability of forecasting led to further developments in strategic thinking. Taylor argues that the energy crisis and the oil price increases represented 'a watershed in planning', as the prospect for stable and continuous growth evaporated.[25]

Strategic planning

The period to be covered by this phase is approximately from the mid-1970s to the early 1980s. The concerns of many of the larger companies, because of their growing complexity, were seen to be different, by comparison with those smaller firms that had a much narrower scope. Conglomerates, groups consisting of unrelated businesses, had emerged as a form of business, which allowed risks to be spread through the distribution of investments in different business fields. This strategy appeared to some to be preferable to either horizontal or vertical integration. Recognition was given to the split between corporate and business strategies. At one level, therefore, corporate interests centred on the management of a range of separate businesses. One question at corporate headquarters was concerned with what businesses to add to or delete from the corporate portfolio. Thus, the need to evaluate the prospects of the individual businesses to help to provide answers to this question was perceived. Another question was concerned with determining the level of resources to allocate to each business in the portfolio. The Japanese onslaught in western markets had also become apparent as shipbuilding and motor cycle industries suffered, for example. The search for explanations of these events was begun. What ideas and techniques were developed to tackle these kinds of problems?

Three different topics with regard to the development of the strategic planning approach will be considered:

1 Developments in analytical approaches
2 Evaluation of strategic options
3 Organisational structures

Developments in analytical approaches – scenarios and SWOT

The first of the topics is that of a heightened concern with assessing conditions in the environment. The technique of scenario analysis was one response to the problem of growing uncertainty and the problems of errors in predicting the future. Instead of looking for one picture of what was expected to happen and then basing a plan upon it, a more circumspect approach was adopted. Adopting this approach allows a range of possibilities or scenarios of situations, which are likely to be confronted, to be depicted and strategies could then be evaluated in the light of each one and the risks assessed.

Another technique, which gained popularity in recommendations of how to tackle strategic problems, is the one known as SWOT – strengths, weaknesses, opportunities and threats. Firms are expected to analyse the external environment, to identify and assess what might lie in store in the form of factors which, on the one hand, pose a threat to the prospects of the firm and, on the other hand, may represent favourable opportunities to be exploited.

Technological change, a threat from a new competitor or a reduction in demand as a result of a change in government economic policy are examples of possible threats. A booming economy and growing demand, the collapse of a competitor firm or a change in customer fashions might open up more encouraging market growth prospects. At the same time as the external environment is being assessed, the capabilities of the firm itself are subjected to investigation to assess its strengths and weaknesses. The quality of its products or services may or may not compare favourably with its competitors in the eyes of its customers. The state of its facilities may or may not place it in a strong position, and the same might be said for the level of skill and expertise possessed by its workforce. However, the success of this technique is partly dependent on the effectiveness of the surveillance in identifying the key factors that may be relevant. It is also affected by the ability to interpret the information in the light of future trends and implications.

Evaluation of strategic options – portfolio and gap analysis

The second area of development in the strategic planning stage is concerned with the identification and evaluation of strategic options. The Boston Consulting Group (BCG) became prominent because of two particular contributions which were made in the strategic field; these are the experience curve and the growth share matrix, as follows:

1 **The experience curve.** The basic conclusion arising from this analysis is that the unit cost of producing a product declines as the cumulative total number of units rises. BCG suggest that the following three factors, at least, contribute to this result:
   - The learning function. A person doing a job over a period of time becomes more efficient as a result of learning by experience. Thus, unit labour costs might decline by 10–15 per cent each time cumulative experience doubles. (The learning curve has been long recognised in purchasing textbooks and is seen to have value in supplier cost analysis and price negotiations.[26]) Learning leading to improvements might also be encouraged by techniques such as value analysis.
   - Specialisation. Increasing job specialisation is associated with a rise in the scale of production and efficiency increases as a result.
   - Scale. As capacity is enlarged, capital costs needed to achieve the additional output decline.

   Reflection on the implications of the general proposition of the experience curve offers the view that if output and sales can grow, the advantages of an expected long run cost reduction can be exploited. Pricing policies can be adjusted in the light of this understanding in order to pursue objectives of growth and profitability.
2 **The growth share matrix.** The pursuit of market domination and the growth of sales as objectives and the corresponding growth in output appeared to offer promising prospects for increased profit. Thus, the external appraisal

of markets with regard to assessing growth potential for the firm became a subject of concern. The BCG growth share matrix offered an approach to this problem.

The matrix focuses on the growth rate of the market and relative market share. Four possible positions were identified and conclusions were drawn with regard to the strategic implications of each one. These were labelled and described as follows:

- 'Dogs' – products with low market share and static or no market growth. The inference is that earnings will be low and little or no profit will be made. The strategic conclusion is to disinvest or withdraw.
- 'Stars' – products with a high market share in a high growing market, offering good prospects for growth. Invest for growth is the option to follow in this position.
- '?' – a question mark arises with regard to products in this position. There is potential for high market growth, but the firm has a low market share. The prospects for a rapid increase in market share need to be evaluated, to assess whether there is potential for the product to become a 'star' or a 'dog'.
- 'Cash cows' – the product enjoys a high market share, but in a low or zero growth market. The strategic implication is to exploit the strong positive cashflow situation, but not to devote any significant new investment to it.

In summary, the analysis concludes: 'milk the cows, invest in the stars, divest the dogs and analyse the question marks to determine whether they can be grown into stars or whether they will degenerate into dogs'.[27]

Thus, the growth share matrix offered a way of managing a portfolio of products and identifying strategies to be adopted, depending on the assessment of the potential of each product. It indicated how resources should be allocated in each case. In addition, the approach assists in the setting of performance targets for each one. Finally, the balance of the portfolio as a whole, with regard to cashflow, risk and profit potential, can be evaluated. 'Gap' analysis may then reveal whether there is a difference between forecasted and desired level of performance.

Other portfolio techniques

In addition to the BCG framework, others have been produced for similar purposes to evaluate the potential of their unit businesses or products. They are described in most books on strategic management and include:

1 General Electric's business screen – this matrix compares industry attractiveness with the competitive position and strengths of the business.
2 The Shell directional policy matrix – this has business sector prospects and the company's competitive capabilities as the two dimensions.
3 The strategic condition matrix of AD Little Inc – this matrix identifies stages of industry maturity and competitive position as the factors to be analysed.

The product life cycle

The analogy of biological life cycles has stimulated interest in business in visualising product life cycles and identifying different stages as a basis for planning. The stages which are designated in many of the life cycle models are: introduction, growth, maturity and decline.[28] Plans may be developed which are appropriate for each particular stage of a product during its life. However, it is also useful in looking at a portfolio of products with a view to assessing and managing the range to achieve a balance of products at different stages.

Organisational structures

The third and final topic in the discussion of the developments in the strategic planning phase is concerned with organisational issues. As many firms grew in size and complexity with regard to geographic, product and product-use scope, so ideas of how to construct appropriate organisational structures were increased. As firms became more complex, it became necessary to consider other models than one based upon a division of tasks on a functional or departmental basis. The earlier work of Chandler did much to publicise possibilities and to increase understanding of the difficulties of centralisation versus decentralisation in relation to decision making and planning and control in complex companies.[29] Strategy and structure were seen to be related questions in Chandler's view, with decisions about the former being taken into account when determining the latter.

1 **Multi-divisional structures.** Thus, multi-divisional structures, where each division had its own functional organisation and operated as a separate profit centre, had been introduced into some companies. The extent to which headquarters might also have functional units to provide functional co-ordination across the divisions varied. One factor that might influence this issue is the degree of relatedness between product divisions (*see* Fig 3.5).

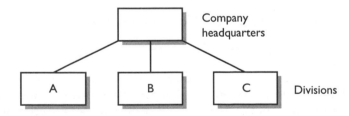

Fig 3.5 Multi-divisional structure

2 **Holding companies.** Other companies existed as holding companies and managed a greater or lesser number of independent businesses. In this position the function of the holding company was to act primarily in a financial capacity. Making judgements of the financial prospects of each subsidiary and acting as a banker in controlling the allocation of funds are the main tasks, as well as trading in the sale or purchase of such subsidiaries (*see* Fig 3.6).

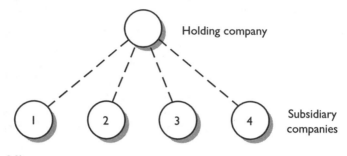

Fig 3.6   Holding company structure

Whatever the particular organisational structure, the task of strategic planning was seen essentially as a central, specialist activity. Planning departments had also emerged in the earlier long-range planning stage in the evolution of strategic management. It might also be pointed out that strategists in consulting firms found many customers who wished to take advantage of their services.

Strategic management

As the 1980s progressed, doubts about the developments of the strategic planning phase began to emerge and disillusionment about the value of specialist central planners began to grow. New problems and new ideas came to the surface and these developments will be examined under this heading of strategic management. It is a phase that appears to be still in a state of development and evolution in its own right. Taylor hinted at the appearance of another phase which he called 'New Frontiers' in his analysis, but the points covered seem to be more of an elaboration of the strategic management approach, as opposed to a distinct break.[30]

Criticisms of the strategic planning approach

Doubts about and a reappraisal of the value of the strategic planning approach were triggered by a number of concerns. First, firms had to face the ravages of the cold winds of recession as the decade of the 1980s commenced. At the same time, Japanese firms demonstrated superior performance and continued to make inroads into both European and American markets. Top managers had to focus attention more directly on individual businesses and to concern themselves with improving their performance. The strategy of diversification and the use of portfolio techniques did not seem to deliver the promised results and expectations were not fulfilled. Central planners were too remote from the businesses and lacked the detailed knowledge of them. The line managers with responsibility for running the businesses needed to be more directly involved in strategic management themselves. Thus, the next stage of development represented a shift of emphasis towards business strategies (*see* Fig 3.7).

One of those who helped to change the direction of developments and to

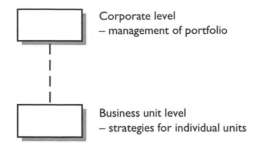

Corporate level
– management of portfolio

Business unit level
– strategies for individual units

Fig 3.7 Corporate and business unit strategies

rethink corporate strategy in the 1980s was Michael Porter. He also contributed to the criticisms of the techniques of experience curves and portfolio planning.[31]

> Portfolio planning is not a panacea for managing a conglomerate, as countless companies have had to admit as they have sold their failed acquisitions.[32]

Porter argued that the techniques lacked substance and their prescriptions were based on too simple a view of competition. Competition occurs at the business unit level and corporate strategy must support and be based upon successful competitive strategies at that level. Strategic plans are needed for each business, therefore. As businesses compete in industries, the starting point is an understanding of competitive conditions in industries. His first main work set out what has become known as the 'five forces' model of competition and it has grown out of the structure-conduct-performance model of industrial economics.[33] He also put forward the notion of generic competitive strategies, based upon considerations of cost leadership and product differentiation. An extension of his thinking was revealed in a later book, which investigated the idea of the value chain and recognised the interconnections of the firm with both suppliers and customers.[34] Subsequently his attention was taken up by concerns for national and international competitiveness.[35]

His analytical interest in competitive advantage, as a cause of success of firms, has moved from an essentially static approach, which analyses the situation at a particular moment in time, to a more dynamic consideration of how competitive advantage can be developed and sustained over a period of time. It is important to look at his ideas in greater depth as there are significant implications arising from Porter's perspective for strategic purchasing and supply management.

The thrust of interest in the strategic management approach has responded to the problem of more rapidly changing conditions by considering innovation and the development of resources and competences in order to improve competitive capability. The broadening of the scope of businesses has opened up the strategic possibilities of international and global postures of operation, including opportunities on a European scale. In addition, in order to implement programmes to develop capabilities and to extend the scope of activities, the problems of coping as independent, self-sufficient businesses were recognised. This has led to the investigation and experiment with co-operative strategies, adopting such forms as alliances and partnerships as possible solutions. An outline of these issues will also be given. Finally, another contributory school of thinking to be taken into account is that of those concerned with putting forward prescriptions of 'excellence' and 'best practice'.

Analysis of competitive advantage

Concern for what makes firms successful is central to Porter's views and the starting point for developing an understanding of a business in the context of the industry in which it operates. Success can be seen in 'attaining a competitive position or series of competitive positions that lead to superior and sustainable financial performance . . . relative to the world's best rivals'.[36]

The immediate contributing factors are seen to be 'the attractiveness of the industry' and 'an attractive relative position' of the business. In other words there are both industry effects and positioning effects. It would appear to be imperative to operate in an industry which offers good prospects and to be better than any rivals. It is perhaps simple to make such a comment, it is far harder to achieve it!

The five forces framework

To analyse an industry structure and its competitors, Porter's framework consists of five competitive forces – the rivalry among existing competitors, which is affected by the bargaining power of suppliers, the bargaining power of buyers, the threat of new entrants and the threat of substitute products or services. Each force, in turn, can be broken down into its constituent elements. The framework can be used by analysts as a guide to the investigation of the particular circumstances of the firm being studied.

1 **Rivalry among existing competitors.** Factors which might affect the nature of competitiveness or 'the jockeying for position' in the industry include:
   - The degree of concentration in the industry (number and relative size of the competitors).
   - The extent and nature of product differentiation.
   - Capacity in relation to demand.
   - Characteristics of demand.
   - Ratio of fixed to variable costs.
   - Height of exit barriers (level of specific assets related to the product and ease of liquidation).
2 **Bargaining power of buyers.** The bargaining power of the buyers (i.e. customers for the products or services produced by the competitors as suppliers) is related to the following features:
   - The degree of concentration relating to the number and relative size of the players on the customer side by comparison with the competing suppliers.
   - The relative significance of the product or service to customers in terms of quality, expenditure and service.

- Relative ease and cost of changing suppliers (switching costs).
- The amount of information possessed by buyers.
- The ability of buyers to integrate backwards.
- Profit levels of buyers.
- The extent to which buyers want differentiated products.

3 **Bargaining power of suppliers.** Factors relevant to the supply side of the industry will be similar to those mentioned on the customer side of the industry, and, thus, include:
- The structure of the supplier side relative to the producer industry.
- The degree of product differentiation/substitutability.
- The potential for forward integration.
- The relative importance of the industry demand to suppliers.
- The feasibility and cost of producers switching suppliers.

4 **Threat of new entrants.** The ease or difficulty for new producers of entering the industry affects the degree to which the structure of the industry can change. In other words, this force is concerned with the height of barriers to entry:
- The extent to which there are economies of scale.
- The amount of capital required.
- The need for product differentiation.
- The level of customer switching costs.
- The accessibility of distribution channels.
- The existence of government and legal barriers.

5 **Threat of substitutes**
- The availability and willingness of buyers to purchase substitute products which have the same functional capability.
- The comparative price of substitutes.

Industry analysis allows the firm to understand the pressures on the industry and their effect on prospects with regard to cost and profit. More specifically, the firm can compare its competitive position with regard to its rivals and can identify its strengths and weaknesses. It can then proceed to consider what strategies to adopt in order to give it a competitive advantage and a position from which to achieve its financial objectives. The next step, therefore, in examining Porter's ideas is to address his concept of generic competitive strategies.

Generic competitive strategies

The approach to identifying generic competitive strategies recognises the relevance of both competitive advantage and competitive scope.

Competitive advantage or an attractive position relative to its competitors can be established on the basis of two basic types. The first is concerned with 'cost leadership' – meeting competitors head-on in providing the same product or service, but achieving greater efficiency. This would enable the firm to cope with any downward pressure on prices better than its rivals. The alternative type of competitive advantage is to foster the ability to differentiate its product offering – 'differentiation' avoids direct competition by creating a unique product or service and commands a higher price.

Competitive scope is concerned with a number of different features, including range of buyer groups or segments, the geographical dimension of markets to be served and the extent of related businesses. Overall, the choice of scope lies between industry wide or single segment possibilities – broad or narrow targets.

The strategic choice that is open to the firm, therefore, is concerned with positions related to both competitive advantage and competitive scope. The selection of a strategy, therefore, pays attention to both customers and competitors. A 2×2 matrix yields four strategies:[37]

1　Cost leadership – lower cost plus broad target
2　Cost focus – lower cost plus narrow target
3　Differentiation – differentiation plus broad target
4　Differentiation focus – differentiation plus narrow target

Porter provides two warnings. First, he suggests that imitation of rivals will not allow a firm to achieve a competitive advantage and mediocre results will be the consequence. Mediocrity is also likely to be the outcome of 'being stuck in the middle', if firms fail to make a clear choice of strategy.

Some doubts have been raised as to whether the four generic strategies are too simplistic. There may be multiple bases of differentiation (quality, service, delivery, etc.), with the associated issue of relative priorities. Another comment is that there is a possibility of pursuing both low cost and differentiation simultaneously. Nevertheless, Porter's work does foster a more conscious effort to consider what the goals of the strategy should be in relation to target customers.

Activities and value chains

Porter's analysis has now suggested that a firm's success is affected by achieving competitive advantage, in the form either of cost leadership or of differentiation. The next step in his thinking is to consider the question of why a firm is able to achieve a competitive advantage. In other words, what is the source of competitive advantage? The answer to this question lies in activities and value chains, according to Porter. He perceives that a firm is a grouping of 'activities' – tasks carried out by different people. They are interrelated and part of a firm's strategy is to organise their configuration and to consider how they should be linked together. Activities are seen as the basic units which create value for customers.

> Competitive advantage results from a firm's ability to perform the required activities at a collectively lower cost than rivals, or perform some activities in unique ways that create buyer value and hence allow the firm to command a premium price.[38]

From the building blocks of individual activities it is then possible to adopt a systemic view and identify sequences of interdependent activities which make up a value chain. Initially the chain may be perceived within the legal boundaries of the firm, where the chain is managed directly by the firm's management hierarchy and planning and control systems. From this vantage point, the perspective can be widened to embrace chains of value creating activities on the supply side, which provide inputs into the internal operations of the firm. Looking in the other direction, there are additional points in the chain until the final customer becomes the recipient of the value of the end product or service. At this point the customer might be seen as receiving not so much a product, but more a 'bundle of values' arising from the use, possession or receipt of the product or service. The purpose of the network of value chains might be seen to be to design, produce and deliver products and services which satisfy or exceed the value expectations of customers in competition with other value chains.

The value chain perspective recognises that it is not just the activities inside the firm that are relevant to securing a competitive advantage, it also involves external activities as well. Furthermore, the linkages and relationships between each activity, internally and externally, are also crucial to the creation of competitive advantage. (Linkages, for Porter, relate to the interdependent effects one part in the chain might have on the efficiency or effectiveness of another part.) An important aspect of strategic management, then, involves the structuring of the value chain and the co-ordination of its parts (*see* Fig 3.8).

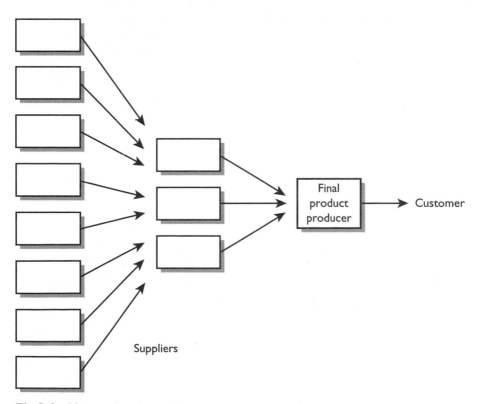

Fig 3.8 Network of suppliers and value creation

A further, and perhaps more controversial, aspect of Porter's analysis of the value chain is the distinction between 'primary' and 'support' activities and the allocation of particular activities to each class. 'Inbound logistics', 'operations', 'outbound logistics', 'marketing and sales' and 'service' are deemed to be primary activities and 'procurement', 'technology development', 'human resource management' and 'firm infrastructure' are designated as support activities.

Further thought about activities in the value chain brings out the point that activities require the use of resources – human, material and capital assets very often, as well as less tangible items such as information, knowledge and routines. A definition of resources can also embrace less tangible assets, such as brand reputation and relationships with other organisations, such as suppliers. Resources involve costs and the structure of the value chain gives a basis on which costs can be identified. The accumulation of total costs can be monitored through each stage in the chain. Activity-based costing is a recent innovation which is an example of how it might be done.

The pursuit of an understanding of competitive advantage and the recognition of the significance of activities and resources as contributing factors have so far been based on a static approach. Firms may assess where they stand in relation to their competitors. 'Benchmarking' emerged as another concept in applying a comparative approach in assessing the performance of a firm. This technique, however, involves not only looking at competitors in the industry, but also investigating best practices in specific activities in unrelated industries. However, interest needs to be turned towards how competitive advantage can be developed and made sustainable over a period of time. Thus, attention must be drawn towards aspects of change and innovation. The basic analysis may establish the current or initial conditions, which will have been affected partially by previous strategic decisions. Managerial choice of strategies will affect the direction of future developments and will influence the extent to which competitive advantage will be achieved. Therefore, a more dynamic perspective is needed.

Resources, innovation and sustainable competitive advantage

Consideration of how firms might defend or pursue competitive advantage identified the development of resources and their use to create innovations as ways which would improve competitive ability. While many economists might emphasise the contribution of macro-economic forces, such as interest rates and labour costs, Porter attaches more emphasis to the ability of the firm to generate streams of innovations. Innovations can occur in many ways. They include product and process changes, as well as the application of new control procedures and changes in organisations. The introduction of improvements covered by the methods of just in time and total quality management is another example. The development of skills and expertise and the application of learning may be central to the stimulation of such innovations. Therefore, learning becomes an important activity. Externally, innovations may be generated elsewhere in the value chain and these may trigger changes in scope with regard to the fields of operation.

Other writers have also paid attention to the resources or competences of the firm and the need to cultivate and enhance them throughout the value chain.[39] Clearly, there are implications for the formation of functional strategies relating to these resources, but these will be discussed further in Chapter 4. However, Porter argues that these resources only take on value if they are able to contribute to competitive advantages in particular industries. He also suggests that other conditions in an industry may help the industry to make progress. He argues that more intense competition can help to speed up the rate of innovation. A supporting cluster of suppliers close at hand may be a helpful aid as well. It is not surprising to find, therefore, that he argues that protection of an industry would be harmful in the long run. Innovation implies the need for changes, either of a gradual, incremental nature or of a more radical, breakthrough kind – or combinations of both. Whatever the case, management of change becomes a task of strategic importance for companies and is part of the implementation phase in strategic processes. Strategies aimed at changing competitive scope and competitive advantage may affect the behaviour of rivals and change the structure of the industry. But there may also be wider environmental developments which will disturb the structural conditions and behaviour of the competitors as well.

Core competences or capabilities

Further developments in strategic thinking, in connection with core competences or core skills, are based on the view that sustainable competitive advantage cannot be obtained in the long run from current products and technologies. These can quickly be copied and leadership founded on them might, thus, be eroded quickly. Companies, it is argued, need to focus on competences which embrace 'know-how' – skills and capabilities which take into account knowledge, procedures and practices, which can foster and bring to commercial development future products and technologies in response to customer requirements.

The notion of 'core' here is related to competences which are thought to be essential to enable an organisation to establish and maintain a competitive edge over its rivals. It follows that there may be other competences which are either no better than, or possibly not as good as, those of other organisations. Part of the strategic task for firms should include, therefore, the analysis of competences, with a view to concentrating on the development of those regarded as core. Competences perceived to be non-core might then be obtained by 'outsourcing' goods and services – buying them from more efficient and more effective suppliers. (See Chapter 5 for further discussion of the 'make-or-buy' question.) The 'legal' boundaries of the firm are determined by the outcome of such decisions and the composition of the purchasing and supply task is also affected.

One final point can be made about the focus of attention on competences. In a dynamic world, radical changes can occur in customers' demands and in the kinds of products that they might purchase. More ambitious strategies may, thus, be needed in order to create new products and to redefine markets. (Current customers may not be of much help with this process, as their 'mindsets' may be framed in terms of today's products, not tomorrow's new possibilities!) The development of new core competences can, therefore, play a crucial role in more radical strategic approaches. Hamel and Prahalad,[40] for example, refer to 'breakthrough strategies' and the creation of 'markets of tomorrow'. From a supply chain point of view, leading firms need to consider how the 'extended enterprise' can develop the necessary total array of competences which are required by such strategies.

Improvement programmes

In recent years, many companies, as well as other organisations in the public sector, have attempted to carry out major programmes of change which have as their main aim the improvement of performance. Such an intention has been achieved with varying degrees of success. For the purposes of this chapter, the nature of such programmes will be mentioned briefly, in order to fit them into the overall discussion of strategic thinking. They will be discussed in more detail in Part Two. The programmes, identified by such terms as total quality management (TQM), just-in-time (JIT) and business process re-engineering (BPR), might have particular applicability in production or operations areas of firms, but they also have more general implications for other parts of the organisation. The present discussion looks in particular at their impact on organisational structures and on styles of management and supervision. These programmes are central to business and corporate strategies and have contributed to the changing face of the organisational world.

International and global operations

Casual observation can reveal that firms have extended their activities on an international and global scale. The emergence of three major economic blocs, Europe, North America and the Pacific Rim countries, has already been noted. This dimension, involving both changes in competitive scope and competitive advantage, needs to be identified as a strategic issue. Scope may involve just the export of products from a home country base to other countries or it may involve the foreign sourcing of supplies. On the other hand, it may involve the development of value chains throughout the world, as operations to make and supply products or services become distributed on a global scale. An intermediate choice may be related to the choice of one or more of the key regional blocs as the focus for the main activities. A number of issues may be relevant to the configuration chosen by a firm, including:

1 The exploitation of factor conditions with regard to the supply of materials and labour
2 The development of economies of scale or scope
3 The exploitation of investments in resources and competences

4 The desire to enhance or defend competitive advantage
5 The degree of commonality in customer needs and tastes in different countries
6 Economic, political and legal conditions in other countries or trading blocs

Co-operation and the development of competitive advantage

It might seem to be paradoxical to talk of co-operation in the same sentence as competitive advantage. However, it has been found that it may not be feasible for individual firms to develop resources as a basis of competitive advantage on a 'go it alone' basis. Rather than relying on a competitive, adversarial mode with external firms, there can be gains to be made through co-operation. Rosabeth Moss Kanter sums up the position in the following quotation:

> Today the strategic challenge of doing more with less leads corporations to look outward as well as inward for solutions to the competitiveness dilemma, improving their ability to compete without adding internal capacity. Lean, agile, post-entrepreneurial companies can stretch in three ways. They can pool resources with others, ally to exploit an opportunity, or link systems in a partnership. In short, they can become better 'PALs' with other organisations – from venture collaborators to suppliers, service contractors, customers, and even unions.[41]

Some of the reasons for considering co-operative developments include the following:

1 Participants in a supply chain recognise their mutual interests in introducing innovations and creating products with values desired by customers.
2 An individual firm recognises that it cannot afford to invest resources in all the innovations necessary and/or is not in a market position to recover the investment. Research and development costs needed to introduce new products and processes are becoming very high, for example:
   – Risks are spread amongst several organisations.
   – There is a less permanent stake in the activity, compared with the full ownership of vertical integration.
   – Access to new markets may be gained.
   – Co-operation with an organisation in another country or trading region may reduce political risk and avoid the application of protective measures.

If co-operative strategies are selected, then there is a need to consider strategies to manage the relationships and to develop the skills of personnel who are involved in establishing efficient and effective co-ordination between the organisations. The achievement of competitive advantage may apply, therefore, not so much to individual businesses, but rather to groups of firms in the same value chain. Competition may exist, nevertheless, between different value chains. Innovation and the success of firms may be spurred on by a mixture of both competition and co-operation.

Prescriptions of excellence

Another strand of thinking which has influenced the development of the strategic management approach is the 'excellence' approach, which Stacey suggests is sometimes referred to as the 'visionary/ideological' model.[42] Tom Peters is the best known representative of this movement.[43] The ten prescriptions of *In Search of Excellence* have become 45 prescriptions in *Thriving on Chaos*. Various attributes and principles of perceived excellent companies have been identified and promoted for adoption. It is to some extent an antidote to the more rigid, analytical and technical approach of the strategic planning school. The difficulty is that there are doubts as to whether their adoption will contribute to long-lasting success and whether there is a positive relationship with success. Many of the companies identified by Peters and Waterman subsequently went under.

In *Thriving on Chaos*, Peters listed the prescriptions for 'dealing with a world turned upside down' under five main headings:

1 Creating total customer responsiveness
2 Pursuing fast-paced innovation
3 Achieving flexibility
4 Learning to love change: a new view of leadership at all levels
5 Building systems for a world turned upside down[44]

Nevertheless, there is value in the approach, in so far as it does draw attention to the 'soft' factors in the functioning of people in organisations. Attitudes, values and styles of management are seen to be important, and the skills and nature of staff are aspects to be taken into account. Strategic management, therefore, should pay attention not only to the 'hard' areas (strategy, structure and systems) but also to the 'soft' areas (style, skills, staff and shared values) i.e. the McKinsey 7–S Framework.[45] The implementation stage of strategic processes is concerned especially with the 'soft' factors. The development of the innovations required to achieve the targeted competitive advantages invariably calls for changes in these areas. Thus, the management of change is a significant element in strategic management.

PROBLEMS OF IMPLEMENTATION AND THE MANAGEMENT OF CHANGE

Mintzberg, as discussed earlier in the chapter, drew attention to the fact that not all elements of a firm's strategies will be realised.[46] Some elements may not prove to be feasible and other outcomes may be influenced by unanticipated, surprise issues. However, some elements may not be carried out, or may not be carried out effectively, because of either a lack of awareness or a lack of resources or because of resistance by those expected to implement them. The implementation of the selected strategies and the changes in the other six Ss (of the McKinsey 7–S Framework) which may be required, need to be managed carefully. The problem is also affected in part by the extent to which people have been involved in the formulation and selection of the strategies in the first place. There is a reciprocal link between strategy and structure, with each exercising an influence on the other. The relationship of corporate and business strategies to functional strategies and the involvement of functional departments will be examined in Chapter 4. Participation may assist in gaining commitment and, thus, helping to lessen the difficulties of carrying out the planned strategies.

The pressures on firms are encouraging them to improve their effectiveness, as well as efficiency, in meeting the needs of their customers. During the 1980s, interest in philosophies such as just in time and total quality management has helped to shape strategies. These philosophies embrace not only new techniques, but also ideas with regard to management approaches and the kind of involvement and contribution that might be expected from the workforce. These ideas have acted as a catalyst in stimulating attention in the fundamental aspects of management. As the decade of the 1990s proceeds, interest is growing in the concept of 'business process re-engineering'.[47] This interest questions the basic approaches of how technology and people can be combined to carry out particular activities and how individual elements can be interlinked to best achieve the key purpose of the organisation. This section of the chapter will identify some of the key issues in the current debate and will point out some of the choices which may form part of the strategic agenda. The 7–S Framework is a convenient way of dealing with them. In this framework, the following six factors are added to that of 'strategy':

Structure

The choice of organisational structure will be affected by the initial position of the firm and by the strategic choices in relation to competitive advantage and competitive scope. Aspects of functional specialisation and the balance between centralisation and decentralisation need to be reflected in decisions. Increasing concern for horizontal interdependencies between activities has focused attention on the development of co-ordinating mechanisms, such as matrix structures, multi-functional teams and committees. The nature of the tasks of some companies may call for the application of a project management approach on a regular basis. In other companies project teams or task forces may be formed for specific projects. The profile of structures, as a result, may have fewer levels and, therefore, be flatter and give less emphasis to vertical relationships.

Systems

Attention to the development of systems and procedures is also an integral part of the problem of co-ordinating efforts to achieve key strategic purposes. The integrating potential of computer systems provides opportunities for managing chains of activities more effectively and coping with linkage problems. It is one of the forces encouraging a radical reappraisal and redesign of business processes, which affects job specifications and skill needs.

Style

Developments in ideas about organisational structures and more optimistic attitudes towards the potential contribution of workers have influenced concern for more democratic and supportive styles of management. Thus, a firm needs to establish policies with regard to the design of tasks and the expectations of what the job holders should contribute. Firms which implement the supportive style of management put more emphasis on expertise being applied at the grass roots level and expect people to have more influence over their work and to contribute ideas towards improvements. Notions of job enlargement and job enrichment are followed in the design of jobs and greater flexibility may be sought. The removal or change of status features between different levels of personnel may also be an area requiring a rethink.

Shared values

A more supportive style of management, which relies less on close control and looks to utilise the skills and expertise of workers as problem solvers, may require other ways of gaining support and commitment. The values of the organisation with regard to such factors as its mission, objectives and approach to management take on extra significance. These may be seen as aspects of the cultural environment of the firm. At the heart of fundamental changes required by strategies may be a need to change the culture of the firm. From a managerial point of view it may be seen as winning over hearts and minds, so that the new values are internalised and affect the behaviour of the workforce at all levels.

Skills

As companies change and as skill and expertise become recognised as major assets of the firm, then heightened efforts in cultivating and enhancing them become a significant part of a developmental strategy. If a more positive role is expected and if activities are redesigned, the need to develop new skills and knowledge has to be recognised in the construction of training and education programmes. This picture reinforces the idea of the learning organisation and also has implications for wider concerns of staffing policy.

Staff

Recruitment and staff development strategies need to support the other aspects which have been outlined. In addition, aspects of job design, reward packages and conditions of work have to be carefully considered to balance the needs of the organisation with conditions of the labour market and the hopes and expectations of people.

It can be seen, therefore, that corporate and business strategies need to entail human relations strategies and there should be an integrated, consistent approach. Nevertheless, there may be more stable situations in which a more bureaucratic, mechanistic approach to management and organisation may be appropriate. Rules for well known situations can be devised and instructions laid down for their treatment. Indeed, some people may also be more comfortable in working in such an environment and may not wish to take on what they might perceive to be more demanding, stressful work. A contingency approach, in which considerations of the environmental demands, the style of management and types of personnel have to be taken together, is perhaps the way forward. There is no one best way that is universally applicable is a conclusion that many might support.

Managing the process of change is an important part of implementing strategies that do call for a change in the current ways of operating. Resistance to change may be anticipated for a variety of reasons. Fear of change and the unknown, any change, is a common reaction. Some may fear that their jobs might disappear and others might fear redundancy, because of a lack of appropriate skill and knowledge for redesigned jobs. Others may not be able to or may not wish to adapt to new cultural values and styles of management. The fears might be manifest in those in managerial and supervisory levels, as well as those at an operational level. In some cases they have been stronger amongst middle management. Programmes for introducing changes must take on board these concerns and take steps to overcome resistance and to reduce or eliminate the fears that people might have.

The discussion of strategy implementation and the management of change has touched upon many points and has raised many questions about techniques and approaches to be adopted. Within the confines of this book it is not possible to explore them in greater depth. There exists, of course, a more specialist body of literature about management and human relations issues that can be delved into.

SUMMARY

This chapter has made an excursion through the field of strategic management and it is now time to try and extract some relevant points for purchasing and supply management. Chapter 4 will examine the connections between corporate and business strategies, on the one hand, and functional strategies, including purchasing and supply management, on the other. Nevertheless, there are some comments that can be made to conclude this chapter:

1 Ideas about strategy, with regard to it being perceived both as a process and as having specific content, can be transferred to the conceptualisation of strategy at the functional level.
2 The approaches to the problems of implementation and management of change can also be seen as providing guidance at the functional level.
3 Those involved in strategic thinking and the development of strategies at the functional level need an awareness of the broader corporate and business

strategic issues to appreciate the role that a particular functional strategy can play and to assist in the implementation of strategies.

4 Ideas of how to sustain competitive advantage at business and corporate levels have implications for functional contributions.

5 Growing strategic recognition that firms do not exist in isolation, but are part of value chains, has changed the strategic emphasis from simply managing internal operations more efficiently, to a deeper concern with increasing the effectiveness of meeting the requirements of its environment and the needs of its stakeholders.

6 The functions involved with other external organisations in a value chain are being given greater strategic recognition. Managing relationships and managing or influencing the creation of value in other parts of the chain are seen as significant activities.

7 As the strategic management school of thought expands, there has been increased awareness that the content of strategic plans and the process by which they may be formulated should not rely only on the major inputs from the functions of marketing and finance and accounting. Purchasing and supply management is no longer viewed as an area concerned with making relatively low-level administrative decisions, as depicted by Ansoff at one time.[48] It should be involved in the configuration of the value chain and in the determination of decisions with regard to competitive scope and competitive advantage. In other words, positioning decisions should reflect purchasing and supply management considerations.

8 In a rapidly changing environment, innovation is regarded as crucial to the sustainment of competitive advantage. The prospects of an individual firm are affected partly by the quality and speed of innovations in other parts of the chain. Stimulation of these innovations and the effectiveness of their adoption can be enhanced by purchasing and supply management.

9 For the most part, discussions about strategic management have been concerned with firms in the private sector. Nevertheless, there are many relevant aspects for public sector, non-market organisations. There are environmental pressures which the latter have to face which call for the development of strategic changes as a response. Demands for increased levels of service to clients or customers and voices calling for better value for money require the search for and application of innovations in a similar way to the private sector. As was indicated in Chapter 2, initiatives to increase competitive forces have been taken, leading to the reappraisal of competitive and co-operative approaches that are needed. Therefore, questions relating to configuration and co-ordination of the value chain are pertinent. Finally, such organisations are having to manage processes of fundamental change as well.

A final observation to conclude the chapter, is to summarise the nature of strategic management. It should rarely attempt to produce a detailed strategic plan in the form of a rigid blueprint, designed to meet a detailed forecast of expected future conditions. Nor should it allow the firm to develop in an *ad hoc* way as a result of a series of uncoordinated, short-term decisions. There is a middle course that gives a clear general direction for the firm, which allows details to be worked out as circumstances permit and which permits some flexibility to cope with 'surprise' events. The implementation process should embody a monitoring process to check progress and to trigger off amendments and further changes as required. Environmental forces are pressuring firms to become 'lean' in both public and private sectors. The question perhaps is whether organisations will become 'lean' and 'mean' in the process, as some maintain, or whether they can be 'lean' but humane at the same time.[49]

NOTES AND REFERENCES

1 Lorenz, K. 'In the Fast Lane', *The Sunday Times*, Section 3, 8 August 1993, p. 3.
2 Hahn, D. 'Strategic Management – Tasks and Challenges in the 1990s', *Long Range Planning*, Vol. 24, No. 4, 1993, pp. 26–39.
3 Mintzberg, H. 'The Design School: Reconsider The Basic Premises of Strategic Management', *Strategic Management Journal*, Vol. 11, 1990, pp. 171–95.
4 Moore, J.I. *Writers on Strategy and Strategic Management*, Penguin (1992), p. xiii. This book sets out the ideas of the main authorities in the field and groups them into the following categories: 'the shapers and movers', 'the consultants', 'the scholars and researchers', 'the developers and teachers', 'the incrementalists' and 'the analysts of decline'.
5 Porter, M.E. 'Towards a Dynamic Theory of Strategy', *Strategic Management Journal*, Vol. 12, 1991, pp. 95–117.
6 Johnson, G. and Scholes, K. *Exploring Corporate Strategy: Text and Cases*, 3rd Edition, Prentice-Hall (1993), p. 10.
7 Grant, R.M. *Contemporary Strategy Analysis: Concepts, Techniques, Applications*, Blackwell (1991), p. 11.
8 Tricker, R.I. 'The Management Accountant as Strategist', *Management Accounting*, December 1989, pp. 26–9.
9 Hax, A.C. 'Redefining the Concept of Strategy and the Strategy Formation Process', *Engineering Management Review*, Spring 1991, pp. 19–24.
   Also, an earlier article sets out thoughts on the concept of strategy:
   Hax, A.C. and Majluf, N.S. 'The Concept of Strategy and the Strategy Process', *Interfaces*, Vol. 18, No. 3, May–June 1988, pp. 99–109.
10 *See* pp. 28–31 of Hahn, D. (1993), as mentioned in note 2 above.
11 Schendel, D.E. and Hofer, C.W. *Strategic Management: A New View of Business Policy and Planning*, Little Brown (1979), p. 11.
12 Gore, C., Murray, K. and Richardson, B. *Strategic Decision-Making*, Cassell (1992).
13 Simon, H.A. *Administrative Behavior*, Macmillan (1961).
   Simon, H.A. 'Rational Decision Making in Business Organizations', *American Economic Review*, Vol. 69, 1979, pp. 493–513.
14 Eisenhardt, K.M. and Zbaracki, M.J. 'Strategic Decision Making', *Strategic Management Journal*, Vol. 13, Winter Special, 1992, pp. 17–37.
15 Glaister, K. and Thwaites, K. 'Managerial Perception and Organizational Strategy', *Journal of General Management*, Vol. 18, No. 3, Summer 1993, pp. 15–33.
16 Cyert, R.M. and March, J.G. *A Behavioral Theory of the Firm*, Prentice-Hall (1965).
17 Wind, Y. 'A Case Study of the Purchase of Industrial Components', in Robinson, P.J. and Faris, C.W. *Industrial Buying and Creative Marketing*, Allyn and Bacon (1967), Chapter 7.

18 Mintzberg, H. 'Crafting Strategy', *Harvard Business Review*, July–August 1987, pp. 66–75.

19 Stacey, R.D. *Strategic Management and Organisational Dynamics*, 2nd Edition, Pitman Publishing (1996).

20 Examples of the popular texts are:
Johnson, G. and Scholes, K. (1991), as mentioned in note 6 above.
Grant, R.M. (1993), as mentioned in note 7 above.
Thompson, J.L. *Strategic Management: Awareness and Change*, 2nd Edition, Chapman & Hall (1993).
Bowman, C. and Asch, D. *Strategic Management*, Macmillan (1987).

21 Ansoff, H.I. and McDonnell, E.J. *Implanting Strategic Management*, 2nd Edition, Prentice-Hall (1990), Chapter 1.

22 Taylor, B. 'Corporate Planning for the 1990s: New Frontiers', *Long Range Planning*, Vol. 19, No. 6, 1986, pp. 13–18.

23 Ansoff, H.I. *Corporate Strategy*, Penguin (1968).

24 Ansoff, H.I. *Corporate Strategy*, Revised edition, McGraw-Hill (1987).

25 Page 13 of Taylor, B. (1986), as mentioned in note 22 above.

26 Baily, P., Farmer, D., Jessop, D. and Jones, D. *Purchasing, Principles and Management*, 7th Edition, Pitman Publishing (1994), pp. 157–8.

27 *See* p. 343 of Grant, R.M. (1991) as mentioned in note 7 above.

28 For accounts of the use of the product life cycle, *see*, for example:
Baker, M.J. *Marketing Strategy and Management*, Macmillan (1992), pp. 61–3, 100–9 and 335–44.

29 Chandler, A.D. *Strategy and Structure*, MIT (1962).

30 *See* the same article by Taylor, B. (1986), as mentioned in note 22 above.

31 *See* the following articles:
Porter, M.E. 'From Competitive Advantage to Corporate Strategy', *Harvard Business Review*, May–June 1987, pp. 43–59.
Porter, M.E. 'Corporate Strategy', *The Economist*, 23 May 1987, pp. 22–8.

32 *See* p. 22 of Porter, M.E. 'Corporate Strategy' (1987) as mentioned in note 31 above.

33 Porter, M.E. *Competitive Strategy: Techniques for Analysing Industries and Competitors,* The Free Press (1980).

34 Porter, M.E. *Competitive Advantage: Creating and Sustaining Superior Performance*, The Free Press (1985).

35 Accounts of his interest in the competitive advantage of nations can be found in:
Porter, M.E. *The Competitive Advantage of Nations*, The Free Press (1990).
Porter, M.E. 'The Competitive Advantage of Nations', *Harvard Business Review*, March–April 1990, pp. 73–93.

36 *See* p. 96 of Porter, M.E. (1991), as mentioned in note 5 above.

37 This list of four is the modified list, which has two different focused strategies, as in note 34 above.

38 *See* p. 102 of Porter, M.E. 'Towards a Dynamic Theory of Strategy', *Strategic Management Journal*, Vol. 12, 1991, pp. 95–117.

39 Prahalad, C.K. and Hamel, G. 'The Core Competence of the Corporation', *Harvard Business Review*, May–June 1990, pp. 71–91.

40 Hamel, G. and Prahalad, C.K. *Competing for the Future*, Harvard Business School Press (1994).

41 Kanter, R.M. *When Giants Learn to Dance*, Unwin Hyman (1989), p. 118.

42 *See* Chapter 2 of Stacey, R.D. (1993), as mentioned in note 19 above.

43 *See*, for example:
Peters, T.J. and Waterman, R.H. *In Search of Excellence*, HarperCollins (1982).

Peters, T.J. *Thriving on Chaos*, Macmillan (1988).

44 *See* pp. ix and x of Peters, T.J. (1988), as mentioned in note 43 above.

45 The 7–S Framework is used, for example, in:
Pascale, R.T. and Athos, A.G. *The Art of Japanese Management*, Penguin (1982).

46 *See* note 18 above.

47 Examples of a growing literature in 'business process re-engineering' are:
Hammer, M. 'Re-engineering Work: Don't Automate, Obliterate', *Harvard Business Review*, July–August 1990, pp. 104–12.
Johansson, H.J., McHugh, P., Pendlebury, W.A. and Wheeler III, W.A. *Business Process Re-engineering*, Wiley (1993).

48 *See* Ansoff, H.I. (1968), as mentioned in note 23 above.

49 Wickens, P.D. 'Lean Production and Beyond: The System, its Critics and the Future', *Human Resource Management Journal*, Vol. 3, No. 4, 1993, pp. 75–89.

CHAPTER 4

From corporate strategy to purchasing and supply chain management strategy

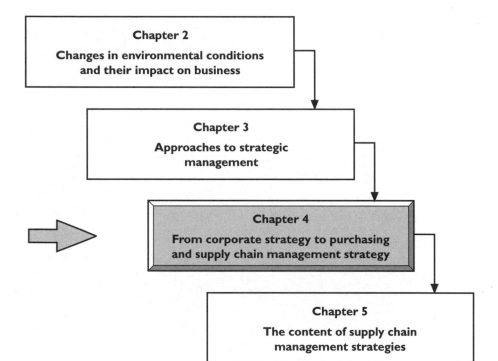

INTRODUCTION

Chapter 3 traced the developments in strategic thinking at corporate and business unit levels and identified the main ideas in the concept of strategic management. It was suggested that the main unit for analysing what made organisations successful was that of each individual business unit. However, to understand how advantages in terms of cost and differentiation can be gained, it is necessary to consider the performance of discrete activities and the development of resources to enhance the level of performance required. Thus, activities might be perceived as the basic building blocks and the business strategy as concerned with providing coherent direction in support of the basic mission and objectives of the business. In organisational terms, the allocation of personnel and the determination of responsibilities for activities is accomplished primarily through the designation of departmental or functional groups. Thus, to understand the formation and content of business strategy it is important to examine the link between the business and functional strategies. It is also necessary to consider the relationship between functional and corporate strategies, and to assess whether there are synergistic benefits to be gained, by examining the potential for interrelationships between different business units and for interrelationships at functional levels as well.

An underlying assumption in this chapter is that, at both business and corporate levels, much of the strategic theory includes considerations of the functions of marketing and financial and cost accounting. More recently, there has also been a growing interest in bringing in aspects of operations/manufacturing strategy. ('Operations' as a term is concerned with processes for generating services as well as goods, whereas manufacturing covers only the production of goods.) On the other hand, while advocates within the purchasing and supply management profession have argued for several decades that this area should be viewed from a strategic point of view, it is an argument which had tended to fall upon deaf ears elsewhere.

John Argenti wrote in 1974:

> I do not hesitate to emphasize that, for some companies, the supplies strategy may be quite as important as its market strategy – a statement that many managers would agree with but which is not reflected in the literature.[1]

In 1989, Graham Stevens of KPMG Peat Marwick McLintock said:

> While businesses often spend a lot of time and thought on strategic issues in the area of manufacturing, finance and marketing, the focus on supply is rarely strategic, it tends to be operational. If the supply issues are disregarded, such that the supply chain is excluded from the strategic debate, there is imbalance, exploitable opportunities are missed and the impact of the competitive threat increased.[2]

There is a difficulty in trying to analyse these issues from a generic standpoint and to cater for the variety of different organisational forms and business types that exist. Also, the perceptions of practitioners will tend to be shaped by their own experiences and by the particular organisational contexts in which they have operated. In the sense that strategic thinking is about trying to determine what the business should be doing and how it should be operating, current structures and approaches may not offer the best prospects. It is important to build up visions of other possibilities. Thus, it is important to stand back from the existing situation and consider other models.

Where purchasing and supply management is concerned, there is the problem of deciding what activities to embrace in a strategic perspective and this will be one of the issues to be discussed in this chapter. The general view to be developed takes into account a broad supply chain perspective. The justification for this is that, whatever particular activity a person may be involved in directly, as a result of a particular organisational arrangement, for decision-making purposes that person will need to be aware of implications elsewhere along the chain. A supply chain perspective is important at both operational and strategic levels.

OBJECTIVES OF THIS CHAPTER

The specific objectives of this chapter are as follows:

1 To examine the basic relationship between functional strategies and business and corporate strategies
2 To examine the problem of identifying 'activities' and 'functions'
3 To account for the development of operations management and manufacturing management strategies and the implications for purchasing and supply management
4 To assess the strategic role for purchasing and supply management in relation to other functional strategies and to business and corporate strategies

BASIC RELATIONSHIPS BETWEEN FUNCTIONAL, BUSINESS AND CORPORATE STRATEGIES

Before entering into a detailed discussion of the nature and content of functional strategies, it will be helpful to recap on some of the basic points about strategic management that were examined in Chapter 3. These provide a framework for the appreciation and development of strategic thinking at the functional level. The key points are as follows:

1 Strategies are concerned with decisions that are significant with respect to long-term development and the employment of both financial and other resources. They are broader in scope than tactical and operational decisions and are likely to involve higher levels of management, at least with regard to final choice.
2 In so far as strategies are deliberate and intentional, the process of formulating strategies involves the basic steps of:
   – establishing the basic mission;
   – setting goals and objectives;

- analysing the environment;
- assessing the capability of the firm;
- identifying options with regard to competitive advantage and competitive scope;
- selecting options;
- implementing strategies.

3 Strategies can be perceived and classified into corporate, business and functional levels.

4 The environment, characterised by growing globalisation of markets, shorter product life cycles, and more demanding customers, emphasises the need to improve capabilities continually in order to pursue competitive advantage and competitive scope.

5 The firm is perceived as a value chain, made up of a collection of activities. The firm's value chain is part of a wider value system, consisting of the value chains of upstream suppliers and the chains of other firms in the downstream channel towards the final consumer or user.

6 Competitive scope can be deemed to embrace choices in relation to market segments, vertical stages, geographical spread and range of industries.

7 Competitive advantage can be discerned as involving dimensions of cost and of differentiation, the latter being to provide unique features compared to competitors.

8 Value can be perceived in different ways, but what counts are the values attached to products by buyers in relation to what they are prepared to pay for. (The nature of products and customer perceptions are discussed in more detail later in this chapter.)

9 Chains create value and firms achieve objectives of profitability and survival (or value for money in non-market organisations) by satisfying or exceeding customer expectations.

10 Activities provide opportunities to achieve competitive advantages and resources applied in activities are the source of innovations.

Products and customer perceived values

It is all too easy, especially for those in a manufacturing firm, to conceptualise products as being of a physical, tangible kind, such as a television set. Those in service environments, by contrast, might conceive of their outputs for clients or customers as being of an intangible kind, such as health treatment. However, it is dangerous to think of products in terms of a strictly either/or distinction, between a physical good and a service. It is worth elaborating on this point. A product offering, therefore, may be thought of as possessing a mix of features, which will be taken into account by both designers and customers.

A starting point is to see the product as providing a 'bundle of benefits' which the customer might obtain from possessing or using it. These benefits may be functional, arising from the form of the good or service. Clearly, a specification might be drawn up to describe elements of both form and function. Benefits may be associated with other aspects of a less tangible kind, such as time and place, and support or ancillary services. Other valued aspects might involve aesthetic and esteem attributes, which provide psychological rather than functional benefits. Thus, with what might be regarded as physical goods, delivery at the right time and to the right place may also be critical aspects as far as the customer is concerned. Capital goods, as well as including functional characteristics with regard to basic performance, durability, reliability, and maintainability, may be part of a wider package of requirements, which might include installation, commissioning and maintenance. Services, while primarily being of an intangible kind, may also require some physical goods in support. Documents or materials, for example, may be an integral part of the provision of a service. Thus, a product should be looked upon as having a profile of both tangible and intangible dimensions.

One general definition of a product is as follows: 'Product: everything that the customer receives that is of value in terms of a perceived want, need or problem'.[3] The same book distinguishes between the essential benefits (the basic product), the product make-up (the real product) and services and intangible associations (the total product).

When considering the problem of differentiation, it is important to delve into customer requirements and understand customer values and priorities – a task for marketing – to reflect the forces of 'market pull' with regard to product design. The offerings of competitors' products may also enter into the evaluation process by customers, with varying degrees of consciousness. Customer perceptions may, thus, be relative to other market offers. There are dangers of giving too much weight to the forces of production or technology 'push' in the design of and in the evaluation of products. It will be seen later that product policy and the design details of product offerings play a central role in developing an integrated perspective of functional strategies and business strategies.

Relationships between functional and business strategies

Porter suggested that a firm has a chain of activities which create value and which are 'performed to design, produce, market, deliver and support its product'.[4] He also points out that each activity employs purchased inputs, human resources and some form of technology. A business strategy needs to give direction to these activities and to ensure that the interrelationships between them are taken into account. Thus, the strategies for these activities should support the overall strategy of the business with regard to mission, objectives, competitive scope and competitive advantage. At the same time, they should support each other and problems of linkages, in the sense of co-ordination and overall optimisation, should be taken into account and resolved.

The nature of the relationship between business and functional strategies might be viewed as 'top-down' or 'bottom-up', in terms of initiatives in formulating strategies. A more appropriate picture is to see it as an interactive or circular process between the levels. Personnel with direct responsibilities for activities need to be involved so that expertise from each area can be contributed. Remote specialist planners may not have accurate perceptions of the problems and circumstances and are not directly involved in implementation. If the view is accepted that functional representatives should be involved, a requirement would seem to be that they can think strategically both about their own function, but also about the business as a whole.

Corporate strategies and functional strategies

For some organisations, the business strategy will be the corporate strategy, because of the limited scope of their operations. For others, however, there arises the question as to how far steps to co-ordinate individual businesses and their activities should be taken. At one extreme of the more complex situations is that of the conglomerate firm, which is perceived as consisting of a range of separate and unrelated businesses. Scope for sharing of resources and adopting mechanisms to co-ordinate activities is severely limited. At the centre is a holding company, which relies primarily on financial strategies and controls to provide a link between them. Opportunities for co-operation between other functions are very few, as the nature of resources used in each business is different. In other cases there may be common features between business units which provide opportunities for central co-ordination and which may be reflected in organisational structures (*see* Fig 4.1).

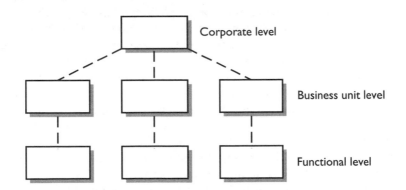

Fig 4.1 Corporate, business and functional strategies

Examples to illustrate the point might include the same markets served with a range of different products, similar manufacturing technologies to produce a range of different products and the same distribution facilities used for different products. On the purchasing and supply side, there may be scope for some co-ordination of purchasing because of the use of common purchased items from the same supply markets. Other forms of integration may involve the possibility of intra-company trading and the establishment of policies to govern relationships and arrangements between supplier and customer units.

PROBLEMS OF IDENTIFYING 'ACTIVITIES' AND 'FUNCTIONS'

Most organisations are already in existence and, therefore, have to start from the initial conditions at a particular moment in time, which have emerged as a result of past events and decisions. There is an existing organisation structure which reflects past views of how to group activities into functional or departmental groupings. The decisions made about the design of the organisational structure also indicate relative priorities with regard to these activities. Some activities may be given a subordinate position as a subsection of another department, rather than being allocated to a department as an independent entity. The positions of heads of department in the hierarchy and the designated reporting relationships also give indications of relative importance. A variety of influences may have contributed to the preferences of those who had been in a position to shape the structure. These might include careful assessment of the significance of the contribution of each activity, as well as knowledge and experience of each. However, an organisational arrangement can reflect political and career considerations and the power relationships of personnel at the time. The current procedures and planning and control systems also help to influence the way in which activities are co-ordinated and provide signals with regard to expectations and performance criteria.

The point that can be made concerning initial conditions is that they are likely to influence the strategic perceptions of people in the business. Each person has a different vantage point, which will reflect to a greater or lesser extent views of the direction of future strategy and structure. Protection of departmental boundaries and career paths may block perceptions of a wider business or corporate vision. Particular ways of looking at situations may thus act as a constraint on the potential role that certain activities might play. Reference to the lack of recognition of purchasing and supply management is a case in point. Different organisations with basically different purposes (manufacturing as opposed to retailing, for instance) will also tend to adopt different perceptions relating to activities and functions. 'Bottom-up' flows of ideas are likely to promote viewpoints that are advantageous to the positions occupied by those promoting them. Strategy might determine structure, but in turn structure might determine strategy. These processes involve both rational, analytical business considerations but also interpersonal, social and political influences. In the end, each organisation will develop its own arrangements and will be unique in some ways.

Another problem with organisational structures is that particular activities might appear to be undertaken by personnel in a certain specialist department, but that may not be the case for all occurrences of them. There may be a purchasing department, but some purchasing might be carried out elsewhere. User departments might buy their own capital equipment, marketing might purchase advertising materials.

A further difficulty is now coming to the forefront, as businesses attempt to break down the barriers between functions and departments and look for ways of fostering closer integration between activities. Thus, multi-functional teams bring together people from different specialisms to carry out an activity jointly, e.g. design engineers, production personnel and quality assurance engineers may come together with buyers to make purchasing arrangements. Similarly, the notion of simultaneous engineering can bring design engineers, process or industrial engineers, marketing and purchasing personnel, and even suppliers' and customers' representatives into a project team to design new products.

There is a problem, therefore, in developing generic viewpoints which avoid elements of arbitrariness and subjectivity. Different frameworks based upon different rationales are likely to be proffered for consideration by both students and practitioners alike. Porter's picture of the make-up of the value chain sets a scheme that reflects his views and justifications.

One way of attempting to break free of particular preconceptions, based upon actual circumstances of an ongoing organisation, is to take the start-up position of a new business. In other words, by taking a clean sheet of paper, it is possible to revert to basic thinking about the possibilities. This tactic may allow people to visualise a different way of evaluating the worth of activities, independently of a particular organisational context. In addition, it will help to focus attention on basic strategic questions about the scope and capabilities that will be required to launch the new business. Of course, it is recognised that most companies do not have the opportunity to start from a 'greenfield' situation and have to decide in which direction to move from a position which has been inherited.

Starting a business

How might a putative entrepreneur plan the start of a business and what activities would need to be taken into account? The initial perspective will need to consider potential customers and their needs which are not being fully met or are not being met satisfactorily. Assessment of such needs leads to thoughts about the type of good or service that might attract customer patronage and this implies attention to design of the features of the package to be offered. The next aspect is to consider how the physical product is to be supplied or the service delivered. Taking the case of the physical product, the notion of supply can be broken down into two basic possibilities with regard to the scope of operations to be undertaken by the new firm. One possibility is to act only as a distributor and buy, stock and sell the selected products that are to be manufactured by suppliers. On the other hand, some of the manufacturing tasks might be taken on by the firm itself. If the latter is the case, it will be necessary to buy in appropriate parts and materials to be consumed in the manufacturing stages inside the firm's boundaries. Also, plans will need to be drawn up with regard to transportation of the parts and materials and the finished product.

In this perspective, supply as a physical system involves the basic activities of 'make', 'move' and 'store'. The start-up firm needs to plan which elements are to be included in the 'value chain' of the firm itself and which elements will need to be performed by other firms. The supply system can be conceived as a pipeline, or as a chain or network of chains. Thus, the strategic plans for the firm provide a basic configuration of the internal operations to be carried out. This configuration determines the value contributions to be made by suppliers' and the firm's own value chains. Some firms that call themselves manufacturers may contribute a relatively small percentage of the total value passed on down the chain. Other resources, as well, will be needed to enable these operations to be carried out, namely, labour, finance, consumable supplies and equipment.

Other activities to be carried out in the firm are needed to control the basic physical supply system. Purchasing and marketing are needed to make the links with upstream suppliers' and downstream customers' value chains. Product and process design and production are required to co-ordinate internal flows of goods, as well as finance and personnel to manage flows of money and inputs of labour.

The basic model that emerges from this account is one that is often seen as an input-output system, with transformation or conversion operations being managed inside the firm (*see* Fig 4.2).

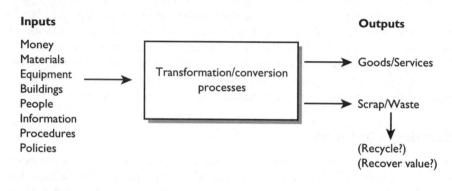

Fig 4.2 Input-output model

It also suggests a different way of depicting the value chain of the firm, compared to that of Porter's model. The key distinction is between physical structural elements and the supporting infrastructural activities concerned with people, systems, and procedures that plan and control operations and cause flows of goods along the chains. This distinction does not imply any differentiation between primary and secondary categories of activity.

However, rather than focusing on the firm alone, which emphasises internal operations, the point of the discussion here is to locate it in a wider system, the supply chain as a whole. This permits a more balanced perspective of the relative importance of internal activities and the boundary-spanning activities that influence the contribution of external value chains. Internal manufacturing operations may be more visible through the manifestation of the plant and equipment and the labour force, but the internal costs of these resources tend, on average, to be a smaller percentage of the total manufactured cost of the product, compared to the cost of bought-out supplies.

A further point to make is that the identification and selection of customer needs to be satisfied will position the firm in the total supply chain, somewhere from raw material stages to the final consumer or user of the product. If the product is in its final state, then the firm will be located near the customer end. Alternatively it might be an intermediate part to be used by a manufacturer. The position in the supply chain will influence the nature of the problems of co-ordination and relative power relationships between the different firms.

The twin fundamental tasks of the firm might be summarised as, on the one hand, managing customer demand and, on the other hand, managing the flow of supplies. Overall, the entrepreneur will want to ensure that the demands emanating from customers can be met by a matching flow of supplies, while retaining a balanced flow in the supply chain. While managing the product flow, the entrepreneur will want to obtain a positive cashflow and earn a return on the investments that have been made.

However, before we return to strategic issues concerned with the supply chain, we will look first towards developments regarding the theory and application of operations management and manufacturing management strategies. This will have an immediate relevance to those operating in a manufacturing environment. There is also a value to purchasing and supply personnel in other spheres, in as much as the latter can gain from understanding and assessing the manufacturing developments of their suppliers.

OPERATIONS MANAGEMENT AND MANUFACTURING MANAGEMENT STRATEGIES

Key phrases sometimes act as a clarion call for new approaches to be adopted and help to promote their adoption. Wickham Skinner is generally credited with being first to articulate the concept of manufacturing strategy and referred to it as 'Manufacturing – Missing Link in Corporate Strategy'.[5] As concern for the lack of a competitive edge by comparison with Japanese manufacturers spread, manufacturing activities were seen in Europe and America to be a cause of the problems in businesses. Low productivity, poor quality, badly managed new product introductions and an inability to deliver on time were just some of the performance deficiencies that firms wished to rectify. (*See* Fig 4.3 for a list of manufacturing strategy topics to be discussed.)

1	The role of manufacturing strategy
2	Factors hindering the development of manufacturing strategy
3	Stages in the evolution of manufacturing strategy
4	The 'content'
5	The 'process'
6	The 'context'
7	Generic manufacturing strategies
8	Implications for purchasing and supply management

Fig 4.3 Discussion topics in manufacturing strategy

The role of manufacturing strategy

Skinner argued that it is important to consider what standards of performance are needed from manufacturing in order that the firm can be competitive and then to configure its facilities accordingly. He also made the point that varying performance priorities call for different manufacturing configurations. Since Skinner first drew attention to the need, there have been many efforts to develop ideas with regard to both the decision content of and the processes of formulating manufacturing strategy. The starting point has been to relate manufacturing to business strategies, with a view to countering the former domination of finance and marketing in strategic thinking. By 1992, Skinner was able to write:

> Enthusiasm for the concepts of 'manufacturing strategy' has never run higher. Academic papers, executive courses, and case studies of industry practice are bursting out all over.[6]

However, Skinner expressed concern that the adoption of a strategic perspective of manufacturing in industry had not progressed as rapidly. He suggests that manufacturing tends to be managed by:

1 Piecemeal decisions, concentrating on local areas of performance rather than considering the overall effect in relation to business objectives.
2 Emphasis on the setting of short-term objectives and measuring performance likewise.
3 Efforts to optimise all aspects of performance, assuming that there are no trade-offs between different goals.
4 Command and control workforce management.
5 A primary focus on reducing costs and increasing productivity.
6 Adoption of the latest fashionable techniques without having a coherent, integrated strategic framework – a 'quick fix' mentality, in other words.

Thus, manufacturing may be left to operate on a reactive basis and its neglect in the formation of business strategies may prevent the development of the very capabilities which such strategies actually need, if they are to be successful.

Performance objectives

Wickham Skinner suggests that the manufacturing 'task' in a strategy is likely to be based upon one or two of seven performance objectives. These are as follows:

1 Cost, efficiency, productivity
2 Delivery leadtimes
3 Quality
4 Service, reliability
5 Flexibility for product change
6 Flexibility for volume change
7 Investment required in the production system

Priorities depend on the competitive strategy, technological opportunities and economic conditions. 'To meet the task, the operations system is designed and tailored to focus on that task, with limited ranges of products, markets, technologies, degrees of process demands and order quantities'.[7]

Elizabeth Haas made similar comments:

> It is only by managing the operational components as an integrated system that manufacturers can exploit their full potential for delivering added value to customers through lower prices, greater service responsiveness, or higher quality.[8]

Factors hindering the development of manufacturing strategy

It is instructive to consider some of the reasons, which both Wickham Skinner and Terry Hill[9] have put forward, which have held back the inclusion of manufacturing strategy in a properly integrated business strategy.

1 Strategic perceptions of top management tend to be outward looking because of the focus of traditional strategic thinking. Manufacturing has arrived late in the debate and has not yet affected all mindsets. There is generally a failure to recognise that the development of manufacturing as a whole can be a competitive weapon which needs to be linked to the requirements of the business strategy.
2 Decisions about manufacturing are believed to be more concerned with tactical and operational issues and, thus, a strategic role is not sought from manufacturing.
3 Personnel in manufacturing have not developed an ability to think strategically about the firm and have not learnt to develop appropriate language to discuss how manufacturing should contribute to business strategy.
4 Functional goals and measures emphasise efficiency rather than business effectiveness, and provide a focus for the attention of manufacturing personnel.

Elizabeth Haas reinforces the latter point, when she says:

> Typically, manufacturing decisions are still taken in an operational framework defined by internal performance standards – machine downtime, scrap rate, work in process inventories, and the like.[10]

Stages in the evolution of manufacturing strategy

Hayes and Wheelwright gave some thought to the pattern of evolution of the role of manufacturing strategy, and suggested that there are four stages.[11]

Stage 1 – 'internally neutral' – minimise manufacturing's negative potential. Manufacturing is essentially in a reactive mode, attempting not to prevent achievement of the business objectives and concentrating mainly on efficiency and improving operational performance.

Stage 2 – 'externally neutral' – achieve parity with competitors.

Manufacturing may attempt to follow industry practice with regard to the workforce, equipment and extension of product range.

Stage 3 – 'internally supportive' – provide credible support to the business strategy.

The strategic role for manufacturing in support of business strategy is recognised. Investments and longer-term developments in manufacturing are examined in relation to changes in business strategy.

Stage 4 – 'externally supportive' – pursue a manufacturing-based competitive advantage.

All functions have a part to play in the development of strategy and manufacturing should be involved as well. Attempts to anticipate the potential of new technologies and manufacturing practices influence the formation of business strategies and may give the firm a competitive edge. Manufacturing is seen as a strategic resource and development of capabilities is important. This may open up new market opportunities.

In short, movement through the stages shows a transition from a reactive to a proactive role. In the last section of this chapter, a review is made of efforts to trace a similar evolutionary development in purchasing and supply management.

The content of manufacturing strategy

While the detailed lists of topics might vary slightly, there has been a strong measure of agreement as to the main aspects that should be covered in an integrated strategy. The list, produced by Hayes, Wheelwright and Clark, might be taken as an indication of the decisions that need to be addressed.[12] These are of two types.

Structural features

The first group are the structural or 'bricks and mortar' decisions:

1 Amount of production capacity
2 Division of capacity into specific facilities and locations
3 Type of production equipment and layout
4 Identification of materials, systems and services to be produced internally, those to be sourced from outside the organisation and the kinds of supplier relationships to be established.

Infrastructural features

The second group are decisions related to the infrastructure:

1 Policies with regard to human resources
2 Quality assurance and control systems

3 Processes for new product development
4 Performance measurement systems and reward policies
5 Design of the organisational structure

Although it is possible analytically to separate out structural and infrastructural features, it is important to appreciate that, in practice, there are interactions and interrelationships between them. An integrated strategy has to take into account the way in which combinations of features harmonise or come into conflict with each other. In recent years, for example, many firms have changed factory layouts to a cellular or group technology approach and have abandoned layouts based upon a process or functional principle. Firms have recognised that such a move opens up different possibilities from the point of view of the deployment of workers. To obtain full benefits, greater flexibility is needed and workers need to operate within teams.

Consideration of the content of manufacturing strategy leads on to the question of how firms might manage the process of formulating the details of it, so that it is integrated into an effective business strategy.

The process of formulating manufacturing strategy

The objective is to develop a manufacturing strategy that aligns competitive advantage with competitive scope, with particular attention being paid to the interface between manufacturing and marketing. Terry Hill has proposed a five-part framework, which is designed to make this link.

Hill's framework

Hill's approach is to consider five basic aspects, which are as follows:[13]

1 **Define corporate objectives.** Among the list of possibilities for consideration are growth, survival, profit, return on investment.
2 **Determine marketing strategies to meet these objectives.** Features to be taken into account include product markets and segments, as well as the range, mix and volumes of products. Further points include questions of product standardisation versus customisation, the level of innovation, and whether the firm should act as a leader or follower.
3 **Assess how different products win orders against competitors.** This task is perhaps the most novel ingredient of Hill's approach and leads to a particular way of categorising priorities in a situation where there are multiple objectives. He suggests that there are certain criteria which will act as 'order qualifiers' and certain others that will be 'order winners' with regard to the product offerings. In other words, it is necessary to meet requirements in relation to some features (the order qualifiers), in order to qualify for consideration as a supplier, but this will not be sufficient to win the order. An example might be a local government authority or other organisation which has a stated policy that a supplier should have been registered as meeting the quality standard BS 5750 (or the equivalent in ISO 9000 or EN 29000

series). Other criteria however, the 'order winners', are the key features that will determine who receives the order from a customer. With 'order qualifiers', a firm has just to satisfy requirements and be no better than competitors. It follows that the firm needs to be superior to competitors in the case of 'order winners', but relative weightings of each criterion also need to be determined.

4 **Establish the most appropriate mode to manufacture these sets of products – i.e. process choice.** This task involves configuration of the structure of manufacturing and attention is drawn to a similar set of factors as indicated by Hayes, Wheelwright and Clark, as listed above.

5 **Provide the manufacturing infrastructure required to support production.** Once again the infrastructural content of the manufacturing strategy covers similar concerns as in the Hayes, Wheelwright and Clark scheme.

In terms of applying the framework, Hill recommends that there should be an interactive, as opposed to sequential, process in considering the five steps and forming a balanced business strategy in which the functional elements support each other.

The Cranfield competitive-edge manufacturing model

Colin New, reporting on the Cranfield competitive-edge manufacturing model,[14] adopts a similar approach to Hill, but refers to 'competitive edge criteria' as the linchpin – 'what could we try to be good at?' The model suggests seven criteria, under four basic headings, as follows:

1 Delivery:
   – leadtime
   – reliability
2 Quality:
   – capability
   – reliability
3 Flexibility:
   – design
   – volume
4 Price

The firm should determine its priorities, having analysed competitors' strategies, market characteristics, corporate objectives and environmental pressures. He reinforces the viewpoint that not all criteria can be pursued simultaneously with equal vigour. Perhaps the problem is similar to that of devising national economic policies. Governments have not been able to give equal attention to multiple goals, such as growth, stable prices, a stable balance of payments situation and low unemployment. New also suggests that relative rankings need to be made and he also suggests that some criteria may be 'hygiene' factors, along the lines of Herzberg in writing about management. These have the same role as 'order qualifiers' in the Hill scheme.

The Cranfield approach disagrees with other writers, such as Schonberger,[15] with regard to the controversial issue of trade-offs. The latter, in promulgating ideas of world-class manufacturing, claims that his 19 principles have general applicability and that there is no trade-off problem. Research carried out at Cranfield indicates that modern practices may have altered the areas of conflict, but that there may still be difficulties with such pairings as quality capability versus price, design flexibility versus leadtime and design flexibility versus price, and in the case of leadtime versus volume flexibility, the level of difficulty may be reduced.[16]

Both marketing strategies (relating to the conventional marketing mix of product, promotion, price and place) and manufacturing strategies (concerned with plant, process, people and product) are devised to support the targeted criteria.

Human resource issues

An important thrust of Hill's approach, as already outlined, has been to focus on the link between marketing and manufacturing when determining developments in structural and infrastructural features of a manufacturing system. Some writers,[17] however, have chosen to give more weight to human resource policies and have separated this factor from the list of infrastructural items. The justification for this is founded on the view that manufacturing systems need to give balanced weight to 'technical' and 'social' issues. Deployment of appropriate human resource strategies in relation to those employed in the manufacturing area is seen to be a vital component in plans.

The context of manufacturing strategies

A further development in the treatment of manufacturing strategy is to highlight the significance of the context in which an organisation is placed and to recognise the 'starting' conditions. In this regard reference can be made to the work of Platts and Gregory,[18] who devised a manufacturing audit tool to diagnose requirements and to guide the development of manufacturing strategies. Using a series of worksheets, an analyst is able to follow a 'logical process of identifying and measuring current manufacturing performance, determining the effects of current manufacturing practices, identifying manufacturing objectives and identifying where changes are required'.[19] A more complete review of their ideas can be found in Mills, Platts and Gregory.[20]

Generic manufacturing strategies

The debate about trade-offs with regard to objectives leads on to the suggestion that differentiated strategies exist for different sets of priorities. Thus, just as Porter tried to identify generic competitive strategies at the business level, so others have tried to identify different types for manufacturing. Sweeney has distilled, from both his own research and the work of others,[21] four basic generic types which have some commonality with the four evolutionary stages of Hayes and Wheelwright, discussed previously.[22]

Caretaker strategy

This approach is in keeping with a least-cost producer-competitive strategy, and top management look to manufacturing primarily to be efficient and reliable – 'internally neutral'. The emphasis will tend to be on improvements in the use of existing facilities, but with some occasional piecemeal investment in processes.

The marketeer strategy

This approach is mainly a response to marketing's request to meet competition by improved customer service, in the form of broader product lines, improved quality and expanded distribution. Sweeney suggests that the manufacturing response is mainly 'externally neutral'. To meet the demands for a more differentiated service, changes may be made in infrastructural features, such as total quality management, working practices and information systems to cope with increased complexity arising from increased product variety. It is an incremental approach, which does not require major changes to the existing facilities and, thus, no major capital investment. There is a risk that changes to the profile of output requirements may stretch the capabilities of the plant too much.

The reorganiser strategy

This 'internally supportive' strategy, to meet demands for enhanced performance in quality and product performance and delivery leadtime, concentrates on structural changes in plant layout and equipment. High throughput efficiency and flexibility are sought from the changes.

The innovator strategy

Manufacturing is seen as a competitive weapon in line with the 'externally supportive' fourth stage of Hayes and Wheelwright's scheme. A clear customer focus drives an integrated approach for improvements in both structural and infrastructural features. It is, perhaps, represented by a combination of total quality management and just in time methods. As a result, short manufacturing cycle times and flexible use of labour are designed to provide a faster response to changing customer requirements. In short, it combines an enhanced customer focus with high throughput efficiency and continuous improvement – the pursuit of world-class manufacturing standards, combining low cost with differentiation.

Implications for purchasing and supply management

It may be helpful to identify and summarise, from the point of view of purchasing and supply management, some of the key messages that seem to be embodied in developments of manufacturing strategy.

General impact of developments in manufacturing strategy

The developments in manufacturing strategy, in both the theory and practice of better companies, have done much to bring a more balanced perspective to business strategy. They strengthen the view of business strategy as being concerned with the development of capabilities in pursuit of competitive advantage. An integrated perspective of the combination of structural and infrastructural factors also comes through strongly. The need to consider the human implications of technological change is an issue which receives particular attention.

Vertical integration

Ideas about the content of manufacturing strategy recognise the significance of bought-out supplies and the importance of relationships with and the performance of suppliers. The strategic problem of determining the span of internal processes (i.e. the extent of vertical integration, addressed through the make-or-buy question) is recognised as one of the important structural aspects. Thus, positioning issues draw attention to external sourcing possibilities.

Integration of the supply chain

Holistic perceptions give encouragement to achieving integration of material and information flows, both internally and externally. Consideration is given to the performance of the manufacturing system as a whole in relation to articulated competitive requirements. There is, therefore, a growing interest in broader supply chain integration.

Several aspects of integration can be highlighted. First, the desire to obtain a better balance of supply with demand has stimulated the search for and development of integrated planning and control systems, such as manufacturing resource planning (MRP2 and its predecessor MRP1 – material requirements planning), distribution resource planning (DRP) packages and the Kanban method in just in time approaches. Developments in electronic data interchange (EDI) techniques have improved the speed and cost of the communication and handling of information on an interorganisational basis. As well as the linking of planning systems to gain more effective control of material flow in supply chains and distribution channels, such links can also enhance co-ordination of product development processes.

Product innovation

The significance of product development, as well as the management of new product introductions and the phasing in of product modifications, has been given increased recognition in maintaining a competitive position in markets. The value of close integration between design and development activities, on the one hand, and manufacturing and supply processes, on the other, has also been perceived, especially as a result of studies of Japanese practices. Multi-functional team approaches have demonstrated their effectiveness in terms of better quality, lower cost and shorter leadtimes. Such approaches, which encourage a pooling of expertise and the solving of problems jointly, represent a significant change to traditional practices, which were carried out on a sequential basis, with little co-operation and a low level of communication between the functions.

Each product cycle offers opportunities for cost reductions and other improvements, as the interrelationships between product design, manufacturing processes and supplier operations are jointly investigated. It has been discovered that about 70 per cent of product costs are determined or built in at the design stage, because of the design implications for the costs of parts and the required manufacturing processes. Thus, it is important to apply simultaneous (or concurrent) engineering and value engineering techniques before product launch, as there is less scope for efficiency improvements afterwards. As product life cycles become shorter and new and modified products are introduced more frequently, so the opportunities for major performance improvements increase. A firm which has a slower rate of new product introductions may not only lag behind competitors' products in terms of design; it may also have fewer opportunities for other improvements in performance. Finally, being early to market with new product designs is a tactic that is likely to generate higher profits before competitors catch up. It cannot be stressed too strongly, therefore, that product innovation plays a vital part in sustaining competitive advantage. Furthermore, co-ordination of all stages in the supply chain is a necessary ingredient of managing such innovation processes successfully.

A perspective which highlights product development processes runs counter to traditional standard cost accounting approaches of managing costs of current products and current manufacturing operations. While some improvements can be obtained in the short term by such approaches, major advances through product innovation and the need to sustain a flow of viable products should not be neglected. Such strategies can play a crucial part in having a successful business strategy, relevant to the needs of the firm's environment. Wheelwright and Clark sum up the position when they say:

> In a turbulent environment, excelling at product and process development becomes a requirement for being a player in the competitive game; doing development extraordinarily well can provide a sustainable competitive advantage.[23]

Dangers for purchasing and supply management

It can be argued that developments in strategic manufacturing management generally attach a subordinate status to the purchasing and supply function. There seems to be an unrecognised paradox in the ideas being put forward. On the one hand, there is a tendency to perceive purchasing and supply affairs as a sub-function of manufacturing. On the other hand, there is a growing recognition of the increasing importance of the value added to products by suppliers. For a variety of reasons, the bought-out content of products made by firms has been increasing, thus reducing the significance of internal operations. Reductions in levels of vertical integration, therefore, alter the balance of a firm's activities. The product design and purchasing activities become more important in co-ordinating the efforts of suppliers. Yet how many companies devote a level of resources that would seem to be warranted by the proportion of bought-out content to the control and influence of the 'external' manufacturing operations of suppliers? (*See* Fig 4.4.)

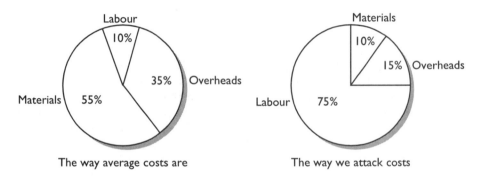

Fig 4.4 Labour, material and overhead costs

Companies have pursued policies of concentrating on 'core' manufacturing processes in which they appear to excel and of buying in more expertise in the form of products sourced from external suppliers. Expertise, in both design and manufacturing services, is being purchased in the bought-out goods. At the same time, technological changes have contributed to a decline in direct labour costs and a higher impact of manufacturing overheads in the profiles of the firm's costs of making products. However, actions and performance assessments by top management in many companies still tend to focus on direct labour as the major factor to control! Many so-called manufacturing firms have become 'purchasing intensive' and harnessing the value creating capabilities of other stages of the supply chain can have a greater effect on competitive advantage than giving attention to internal manufacturing activities alone. This point will be picked up again in the final main section of this chapter, which will focus on the role of purchasing and supply management strategy in relation to business strategy.

Service operations

In spite of the fact that the tertiary or services sector of the economies of advanced industrial nations now provide more than 50 per cent of the gross domestic product, the strategic theory for service operations is less developed compared with manufacturing operations.[24] It is argued that similar approaches can be adopted, but with some allowances made for the differences in providing services, as opposed to goods. Services as products tend to put more emphasis on intangible aspects and there may be problems in creating clear specifications of what is to be delivered. The product may involve the customer as part of the delivery process and this means that the product cannot be uncoupled from demand by the introduction of a storage function. Thus, the problem of managing capacity is different, though there may be a possibility of allowing customers to queue or of delaying their arrival. A distinction can be made between 'front office' and 'back office' activities. The first covers those activities that involve the customer directly, and the point just made about capacity refers to these. Ward or theatre operations in a hospital are typical examples. On the other hand, the examination of specimens in a pathology laboratory is a 'back office' activity, and there is more freedom to schedule work without the presence of patients.

Having recognised that there may be some differences, there is nevertheless the possibility both of applying the basic input-output model to service operations and of developing strategies that give attention to combinations of structural and infrastructural factors. Service criteria, based on an analysis of customer perceptions of value, can be determined to guide the development and improvement of operations processes. There can be a wide diversity of mixes of labour and capital equipment in comparing different types of service firms. The introduction of technological innovations can radically alter the mix and lead to major tasks of managing change. Consider, for example, the banking industry, and the application of information technology generally, and the switch to automatic teller machines in particular. Such changes have altered the cost profile of providing banking services, with a reduction in labour costs and an increase in the use of equipment and supplies. The task of purchasing has grown as a result. In retail and wholesale operations the purchase cost of goods being sold and the significance of purchasing activities has long been recognised.

STRATEGIC PURCHASING AND SUPPLY MANAGEMENT IN THE CONTEXT OF BUSINESS AND CORPORATE STRATEGY

Now that the analysis of strategies for manufacturing and service operations has been completed, it is time to consider strategies for purchasing and supply management in relation to business and corporate strategies. The aim for this chapter is to trace the development of strategic approaches in purchasing and supply management and relate them to the wider strategic management context.

The main focus will be to trace evolutionary patterns which have been proposed and to explore the possible strategic roles that might be given to purchasing and supply management. The detailed treatment of the content and processes for formulating strategies for purchasing and supply management is considered in Chapter 5. Figure 4.5 identifies topics for discussion in this chapter.

1 General observations
2 Links to corporate and business strategy
3 Stage models in the evolution of purchasing and supply management
   ● Reck and Long
   ● Syson
   ● Cammish and Keogh
   ● Burt and Doyle
4 Portfolio approach
   ● Kraljic

Fig 4.5 Strategic purchasing and supply management topics for discussion

General observations

To begin with, some general observations will be advanced about the pattern of developments in strategic thinking about purchasing and supply management. At the same time, some comments will be made which may help to clarify some of the problems in evaluating the progress and direction of these developments.

Forces stimulating developments

Several forces can be detected as having had an influence on the paths of development. The first point to note is that there have been developments closely in line with the evolution in ideas about strategic management in general. Ideas have been transported into the functional area and applied to purchasing and supply management. The question of how the function can be linked into the business and corporate plans has been considered at the same time. A critique of some of the main contributions will follow shortly.

Parallel with and blending in with these theoretical developments have been changes in purchasing and supply management practices, which have also led to the reappraisal of the strategic role of the function. In particular, observation and, at least partial, emulation of Japanese supply practices have introduced new techniques. Reduction in the number of suppliers and the introduction of partnership sourcing, for instance, have altered the nature of work and the balance of activities. In addition, other developments in western manufacturing industries, such as computerised planning and control techniques, have stimulated new perceptions of the scope of the function.

Finally, external environmental difficulties have awakened a more general interest from time to time and have increased awareness of the strategic corporate significance of supply issues. Inflationary effects on material prices, interest rates in relation to inventory and purchasing commitments, fluctuations in exchange rates and fears of material shortages are just some of the examples of these issues.

Nevertheless, the rate of progress in the adoption of a strategic perspective of purchasing and supply management has been variable. Personnel within the function often still concern themselves with short-term activities. Managers outside the function may continue to encourage the perpetuation of these perceptions by the expectations they hold in relation to the function and by the measures of performance they use in making judgements. Occasional periods of recession have reinforced this shorter-term outlook as well. Longer-term requirements should not be neglected, however. Reference was made earlier in the book to the campaign which the Department of Trade and Industry believed to be necessary to widen appreciation of the importance of the function. A comment about purchasing strategy is as follows:

> In the longer term, better purchasing and supply can affect what markets you are in and whether you are competitive enough to stay in them. It's no coincidence, therefore, that many of today's most successful firms have taken a wider, strategic attitude towards the goods and services they buy, and towards the people who supply them.[25]

Conceptual problems

One of the difficulties in the analysis of progress of strategic thinking about purchasing and supply management is the lack of a commonly agreed framework of concepts and terms. Frequently, the meanings of ideas which are being proffered are not made clear and terms often are not used in a consistent fashion. New terms are occasionally coined to give the appearance (and perhaps the reality sometimes) of something new being offered. Thus, as people and organisations have perceived the role of purchasing and supply management changing, so new phrases have appeared, such as 'supplier management', 'resource management', 'source management', 'supply base management' and 'supply chain management'. In attempting to cut through this confusion, several trends may be detected in these developments. They include:

1 The progression of purchasing or buying as a department from just a tactical/operational plane to a strategic level, considered from the point of view of managing the function as a whole.
2 The development of a strategic approach to purchasing at the buyer level, in relation to a particular product or group of products or to the management of the link with a particular supplier.
3 Ideas that broaden the scope of purchasing, by taking into the picture aspects other than buying in the supply chain – increasing the range of factors, such as inventory and transportation arrangements, which are taken into account in a more integrated systemic perspective. In some cases, this broadening of

the field of vision is expressed in organisational terms. In other cases, the wider perspective is more to do with a conceptual or philosophical approach to guide decision making – breaking down narrow functional thinking without redrawing the departmental boundaries.

What is clear in the developments is the need to progress from just a narrowly defined, order placing, buying perspective, which emphasises the acquisition of supplies on an essentially short-term basis.

Links to corporate and business strategy

As in the case of manufacturing strategy, so in the case of purchasing and supply management, a flow of suggestions has been forthcoming to integrate the functional aspect to the wider business concerns. There are also comments about the lack of attention given in the more general literature on company strategy to the need to include the purchasing and supply area.

Purchasing and corporate planning

The early groundwork in establishing a strategic view of purchasing was carried out mainly in the 1970s, when the corporate and strategic planning phase was in progress. The person who has probably done most in the United Kingdom to foster strategic thinking in relation to purchasing and supply management is David Farmer. Several articles, based upon his research, explored the need to include purchasing in corporate planning and schemes were mapped out as to how this might be achieved.[26] Similar work appeared in America and a number of references are included in the notes.[27] Many central ideas emerge in this early phase. Purchasing is accounted for as a significant function, which needs to be considered as part of the corporate planning process to ensure that supply conditions are reflected in it. Purchasing plans need to be prepared after careful analysis of supply markets and these should take a long-term view of developments. Supply markets provide both threats and opportunities and neglect of supply matters can put companies at risk. Kiser, for example, pointed to tasks, such as protecting the cost structure of the company, minimising purchasing costs, assuring long-range sources of supply and maintaining good relationships with suppliers, as having strategic implications.[28] Fox and Rink also suggested that the product life cycle model might be used as a basis for selecting different strategies for different stages.[29] In short, a strategic mode is shown to be both different to an operational one and one which should be implemented.

Purchasing and competitive advantage

As the 1980s proceeded, further developments in strategic purchasing and supply management tended to stress the theme of competitive advantage. As a function, purchasing was claimed to be capable of being a source of competitive advantage for the business. The tasks of managing suppliers and supplier relationships start to come to the forefront with regard to strategies for achieving competitive advantage in purchasing. As a function, it was seen to be in competition with the same function in competitor companies, but strategic direction, and not just concentration on short-term operational problems, was deemed to be necessary for success. Farmer, for example, set out ideas for the competitive analysis of markets and for strategic interventions as part of supply market planning.[30]

The call for the inclusion of purchasing on an equal level with finance, marketing and manufacturing in the formation of business strategies was sounded. The distinction between corporate and business unit strategies entered into suggestions for strategies in the purchasing area as well. Browning *et al.* suggested that purchasing could contribute in at least four significant ways:[31]

1 Monitor supply market trends
2 Interpret the meaning of these trends for the firm
3 Identify the materials and services required to support company and strategic business unit strategies
4 Develop supply options

This article also states that a strategic role for purchasing professionals has implications with regard to the development of appropriate strategic management skills.

Spekman discussed the contribution of purchasing in terms of strategic resources and the need to manage key materials in relation to product/market objectives of the particular businesses.[32] 'At the very least corporate managers must begin to consider external resources availability as a major component of their product/market decisions'.[33]

As the 1980s drew to a close, Robert Monczka captured the spirit of the pursuit of world-class manufacturing and the need for continuous improvement year after year, in terms of cost reductions and improvements in quality, delivery, getting new products to market faster and customer responsiveness.[34] 'Supply base management' and supplier development on a long-term basis, tied to manufacturing and engineering strategies, have the potential to contribute to the achievement of these aims. The need to work in multi-functional teams is noted and he suggests that make or buy decisions need to be considered in relation to design, build and sourcing capabilities. A part of purchasing in a changing environment is 'leverage of information' – collecting, analysing and applying it to business situations. Emphasis is given to 'upstream' activities in meeting customer wants and maintaining a competitive advantage. This means that purchasing needs to be more involved in the design of products and should become more involved in working with suppliers within partnership arrangements. It should aim to drive out waste early in the design process and to reduce costs of the suppliers' manufacturing operations, while at the same time speeding up product flow. Joint problem solving, both internally and externally, is an integral part of this approach.

A number of frameworks were proposed early in the 1990s to make more explicit the link between specific business competitive strategies and the contribution of strategic purchasing. Thus, it is recommended that purchasing should be aligned to the competitive priorities of the product strategy. Watts *et al*. stated:

> The purchasing strategy can be viewed as the pattern of decisions relating to acquiring required materials and services to support operations activities that are consistent with the overall corporate competitive strategy.[35]

Monczka also developed a scheme to guide the integration of procurement strategy to business strategies.[36] This also allowed for the prioritisation of objectives and reinforced the idea of a differentiated approach at the functional level. The phrase 'strategic sourcing management' is used in this presentation, and this was defined as:

> In simplest terms, strategic sourcing management involves the integration of all decisions that affect the design and flow of purchased items/materials into and through a corporate entity to finished products aimed at specific customers.[37]

Supply chain perspectives

The last quotation, by Monczka, serves to underline the third trend that is emerging in the development of strategic thinking in purchasing. As well as building up the strategic tasks both at the level of managing the department and at the level of particular resources and suppliers, there is also a widening of perspectives to embrace a more comprehensive supply chain view, so that planning takes into account a wide range of activities within it.

Djon *et al*. commented that the pursuit of just in time approaches has changed the role of purchasing.[38] It puts less emphasis on transactions and enlarges the buyer's participation in competitive strategies and is more concerned with flows of materials – the overall management of buyer-supplier logistics activities. Cavinato suggests that the role of purchasing becomes that of 'evaluator, creator and manager of interfirm supply links'.[39] Analysis and management of the total costs is seen to be part of this agenda. Towill and Naim argue in favour of a wider systemic view of modelling and operating integrated supply chains and suggest that partnership sourcing may provide a basis for co-operating with suppliers.[40]

Developments with regard to materials management and logistics management have also reinforced the need for a wider perspective, but these concepts are seen more in organisational terms and will be dealt with in Chapter 5, in discussions of organisational structures for purchasing and supply management. Nevertheless, these structures may allow also the potential conflicts between, for instance, customer service levels, low stock levels, short leadtimes, low administrative costs and low prices to be faced and resolved. Structuring of supply chains, with regard to location and operation of warehouses, management of inventory and methods of transportation, as well as the location of suppliers, are important aspects of strategy. Logistics considerations strengthen the need for an integrated perspective so that the interactive effects of these factors can be taken into account. Questions of ownership of different parts of the pipelines and their interrelationships have to be resolved. Implications with regard to planning and control systems, total costs, packaging and materials handling are similarly part of the total picture.

Stage models and the evolution of purchasing and supply management

An account has been given of the developments in strategic thinking about purchasing and supply management. Various authors have tried to portray the way that the role of the function has changed over time and in different organisations.

Robert Reck and Brian Long

Robert Reck and Brian Long have produced a four-stage classification scheme, which is broadly comparable to the scheme of Hayes and Wheelwright for manufacturing.[41] The four stages are as follows:

1 **'Passive'** – no strategic direction and primarily reacts to the requests of other functions. Focus on quick-fix and routine operations, with price and availability the main basis of supplier selection.
2 **'Independent'** – the function adopts the latest techniques, but its strategic direction is independent of the firm's competitive strategy. Cost reduction and efficiency measures are adopted and opportunities for profitability are recognised by top management.
3 **'Supportive'** – techniques and practices are adopted which strengthen the firm's competitive position, suppliers are seen as a resource and are carefully selected. The supply environment is monitored and analysed.
4 **'Integrative'** – purchasing's strategy is fully integrated with those of other functions and with the competitive strategy. Professional development is related to both cross-functional and strategic needs. 'Before purchasing can become a competitive weapon in the battle for markets, it must first develop its own capabilities'.[42]

Russell Syson

Russell Syson proposes three phases of development, as policies, departmental focus and measure of performance change.[43] The scheme may help firms to position themselves as a step to developing an improvement programme.

1 **Clerical (transactional)** – purchasing is perceived as a routine function and not ranked highly. Adherence to routine, monitoring of numbers of orders placed and administrative efficiency in carrying out transactions are points of concern.
2 **Commercial** – attention is brought to bear on price and savings, which are obtained mainly through adversarial treatment of suppliers and through the exploitation of short-term tactical advantages.

3 **Strategic (proactivity focus)** – purchasing managers are concerned with effectiveness and contribution to competitive advantage. Strategies are introduced to improve the performance of supply chain logistics and procurement engineering teams are established.

Robin Cammish and Mark Keough

Robin Cammish and Mark Keough say that:

> The evidence that purchasing can play a strategic role is compelling: companies are finding that world-class purchasing practices can not only boost long-term competitiveness, but can also raise short-term profitability.[44]

Their 'Procurement Developmental Model' compares differences in organisational form, key skills used and activities carried out and it has four stages. The belief is that purchasing should expand and take on extra features in a progression from Stage 1 to Stage 4. Support on a day-to-day basis is important and has to be maintained as roles are expanded to strengthen the application of strategic activities.

1 **'Serve the factory'** – factory-based operations, concentrating on clerical transactions and basic logistics.
2 **'Lowest unit cost'** – purchasing departments at strategic business unit level, which emphasise cost analysis and negotiation.
3 **'Co-ordinate purchasing'** – purchasing is co-ordinated in a variety of ways, centralising it within a unit and between units, via lead buyer and purchasing committees, for example. Development of corporate policies and national contracts help to implement this approach.
4 **'Strategic procurement'** – led from the centre, executed in the business units and use of cross-functional teams exemplify this phase. Emphasis is placed on the application of supplier certification and supplier development programmes. Buyers are involved in challenging specifications and in carrying out total cost analysis. Attention is given to make or buy issues.

Burt and Doyle

The American writers, Burt and Doyle,[45] have produced a four-stage model as a way of demonstrating the rise in the importance of purchasing and supply management. Their fourth stage, the most advanced, emphasises involvement in strategic issues. In addition, the stages show how the range of techniques has expanded to implement more sophisticated approaches. The stages are:

Stage 1 – reactive
Stage 2 – mechanical
Stage 3 – proactive
Stage 4 – strategic supply management

The various stage models share a common viewpoint. They indicate that there has been a gradual evolution in the development of both ideas and practice with regard to the role that the function can and should play. They might all be regarded as ideal types which differ in detail, but which, nevertheless, provide a guide to the development of specific programmes to expand the horizons of the function in specific contexts.

Other schemes

Some additional schemes which follow along similar lines can be introduced briefly. Michiel Leenders and David Blenkhorn, for example, differentiate between 'negative', 'neutral' and 'positive' stages, with the latter embracing the strategic perspective.[46] Michael Morris and Roger Calantone recognise 'clerical', 'asset management and profitability' and 'core strategic function' stages.[47] Virginia Freeman and Joseph Cavinato relate four stages of purchasing (buying, purchasing, procurement and supply) to stages in the development of strategic management (basic financial planning, forecast-based planning, externally oriented planning and strategic management).[48]

Portfolio approach – Peter Kraljic

Peter Kraljic is also conscious of different purchasing approaches, but he sets out a scheme that relates different strategies to different classes of purchase.[49] In other words, he suggests a differentiated approach based upon the type of problem to be resolved. His portfolio of problems is based upon a 2×2 matrix which relates the relative importance of purchasing to the relative complexity of the supply market. He then identifies four stages of 'purchasing sophistication' – 'purchasing', 'materials management', 'sourcing management' and 'supply management'. This approach is analysed in more detail in Chapter 5.

SUMMARY

It can be seen that there has been a steady flow of ideas regarding the strategic development of purchasing and supply management and the profession is undergoing a period of transition as the new possibilities are absorbed. Companies are showing increasing interest in the integration of functional strategies into the broader framework of business and corporate strategic plans. Greater recognition is being given to the need to have a clear customer focus, through marketing, and to manage internal operations and the supply chain as a whole, in order to be competitive in satisfying customer requirements. The capabilities to compete in terms of quality, time, flexibility and price, and, simultaneously, to be successful financially, have to be cultivated and shaped by a clear strategic vision. The high walls, that traditionally separated departments in many companies, are being knocked down and ways of increasing interfunctional co-operation are being fostered. At the same time, strategic views of the external supply chain reinforce the need to explore ways of purchasers working more closely with suppliers to gain advantages that can help both parties.

It is not only manufacturers who are looking for closer links in the supply chain. In the world of retailing, great strides have been made in building more effective supply chains through closer integration between the retailer, its manufacturers and the connecting distribution arrangements. Especially in the case of retailers' 'own brand' products, closer involvement in product designs and in the manufacturing processes used by their suppliers has become a way of life. Marks and Spencer, for example, has been described as being 'more than a retailer – a manufacturer without factories'.[50] In getting the right supplies for its customers, this company is concerned with creating rather than buying products. It has been operating much of the modern thinking about purchasing for many years. The 'blurring' of the apparent functions of firms is also affecting some manufacturers, where much of the creative work is done by their suppliers.

What has emerged in this chapter is the view that the destiny of an individual firm is not bound up only with its own internal operations. To a greater or lesser extent, the value of goods and services sold (or provided in the case of non-market organisations) to its customers is dependent on the contribution of others in the supply chain. Thus, a firm is part of a 'productive confederation', according to Hayes and Wheelwright.[50] In rapidly changing markets, in which customer tastes are becoming more varied and new products are being introduced more frequently and quickly, the need to manage innovation throughout such confederations is crucial. The major task is not so much controlling the added value at each stage, though this is important at the operational level, it is more concerned with 'creating value' and creating the chains to achieve this. Normann and Ramirez refer to 'value constellations' and suggest that the resources that really matter are knowledge and relationships with customers and suppliers.[51] They demonstrate their views through a number of case studies, including the home furnishings retailer, IKEA.

NOTES AND REFERENCES

1 Argenti, J. *Systematic Corporate Planning*, Nelson (1974), p. 264.
2 Stevens, G.C. 'Integrating the Supply Chain', *International Journal of Physical Distribution & Materials Management*, Vol. 19, No. 8, 1989, pp. 3–8.
3 Adcock, D., Bradfield, R., Halborg, A. and Ross, C. *Marketing: Principles and Practice*, Pitman Publishing (1995), p. 137.
4 Porter, M.E. *Competitive Advantage: Creating and Sustaining Superior Performance*, The Free Press (1985), p. 36.
5 Skinner, W. 'Manufacturing – Missing Link in Corporate Strategy', *Harvard Business Review*, May–June 1969, pp. 136–45.
6 Skinner, W. 'Missing the Links in Manufacturing Strategy', in *Manufacturing Strategy – Process and Content* (editor C.A. Voss), Chapman & Hall (1992), pp. 12–25.
7 *See* p. 23 of Skinner, W. (1992), as mentioned in note 6 above.

8 Haas, E.A. 'Breakthrough Manufacturing', *Harvard Business Review*, March–April 1987, pp. 75–81.

9 Hill, T. *Manufacturing Strategy*, 2nd Edition, Macmillan (1993), Chapter 2.
   Hill, T. *The Essence of Operations Management*, Prentice-Hall (1993), Chapter 2.

10 *See* p. 75 of Haas, E.A. (1987), as mentioned in note 8 above.

11 Hayes, R.H. and Wheelwright, S.C. *Restoring Our Competitive Edge: Competing Through Manufacturing*, Wiley (1984), p. 396.

12 Hayes, R.H., Wheelwright, S.C. and Clark, K.B. *Dynamic Manufacturing: Creating the Learning Organization*, The Free Press (1988), p. 21.

13 *See* pp. 36–45 and Table 2.1 on p. 38 of Hill, T. *Manufacturing Strategy* (1993), as mentioned in note 9 above.

14 New, C. 'World-class Manufacturing versus Strategic Trade-offs', *International Journal of Operations and Production Management*, Vol. 12, No. 6, 1992, pp. 19–31.

15 *See* Table III on p. 28 of New, C. (1992), as mentioned in note 14 above.

16 *See* note 15.

17 The following references discuss the importance of human resource issues in manufacturing systems:
   Kinne, N. and Staughton, R. 'The Problem of Implementing Manufacturing Strategy', in *New Wave Manufacturing Strategies* (editor J. Storey.) Paul Chapman Publishing (1994).
   Harrison, A. and Storey, J. 'New Wave Manufacturing Strategies: Operational, Organisational and Human Dimensions', *International Journal of Operations and Production Management*, Vol. 16, No. 2, 1996, pp. 63–76.
   Storey, J. (editor). *New Wave Manufacturing Strategies*, Paul Chapman Publishing (1994).

18 Platts, K.W. and Gregory, M.J. 'Manufacturing Audit in the Process of Strategy Formulation', *International Journal of Operations and Production Management*, Vol. 10, No. 9, 1992, pp. 5–26.
   The audit scheme was also published as a workbook by:
   DTI. *Competitive Manufacturing – A Practical Approach to the Development of a Manufacturing Strategy*, IFS Kempston (1988).

19 *See* p. 17 of Platts, K.W. and Gregory, M.J. (1992), as mentioned in note 18 above.

20 *See* Mills, J., Platts, K. and Gregory, M. 'A Framework for the Design of Manufacturing Strategy Processes: A Contingency Approach', *International Journal of Operations and Production Management*, Vol. 15, No. 4. 1995, pp. 17–49.
   For a review of the main approaches to manufacturing strategy, the following gives a helpful overview:
   Voss, C.A. 'Alternative Paradigms for Manufacturing Strategy', *International Journal of Operations and Production Management*, Vol. 15, No. 4, 1995, pp. 5–16.

21 Sweeney, M.T. 'Towards a Unified Theory of Strategic Manufacturing Management', *International Journal of Operations Management*, Vol. 11, No. 8, 1991, pp. 6–22.

22 *See* note 11.

23 Wheelwright, S.C. and Clark, K.B. 'Competing through Development Capability in a Manufacturing-based Organisation', *Business Horizons*, July–August 1992, p. 29.

24 See a review of strategic management for both manufacturing and service operations by:
   Adam Jnr, E.E. and Swamidass, P.M. 'Assessing Operations Management from a Strategic Perspective', in *Manufacturing Strategy – Process and Content* (editor C.A. Voss), Chapman & Hall (1992), pp. 373–400.

25 DTI. *Building a Purchasing Strategy* (1991), p. 1
26 Examples of these articles include:
   Farmer, D.H. 'Source Decision-Making in the Multi-National Company Environment', *Journal of Purchasing*, Vol. 8, February 1972, pp. 5–17.
   Farmer, D.H. 'The Impact of Supply Markets on Corporate Planning', *Long Range Planning*, March 1972, pp. 10–16.
   Farmer, D.H. 'Corporate Planning and Procurement in Multi-National Firms', *Journal of Purchasing and Materials Management*, Vol. 10, No. 2, 1974, pp. 55–67.
   Farmer, D.H. 'The Role of Procurement in Corporate Planning', *Purchasing and Supply*, November 1976, pp. 44–6.
   Farmer, D.H. 'Developing Purchasing Strategies', *Journal of Purchasing and Materials Management*, Fall 1978, pp. 6–11.
   David Farmer was also a joint editor of:
   Farmer, D.H. and Taylor, B. *Corporate Planning and Procurement*, Heinemann (1975).
27 Examples of articles in America are as follows:
   Kiser, G.E. 'Elements of Purchasing Strategy', *Journal of Purchasing and Materials Management*, Fall 1976, pp. 3–7.
   Bauer, F.L. 'Managerial Planning in Procurement', *Journal of Purchasing and Materials Management*, Vol. 13, Fall 1977, pp. 3–8.
   Adamson, J. 'Corporate Long-Range Planning Must Include Procurement', *Journal of Purchasing and Materials Management*, Spring 1980, pp. 25–32.
28 *See* Kiser, G.E. (1976), as mentioned in note 27 above.
29 *See*, for example:
   Fox, H.W. and Rink, D.R. 'Guidelines for Developing A Purchasing Portfolio,' *Purchasing and Supply*, October 1977, pp. 42–6.
   Fox, H.W. and Rink, D.R. 'Effective Implementation of Purchasing Operations', *International Journal of Physical Distribution and Materials Management*, Vol. 9, No. 1, 1979, pp. 62–73.
   Rink, D.R. 'The Product Life Cycle: Vehicle For Fashioning a Purchasing Strategy', *International Journal of Physical Distribution and Materials Management*, Vol. 8, No. 4, 1978, pp. 200–14.
   John Ramsey also discussed this theme in later articles:
   Ramsey, J. 'The Product Purchase Life Cycle', *Purchasing and Supply Management*, October 1988, pp. 22–4.
   Ramsey, J. 'Pricing, Sourcing and Power', *Purchasing and Supply Management*, November 1988, pp. 34–6.
30 Farmer, D. 'Competitive Analysis – Its Role in Purchasing', *Long Range Planning*, Vol. 17, No. 3, 1984, pp. 72–4.
31 Browning, J.M., Zabriskie, N.B. and Huellmantel, A.B. 'Strategic Purchasing Planning', *Journal of Purchasing and Materials Management*, Spring 1983, pp. 19–24.
32 Spekman, R.E. 'Competitive Procurement Strategies: Building Strength and Reducing Vulnerability', *Long Range Planning*, Vol. 18, No. 1, 1985, pp. 94–9.
33 *See* p. 95 of Spekman, R.E. (1985), as mentioned in note 32 above.
34 Morgan, J.P. 'Are You Aggressive Enough for the 1990s', *Purchasing*, 6 April 1989, pp. 50–57. This article is based on an interview with Dr Monczka and discusses some of his research findings.
35 Watts, C.A., Kim, K.Y. and Hahn, C.K. 'Linking Purchasing to Corporate Competitive Strategy', *International Journal of Purchasing and Materials Management*, Fall 1992, pp. 2–8.
36 Monczka, R.M. and Morgan, J.P. 'Strategic Sourcing Management', *Purchasing*,

Part 1, 18 June 1992, pp. 52–5, Part 2, 16 July 1992, pp. 64–7 and Part 3, 13 August 1992, pp. 70–2.

37 *See* p. 52 of Part 1 of Monczka, R.M. and Morgan, J.P. (1992), as mentioned in note 36 above.

38 Djon, P.A., Banting, P.M., Picard, S. and Blenkhorn, D.L. 'JIT Implementation: A Growth Opportunity for Purchasing', *International Journal of Purchasing and Materials Management*, Fall 1992, pp. 2–8.

39 Cavinato, J.L. 'Identifying Interfirm Cost Advantages for Supply Chain Competitiveness', *International Journal of Purchasing and Materials Management*, Fall 1991, pp. 10–15.

40 Towill, D. and Naim, M. 'Partnership Sourcing', *Purchasing and Supply Management*, July 1993, pp. 38–42.

41 Reck, R.F. and Long, B.G. 'Purchasing: A Competitive Weapon', *Journal of Purchasing and Materials Management*, Fall 1988, pp. 2–8.

42 *See* p. 8 of Reck, R.F. and Long, B.G. (1988), as mentioned in note 41 above.

43 Syson, R. *Improving Purchase Performance*, Pitman Publishing (1989 and 1992).

44 Cammish, R. and Keough, M. 'A Strategic Role For Purchasing', *The McKinsey Quarterly*, No. 3, 1991, pp. 22–39.

45 This model was published in: Burt, D.N. and Doyle, M.F. *The American Keiretsu*, Business One: Irwin (1992). It also appears in Dobler, D.W. and Burt, D.N. *Purchasing and Supply Management*, McGraw-Hill (1996).

46 Leenders, M.R. and Blenkhorn, D.L. *Reverse Marketing*, The Free Press (1988).

47 Morris, M.H. and Calantone, R.J. 'Redefining the Purchasing Function: An Entrepreneurial Perspective', *International Journal of Purchasing and Materials Management*, Fall 1991, pp. 2–9.

48 Freeman, V.T. and Cavinato, J.L. 'Fitting Purchasing to the Strategic Firm: Frameworks, Processes, and Values', *Journal of Purchasing and Materials Management*, Winter 1990, pp. 6–10.

49 Kraljic, P. 'Purchasing Must Become Supply Management', *Harvard Business Review*, September–October 1983, pp. 109–17.

50 Tse, K.K. *Marks and Spencer*, Pergamon (1985), p. 84.

51 *See* Hayes, R.H. and Wheelwright, S.C. (1984), as mentioned in note 11 above.

52 Normann, R. and Ramirez, R. 'From Value Chain to Value Constellation: Designing Interactive Strategy', *Harvard Business Review*, July–August 1993, pp. 65–77.

CHAPTER 5

The content of supply chain management strategies

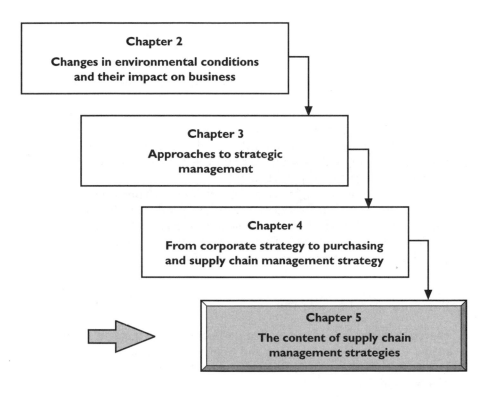

INTRODUCTION

The main failure of the purchasing function is its concentration on negotiation and market price, and in emphasising short-term opportunistic decision making. Such an emphasis ignores a strategic holistic approach to purchasing and falls well short of any long-range planning horizons.[1]

Owen Davies developed the view quoted above in the mid-1980s. Nevertheless, for many companies it is still applicable. According to Farmer and Amstel in 1991, while some companies had emulated the Japanese and had adopted a longer-term view of managing pipelines, many managers in the logistics field 'still have the tendency to focus on day-to-day issues'.[2]

The purpose of this chapter is to consider how this longer-term, strategic, more holistic perspective can be developed. As mentioned elsewhere, there is a need to contemplate the scope of strategic thinking and action at two levels. The first level concerns the purchasing and supply management function as a whole – strategic management of the function. The emphasis at this level is to provide a link to business and corporate strategy and to provide strategic direction to those working within the function. The second level refers to strategic approaches to be adopted by those involved with sourcing and supply plans for particular products (goods or services) or groups of products and with managing suppliers in particular supply chains.

Fundamental to the strategic perspective of supply chains is the determination of which goods and services are to be produced through internal operations and those which are to be acquired from external sources – the 'make/do versus buy' question. This question has a prominent place in this chapter. Figure 5.1 identifies the topics to be discussed.

OBJECTIVES OF THIS CHAPTER

1 To establish the link of purchasing and supply management strategies to business and corporate strategies and to other functional strategies
2 To provide guidelines for strategic 'make/do versus buy' decisions in supply chains
3 To consider the strategic management of the purchasing and supply function
4 To set out policies to guide strategic sourcing and strategic supplier management

STRATEGIC PURCHASING AND SUPPLY MANAGEMENT IN THE CONTEXT OF BUSINESS AND CORPORATE STRATEGIC MANAGEMENT

It was established in Chapter 4 that strategic approaches for a particular function need to be:

1 linked to other functional strategies

1   Strategic purchasing and supply chain management in the context of business and corporate strategies
2   Positioning the firm in the supply chain
3   Strategic management of purchasing and supply and the supply chain
    ● strategic development
    ● identifying priorities – the supply portfolio
    ● strategic planning – structural aspects
    ● strategic planning – infrastructural aspects
    ● organisational arrangements
    ● planning and control systems
    ● human resource management in purchasing and supply
    ● information systems
    ● monitoring performance
4   Policy guidelines
    ● ethics
    ● environmental policies
    ● intracompany trading
    ● commodities

Fig 5.1   Outline of strategic topics

2   linked to strategies for particular business units
3   linked at the corporate level where there are perceived synergistic benefits

Interrelated strategies

The linchpin in connecting functional strategies to the business strategies, whose intention is to provide competitive advantage and competitive scope, is the product strategies. Figure 5.2 illustrates these connections in relation to the basic functions of a manufacturing firm.

Fig 5.2   Interrelated strategies framework

Supply chain strategy

It is possible to break out of the conventional functional differentiation between purchasing and supply and manufacturing and consider a more integrated perspective, which links them together in a framework for supply chain strategy. This is illustrated in Fig 5.3. This approach is partially influenced by the work of John Parnaby and the systems engineering approach to manufacturing, developed in Lucas.[3] In this, importance is given to strategies in both manufacturing and buying in order to meet the standards of world-class competition. The framework is also influenced by Terry Hill's approach to manufacturing strategy,[4] but it does attempt to bring the external supply chain into a more balanced perspective.

Strictly speaking, the often used phrase 'supply chain' is inadequate to capture the full complexities of the interconnections between different organisations. The idea of a network with various nodes might be a more appropriate analogy and description. However, perhaps the most popular convention is the term 'supply chain' and this is used in the figures in this chapter.

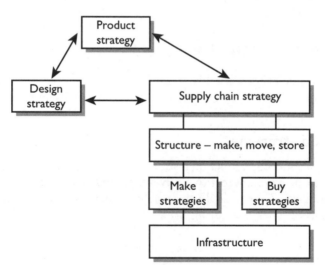

Fig 5.3 Supply chain strategy framework

Product strategies establish the basic task for the supply chain, which, therefore, encompasses both internal and external activities. They include the determination of priorities, with regard to product objectives, needed to meet customer requirements and to beat the offerings of competitors. Differentiated strategies, with regard to quality, cost, time and product innovation, impose different requirements on the supply chain. They should play an important part in the design and development of both the structural and infrastructural features of the supply chain.

Functions of the supply chain

The primary function of the supply chain might be said to be the provision of goods and/or services required by customers and to provide appropriate form, time, place and quantity utilities in the package offered. However, the chain also acts as a medium for the exchange of information and the communication of orders or instructions. Also, as well as providing for the flow of goods, it provides a channel for the flow of money from customers, which is the normal reward for the supplier. There is a fourth object of exchange, according to the interaction model of the Industrial Marketing and Purchasing Group, and this incorporates social values which are involved in the interpersonal relationships between suppliers and customers.

Structural and infrastructural features

The structural features encompass the fundamental physical activities of 'make' or 'transform', 'move' and 'store'. Factors such as capacity, location of activities, types of plant and machinery are relevant to the 'make' activity. Logistics factors, encompassed by decisions, for example, with regard to transport media, materials handling equipment and the location and type of storage facilities, provide the flow of goods from suppliers into and through the operational areas of the chain out to customers. The supply chain structures of more complex organisations may require internal movement of supplies between different sites on a national, regional or global basis, where there are sequential interdependencies between operations. Where the same operations are duplicated at different sites, suppliers may be required to deliver the same items to each of them.

Infrastructural features cover aspects concerned with controlling the operation of the physical system and include, as was seen in Chapter 4, planning and control systems, human resource policies and communications approaches. The framework is intended to show the need to maintain integrated control of the supply chain and to provide the interface between internal operations and those conducted by members on both upstream and downstream sides.

The temptation to consider these structural and infrastructural features from a narrow production and/or supply orientated viewpoint, in isolation from knowledge of the customer and competitor requirements, can have harmful, possibly disastrous consequences. Capabilities and product output performance may not be synchronised with what the market wants. Also, equally damaging consequences may arise from the marketing function attempting to change product strategies, without any adjustments to the supply chain.

Primary and support supply chains

It is helpful to distinguish between primary and support supply chains for an organisation. Primary supply chains might be said to be those that ultimately provide supplies to the external customers. Thus, production materials, parts, components and subassemblies, and then, finally, the finished product may be seen to be flowing in the primary chains of a manufacturer. In the case of wholesale and retail distributors, goods sold on to their customers flow through their primary chains.

Chains, on the other hand, which involve the inward flow of consumable or MRO items and capital plant and equipment might be called support chains. These provide necessary supplies for the organisation to be able to carry out its main function and they have a terminal point inside the organisation. The very label, consumables, expresses the point that such items are used up or consumed by the internal activities of the organisation. For practical purposes, capital equipment may also be said to be used inside the organisation. (It is recognised that plant and equipment may be sold eventually to external customers before their useful working life has been exhausted.) The key point is that these support supply chains do not involve outward logistics and, generally, do not involve customers/clients in decision-making processes.

Much of the discussion about supply chain management in recent years has tended to be concerned implicitly, if not explicitly, with what have been labelled here as primary chains. Nevertheless, strategies need to be developed by purchasing and supply management for the support chains as well. Though called support chains here, they can still have a significant role in organisations and can affect their effectiveness and efficiency. In service organisations, such as the National Health Service, the task of controlling the flow of supplies to support the provision of services to clients and customers has important implications with regard to such features as quality, availability and cost of supply. The provision of spare parts for plant and equipment plays an important part in effective management of maintenance operations and can contribute to high levels of availability of plant and facilities. The purchase of building and construction work, plant and equipment can also have significance within the context of the management of important projects. Strategic purchasing and supply management, therefore, should embrace support chains as well.

Design and technology strategies

An additional feature of Fig 5.3 is the inclusion of the element concerned with design and technology strategies. Questions tackled in this area help to shape which activities will be carried out internally and which by external suppliers. A broad interpretation of design includes here both product and process design activities. In the context of long-term strategy, the 'make/do versus buy' strategy really embraces three key services – 'design' and 'make' services, and also 'logistics' services. It is decisions about these services which are being determined at the design and planning stage. What design work and which parts are to be made internally? What design work and manufacturing operations are to be undertaken by suppliers? What design and technological competences are to be fostered inside the business? To what extent does the business wish to become dependent on, and encourage development of, supplier contributions to innovation and to the added value in the final output?

Questions can also be asked about logistics activities, which cater for the movement of goods at three basic stages – inbound and outbound as regards the firm, but also inside the firm on both an intra- and interplant basis. Should logistics services be bought from third parties on either a general or a dedicated basis? Should the firm operate its own transport and distribution facilities? Should suppliers take responsibility for shipments of goods to their customers? These are just some of the questions that may need to be examined and which are, clearly, of major strategic importance. The output from both design and manufacturing services will be the flow of products in the future – products possibly quite different to those currently flowing through the chain, as a result of technological change.

This make/do versus buy aspect will be dealt with shortly as part of a more general treatment of the strategic make/do or buy issue. In the meantime, other aspects of design strategies which can influence the supply chain strategy need to be brought into the picture.

1 Increasingly firms are considering the use of simultaneous or concurrent engineering approaches, to increase both efficiency and effectiveness in the overall management of processes for the introduction of new and modified products. This makes use of multi-functional teams and these may be part of the infrastructural features for the supply chain, involving both internal and external representatives.

2 Suppliers may be part of the design teams and participate in such things as supplier days, as ways of implementing the concept of 'early supplier involvement' (ESI). Buyers also may spend more time on these 'upstream activities' as they work closely with suppliers.

3 Simultaneous engineering is concerned with putting into effect other jargon phrases such as 'design for economic manufacture', 'design for assembly' and 'design for quality'. The point behind these concepts is to try and ensure that design processes reflect the implications of designs from the point of view of the ease and cost of manufacturing processes, which will eventually be needed to produce the product. Control of time, cost and quality are all relevant issues and the objective is to anticipate and resolve problems before scheduling of purchasing and production begins. Resolution of design possibilities should be achieved by giving adequate consideration to both technical and commercial aspects in the supply chain.

4 Design strategies affect the basic architecture of products and involve the assessment of possibilities with regard to a number of techniques. These include product simplification to reduce the number of parts, as well as standardisation of parts and materials to reduce the range required. The adoption of modular approaches is a way of coping with the conflicting aspects of standardisation, on the one hand, and flexibility and customisation with regard to end products, on the other.

5 Design and make or buy decisions help to demarcate the boundaries for supply markets and in this sense influence which potential suppliers might be considered in sourcing questions. Robinson and Faris referred to the idea of

'creeping commitment' with regard to purchasing decisions.[5] As the details of the product and component specifications are worked out, so the number of potential suppliers becomes restricted.

6   Computer-aided design (CAD) and computer-aided engineering (CAE) techniques have implications with regard to storage, retrieval, analysis and communication of design data. Infrastructural questions arise with regard to how to co-ordinate design processes in the supply chain, using EDI techniques, for example.

Short-term static analysis of the supply chain and the solution of operational problems tend to underplay the design and planning aspect and to focus on increasing efficiency of current activities. For long-term strategic considerations, a dynamic perspective perceives product and process design as the crucial issues with regard to improvements in performance and the pursuit of sustainable competitive advantage. Supply chains can be altered fundamentally by such issues. They are issues which should involve all the functions, however, and not just the technical functions.

The environment for the supply chain

While a framework, designed to assist in the analysis of supply chain strategy, has just been discussed, the framework can be enriched by introducing the wider environmental aspects with which there are interactive effects. Conditions in the wider environment, which cannot be altered or influenced by the firm, impose constraints on the feasibility of strategies. Some of these developments may pose threats and others opportunities to be exploited. However, there may be scope for some strategies to influence and change the direction of developments. Environmental analysis of these threats and opportunities has long been a part of the baggage of strategic management. Benchmarking is another technique being used by many firms to establish best practices and to identify gaps that need to be bridged in terms of performance. Figure 5.4, therefore, embeds the supply chain in an extended framework.

While product strategies partly determine, and at the same time are partly shaped by, the nature of the tasks for the supply chain, it is the strategic 'make/do versus buy' questions which determine the division of the tasks between external and internal operations. Decisions about what to make and what services to provide within the firm locate or position the firm in its supply chains. In effect they draw the boundaries of the firm! These questions will now be examined in more depth.

POSITIONING THE FIRM IN THE SUPPLY CHAIN

The last paragraph suggests that it is strategic decisions that should determine which activities are conducted within the firm and which activities are carried out by suppliers and customers. While this might be a perfectly laudable prescriptive

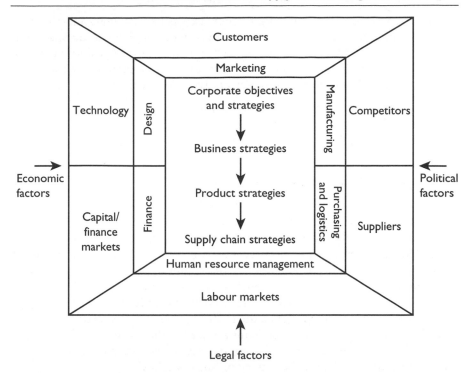

Fig 5.4 Environmental framework for the supply chain

principle, evidence suggests that firms do not necessarily apply such a rational, analytical approach in practice. Most businesses, of course, usually find themselves with an initial position which has been inherited from the past. Their position in the supply chain is already established and the extent of vertical and horizontal integration has been mapped out. This may have emerged from a series of fragmented, piecemeal decisions, taken with no clear co-ordinated sense of strategic direction. Research carried out by David Ford and David Farmer showed wide variations,[6] but findings generally doubted whether make-or-buy decisions were taken within a carefully thought out strategic perspective. Even a subsequent international study by Ford *et al.*, comparing US, UK, Australian and Canadian practices, reinforced this earlier conclusion.[7] It has been suggested that many firms adopt a short-term perspective and are motivated primarily by the search for short-term cost reductions.

Introduction to 'make/do or buy' decisions

Strategic consideration of 'make/do or buy' decisions, with regard to goods and services, is central to supply chain positioning for organisations in both private and public sectors. The outcome of a firm's investigations of these issues will define the scope of that part of the chain which falls under direct control and which will require resource investments in order to develop its internal capabilities. It follows that other assets, both human and material kinds, will need to be cultivated by either 'upstream' suppliers or 'downstream' customers. Thus, strategic changes of direction with regard to positioning in the supply chain can affect purchasing and supply. In this section, the following topics will provide a framework for the analysis of such decisions:

1 the nature of 'make/do or buy' decisions
2 triggers of 'make/do or buy' decisions
3 managing the portfolio of 'make/do or buy' decisions

The nature of 'make/do or buy' decisions

Before proceeding with an analysis of the make-or-buy decision, it is necessary to bring into the discussion another related term – subcontracting. Use of this term can vary, but there can be a degree of overlap in some interpretations. In the building and construction industry it usually means the subletting of part of the main contract to subcontractors. In the engineering industry it has sometimes been used to refer to the outsourcing of work that could be done internally, in times of a shortage of capacity, for instance. However, in studies of Japanese sourcing arrangements, the term has been broadened to cover items made by suppliers, especially those items tailored to the specific requirements of a particular purchaser (as opposed to more general, 'commodity' items). In this sense 'subcontracting' is a subcategory of 'make-or-buy'.

Make-or-buy decisions are varied in nature and several different ways of classifying them will be considered. They are also multi-faceted, in the sense that there is a varied range of implications. They affect not only the ownership and employment of physical assets, but also the quantity and quality of human assets directly controlled within the firm. The question of 'make/do' internally may have to be compared to a variety of external arrangements, ranging from basic market exchanges to co-operative partnerships and joint ventures. Thus, Terry Hill suggests that there is not only the question of the breadth of the span of processes to be performed internally, but also the form of control to be used.[8] Risk and risk management are also involved in the decision. On the one hand, risk is involved in buying, by becoming dependent on arrangements with outside suppliers. However, investing in internal assets may carry risks of such assets becoming outdated, less efficient, or underutilised. Levels of risk and the amount of resources implicated in particular decisions vary, so that some are not really of a significant strategic nature, whereas others are strategic, because they affect the fundamental nature of the business and the direction of its investments. They go to the heart of what distinctive competences the business may or may not be able to develop as a basis of competitive advantage. In a dynamic world, conditions can change, and there is a risk that a decision which appeared to be right at one moment can be seen to have been a mistake later on. Uncertainty is, thus, another characteristic of the strategic scene.

There are a number of different ways of categorising make-or-buy decisions. In the first place, there is the nature of the good or service. Is it something fundamental to the basic function or essence of the business or is it merely a support item? Take the case of a manufacturing firm and production items. The degree of significance expands as one considers the case of individual parts, a component, a subassembly and a complete assembly. In an extreme case a business might become a stockist/distributor rather than a manufacturer. This happened, for example, to the part of GKN involved in standard industrial fasteners. As Far Eastern sources became more competitive, it was decided that costs could not be brought down to their level by continuing to manufacture in the UK. Support items include making or acquiring process equipment, making or buying consumables, such as printing of forms. Services might include minor items such as cleaning or more significant questions of whether to own and operate a transport and distribution system or buy in the services of a third party distributor. In a service organisation, on the other hand, the possibility of outsourcing services may not only affect ancillary support services, but may even affect the basic composition of the business. Compulsory competitive tendering policies in the public sector, designed to compare outside contractors to internal direct labour organisations, are pertinent in this respect. A primary task of an organisation might, therefore, become that of contracting for the supply of services for clients or customers – an 'enabling' activity.

Peter Baily and David Farmer consider varying levels of significance and suggest that there can be differences in the level at which decisions are made.[9] The level may have implications with regard to changes in resources employed in the firm. Thus, they differentiate between departmental, intermediate and top management. Departmental decisions imply no change of policy and no change in existing facilities. Intermediate level decisions involve some investment or divestment in internal resources, whereas top management may enter into questions of investing or disinvesting in whole businesses in relation to vertical integration.

Both research studies, mentioned above by Ford et al.,[10] make use of a classification scheme relating to the approach used in the make-or-buy decision. They are as follows:

1 **Operational cost-based approach**. Cost savings and operational benefits, in adjusting, for example, to existing capacity shortages or surpluses are examined, but with no concern for overall strategy. The problems looked at are often in relation to less essential and less significant activities.
2 **Business approach**. A more proactive approach is demonstrated, with a system of continuing evaluation of parts of the business in relation to possible suppliers. Multi-functional teams might be used and a longer time horizon and a wider range of criteria might be taken into account.
3 **Policy approach**. Assessment is based on views of the strategic direction and technological capabilities of the business, but there may be problems of gaining full functional integration. It is this approach that is most germane to the purpose of this chapter.

Approaches 2 and 3 are most relevant to the discussions in this chapter.

Triggers of make-or-buy questions

A consciously organised strategic approach to the formation of business strategies could include within it scope for regular monitoring of comparative performance of internal and external capabilities. At the same time checks on progress with the implementation of development plans could keep the issue of make or buy under surveillance. Often firms tend to carry on doing what they have always done, without examining whether such positions in the supply chain are the most favourable. In many companies, therefore, it may be *ad hoc* events which draw attention to problems and trigger off studies. Awareness of new technology, supplier suggestions and concern with poor performance are illustrative of such events. Buyers, through their knowledge of supply markets, are often in a good position to be able to put forward propositions for consideration.

In recent years, many companies, which have had a high degree of vertical integration, have pursued a policy of vertical disintegration, though the extent of this might vary from country to country.[11] Stuckey and White suggest that a number of reasons for this trend are:[12]

1 Recognition that past decisions were wrong
2 Pressure from financial markets to restructure
3 Changes in world markets have reduced the risk and costs of buying
4 Acceptance of the difficulty in maintaining excellence in all areas

There is a danger that decisions have been taken without thinking carefully about the long-term strategic implications of the erosion of internal capabilities. The failure to identify developments of distinctive competences necessary to secure the future survival of the firm may contribute to the build-up of threats in the future which may be difficult to counter. 'Hollowing out' of the firm may be fashionable and may produce short-term benefits, but it may create positions in the future which cannot be defended against competitors. As Kumpe and Bolwijn say, 'the central strategic problem is to find the right balance between investing in vertical integration and encouraging process technology development among suppliers'.[13]

Managing the portfolio of make-or-buy questions

A firm will normally have a wide range of make-or-buy questions and it is sensible, therefore, to consider the drawing up of guidelines for managing them. Firms have not found a logical way of dealing with a large number of items, and according to Venkatesan, this is a cause of the lack of a coherent approach.[14] The position has often been aggravated by a failure to co-ordinate the differing views and interests of the various functions which can be affected. Not all questions are of equal importance, as suggested already, so a differentiated approach based on different types of problem situation would be worth while. Such guidelines should include:

1 A scheme to determine and classify situations
2 Identification of personnel to be involved
3 Establishment of procedures to analyse situations and develop solutions

Classification of situations

1 **Short term v long term.** Initially, there is a need to differentiate between short-term, operational and long-term situations. The first is concerned with maintaining a high usage of current capacity and with varying the levels of outsourcing to adjust to changes in levels of demand. Long-term perspectives are concerned with more permanent employment and development of internal resources, as opposed to using the resources of suppliers. Comparisons between in-house supply and outsourcing in the long-term case are less concerned with specific products, more with design and manufacturing capabilities and their potential for future supplies.

2 **Long term**
    – **Strategic.** Some activities involve a significant level of resources from the overall business point of view and decisions in this category may have a profound effect on the boundaries of the company. Furthermore, these key activities, and output from them, might be seen to have a crucial impact on the competitive position of the company and its ability to satisfy its customers. Design and process skills, as well as investment in specialised assets, may be the basis for establishing distinctive capabilities. In other words, there is an underlying issue with regard to the technology strategy of the business.
    – **Non-strategic.** These activities may be regarded as less significant from the point of view of customer requirements and are not seen as a basis for establishing a competitive advantage. External suppliers are likely to be able to provide similar offerings, which might be regarded as commodity items. In the public sector, it might be said that the early phase of compulsory competitive tendering was involved in non-strategic services, such as cleaning, catering and dining services.

As far as manufactured goods are concerned, Venkatesan argues that the structure of the product and the stages of build-up from parts, components and subassemblies should be taken into account. For the case of original equipment manufacturers (OEMs), he suggests that the end product breaks down into distinct subsystems, such as an engine in a vehicle. In turn, a subsystem is composed of components. Each subsystem may have its own unique technological features with regard to design, development and manufacture. There is a strategic issue as to whether the complete subsystem or just some, all or none of the components should be assessed from the point of view of make or buy. Both subsystems and components may be investigated and divided into strategic and non-strategic categories.

Identification of personnel

For the strategic items, there is a clear case for involving a high-level multi-functional team, which might consist of top executives and representatives from at least marketing, purchasing, product design, process design and production. Lower-level and a narrower grouping may be sufficient on less important and short-term items.

Analysis of situations

1 **Short term.** Comparison of proposals with regard to internal and external supply possibilities will tend to be based on relevant technical and commercial assessment of current capabilities. In the short term, an argument can be justified for basing costing and pricing analysis on short-term variable costs for in-house manufacture. This will, not surprisingly, tend to give an advantage to the internal supplier. As long as there is no conflict between such immediate considerations and the securing of future supplies, this provides a way of utilising what might otherwise be unused capacity – plant and labour.

2 **Long term – strategic.** As regards the long-term sourcing of strategic items, it may be necessary to make a distinction between the design skills and the process capabilities, when comparing internal and external candidates. The two might be considered as a combination for either subsystems or components, but there is the chance of retaining much of the design capability and only subcontracting the 'make' portion of the work. Indeed, as in the case of 'own brand' products bought by some retailers, there is scope for subcontracting the manufacture of the complete product, but retaining technical knowledge and design skills. Marks and Spencer adopts the view that it knows better than its suppliers what its customers want and is able, through its merchandising teams, to translate those needs into product and process specifications. These are then used as a basis of the arrangements for the control of suppliers' operations.

Both technical and commercial capabilities of external suppliers need to be evaluated to establish whether the firm is a leader or whether there is a capability gap. If there is a gap, an assessment of the feasibility of closing the gap, in the light of future trends and the resources needed to do so, should be made. One of the difficulties in some areas of technology is the high cost of new product development, and firms may find that they do not have sufficient volume of sales to be able to justify the investment on a 'go it alone' basis. Other opportunities for economies of scale may be available to outside sources.

An outcome of the analysis could be that some subsystems and components and parts need to be outsourced, possibly through partnership or joint venture arrangements, and investments for the future concentrated in other strategic areas where leadership can be maintained. The latter then become the core areas of the business.

It is worth considering the following comment from a consultant regarding the manufacture of trucks in the commercial vehicle industry.

> The reasons for moving from manufacture to design and assembly are clear. The demands of low inventory manufacture, be it just in time (JIT) or otherwise, and limits on investment capital mean that the 'make or buy' equation moves towards the latter, especially when volumes are small . . . Much better, therefore, for a low/medium-volume builder to concentrate on product development, make crucial items in-house and organise its assembly.[15]

3 **Long term – non-strategic.** There are no strong reasons for continuing to make commodity items, for which the firm has no particular advantage. Margins are likely to be low on these activities and often smaller suppliers which have lower overheads and lower wages may offer better prospects. Thus, instead of remaining locked into such facilities, steps may be taken to run them down gradually without making any new investments, and allow natural wastage or transfers of labour to take their course.

The significance of make-or-buy questions

Positioning decisions and sourcing decisions in the supply chain play a fundamental part in determining the future success of the firm. They determine the locations of participants in the chain and the points where product value will be created. The reverse side of the coin is that the points also identify where costs are incurred. Each firm can perhaps develop its own unique approach, depending on the competitive advantages it is trying to establish and the profiles of competitive scope it decides to pursue. Different solutions can succeed at different times.

It is interesting to compare the strategy of Henry Ford I in an earlier era with that of Toyota in more modern times. Ford adopted a strategy of vertical integration as a solution for a lower-cost, high-volume car production system to meet the needs of a mass market for lower-priced cars. He set up his own upstream facilities to produce high-volume, standardised, interchangeable parts at a time when suppliers still operated on a low-volume, craft basis. Toyota, on the other hand, faced initially with supply difficulties, but also lack of capital and space, adopted supplier development through partnership arrangements as the way forward. In the textile industry, Benetton has developed a closely linked network of small suppliers, to retain flexibility in coping with the problems of the fashion industry, in which product life cycles are short and forecasting of customer tastes is notoriously difficult.

Implications for purchasing

Purchasing has a valuable role to play in all of the make/do or buy decision situations. Personnel in purchasing and supply can initiate studies, be involved in the analysis and preparation of sourcing options, as well as in the determination of the solution to be implemented. The main contribution, in terms of information, will be in relation to the purchasing and logistics opportunities and the evaluation of supplier capabilities. However, the decisions affect the business as a whole and an integrated team approach is needed. It is important that the choice of criteria governing the final selection of a sourcing plan should not be dominated by any one particular function.

In the cases where the sourcing decision outcome is to use external suppliers, purchasing can be confronted with a variety of problem types depending on the extent of supplier input that is required in relation to design and manufacturing services. These will have a varying impact on the nature of the arrangements and relationships that will have to be developed with suppliers in resolving the problems. The following gives a list of different types:

1 **Design and manufacturing services – design and make to order.** The selected supplier is expected to design and develop products, so that design and manufacturing services are being purchased, the outcome of which will be products tailored to the needs of the purchaser. For this strategic approach to be successful, it will be necessary to form close working relationships on a multi-functional basis between the supplier and the purchaser organisations. The accent will be on both technical and commercial co-operation and a sharing of information on an open book basis. A particular concern may arise with regard to confidentiality and the risk of innovatory ideas being passed on to the competitors of the purchaser.

2 **Manufacturing services – make to order.** The purchaser firm may decide in some instances to keep the main design initiative inside the firm and the sourcing situation is one in which the supplier is expected to provide the manufacturing service to make to the purchaser's specification. Therefore, liaison with suppliers will focus primarily on production issues.

3 **Supplier's proprietary products.** The supplier is responsible for design and manufacture, but in this case the supplier also sells these products into a more general market. The degree of involvement needed between buyer and seller is less, and is likely to be mainly concerned with purchasing, scheduling and logistics issues.

4 **'Commodity products'.** What is being purchased is a standard item which many suppliers make and sell to a general market. A more distant and less intensive relationship may be sufficient in this respect and purchasing will be the main point of contact with the supplier.

Shaping the structure of the supply chain – tiers

The purchase of a complete subsystem, as a product for assembly into a finished product, obviously results in just one buyer-supplier link (assuming for the moment that it is to be bought from a single source). The subsystem supplier will have responsibility for the procurement of all the necessary components. On the other hand, if the purchasing firm decides to buy in parts and components and assemble the subsystem in its own factory then direct links with a larger number of suppliers will be necessary. Figure 5.5 illustrates the two possibilities.

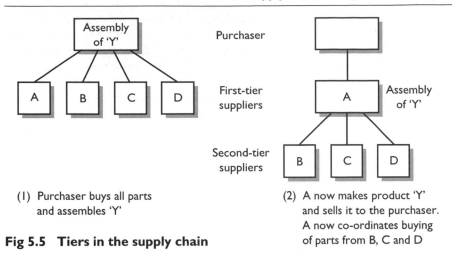

(1) Purchaser buys all parts and assembles 'Y'

(2) A now makes product 'Y' and sells it to the purchaser. A now co-ordinates buying of parts from B, C and D

Fig 5.5   Tiers in the supply chain

It can be seen that decisions to outsource subsystems reduce the number of immediate suppliers to be managed by the purchaser. This reduces the number of transactions from an operational point of view and slims down the number of buyer-supplier relationships that have to be managed. On the other hand, the relationship is likely to be more intensive, especially if both design and manufacturing services are being procured. While it will be the responsibility of the first-tier supplier to manage sourcing relationships with its suppliers, the purchaser of the subsystem may wish to influence policies, methods and performance standards of second-tier suppliers as well. Indeed, the purchaser may wish to extend influence further upstream to third-tier suppliers.

From a strategic purchasing and supply management point of view, make-or-buy decisions in firms, which are positioned in downstream stages in the supply chain, not only affect the nature of what is being sourced from immediate suppliers, but also have implications for managing and influencing links further upstream in the supply chain. Those firms that are in the first and second tiers etc. may find that upstream customers can exercise some influence over both their internal and external sourcing operations. Position in the supply chain and the relative power of participants partly determine the amount of freedom a firm has over its own destiny.

Shaping the structure of supply chains – geographical features

The external sourcing possibilities in make-or-buy situations may include suppliers in other parts of the world. If cost is a key issue, then the decision to outsource may be influenced by the desire to move the manufacturing of labour-intensive items to other countries which have lower wage costs. If this lengthens the distance of the supply chain, any benefits of low-cost manufacture may have to be offset by increased logistics costs – higher transport costs, costs of higher inventory and longer replenishment times.

A second issue is that for more complex organisations the sourcing decision may require the external source to be able to supply to several or indeed many purchaser locations that consume the same item. Co-ordinated policies may have national, regional or even global dimensions. Manufacturing strategies for internal production may involve changes of location or the opening up of additional facilities in new locations. Such developments need to be assessed in the light of supply considerations and the logistics costs that might arise. The expansion of firms into developing countries can lead to supply problems if there are no supporting supplier industries in that country. Problems of importing parts and components should be evaluated as part of the overall strategy.

A general conclusion that emerges from this section of the chapter is that firms need to apply strategic thinking to the key make-or-buy questions, something which is not being done by many companies. Those involved either in directing the purchasing function or in making strategic sourcing decisions likewise need to develop such a perspective. Furthermore, strategies not only direct the nature of relationships in links with immediate first-tier suppliers; they can also be devised to affect links further up the chain.

STRATEGIC MANAGEMENT OF PURCHASING AND SUPPLY AND THE SUPPLY CHAIN

The next step in this chapter is to start looking more directly at the strategic management of tasks in purchasing and supply, which arise from the strategic plans of the business and the resolution of the 'make/do or buy' decisions. A 'top-down' perspective has to encompass the wide and heterogeneous nature of the goods and services which are required as inputs into any organisation. The basic management task is to plan, organise and direct resources, which will be needed to manage the flow of supplies for immediate requirements, but also to prepare and implement strategies which will govern future supplies. Cammish and Keogh make the point that it is purchasing involvement in the development of products, preparation of specifications and the development of sourcing strategies (the upstream activities) which increases the leverage on performance and produces world-class performance.[16] The overall management problem is to find ways of providing control of day-to-day current requirements, but at the same time exercising leverage to obtain advantages in the future. Major improvements can rarely be gained overnight; the necessary measures to achieve them take time before the fruits are harvested. Plans have to take into account the state of the organisation and its circumstances – the starting position.

Strategic development of purchasing and supply

The way forward in developing the firm's approach to purchasing and supply activities depends on the needs of the business plan and the current mode or stage of development of the function. A comprehensive development programme might be needed by some to take the function from a basic clerical, reactive style to a proactive, strategic style. Business strategies may be guided by visions of moving towards world-class standards through the adoption of just in time and total quality management initiatives in order to pursue targets, such as improvements in quality, lower costs and faster, more flexible responses to customer demands. The same approaches may be required from the upstream supply side as well. Others might find themselves in circumstances that call for a more radical, root and branch reappraisal of the supply chain structure. Specific programmes, in other words, have to be tailored to the particular exigencies of the individual firm.

To give concrete direction it is recommended that the basic vision of the way forward needs to be translated into a mission statement, which gives a concise description of what the function is aiming to achieve. Then, a more specific set of objectives can be formulated which provide quantified targets, against which performance can be measured and compared. (Stage models discussed in the previous chapter provide a guide to the development steps which might be needed.)

Identifying priorities – the supply portfolio

Many of the inputs do not warrant strategic treatment because they are not significant in either technical or commercial terms and so it is necessary to prioritise the tasks that have to be carried out and to identify different approaches to be used.

1 **Categories of requirements.** Initially, however, it is useful to recognise the division of the total portfolio of supply tasks into the different categories that are relevant to the particular organisation, which were identified in Chapter 1; these categories are inputs to production, consumables or MRO items, capital plant and equipment, services and goods for resale. The nature of their supply chains vary and different sourcing policies, contracting approaches and purchasing techniques may be used. Priorities vary from organisation to organisation and they vary both within each category and also between categories. Pareto analysis can provide an initial picture, by identifying relative importance in terms of annual expenditure. However, other characteristics such as technical significance and whether it is a repeat item or not can be taken into account.
2 **Matrix analysis.** Several schemes based upon matrix analysis have been developed to identify different classes of problem and to apply different sourcing approaches and actions. These investigate the relative purchasing importance of the item in comparison to the conditions in the supply market.
   - **Kraljic's portfolio.** In his 2×2 matrix, he compares low to high levels of 'importance of purchasing' against low to high levels of 'complexity of the supply market'.[17] (*See* Fig 5.6.)
   - **Procurement positioning overview.** Elliott-Shircore and Steele adopted a not dissimilar approach and developed what they called the positioning overview.[18] They considered the relationships between 'supply vulnerability' and 'value potential/profit'. (*See* Fig 5.7.)

These approaches underline the value of recognising different priorities and can give a guide to the allocation of time and effort and the selection of appropriate courses of action. They also serve as a warning against the promotion of any one particular approach as a panacea for all situations. Staff need to be able to diagnose problems and select solutions from a wide repertoire of possibilities.

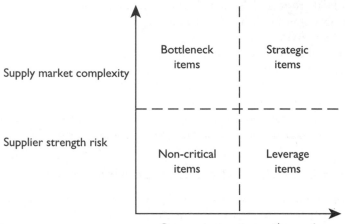

Fig 5.6 Purchase portfolio
(*Source*: Reprinted by permission of *Harvard Business Review*. Adapted from Kraljic, P. 'Purchasing Must Become Supply Management', *Harvard Business Review*, September–October 1983, p. 111. Copyright © 1983 by the President and Fellows of Harvard College.)

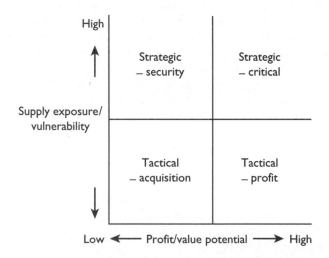

Fig 5.7 Procurement positioning
(*Source*: Adapted from Elliott-Shircore, T.I. and Steele, P.T. (1985) 'Procurement Positioning Overview', *Purchasing and Supply Management*, December, pp. 23–6. Copyright © 1985 The Chartered Institute of Purchasing and Supply. Reprinted with permission.)

Strategic planning – structural aspects

As far as structural aspects are concerned, purchasing and supply management is concerned primarily with the 'move' and 'store' aspects in parts of the supply chain, which are under direct ownership. Strategic thinking needs to take into account the interrelationships between them and to develop integrated logistics systems. Issues with regard to materials handling and packaging are additional facets of such systems. Operations departments will have the main responsibility for the development of structural and infrastructural strategies for the internal 'make/transform' facilities. It will also be shown in Part Two that purchasing strategies may be able to exercise significant influence over parts of the supply chain controlled directly by suppliers of both goods and services.

1 **'Store'.** Plans for provision of storage facilities need to be based on estimates of the future range, type and volume of goods to be stored. While the guiding principle might be to avoid having investment tied up in stocks in storage points in the supply chain, it must be remembered that even kanban systems have small stocks close to the work area. The following points should be catered for in the development of appropriate premises:
   - geographical locations and positions in the supply chain;
   - siting in proximity to operations and points of use;
   - capacity;
   - type of construction and structural dimensions;
   - conditions and provisions with regard to health and safety;
   - operating conditions with regard to temperature and light;
   - security aspects;
   - access and exit points;
   - storage equipment;
   - materials handling equipment;
   - layout approach – fixed, random or zoned;
   - degree methods of automation.
2 **'Move'**
   - equipment and vehicles for internal movement;
   - type of transportation externally – road, rail, air or water – and multimodal possibilities;
   - unitisation of loads – containerisation, palletisation.

Strategic planning – infrastructural features

Key areas requiring attention from the strategic planning point of view include the topics of organisation, planning and control systems, human resource management, performance monitoring systems, information systems and interorganisational relationships.

Organisational arrangements

Attention to organisational arrangements needs to focus on a variety of aspects, such as the following issues:

1 The degree of horizontal integration of purchasing and supply subfunctions into a unified management structure (subfunctions of purchasing, stores and stock control, transport and distribution and production planning and control/material control, for example). Writers such as Peter Baily and David Farmer,[19] Donald Dobler, David Burt and Lamar Lee,[20] Stuart Heinritz, Paul Farrell, Larry Giunipero and Michael Kolchin[21] and David Farmer[22] have discussed the merits of different structures for a variety of situations. The main problem lies in the need to ensure that the pursuit of overall performance of the supply chain as a whole through integrated control and does not lead to neglect of the interests of particular specialisms.

2 The level of managers within the hierarchy of the organisation. The level affects perceptions of the importance of the function and the extent to which the function might be involved in the strategic planning and direction of the organisation.

3 The grouping of personnel within subfunctions to reflect considerations of commodity specialisation, geographical spread of operations and service to different product lines.

4 The division of tasks on the basis of strategic, tactical and operational time horizons. In purchasing, for example, responsibilities for short-term scheduling and expediting of supplies can be separated from those concerned with market and product research and the formulation and implementation of commodity plans and policies with major suppliers.

5 Choice of centralised, decentralised or mixed structures in multi-site and/or multi-product situations with regard to permanent divisions of staff and linkages between different businesses. Alternatively, co-ordination might be achieved through less permanent, more informal mechanisms, such as committees or appointed leaders for particular tasks.

6 The use of multi-functional teams to link purchasing and supply management personnel with other functions for design and material selection purposes, and also for supplier evaluation and supplier management purposes.

7 The possibility of allocating staff on a project management or matrix basis.

8 Responsibility, especially for the application of routine procedures, may be delegated to user departments, subject to guidance, training and contractual arrangements provided by the specialist function.

As firms develop flatter organisational structures for individual businesses, more emphasis is being placed upon horizontal integration and the use of multi-functional teams to improve understanding and co-operation. The extent of integration between businesses depends on the degree to which their activities are linked or the extent to which common resources and common supply chains are used.

As firms analyse the characteristics of the purchasing and supply circumstances and the needs of the operations areas with which they are confronted, the goal will be to find the right balance between centralising and decentralising forces. Factors pointing towards centralisation include the benefits of co-ordination and leverage of buying power in supply markets, the development and sharing of integrated logistics systems, the adoption of common procedures, policies and systems, the development of co-ordinated human resource policies and representation of the function at a high level in the organisation. On the other hand, counter forces favouring decentralisation include the focus of responsibility and the provision of service to users and customers at the local level, as well as the encouragement of individual initiatives. While there are 'typical models' for purchasing and supply structures, in the last analysis, organisational strategies have to be tailored to the contingencies and requirements of individual firms.

It has to be recognised that there can be considerable tension and conflict between local and central units, arising from different interests and loyalties. Those charged with responsibilities for developing integrated plans will need to exercise sensitive negotiating skills to minimise the effect of such tensions.

Formal organisational arrangements play a powerful part in determining the performance of purchasing and supply management and the behaviour of personnel in the conduct of activities. They also play a part in the degree of integration achieved between different activities. However, integration can also be achieved through the choice and operation of planning and control systems. This topic will now be given some attention.

Planning and control systems

Significant determinants of the levels of performance and productivity of the basic 'move', 'store' and 'make/transform' activities are the types of planning and control systems in use. Selection of requisitioning and purchasing systems, stock control systems, production scheduling systems, vehicle routing and vehicle scheduling systems are examples of applications which can enter into the picture. Choices of systems and techniques, however, should take into account not only the needs of particular subfunctions, but also the potential for integrated planning and control of the supply chain as a whole and the interfaces with other functions not directly involved. Approaches, such as material requirements planning (MRP 1), manufacturing resource planning (MRP 2), distribution requirements planning (DRP) and kanban are examples in a manufacturing environment. Major retailers have developed integrated control of stock replenishment processes for their sales outlets using data generated by electronic point of sale (EPOS) devices.

As well as scheduling systems to plan and control material and product flows, other types of control system are also needed. Systems to control and manage quality need to be devised. Also, appropriate costing systems need to be created to assist decision making in the purchasing and supply management field. The potential of new approaches, such as activity-based costing, which may give a more accurate picture of costs to guide the improvement of working practices, may need to be explored. Consideration should also be given to the development and operation of suitable flexible budgetary control systems.

The introduction, enhancement or replacement of such systems in purchasing and supply management are tasks which need to be carefully thought out as part of the strategic planning process. Their successful operation, however, is partly dependent on the coherent development of other infrastructural factors such as human resources.

Human resource management in purchasing and supply

It can be argued that, in the last analysis, the successful functioning of organisational structures and the effective operation of planning and control systems is dependent on the quality and ability of the staff employed. Thus, strategic plans for purchasing and supply management should include the formation of plans to cover the acquisition, development, use and reward of human assets. Plans need to take into account the current state of development of the purchasing and supply function and the strategic direction in which its state might change. In Chapter 4 patterns of evolution were discussed and these can provide suggestions for future progress. Strategic plans for the development of human resources might emerge from the pursuit of the following steps:

1 Carry out an audit of the existing staffing situation. The audit should include the profiling of staff in terms of demographic characteristics such as age, achievements with regard to education and qualifications, skills and experiences of different tasks. The range of current job positions and their knowledge and skill requirements need to be identified and accounted for.
2 Assess the implications of strategic plans for changes in the expected profile of job positions and the changes in knowledge and skill requirements.
3 Identify gaps in staff requirements in terms of numbers and skills and knowledge.
4 Develop plans to fill the gaps by recruitment, training and education and job progression.

The trend in raising the standards of performance in purchasing and supply management is to look for higher levels of skill and knowledge. More sophisticated approaches in developing and managing supplier relationships, in planning supply arrangements and in fostering improvements in performance, place an emphasis on the enhancement of staff capabilities. The appropriate combinations of technical, commercial and interpersonal skills and knowledge need to be analysed and developed. Interactions between people in the supply chain, in the context of 'partnerships' and team approaches, have heightened the importance of such social skills as negotiation and participation in team activities. The concept of 'reverse marketing', for example, implies the ability to promote and gain acceptance for propositions through persuasion rather than reliance on organisational position and power based on authority.[23] The changing role of purchasing and supply management involves the purchaser in taking

the initiative in developing arrangements in supply markets
passive purchasing approach permitted the sellers to take

Wider involvement in joint planning and management
tions, based upon a clear understanding of the technical and com
calls for a wider range of ability than just concern for basic purcha
and knowledge. Buyers of strategic supplies need to be able to manage 'th
side factory' and to have an understanding of suppliers' businesses as a whol

Developments in planning and control systems and the use of information
technology provide opportunities to reduce the time spent on clerical and
administrative activities. More attention can be devoted to these more fundamental issues and to influencing the growth of supplier capabilities to contribute
to the purchaser's own competitive edge.

Reward systems, whose packages should involve concern for salary, working
conditions and career advancement, naturally need to be tailored to support the
strategic direction planned for the function. People with the right motivation
and ability are required if a strategic approach to purchasing and supply management is to be successful. Performance appraisal techniques can be helpful
both in identifying training needs and also in relating rewards to performance.

A final aspect relating to human resource strategies, which is no less important than any of the issues already discussed, is concerned with management
style and attitude towards staff. Broadly speaking it is possible to identify two
contrasting approaches – an authoritarian, autocratic style and a democratic,
supportive style. The former relies on a command and control approach and
perhaps takes a more pessimistic view of human nature. Workers are simply
required to do as they are instructed. The latter encourages a more positive contribution from subordinates and encourages the adoption of a problem solving
approach, in which their initiatives and expertise can lead to improvements in
performance. Strategic management of supplies and suppliers within the context
of buyer-supplier partnerships requires staff to apply the latter approach.

Information systems

Purchasing and supply management is an area that generally has benefited
greatly from developments in information technology (IT). There have been dis-
asters along the path of progress, with such potential dangers as the selection of
inappropriate software and hardware and also the poor management of implementation phases, for instance. *Caveat emptor* is a phrase that is just as
applicable here as in other fields. However, applications of information technology, both within and between organisations, provide opportunities for
improvements in data storage, analysis and communication in many areas of
supply chain activities. The increased speed of transmission of data can shorten
leadtimes and bring about improvements in the synchronisation of activities at
different points. Reductions in the duplication of data generation and in the volumes of paperwork can reduce costs. The adoption of processes for the electronic
exchange of commercial and technical information can lead to improvements in
both the efficiency and the effectiveness of purchasing and supply management.

hile the speed of developments in IT has been rapid, history is likely to confirm ventually that we are still in the early stages of the electronic revolution and strategies will need to keep abreast of future developments.

While communications based on the exchange of Fax messages have speeded up the flow of information, the main revolution in business affairs has been caused by the development of computer-based systems. From a strategic point of view it is worth identifying the main developmental stages that have occurred so far. Venkatraman,[24] for example, has suggested the following steps:

1 **Localised exploitation** – leading to isolated systems at a local level.
2 **Internal integration** – linking up separate systems in relation to more holistic operating processes.
3 **Business process redesign** – designing systems for redesigned processes, often accompanied by changes in organisational structure.
4 **Business network redesign** – extending changes to the external supply chain to integrate operations with suppliers and/or customers.
5 **Business scope redefinition** – leading to changes in the roles of firms and developing more flexible linkages – the 'virtual organisation'.

In terms of the extent of business transformation, it is suggested Stages 1 and 2 represent evolutionary steps and have been most common in applications to date. The remaining three steps are more revolutionary in impact and there are fewer examples of these so far.

As far as supply chain management is concerned, the more revolutionary steps now offer the best scope for further advances. Electronic data interchange (EDI) permits the exchange of information on a wide variety of supply matters, with regard to both technical and commercial operations. The potential for closer co-operation is available between buyers and sellers in product design and development processes. There is scope also for sharing logistics information about demand and stock levels in order to develop more responsive supply capabilities in meeting customer requirements.

It is, perhaps, important to appreciate that IT does not simply offer a straight replacement for earlier forms of communication. Its effects are qualitatively different. It changes what people do and it alters the environment for decision-making purposes by opening up possibilities that would not have been available before. Take, for example, the integrated stock replenishment systems used by major retailers. Close tracking of actual sales, together with the fast, responsive logistics systems, has improved the co-ordination of manufacturing output by suppliers with customer demands in ways that could not have been contemplated in an earlier age.

Monitoring of performance

What is measured not only provides data that can inform judgements about the standards of performance achieved, but also provides signals about what is important. Measurements have a motivational influence, therefore, and they help to shape perceptions of what is important and to concentrate energies on actions relevant to them. It follows from this viewpoint that care needs to be taken in the construction of the set of measures which are to be used. Schemes are needed to cover the performance of suppliers, the performance of the function of purchasing and supply management both as a whole and of its subfunctions, and finally, the performance of individual personnel.

Choice of the wrong factors for measurement may divert attention away from important goals, which have not been covered. Cynics might say that some companies, which claim that quality is important, are only paying lip-service to what is fashionable, unless they monitor and report quality performance, along with other data, such as financial performance.

The conclusion of this discussion is that measures should be related to the objectives chosen for the function and that an array of measures should relate to performance at both operational and strategic levels. Conventional measures of quality, delivery and availability, as well as costs of the activities in different parts of purchasing and supply management, may be appropriate with regard to current performance, but others need to be devised to monitor strategic developments. Programmes with regard to supplier and product development are concerned more with the capabilities of the supplier than with product deliveries. Total cost of supply is a more relevant measure in the analysis of supply chains than a focus which emphasises only the purchase price. Weighted points plans and cost-ratio approaches are based upon the recognition that problems of quality and delivery can offset any benefits achieved from a lower priced supplier. Useful references which provide more detail of measurement systems include Peter Baily and David Farmer,[25] Russell Syson[26] and John Stevens.[27]

Benchmarking is an approach that can enable managers to compare performance of working practices and standards achieved in their own companies with 'best in class' and to identify competitive gaps which need to be overcome. Rank Xerox played a part in the development of this technique in the 1980s as the company became aware of deficiencies in terms of the quality and cost of its products, in comparison with Japanese competitors. European car assembly companies have also realised that costs of bought-out components put them at a 30 per cent cost disadvantage by comparison with leading competitors. Detailed analysis and comparison of various facets of suppliers' operations has enabled them to identify targets for overall cost improvements and to pinpoint particular aspects of operations, which have scope to contribute to these efficiency gains. The approach is equally applicable to service businesses.

POLICY GUIDELINES

The main purchasing and supply management strategies to manage the supply of products and to manage suppliers form the content of Part Two. These strategies are covered under the main topics of:

1 Managing quality, including product innovation (Chapter 6)
2 Managing material flow (Chapter 7)

3 Managing costs and added value (Chapter 8)
4 Managing supplier relationships (Chapter 9)

In the last section of this chapter attention is focused briefly on several general policy issues which should be developed to give guidance to personnel.

Ethics

An aspect of purchasing and supply work, which can be controversial and also damaging to the image of the function, concerns ethical standards of behaviour or conduct, in relation to a number of key topics with which personnel may be confronted. Rumours of unethical behaviour, even if they are not true, can do much harm to the reputation of personnel and the integrity of the function. It is recommended that firms develop clearly stated codes of conduct, so that requirements are indicated to personnel inside the function, but also to outsiders in the rest of the organisation and in supplier firms as well.

The Chartered Institute of Purchasing and Supply has developed a code of conduct to be adopted by its members. Organisations in the public sector also draw up statements of practices which are unacceptable, in order to protect the public interest and to assist the pursuit of value for money. Many private sector firms, however, fail to make explicit policy statements and it is less clear what their expectations are. The following are the main areas of concern:

1 Declaration of interests in supplier firms
2 Fair treatment of suppliers and confidentiality
3 Receipt of hospitality
4 Receipt of gifts

It is the last item that can cause most difficulty if firms try to establish a dividing line between courteous custom and practice, on the one hand, and deliberate acceptance of excessive hospitality and/or valuable gifts as incentives or bribes to sign contracts, on the other.

Environmental policies

As the century draws to a close, one of the most significant issues for society as a whole, and for business in particular, is the growing concern for the protection of the environment. Political parties, governments, customers, and responsible business people as well are anxious to consider the potential harm that their activities might have on the environment. A mixture of forces, including legislation and regulations, the threat of penal sanctions, the development of standards, such as BS 7750,[28] and changing customer tastes and preferences are having to be responded to. Purchasing and supply management is an area in which environmental issues can have a direct bearing. The following list identifies many of the concerns that need to be covered by purchasing and supply strategies in relation to environmental goals:

1 The recovery, recycling and reusing of materials and waste products.
2 The safe disposal of waste products that cannot be recycled.
3 Supplier selection policies to support firms that conform to environmental standards with regard to air, water and noise pollution.
4 Supplier and product selection policies that reflect concern for conservation and renewal of resources.
5 The safe testing of products and materials.
6 Concern for noise, spray, dirt and vibration in the operation of transportation facilities.

As an example, B&Q, the DIY subsidiary of the Kingfisher group, has developed purchasing policies for the supply of such products as timber, peat and paints, which conform to its environmental objectives. The suppliers to B&Q have to fill out a questionnaire as part of a supplier environmental audit, which helps B&Q buyers to evaluate the concern of their suppliers for the environment.

Intracompany trading

More complex organisations can have situations in which one business can become a supplier to another business within the same group. This leads to policy implications in relation to the basis on which the two parts should attempt to trade. The main approaches are as follows:

1 It can be made mandatory to purchase within the group, where such purchasing possibilities exist.
2 The supplier unit has to win business against competition from external suppliers.
3 Transfer prices might be based upon actual costs or competitive quotations or be arrived at as a result of negotiation. Complications can occur in cases where tax and tariff considerations are involved, if the goods have to cross boundaries between different countries.

Commodities

For some companies, primary commodities, such as cocoa, coffee and copper, are significant to their operations. Thus, trading operations on the international Commodity Exchanges may be relevant to purchasing and supply strategies. Manufacturers of confectionery products and electrical engineering companies are examples of firms for whom this area of trading is important. 'Spot' and 'futures' trading operations in such markets are, of course, quite different to other supply situations. Trading policies designed, for example, to protect the availability of supplies, to manage buying prices or to cover stock values may need to be developed. A more detailed account of the issues that may be involved is given in Baily et al.[29]

SUMMARY

The current state of knowledge with regard to strategic purchasing and supply management has not dealt adequately with the linkage to business and other functional strategies. This chapter has attempted to remedy this deficiency by providing a way to conceptualise the relationships and, at the same time, to present a more balanced perspective of the relative importance of internal and external supply activities. For many organisations, the external supply chain contributes a higher percentage of the value of the finished product than do the internal processes. In spite of this, many such firms continue to concentrate more effort on this internal area in which the impact is smaller.

Attention has been given to the key strategic issue of determining what tasks should be carried out internally and which operations should be conducted by external suppliers. The main structural and infrastructural questions for purchasing and supply management were also identified.

This chapter concludes Part One of the book. This has taken readers on a journey which first identified the need for a strategic approach to business and to purchasing and supply management in particular. Ideas, which have evolved in the field of strategic management in general, were examined to assess their value for directing businesses as a whole and to investigate their treatment of functional areas, including purchasing and supply management. Attention was then narrowed to allow the spotlight to be directed on the development of strategies for the purchasing and supply function. Part Two of the book focuses on the development of specific strategies to manage particular suppliers and to manage the flow of important commodities.

NOTES AND REFERENCES

1 Davies, O. 'Strategic Purchasing', in *Purchasing Management Handbook* (editor D. Farmer), Gower (1985), pp. 59–83.
2 Farmer, D. and Van Amstel, R.P. *Effective Pipeline Management*, Gower (1991), p. 182.
3 The approach of John Parnaby and Lucas is described, for instance in:
Oliver, N. and Wilkinson, B. *The Japanisation of British Industry*, 2nd Edition, Blackwell (1992), pp. 92–4.
4 Hill, T. *Production/Operations Management*, 2nd Edition, Prentice-Hall (1991).
Hill, T. *Manufacturing Strategy*, 2nd Edition, Macmillan (1993a).
Hill, T. *The Essence of Operations Management*, Prentice-Hall (1993b).
5 Robinson, P.J. and Faris, C.W. *Industrial Buying and Creative Marketing*, Allyn and Bacon (1967).
6 Ford, D. and Farmer, D. 'Make or Buy – A Key Strategic Issue', *Long Range Planning*, Vol. 19, No. 5, 1986, pp. 54–62.
7 Ford, D., Cotton, B., Farmer, D., Gross, A. and Wilkinson, I. 'Make-Or-Buy Decisions and their Implications', *Industrial Marketing Management*, Vol. 22, 1993, pp. 207–14.
8 *See* Chapter 6, p. 195, of Hill, T. (1993), *Manufacturing Strategy*, 2nd Edition, Macmillan.

9 Baily, P., Farmer, D., Jessop, D. and Jones, D. *Purchasing, Principles and Management*, 7th Edition, Pitman Publishing (1994), Chapter 11.

10. *See* Ford, D. and Farmer, D. (1986), as mentioned in note 6 above, and Ford, D. *et al.* (1993), in particular Table 9 on p. 212, as mentioned in note 7 above.

11 *See* Ford, D. *et al.* (1993), for their analysis of this issue, as mentioned in note 7 above.

12 Stuckey, J. and White, D. 'When and When Not to Vertically Integrate', *Sloan Management Review*, Spring 1993, pp. 71–83.

13 Kumpe, T. and Bolwijn, P.T. 'Manufacturing: The New Case for Vertical Integration', *Harvard Business Review*, March–April 1988, pp. 75–81.

14 Venkatesan, R. 'Strategic Sourcing: To Make Or Not To Make', *Harvard Business Review*, November–December 1992, pp. 98–107.

15 'Sub-Contract Trend Makes More Sense', *Machinery and Production Engineering*, 15 February 1990, pp. 108–13.

16 Cammish, R. and Keogh, M. 'A Strategic Role for Purchasing', *The McKinsey Quarterly*, No. 3, 1991, pp. 22–39.

17 Kraljic, P. 'Purchasing Must Become Supply Management', *Harvard Business Review*, September–October 1983, p. 111.

18 Elliott-Shircore, T.I. and Steele, P.T. 'Procurement Positioning Overview', *Purchasing and Supply Management*, December 1985, pp. 23–6.

19 *See* Chapter 2 of Baily, P and Farmer, D. (1990), as mentioned in note 9 above.

20 Dobler, D.W., Burt, D.N. and Lee, L. *Purchasing and Materials Management*, 5th Edition, McGraw-Hill (1990), Chapter 5.

21 Heinritz, S., Farrell, P.V., Giunipero, L. and Kolchin, M. *Purchasing: Principles and Applications*, Prentice-Hall (1991), Chapter 7.

22 Farmer, D. 'Organising for Purchasing', in *Purchasing Management Handbook* (editor D. Farmer), Gower (1985), Chapter 4.

23 Leenders, M.R. and Blenkhorn, D.L. *Reverse Marketing*, Free Press (1988).

24 *See*: Venktraman, N. 'IT-Enabled Business Transformation: From Automation to Business Scope Redefinition', *Sloan Management Review*, Winter 1994, pp. 75–87.

25 See Chapter 17 of Baily, P. and Farmer, D. (1990), as mentioned in note 9 above.

26 Syson, R. *Improving Purchase Performance*, Pitman Publishing (1992), Chapter 7.

27 Stevens, J. *Measuring Purchasing Performance*, Business Books (1978).

28 BS 7750 Environmental Management Systems is a standard which operates in a similar way to BS 5750 in relation to quality management systems.

29 For more information about commodity trading, *see* Chapter 12 in Baily, P., Farmer, D., Jessop, D. and Jones, D. *Purchasing, Principles and Management*, 7th Edition, Pitman Publishing (1994).

PART TWO

The implications of purchasing and supply chain management strategies

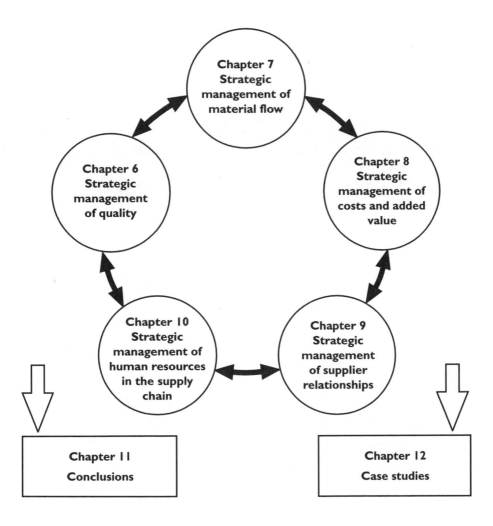

INTRODUCTION

The main message from Part One is that organisations need to develop capabilities to be able to meet customer requirements with regard to quality, delivery and price and that purchasing and supply management has a major role to play in enabling their organisations to do so. As far as strategic purchasing and supply management is concerned, the chapters in Part One had the purpose of establishing strategies for the level of the function as a whole. In Part Two, the emphasis switches to the level of the strategic management of particular products or groups of similar products and the strategic management of suppliers. The ability to think strategically and to develop long-term plans with respect to these matters is, thus, required from many more people than just functional managers. Also, such issues will involve not only personnel directly grouped within the purchasing and supply function, but also others nominally located in other functions, such as design and production, who may be members of supplier management teams.

It is both convenient and logical to create separate chapters for the different dimensions of capability – quality, material flow and cost/price. From a practical point of view, however, these issues are interrelated and a total strategic plan has to be formulated and put into operation. Measures to manage quality may impact on material flow, and both may have an influence on cost outcomes. The implementation of initiatives, such as total quality management and just in time, call for and produce improvements on all fronts as part of an integrated approach. Chapter 9 is concerned with the management of supplier relationships and enables a more holistic perspective to be adopted. Indeed, it will be seen that the expanding view of what constitutes quality, as embraced by the notion of total quality management, acts as an umbrella for all dimensions of the service offered and provided to customers.

Part One also put forward the view that the relative priorities with regard to quality, delivery and price might vary in line with the particular business and corporate strategies that have been selected by the firm. Nevertheless, a focus on satisfying customer needs is essential in successfully managing supply chains. Only by being able to do that on a long-term basis and by simultaneously achieving its financial goals can an organisation hope to remain viable. This might be summed up as providing value for money to customers and clients and satisfying those who provide financial resources to enable the organisation to proceed. Both private and public sector organisations can share such a view. Strategic purchasing and supply management is relevant to both at both functional and commodity levels.

CHAPTER 6

Strategic management of quality

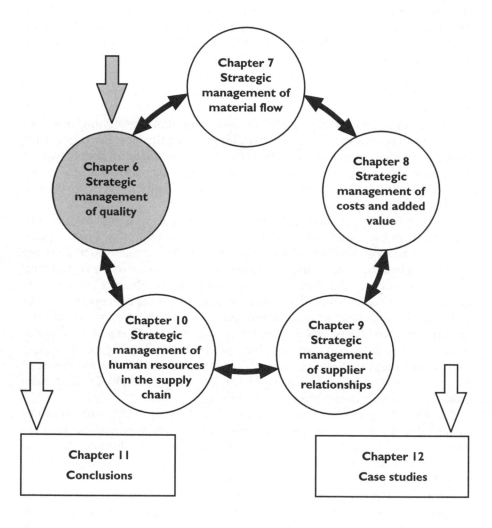

INTRODUCTION

A strategic use of purchasing links a company to its environment, especially as the environment affects future procurement requirements. Sensible decisions about such requirements call for buyers and suppliers to share information.[1]

Management of the quality of bought-out items calls for such sharing of information.

THE SIGNIFICANCE OF QUALITY

It was argued in Part One that product differentiation can provide a basis for achieving competitive advantage and, thus, quality can be brought into a central position in strategic plans. Japanese companies demonstrated how a concerted effort on this front can, over a period of time, bring about a dramatic change in reputation. From being regarded as suppliers of poor quality products, often of cheap copies of those supplied by western manufacturers, they are now regarded as world-class leaders. Especially during the 1980s, phrases such as 'right first time' and 'zero defects' became widely used in campaigns to promote changes of approach in Europe and America. Ironically, many ideas that contributed to the reversal of the perceived image of Japanese quality originated in the West. It must be said, however, that further developments have been built upon such foundations by the Japanese themselves.

A failure to recognise quality problems and too much emphasis on price competition undoubtedly contributed to the decline of manufacturing in the UK. It might be said that purchasing policies played a part by not providing the right lead and incentives to suppliers to improve the quality of their supplies. Progress in restoring competitive capabilities has been made by many western firms, as a result of investing considerable resources to do so as part of their strategic plans. UK government and bodies, such as the British Standards Institution, have also implemented quality initiatives to encourage firms to develop programmes to improve quality. More recent purchasing strategies have also had a beneficial impact on the improvement of performance in supply chains. Indeed, some argue that quality is now, not so much an 'order winner', but rather an 'order qualifier'. Unfortunately, there may be too many companies that are not in a position to qualify in the eyes of their customers!

So far, this chapter has begged the question of what is meant by quality. Expressions like 'good' or 'bad' quality, or even the 'right quality', do not take us far in our understanding, even though they are frequently used in all walks of life. It is not easy to arrive at a satisfactory single definition, but it is, nevertheless, important to consider this question before moving on to discuss the involvement of the purchasing and supply function in quality matters. Thus, the first objective of this chapter will be to analyse the meaning of quality as a necessary task before considering the strategic management of quality in purchasing and supply work. *See* Fig 6.1 for a list of topics to be discussed.

1 The meaning of quality
- as conformance to specification
- as a feature of 'excellence'
- as 'fitness for purpose' or 'fitness for use'
- as conformance to customer requirements
- total quality
- an overview of quality
- costs of quality

2 Involvement in the development of product specifications
- the creation of value
- mechanisms for the involvement of purchasing and supply
- objectives at the specification stage
- establishing the feasibility of specifications

3 Assessment and development of supplier quality capabilities
- assessment of capabilities
- development of suppliers

4 Monitoring quality performance

Fig 6.1 Topics on quality

OBJECTIVES OF THIS CHAPTER

1 To consider the meanings of 'quality'
2 To analyse the potential for the strategic involvement of purchasing and supply management in the development of specifications
3 To investigate strategies to assess and develop supplier quality capabilities
4 To examine strategies for monitoring the quality of supplies
5 To identify the benefits of quality management

THE MEANING OF QUALITY

The following analysis of the meaning of quality draws on the discussions presented in some of the texts on quality and total quality management, such as those of John Oakland,[2] Joseph Juran,[3] Armand Feigenbaum[4] and Barrie Dale.[5]

Quality as 'conformance to specification'

It has to be recognised that ideas about quality have evolved over time, so that definitions of 20 or 30 years ago tend to have a much narrower scope. Quality controllers, for example, considered quality to be concerned with the degree to which a product conformed to its specification – a description of what is required. This is clearly one important dimension that has relevance to purchasing and supply management and strategies for the management of the quality of supplies will need to cover this aspect. Some people argue that this is the main issue as far as buyers are concerned. They take the view that the objective of the buyer is simply to enter supply markets and purchase supplies that conform to the specification as requested, for instance, in a purchase requisition. Supporters of this argument place more emphasis on the development and application of commercial competences in buyers. Wider involvement in quality issues is seen to be a distraction and should be left to technical experts. However, this perspective tends to be more appropriate for a short-term operational role for purchasing.

The definition of quality, as conformance to specification, leads to the quantitative analysis of the extent to which all items in a batch of a product conform to the specification. Objectives and results can be expressed in relation to an acceptable quality level (AQL). Thus, inspection plans can be prepared, based upon the use of statistical tables, to guide inspection work. Judgements of the quality of a batch of goods are based on the evaluation of data from the checks for conformance of a small sample of goods, with respect to selected characteristics of the specification. Acceptance or inspection sampling techniques represent one way in which statistical approaches can be applied in supply chains. The findings of the sample are used to predict the level of quality of the batch as a whole. Use of AQLs can encourage complacency, however, unless the required rates are tightened from time to time.

Inspection, at best, can only demonstrate whether products conform to the specification or not. Though there are benefits to be obtained from knowing this, costs are generated in the detection process and any defective goods that are discovered still have to be put right or replaced. Inspection work does not change or improve the product directly. If the task of inspection can be eliminated at a point in the supply chain, then there is a cost saving to be made.

A 'conformance to specification' approach to the definition of quality has a major limitation, because it does not permit questions to be asked with regard to the correctness or appropriateness of the specification. Other definitions open up these aspects, as the level or grade of quality built into specifications by designers comes into consideration.

Quality as a feature of 'excellence'

In popular usage, the word 'quality' implies the possession of features of excellence in the product and can be used as a standard of comparison with other apparently inferior products. In this sense it is often used in a somewhat vague and subjective way and this approach does not lend itself easily to the development of operational definitions for practical purposes.

A quality product may be assessed in relation to the best that can be achieved with regard to existing knowledge and technology. This approach can have an attraction to professional designers and engineers, who may gain understandable professional satisfaction and pride from developing something which is 'best in the field'. The problem is that pursuit of this view of quality may lead to the selection of the best, most expensive materials and the highest standards of accuracy with regard to their dimensions and composition. These demands are not a problem in themselves, as long as there is no money constraint. Unfortunately, design decisions normally have to be taken in the light of the costs of making the product and the prices customers are prepared to pay.

An architect can design a building with an appearance that is aesthetically appealing, and which is fitted out with luxurious fittings and furnishings, but, if the cost to the client is much higher than a planned budget figure, it will be unacceptable. Aspects of quality cannot be assessed separately from cost and price in a world of scarce resources. Everyone might like to buy and run a Rolls Royce, but most people lack sufficient resources to do so. A Mini may be adequate as a form of independent transport, at an affordable cost to a wider range of customers. Consistency of quality achieved in relation to a targeted grade is a more useful view of quality, therefore. In some cases the chosen grade may coincide with what is also perceived to be the best from an excellence point of view. This line of reasoning is beginning to open up another approach to the definition of quality – fitness for purpose.

Quality as 'fitness for purpose' or 'fitness for use'

The concept of quality underlying this approach is to regard a product as possessing certain functional characteristics when the product is used. Many will recognise this as a phrase encountered in the Sale of Goods Act 1979 and consumers may gain some comfort from it, in the right circumstances, in disputes with sellers. The more general point is to recognise that it is less important to focus on the nature of the product itself, and more important to evaluate its performance in relation to the use to which it is to be applied. Copper and aluminium, or indeed gold or silver, are metals that have the property of conducting electricity. In principle, the materials are to some extent substitutable, though clearly there are differences in both technical and commercial features. This analysis raises the question of how best to describe or specify requirements. Should specifications concentrate on the characteristics of the composition and dimensions of the product and its constituent parts or should they be based upon descriptions of performance features and the operating conditions in which the product is to be used?

Performance, in the context of plant and equipment, also entails aspects with regard to continuing use and the life of the product. Included in such considerations are reliability, durability, maintainability and length of life – continuing fitness for use, in other words.

The problem with the definition of 'fitness for purpose' or 'fitness for use' is that it does not clearly address the problem of determining the characteristics of purpose or use. It is possible for designers to develop products that they believe have useful and desirable functional properties, but, unless they have a clear understanding of what customers want, these properties might not be completely suitable for the uses the customer has in mind. Such a product would not match the requirements of the customer, therefore. Skilful market research can prevent such a mismatch from happening.

Quality as 'conformance to customer requirements'

This approach to quality clearly emphasises the prominent position of customers in concerns about quality and the need for suppliers to penetrate the perceptions they may have with regard to their requirements in a product or service. This line of thought leads to the view that quality is concerned with providing the features that satisfy or exceed customer expectations in comparison with other offerings from competitors. Price/cost considerations are likely to be included in those perceptions and, thus, different groups of customers may be satisfied by products of different grades or levels of performance. It follows that firms need to carry out research to enrich their understanding of customer requirements. A design brief, developed from studies of customer requirements, can then be converted into a product specification and a specification of all its constituent parts. Other factors, such as health and safety requirements arising from government regulations, may also need to be taken on board in a design brief.

This perspective of 'conformance to customer requirements' assumes that customers have a clear view of their requirements and that they can discriminate carefully between different offers. This may not always be the case. Marketing communications may be able, however, to go some way in influencing and helping to form customer perceptions and expectations. In some cases, consumers of products or services may have 'agents' who make decisions on their behalf. Doctors in general practices or 'purchaser' units in the National Health Service may purchase services on behalf of patients for whom they have responsibility. This complicates the picture as to whose views are to be listened to – the agent or the consumer, or both?

'Total quality'

The development of ideas about quality has been concerned, so far, with the characteristics of the product. The concept of total quality, however, widens attention to include all aspects of the offering, including service and delivery time. The main interest in this chapter, however, is with the technical aspects of product quality, especially in relation to the quality of bought-out supplies. There are other aspects to total quality, which are not directly relevant to the current discussion, but these are referred to later in this chapter.

An overview of quality

Barrie Dale has provided an overview of issues in quality management and suggests that there are four levels in the evolution of ideas.[6] These levels feature different aspects (*see* Fig 6.2) and are as follows:

1 Inspection:
   – Salvage
   – Sorting, grading, reblending
   – Corrective actions
   – Identify sources of non-conformance

2 Quality control:
 - Develop quality manual
 - Process performance data
 - Self-inspection
 - Product testing
 - Basic quality planning
 - Use of basic statistics
 - Paperwork controls
3 Quality assurance:
 - Quality systems development
 - Advanced quality planning
 - Comprehensive quality manuals
 - Use of quality costs
 - Involvement of non-production operations
 - Failure mode and effects analysis
 - Statistical process control
4 Total quality management:
 - Policy deployment
 - Involve suppliers and customers
 - Process management
 - Performance measurement
 - Teamwork
 - Employee involvement

Fig 6.2 Expansion of the content of 'quality'

As firms progress and adopt total quality management, emphasis switches away from the tools and techniques side towards the involvement and empowerment of people. Attitudes and the internalisation of values concerned with care for quality and a desire to seek continuous improvement become important. Quality is seen to be the concern of everybody in the organisation. Reliance only on the 'hard' factors and neglect of these 'soft' factors will not produce the best results, it is claimed. This picture also reinforces the view put forward by Edwards Deming, an American who has been awarded 'hero' status in Japan, that firms should move away from blaming people for poor quality.[7]

He argues that the main causes of quality problems are to be found in faulty processes and are the responsibility of management in the last analysis. Control of processes is vital in his view. 'Top-down' influences are important and managers can take the lead in encouraging the right approach. However, by allowing 'bottom-up' influences to surface, previously untapped talents of the workforce can be released and permitted to make a valuable contribution to innovation and improvement.

Summary of the meanings of 'quality'

The meaning of 'quality' can be seen to include two basic considerations which are helpful in purchasing and supply work. First, it involves the setting of a specification that establishes the features or requirements that are desired. These should coincide with customer requirements. As regards the specifications of constituent parts, which are in the bill of materials for a product, their contribution towards satisfying customer requirements needs to be evaluated. Second, there is a need to ensure that products and services which are produced have a high degree of conformance to the specified requirements.

Strategic management of quality should involve personnel in purchasing and supply management in both of these considerations. The justification for this viewpoint will be brought out in subsequent parts of this chapter. Early involvement of both purchasers and sellers in product development can pay off handsomely.

Manufacturers of products, if they were to analyse product faults as perceived by their customers, will be able to trace three basic causes of the problems:

1 Weaknesses due to poor design
2 Defects due to internal manufacturing errors
3 Defects in parts and components supplied by vendors

For example, when Jaguar carried out an investigation of its quality problems in the early 1980s it found that 60 per cent of the problems could be traced back to poor quality suppliers. Naturally, awareness of these difficulties triggered off strategies to improve supplier performance with respect to quality. Sadly, perhaps, many companies do not take the trouble to communicate effectively with customers at the end of supply chains, who use their products, in order to collect data that would allow them to build up an understanding of their quality problems.

Prevention rather than detection

Another theme relevant to managing quality is a switch in emphasis from investment in methods of detection to efforts to prevent problems of quality arising in the first place. Purchasing strategies can reflect this trend by placing responsibility on the shoulders of suppliers for both preventive and inspection measures. The guiding principle is to develop quality programmes with suppliers that build in quality at the source. While this policy externalises some of the costs of quality, as far as the purchaser is concerned, costs can be lower overall for both buyers and sellers. Contractual arrangements and the development of appropriate buyer-supplier relationships can implement this approach.

The costs of quality

Few companies take the trouble to investigate the costs of quality. Perhaps the main reason for this lies in the fact that most accounting systems have not been structured with an ability to provide easily an aggregated figure of all the relevant costs. Quality costs are generated in a variety of ways. The processing of defective products before the defects are discovered, the activity of inspecting goods and the work involved in putting the problems right are but a few of these. Scrap and unusable materials also add to the cost of non-conformance. Studies have suggested that the cost of quality may be as high as 25 per cent of total cost! A significant level of resources, therefore, can be wasted by doing things wrongly and then having to carry out corrective and remedial measures. It is also worth noting that the costs may be just as high in service organisations as well. The main cost categories, each of which can be broken down into many elements in a cost study (*see* Fig 6.3), are as follows:

1 **Appraisal costs.** These include the costs of inspection processes – labour, equipment, training, etc.
2 **Prevention costs.** Costs of personnel and the application of methods to prevent problems occurring etc.
3 **Failure costs – internal.** Costs of processing faulty goods, rectification areas, delays, scrap, putting the problem right, etc.
4 **Failure costs – external.** Warranty costs and loss of reputation, sales because of delays, etc.

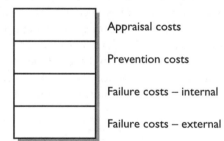

Fig 6.3 Total cost of quality

Generally, the costs of poor quality increase exponentially, the further down the supply chain the product travels before defects come to light. The most harm and the highest expense arise when the defective goods reach the hands of the final consumer. The overall goal is to improve standards of quality and to reduce costs at the same time. 'Quality is free', is the claim made by Philip Crosby.[8] This is a reversal of the traditional view that better quality costs more. However, the reasoning behind Crosby's claim is that costly wasteful activities will be eliminated by taking the necessary steps to prevent quality problems arising in the first place. Therefore, this argument strengthens the case for implementing strategies that support preventive approaches.

INVOLVEMENT IN THE DEVELOPMENT OF PRODUCT SPECIFICATIONS

It has been argued that product innovation and the ability of firms to manage the development and introduction of new and modified products in an efficient and effective manner are essential prerequisites of sustaining competitive advantage in the long term. Furthermore, the best Japanese firms have demonstrated both superior speed and productivity in this field.[9] The role of both purchasing and suppliers in supporting processes of innovation is important. A shift in the amount of value added from the purchaser to supplier organisations in the supply chain adds even more weight to the level of significance.

'In today's environment, product development must become a co-operative venture by the primary developer and its key suppliers', according to David Burt and William Soukup.[10]

Creation of value

The degree and nature of supplier involvement in design deliberations depends on the extent to which design services are sought from the supplier. In some cases the supplier will be given a specification and asked to make goods to it. The other extreme situation is where the choice is simply to select a standard proprietary item which the supplier offers. In either case, the amount of interaction to discuss variations in the specification is limited. In between, the degree of involvement can increase. A basic proprietary item may be partially customised to suit the particular needs of the purchaser, for instance. When the supplier is requested to provide a full design and development service to make tailor-made items for the purchaser, then the level of interaction between the two firms is likely to be at its greatest. Purchasing personnel can play an effective part in establishing communication with suitable relevant suppliers. 'Supplier days' can provide a way of inviting suppliers to meet representatives of the purchasing company to discuss future developments. They can assist also in establishing a dialogue between suppliers of complementary parts.

As well as making valuable interventions at the initial design stage, purchasing can make further improvements to a product's competitive position in later stages of its life cycle. Modifications to the specifications of bought-out supplies can help to improve the cost/value equation and enhance the appeal of the final product in the market-place. Purchasing can contribute to the ability of the product to win and/or retain customer patronage. As a result, the firm may be able to protect market share at a time when competition from others might be at its peak.

Purchasing involvement in the development of specifications for bought-out items, which will subsequently be inputs into manufacturing processes and become part of the final product, is important in terms of establishing low costs, appropriate quality and satisfactory delivery service. However, in other environments close co-operation with designers, users and suppliers might be just as important. Key consumable supplies in the National Health Service, consumer goods for retailers and capital equipment may also provide opportunities for profitable collaboration.

Mechanisms for involving purchasing and supply management

A variety of ways can be adopted by firms to involve personnel from purchasing and supply management in matters of product design and the development of specifications. These can include the establishment of multi-functional teams on an ongoing basis or simply arrangements of a more intermittent kind.

Multi-functional teams may take various forms.

1 **Project teams.** The adoption of a project management approach would set up a project team and include buyers within it. Responsibility would be allocated to the team to guide the product development process from the initial concept stage right through to product launch and, indeed, the team may continue to have responsibility then for the production stage. It could work closely with suppliers, and their representatives could be involved directly at appropriate times. Stages involved along such a route include preparing designs, product and prototype testing, commercial and market evaluation and market testing.

Such a project team has an opportunity to adopt a simultaneous or concurrent engineering approach. The hoped-for benefits of this approach include reduced cost, better control of quality, faster time to market and less need to cope with production difficulties and design weaknesses in the early introductory stages. Customers should not have to be used, as a general rule, as guinea pigs to test and find the faults! The basic idea behind 'the rugby scrum' approach, as opposed to 'the relay race approach', is that consideration can be given to all the problems anticipated by the functions represented before the design is finalised. More traditional practices followed a path of sequential development. Product designers developed their ideas and their plans were then 'thrown over the departmental wall' to the process engineers. They decided how the product could best be made. Production personnel were then consulted and they decided how the product had to be made, given the equipment they had to work with. At the very last moment somebody might think to ask purchasing to buy the supplies and eventually suppliers would enter the picture. Some readers may be familiar with this picture and are aware of the frequent need to modify ideas as the different steps were tackled.

2 **Value engineering (VE) and value analysis (VA) teams.** Teams may be established to apply techniques of VE/VA. The objective of such studies is to take out any unnecessary costs from designs. Investigations can look for designs which improve the value/cost relationship, taking into account alternative parts and materials and manufacturing process costs.

3 **Merchandising teams.** Retailers may form teams from purchasing, merchandising, marketing and technical sections to consider the range and design of items to stock.

4 **Materials or product user committees.** Such committees can provide a forum in which views can be aired with regard to requirements and the details of specifications determined. These can help to promote the sharing of knowledge and experiences and lead to the adoption of standardised ranges of goods to be supplied.

Objectives at the specification stage

The obvious aim is that of establishing specifications of the total product and its constituent parts that produce a product that is 'fit for the purpose' of the intended customers. It has already been argued that the design process should be market driven. Quality function deployment (QFD) is a method developed in Japan to implement a customer driven engineering approach. 'It employs a step-by-step approach, from customer needs and expectations through product planning and development, process planning and production planning, to manufactured products.'[11] As far as goods or services for internal purposes, the same aim of satisfying the needs of internal customers or clients is valid.

However, as well as satisfying functional objectives, it is suggested that other aims need to be pursued. The product as a whole needs to be commercially viable and, hence, the brief for the design team should contain an indicator of the market price at which the product can be sold. A cost target can then be established for the product as a whole to allow an acceptable margin, and this in turn can be broken down to guide the design of subsystems and parts. A traditional cost-plus approach may not be effective in producing a competitive price. Further aims should include considerations of manufacturability and the control of quality. The involvement of suppliers in design assessments grants them an early opportunity to apply their expertise in putting forward proposals both to satisfy functional needs, but also to take into account these other objectives.

The use of functional specifications

As the level of outsourcing has increased and as the trend of buying complete systems (rather than a group of parts to be assembled internally) has risen, so the use of functional specifications has grown in popularity. Sometimes the expression to buy 'black box' items is used. This method gives freedom to the supplier to develop the most appropriate approach in designing and making the product and scope to best meet the overall set of design objectives. The purchaser is relieved of the responsibility and risk of assessing whether a particular product specification can provide the desired functions or not. Working to functional specifications allows suppliers to be innovative and to apply the most recent ideas.

Establishing the feasibility of specifications with suppliers

Early involvement of purchasing in upstream activities enables buyers to work closely with suppliers to establish that it is feasible for the supplier's manufacturing processes to produce to the standards required. Other steps can be taken to minimise the occurrence of quality problems. An outline of these possibilities for advance planning follows.

Process capability

To establish whether a specification is feasible can involve first the determination of process capabilities. The application of statistical process control (SPC) techniques may be used to establish the capability of a process with respect to a particular feature being produced. While a nominal value will be stated in a specification, it is recognised that every process will tend to display a degree of variation, large or small, in its ability to reproduce the nominal value of that characteristic in the units produced. Hence, normally, specifications will be expressed with stated tolerance limits, which identify an acceptable range of variation. The question to be determined is whether the process, when operating normally, is able to exhibit a range of variation that is less than the specified tolerances. Cp and Cpk indices are often used as indicators of process capability, and suppliers may be asked to provide such data.[12] Control charts can be constructed to track performance subsequently and to compare it with upper and lower control limits for means (averages) and ranges of variation in the characteristic that is to be monitored.

Failure mode and effects analysis (FMEA)

Barrie Dale and Cary Cooper define potential failure mode and effects analysis (FMEA) as 'a systematic and analytical quality-planning tool for identifying, at product, service, and process design stages, what might go wrong either during the manufacture of a product or during its use by the end customer'.[13] It is a formal approach, which documents findings of what perhaps all good engineers should do anyway. However, to ensure that it is carried out as part of a design review and at later stages, companies such as Ford require their suppliers to adopt the approach and to use it as a basis for a dialogue with Ford engineers. Having identified potential causes of failures, action can be taken to prevent failures and to improve quality.

ASSESSMENT AND DEVELOPMENT OF SUPPLIER QUALITY CAPABILITIES

Planning for quality and the establishment of specifications overlaps with the assessment and selection of suppliers. A strategic approach to quality management is concerned with identifying and cultivating networks of preferred suppliers and with sourcing families of commodities from relevant groups of suppliers. Especially if a partnership approach is being followed and commodity strategies have already identified a set of suppliers for particular products, the selection of the supplier for a particular item may not really be a problem. Nevertheless, schemes for the initial assessment and ongoing monitoring of supplier capabilities and performance have an important part to play in the working relationship with suppliers. Assessment goes hand in hand with supplier development and improvement programmes, as the findings in a supplier audit can suggest areas for improvement. Action plans can be drawn up and progress monitored by the partnership.

Assessment of capabilities

In this chapter the main concern is with factors relevant to the ability of suppliers to manage product quality. Clearly, source selection and supplier management strategies have a need to consider a wider array of features with regard to delivery and commercial aspects. Chapter 9 embraces the wider picture in the context of managing supplier relationships. As far as quality is concerned, it can be envisaged that assessment schemes need to be able to cover capabilities and performance in several ways, as follows:

1　Ability to control steps in the planning and introduction of new products.
2　Ability to control and provide assurance for quality during production.
3　More general capabilities, with regard to design and development of new products, the improvement of existing products and the development and improvement of production processes – aspects of total quality management, in other words.

The latter consideration is concerned with the ability of the supplier to support strategic developments, whereas the first two points are associated with more immediate activities. Purchasing personnel throughout need to work closely with other functions within the purchaser's firm and the combined team, likewise, needs to maintain close communication with the supplier. Some firms have deployed specialist expertise in quality matters in the purchasing function itself, bringing responsibility for control of supplier quality clearly into the sphere of responsibility of the purchasing manager.

Steps in the introduction of new products by suppliers

The following steps identify activities to control the launch and ongoing supply of a new product, which is made by the supplier for the purchaser:

1 Feasibility planning – to establish that the specification can be produced effectively.
2 Failure mode and effects analysis – to anticipate and resolve potential problems.
3 Establishment of process capability in relation to the requirements of the specification.
4 Design of quality control plans to monitor production – identifying, for example, manufacturing points and characteristics of items to be inspected and statistical techniques to be used.
5 Decide what documentation should be provided by the supplier, e.g. certificates of conformance.
6 Inspection and approval of samples.
7 Inspection of first production shipments.
8 Feedback of performance data by the purchaser.
9 Review of performance with the supplier.
10 Identification of action plans to tackle identified problems and to develop improvement programmes generally.

Supplier quality assurance approaches

As well as establishing detailed plans and arrangements to manage the supply of particular products, there is also a need to consider processes by which suppliers might be assessed and be awarded 'approved status'. Larger companies and other organisations such as the Ministry of Defence, as purchasers, have conducted their own supplier assessment and approval processes – which might be called 'second party' quality assurance (the supplier being the 'first party').

However, in response to concern that firms were having to receive assessment teams from many of their customers, and thus had to devote significant resources in accommodating them, the idea of 'third party' quality assurance emerged. The British Standards Institution developed BS 5750 Quality Systems, and this contributed to a much wider international and European interest in the approach. This interest took on a more concrete shape in the form of the ISO 9000 series (International Standards Organisation), EN 29000 series (the European standard) and standards of other national standards bodies. BS EN ISO 9000 is the new number for the quality system standard that, in the United Kingdom, used to be called BS 5750. The old number, of course, occurs in much of the literature and use of it has not died out since the official change. ISO 9000 is sometimes adopted for simplicity. The intention of these developments is to encourage assessment by approved independent bodies. The subsequent registration of firms that have been successful in their bids for assessment, together with the use of approved logos on their documentation, allows buyers to become aware of their status. It can be seen, therefore, that a purchasing policy to consider and select only registered suppliers is a possible choice. Local government purchasing units, for example, may insist on registration of suppliers as an 'order qualifier' for products or services which have been covered by the third party process.

One aim of the introduction of BS 5750 was to encourage purchasers to adopt third party assessments as a basis for supplier evaluation. It was intended to demonstrate that registered firms had effective quality management systems. Firms could decide whether to apply for registration under Part 1 (including design, manufacturing, installation and inspection activities), Part 2 (not including design), or Part 3 (inspection only). However, many firms, which have traditionally carried out their own evaluations, no longer consider the standard to be adequate for their strategic items. Interest in the wider aspects of total quality management has broadened the range of factors that they wish to build into a supplier evaluation process. Thus, such firms still desire to continue with their own surveys and to work closely with their suppliers within the framework of long-term partnership relationships. In their view ISO 9000 provides only a minimum level.

It is possible to conclude, therefore, that BS EN ISO 9000 is no longer sufficient to satisfy the quality strategies on key commodities. Nevertheless, the movement can claim to have provided a stimulus to firms to improve their competences in managing quality and maintaining a higher level of consistency in their offerings to customers. Critics emphasise the bureaucratic aspect, with its concentration on manuals and procedures, and, especially for small firms, the cost of developing acceptable systems and the cost of the fees for the assessment process. It has also been voiced that some firms have undertaken the process of registration as a gesture to the demands of their suppliers, but they have not radically altered the attitudes of their workers and have not demonstrated strong support for it. Now, the British Standards Institution has seen fit to introduce BS 7850 Total Quality Management, which gives recognition to additional factors. This is, however, a guidance document only, but it does give weight to the importance of attitudes and human factors, as well as concern for continuous improvement.

Another implication of the quality assurance approach is that it is of relevance to purchasers, not only from the point of view of the assessment of their potential suppliers, but also from the point of view of the obligations in relation to purchasing when their own organisations are being subjected to assessment. Purchasing strategy, from the wider functional view, has to take into account the development of appropriate procedures to comply with the requirements of the standard.

BS 4778 defined quality assurance as:

> All those planned and systematic actions necessary to provide adequate confidence that a product or service will satisfy given requirements of quality.[14]

The main aspects of quality systems, which need to be given attention under the quality assurance approach, are listed below:

- Management responsibilities
- Quality system and statistical techniques
- Contract review
- Design control

- Document control
- Purchasing and supplier selection
- Purchaser-supplied material
- Product identification and traceability
- Process control and goods inward/outward inspection and testing
- Inspection measurement and test equipment
- Inspection and test status and records
- Control of non-conforming product and corrective action
- Handling, storage, packaging and delivery
- Internal quality audit of the operation of the system
- Training and staff development

Companies design their own questionnaires to guide assessment and to grade suppliers as a result of the data collected. The grades may be in terms of acceptable/not acceptable/not immediately acceptable. An alternative approach is to classify firms on the basis of the type of goods inward inspection policy to be applied to supplies. Examples of such policies are no inspection/sample inspection/100 per cent inspection.

Total quality approaches

The broadening of horizons with regard to the scope of quality management takes into account not only 'hard factors', the systems and tools and techniques of quality control and quality assurance, but also the 'soft' factors of human resource management. It is concerned, in short, with the overall culture of the firm and its desire to serve and meet customer requirements. From a strategic purchasing and supply management point of view, attention is directed to the supplier's potential for future performance, as much as at existing performance. It is concerned with abilities to improve and to provide streams of supplies that enable the customer to gain future competitive advantage. It encourages learning and innovation for the benefit of both supplier and customer. It discourages complacency and puts an accent on a dynamic, progressive approach, to stay ahead in the race or, at least, to keep up with competitors.

Total quality management is defined in BS 7850 as:

> The management philosophy and company practices that aim to harness the human and material resources of an organisation in the most effective way to achieve the objectives of the organisation.[15]

From the point of view of quality improvement and product development, the following features would seem to be relevant and to form the basis for the assessment of these more general capabilities. The purchasing strategy should be to identify key suppliers with a view to establishing a foundation for long-term collaboration.

1 **Design and technology strength.** This is particularly important in situations where the buyer is interested in looking to the supplier to take on the main responsibility for product innovation – major first-tier system suppliers, for

example. Expertise with regard to research and development and previous track record, as well as equipment and facilities to support it, are aspects to be taken into account. Compatibility of CAD/CAE (computer-aided design and computer-aided engineering) systems may also be taken into account to increase the speed and efficiency of communication of engineering data. The ability to apply techniques such as quality function deployment and failure mode and effects analysis may also be a requirement.

2 **New product plans.** Strategies and commitment for new product development and the intention and ability to invest in developments are the aspects which need to be investigated under this heading.

3 **Manufacturing skills and capabilities.** This issue includes an assessment of the existing facilities as well as plans for both structural and infrastructural development. The skills and attitudes of the workforce, training and development and management strategies can also impact on future performance.

4 **Quality capability.** The ability of the firm to deploy systems, tools and techniques of quality control are important, but it is also relevant to assess whether the firm has developed approaches that lead to improvements. Cause and effects analysis is a useful first step to the application of problem solving techniques, for example. However, the use of quality circles, quality improvement teams and task forces and other ways of applying the ingenuity of both individuals and teams provide the motivation and integration of efforts for the pursuit of continuous improvements.

5 **Commitment of corporate management.** The positive support and commitment of management for quality strategies are significant factors – but they need to be genuine and not simply empty rhetoric.

6 **Climate and attitude of employees.** Management style and attitude is instrumental in shaping working conditions and releasing the creative potential of their employees. TQM represents a reversal of the classical management approach, by looking to those who carry out activities to contribute to improvements, rather than using independent 'experts'.

Development of suppliers

It can be seen that the assessment of facets of total quality leads to a focus on improvement behaviour. The dynamic outcome of this can be the identification of action plans which are of mutual interest to both the supplier and purchaser. Developments in both product and process areas can enhance the value added by the supplier. Development opportunities can cover improvements in dimensions of performance other than just product quality, such as delivery and cost. The thrust of this kind of supplier assessment is for purchasing personnel to work with the best suppliers to improve all aspects of quality. The reinforcement of innovative behaviour to improve quality and to produce new products can be achieved through close co-operation and intensive interaction between supplier and customer. Incentives need to be given to suppliers to encourage their investment in improvement initiatives and to gain their support. Tangible rewards in the form of future business, but also more symbolic rewards, in the form of 'preferred supplier status' and 'awards of excellence', can play a part. The Ford Q1 rating is coveted, for instance, not only by external suppliers, but also by internal supplier divisions of the Ford company. Feedback of poor performance and the insistence that suppliers rigorously analyse causes of problems help to prevent complacency and a lax attitude from emerging.

MONITORING OF QUALITY PERFORMANCE

Traditional practices of quality control, with regard to bought-out supplies, tended to focus on goods inward inspection – a strategy of detection and one which perhaps did not trust suppliers. It has become apparent that this strategy can be expensive. It can only 'discover' quality problems and, if shipments have to be rejected, delays in obtaining replacements can affect operating plans and lead to the failure to provide an adequate service to customers further downstream in the supply chain. Tactics, such as maintaining safety stocks to provide protection against the contingency of supplier failure, add to the costs of supply, because of the costs incurred in holding the inventory. The search for greater efficiency and effectiveness has, thus, added weight to the view that strategies should switch to ensuring that suppliers get it 'right first time' and that they should accept responsibility for dispatching shipments of goods with 'zero defects'. Preventive approaches are, therefore, introduced by purchasing, to select competent suppliers and to insist on the implementation of supplier programmes that achieve the desired objective.

As well as improving quality *per se*, another objective for many firms is the implementation of the just in time philosophy. Faster response to customer demand and the reduction of inventory have, as a prerequisite of success, the need for reliable and consistent quality. The goal is to adopt 'ship to line' or 'ship to stock' procedures, which eliminate the cost and time involved in goods inward inspection. Confidence in supplier performance may have to be built up gradually, however, by monitoring the quality of deliveries at the goods inward stage initially, but gradually reducing the effort as suppliers prove their reliability.

SUMMARY

To conclude this chapter, a summary of the benefits that might be expected from strategies to manage the quality of supplies is provided.

1 **Technological change and innovation.** In the long run, there seems to be general support for the view that in rapidly changing world markets, product innovation is an essential ingredient in the capability of firms to sustain a competitive advantage. Linkages with suppliers and the relationships that are forged with them can help to stimulate technological changes that can benefit both parties. Close collaboration can provide an effective basis for the

transfer of ideas and can contribute to faster learning processes, through which the needs of customers can be responded to and served more effectively. A key purchaser in the supply chain, such as an original equipment manufacturer (OEM) or retailer, can foster developments through 'clusters' or 'constellations' of suppliers on the upstream supply side and keep ahead of the competition.

Control of both time to market and cost is also important in managing the design and development of new products and their constituent parts at different stages in the supply chain. The automotive and electronics industries have shown the importance of competing in these dimensions, for instance.

2 **Consistency**. It was suggested earlier in the chapter that consistency of quality at a chosen grade or level can be an aspect of good quality. Higher levels of supplier consistency can be achieved, with the consequences of improved end product performance and reputation, as well as enabling stages of production downstream to be carried out without problems of dealing with defective materials. Warranty problems will also be less.

3 **Lower costs**. If the 'quality is free' proposition is true, then the supply chain will experience lower costs of operation. From the point of view of the purchaser, the more visible signs will be in terms of reduced 'non-value-added' activities. The result will be savings from reduced levels of safety stock and reduced costs of inspection, as well as reductions in other failure costs, such as reduced scrap and waste.

4 **Logistics reliability**. Reliable quality permits more effective control of material flow and the operation of the just in time approach.

Edwards Deming has suggested that improvements in quality have a chain effect, culminating in improved profits for the firm. Improved quality and lower costs increase customer satisfaction and this contributes to higher sales, which in turn result in higher profits. A further consequence of the latter, from the point of view of employees, is the protection of job opportunities.

Stewart Judd argued that TQM is 'a concept, which, when adopted successfully, distinguishes world-class companies from the rest, enabling them to win internationally. To be successful, it is a mindset which must cascade right down through an organization, starting with a clear commitment from the top'.[16] Purchasing strategies need to develop a world-class supply base, it can be argued. It is sometimes said that a firm gets the suppliers it deserves. If so, implementation of the right strategies is vital. It has been shown that major purchasers can exercise a significant influence on the performance of their suppliers and they have an opportunity, therefore, to spread ideas about 'best practice'.

NOTES AND REFERENCES

1 Burt, D.N. and Soukup, W.R. 'Purchasing's Role in New Product Development', *Harvard Business Review*, September–October 1985, pp. 90–7.

2 Oakland, J.S. *Total Quality Management*, 2nd Edition, Butterworth-Heinemann (1993).

3 Juran, J.M. (editor). *Quality Control Handbook*, McGraw-Hill (1988).

4 Feigenbaum, A.V. *Total Quality Control*, 3rd Edition, McGraw-Hill (1991).

5 Dale, B.G. and Plunkett, J.J. (editors). *Managing Quality*, Philip Allan (1990).
Dale, B. and Cooper, C. *Total Quality and Human Resources: An Executive Guide*, Blackwell (1992).

6 *See* Fig 1.4 on p. 16 of Dale, B. and Cooper, C. (1992) or Fig 1.1 on p. 4 of Dale, B.G. and Plunkett, J.J. (1990), as mentioned in note 5 above.

7 Deming, W.E. *Out of the Crisis*, Massachusetts Institute of Technology (1986).

8 Crosby, P.B. *Quality is Free*, Mentor (1979).

9 *See* the discussion in Chapter 2 and:
Clarke, K.B. 'Project Scope and Project Performance: The Effect of Parts Strategy and Supplier Involvement on Product Development', *Management Science*, Vol. 35, No. 10, October 1989, pp. 1247–63.

10 Burt, D.N. and Soukup, W.R. 'Purchasing's Role in New Product Development', *Harvard Business Review*, September–October 1985, pp. 90–7.

11 *See* p. 223 of Dale, B. and Cooper, C. (1992), as mentioned in note 5 above. Pages 222–6 give a brief explanation of this approach.
Syson, R. *Improving Purchase Performance*, Pitman Publishing (1992), pp. 163–5 also describes this approach.

12 *See*, for example, Appendix C of Dale, B. and Cooper, C. (1992), as mentioned in note 5 above, for an explanation of these indices and for a more general account of statistical process control. Chapter 4 of Syson, R. (1992), as mentioned in note 11 above, also gives an account of this topic.

13 *See* p. 258 of Appendix D of Dale, B. and Cooper, C. (1992), as mentioned in note 5 above. This appendix gives an account of the nature and uses of FMEA.

14 BS 4778: Part 1. British Standards Institution (1987).

15 BS 7850: Part 1. British Standards Institution (1992).

16 Judd. S. 'Quality – the Key To World Class Performance', *CBI NEWS*, September 1993, p. vii of Manufacturing Bulletin.

CHAPTER 7

Strategic management of material flow

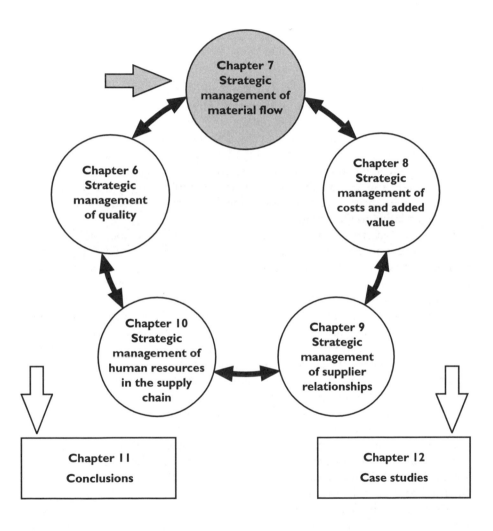

INTRODUCTION

The following paragraph, in an article by Denis Towill,[1] encapsulates some of the key issues to be covered in this chapter.

> with the hope that the European Common Market will become increasingly effective, it is more important than ever for a company to think of itself as one player in an interdependent chain of businesses competing against other chains for the ultimate patronage of the end customer. In doing so they are helping the whole chain compete more effectively and hence are protecting the future of all the 'players' therein. With products, subassemblies and materials (by definition) travelling much greater distances between echelons within the European chain, it should be clear that system integration and rapid dissemination of 'good' information is an integral part of supply chain logistics.

In Chapter 6, attention was focused on the issue of quality and its significance in relation to the supply of goods and services. Thus, 'form' utility has been dealt with. The logistics aspects of 'time', 'place' and 'quantity' utilities, in relation to customer service and competitive edge, will be the main concern of this chapter. The development of strategic commodity plans has to embrace concern for these factors. As the above quotation suggests, interest and responsibilities for managing these factors can involve many firms in complex supply chain networks. Within a single firm, several different specialist groups might be involved in decisions relating to these matters.

In a manufacturing firm, for example, personnel from such units as purchasing, stores management and stock control, material control, production planning and control, materials handling and transport and distribution may all have an influence on the progress (or lack of progress), of material flow.

From a strategic point of view, the fact that decision making can be fragmented poses a real problem in achieving co-ordinated and synchronised flows. Denis Towill has expanded on the earlier work of Forrester,[2] with regard to industrial dynamics and supply chain behaviour. The main point of this type of analysis is that demand changes at the consumer end become amplified as each point further upstream tries independently to adapt to and to compensate for the changes in ordering patterns of its immediate customers. Thus, a small increase or decrease in consumer demand can lead to major swings of production activity in upstream suppliers' operations. Such information distortions lead to inefficiencies because of the unbalanced use of facilities and large fluctuations in levels of stock. Oscillations in boom and slump conditions and swings from stock shortages and surpluses increase the more stages away from the final consumer the firm is.

Decision making can be fragmented, first by the presence of independent firms in the chain, and second by further divisions of responsibilities within firms. The strategic objective, then, is to devise more integrated organisational structures and co-ordinated planning systems, not only internally, but also at the interfaces between different organisations.

While the main interest will be in approaches to achieve the three customer utilities identified, the issue of logistics costs cannot be ignored and these have to be included in the analysis of options that may be available. This is another source of savings that remains relatively untapped in some companies. It is disturbing to find that:

> Only half of the companies surveyed know their current total logistics costs. This is one of the most disturbing findings. Unless a company can quantify its cost base and has formal performance measures in place, it has little hope of measuring the effect of logistics changes on service and cost . . . Rather than championing logistics, many boardrooms are still operating in a logistics Stone Age.[3]

Fortunately, there are some companies who are reported in the same survey as 'tackling key logistics challenges head on, embracing leading edge technology and new business wisdom to "steal" market share'.

Once again it can be observed that firms in Europe and America have been captivated by the outstanding performance of the best Japanese companies, as the latter set world-class standards with regard to the control of material flow in supply chains. Much of this interest is drawn to the philosophy and techniques of the just in time (JIT) approach. The management of 'make/transform', 'move' and 'store' activities has been radically affected by attempts to apply this approach. This chapter will address, therefore, the issues involved in the adoption of JIT approaches. Incidentally, it is worth reiterating that effective management of product quality, covered in Chapter 6, is an important requirement if JIT is to stand a chance of success.

It is easy to be carried away by the enthusiasm and heavy promotion that has been given to the topic of JIT and it is necessary, therefore, to introduce a note of caution. The overall aim of operating low inventory, fast moving, material flow systems, based on small batch quantities and with short leadtimes, might be laudable, but it might not be possible in all circumstances. Discussions of the applicability of JIT concentrate on those areas where it might be successful, but they tend to ignore the rich variety of situations with which purchasing and supply management has to become involved. Nevertheless, pursuit of JIT practices has shown that some remarkable improvements can be made in cutting both leadtimes and inventories, resulting in much leaner supply and production systems.

After these preliminary opening observations about the management of material flow, the specific objectives for this chapter will now be set out. (Figure 7.1 sets out a list of topics to be discussed in this chapter.)

OBJECTIVES OF THIS CHAPTER

1 To identify the objectives in managing material flow
2 To assess the value and relevance of trends and issues in relation to the basic activities of 'make/transform', 'move' and 'store'
3 To analyse ways of categorising different patterns of material flow
4 To examine the strategies for different types of material flow

1 Objectives in managing material flow
- matching demand with supply
- meeting time objectives
- the right quantities
- minimising costs

2 Trends with regard to 'make/transform,' 'store' and 'move' activities
- storage and stock control
- issues in manufacturing
- issues in transport and distribution (logistics)
- lean supply and lean production

3 Different categories of material flow
- characteristics of material flows

4 Strategies for different material flows
- inputs to production
- capital plant, equipment, machinery and buildings
- consumables/MRO supplies
- goods for resale
- service flows

Fig 7.1 Topics for management of material flow

OBJECTIVES IN MANAGING MATERIAL FLOW

The overall objective might be summarised in terms of meeting the service requirements of customers, but this can be dissected into various component elements.

Matching demand with supply

It might appear to be obvious to state that matching customer demand with the supply of the right goods, in the right quantity and at the right time is one of the objectives. However, David Farmer and Rien Ploos Van Amstel have also emphasised the need to achieve a balanced flow and system-wide effectiveness.[4] It must also be remembered that customer demands have become more exacting with regard to flexible and fast responses which suppliers are expected to provide. Add the fact that product variety and the need to customise offerings have accentuated the difficulties, then the basic task of harmonising material flows to meet this basic objective has become more difficult.

Meeting time objectives

Time continues to be an important dimension of competition. The need to offer competitive leadtimes and, afterwards, to meet them in a reliable manner may be 'order winning' features for some companies. To achieve these goals requires co-ordinated efforts and joint planning across the key interfaces of the supply chain. The time to get new products to market was also referred to in the context of product development. However, a further important aspect of managing time is the need to control a related factor – that of cost. Long total manufacturing times allow costs to build up, tying up expensive financial resources, before the firm receives its reward – payment – from its customers. Faster throughput speeds up payment and reduces investment in stocks and work in progress.

It is worth contemplating in more detail the breakdown of time, in relation to the supply chain, into different elements and, then, to consider how total cycle times or leadtimes might be collapsed or compressed. Some amount of time elapses as goods are held in stock or as work in progress at various points along the supply chain. Goods may be delayed waiting to be transported to the next activity point. Machine set-ups and machine breakdowns can also add to the amount of idle time experienced by these goods. Large batch quantities, if moved from activity point to activity point in one batch, can further exacerbate the problem. Time in transit, both internally and externally, is a further element to be considered. The choice of method of transport will affect this element, of course. The main task in which value is being added to the product, that of 'make/transform', has not yet been mentioned, and this clearly generates a process time. The speed with which information regarding requirements is communicated to different stages in the supply chain is also an important factor.

Compression of the leadtimes of a particular task in the sequence of activities can reduce the overall leadtime in meeting customer demands, but only if it is on the critical path. If the total leadtime falls within the agreed customer order leadtime, then the firm can operate on a make to order basis. As the total production and supply time starts to exceed that of the delivery leadtime built into the contract with the customer, so the earlier stages in the sequence have to be planned on the basis of anticipated or forecasted requirements. This increases risk and uncertainty and may lead to the supply and stock build-up of parts which may not be needed in the end. The more activities that can be scheduled to satisfy actual orders, the better the results will be.

To summarise, it can be observed that all of the functions connected with supply chain management can affect the time dimension. It should also be noted that attention to just one element in the chain or network may result in compressing time, but it might only have a small or negligible impact on the total time.

The right quantities

Some definitions of JIT help to get to grips with this objective. For instance, Christopher Voss defined it as 'An approach that ensures that the right quantities are purchased and made at the right time and quality and that there is no waste'.[5] One of the activities that the Japanese refer to as waste is that of the holding of inventory.

Richard Schonberger proposed the following definition:

Produce and deliver finished goods just in time to be sold, subassemblies just in time to be assembled into finished goods, fabricated parts just in time to go into the subassemblies and purchased materials just in time to be transformed into fabricated parts.[6]

This quotation implies that just sufficient quantities should be made to meet immediate needs. It also demonstrates that questions of quantity are closely related to questions of time. An ideal picture might be one of a synchronised flow, in which flows are perfectly balanced and operated on a continuous basis, with batch quantities of one! However, such an ideal will not always be either practically or economically feasible, as will become apparent in later discussions.

Minimising costs

Reference to cost control has already been made above, but the elements of total cost can be identified in more detail. However, it is important to form an integrated view of the interdependent activities and their associated costs. The danger of fragmented control is that decisions relevant to one stage, considered from within a narrow, limited perspective, may appear to be optimal. Yet, if they are examined from a wider supply chain viewpoint, they may be seen to be both dysfunctional and suboptimal. The configuration of activities in supply chains varies, but the main cost elements to be found are encompassed in the following list:

1 Costs of processing goods or the purchase price of goods
2 Set-up or changeover costs
3 Costs of possessing stocks (including money invested, as well as costs of operating the stores), held in stores or as work in progress
4 Costs of materials handling
5 Costs of transport and internal transit
6 Costs of packaging
7 Costs of administration and communication
8 Costs of failure – stockouts and failure to deliver on time
9 Costs of tariff duties, etc., in some cases where international movements are concerned

In the case of relatively low value usage items, C category in the Pareto distribution, costs of controlling the replenishment process can be high in relation to the value of the goods. Thus, strategies that can produce savings may be based less on reducing purchase price and more on lowering other costs of the supply process.

The interactive nature of cost elements should be appreciated. For example, the choice of air transport versus surface transport involves not only the comparison of different freight rates, but also differences in aspects such as variations in forms of packaging, in speed and in stock levels, held both in stock centres and in the pipeline. Control of 'total costs of supply' or 'total logistics cost' or 'total distribution cost' is, thus, an overriding goal to be pursued.

RELEVANT TRENDS WITH REGARD TO 'MAKE/ TRANSFORM', 'STORE' AND 'MOVE' ACTIVITIES

Recent years have been dynamic with regard to the development of ideas and opportunities that can transform standards of performance in relation to the three areas of 'make/transform', 'store' and 'move'. Each will be examined in turn to identify the major trends that have a bearing on the strategic management of material flow. In doing so the interactive implications must not be ignored and, in the last analysis, it is the configuration of the overall chain that is of paramount importance.

Storage and stock control

Awareness of Japanese stock turnover rates and high rates of interest on money in the West have directed attention to the relatively poor standards achieved in Europe and America. Stock is now seen less as an asset (except on balance sheets) and more as a waste of resources. A key strategic aim, therefore, is to dramatically lower average inventory levels where possible. To see how this might be done, it is necessary first to consider traditional approaches to the control of stock and the determination of when to reorder and how much to order.

In an earlier age, it seemed to be possible to regard stock control as a quasi-independent functional area, with its own objectives and with responsibilities of coping with whatever demands and conditions it was confronted with. Stock control involved choosing techniques from within the families of fixed order point (or quantity) or periodic review systems and then applying them as effectively and as efficiently as possible to selected categories of stock.

Selection and application of various statistical techniques were used by some to improve perceptions of expected demand and supply conditions. These scientific approaches were also used to supplement more intuitive, 'rules of thumb' ways of determining levels of safety stock, needed to cope with contingencies, such as late deliveries, rejected shipments of defective goods and uneven patterns of demand. The economic order quantity (EOQ) formula, for bought-out supplies, was one attempt to tackle decisions with regard to an appropriate replenishment quantity in a scientific way. The equivalent, for made-in items, was the economic batch quantity (EBQ) or economic lot size (ELS).

Within the confines of the picture that has been painted, there was scope for improving performance and these approaches are still useful and appropriate in the right circumstances. However, communication with other stages or parts of the chain was limited and little effort was given to attempting to change the basic conditions that had to be taken into account. The latter point is a much more fundamental weakness, as will now be explained.

Reducing the need for a just in case approach

Traditional stock control techniques are now sometimes referred to as the just in case approach (*see* Fig 7.2). This label shows a much greater awareness of the causes of stock levels under such regimes. An examination of the average level of stock held in inventory, managed by this approach, is likely to reveal that safety stock is a significant proportion (possibly between one-third and two-thirds). This safety stock is being held to provide protection when things go wrong, as previously argued. This appears to be a rational response, but it does not direct efforts to an examination of the causes of these basic difficulties. Thus, solutions which remove or reduce such uncertainties are not developed. If more reliable suppliers, in respect of both quality and delivery, are selected, and if demand uncertainties are reduced, then safety stocks can be cut. Improved maintenance policies can reduce machine breakdowns and lost production time and, therefore, help to adhere to production schedules.

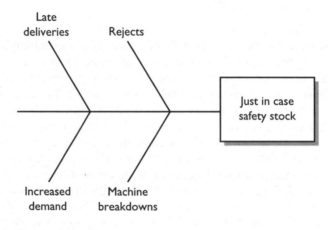

Fig 7.2 'Just-in-case' stock

Reducing order quantities

Purchasing or production solutions may also permit order quantities to be reduced, the other factor that has an immediate and direct effect on average stock level. Both purchasing and production can concentrate efforts on acquiring or making batches of a smaller size, without increasing the unit price or cost. (Note that this is a reversal of the western belief in the efficacy of large batch sizes in order to reap the apparent advantages of economies of scale.) Large batch sizes mean making goods in larger quantities, ahead of immediate demand and, hence, lead to a build-up of inventories. The EOQ/EBQ equation was one rational attempt to balance storage costs with procurement or set-up costs, but it treated the latter as given factors. Thus, western firms did not attempt to tackle the root causes of the problem. The Japanese, on the other hand, saw that if the times and costs of setting up (or preparing) machines and processes for production could be reduced, then batch sizes could be made smaller and more in line with immediate short-term demands.

Large batch sizes also have implications with regard to the management of time. It takes a longer time to produce the whole batch, thus tying up capacity to produce goods in quantities that are not needed immediately. Longer lead-times and longer periods of time held in stock are the outcome for many products. The point to emphasise is that leadtime may not be independent of the quantity decision, an assumption of most stock control techniques.

Eliminating storage stages

Another solution is to eliminate a storage stage in the supply chain. Goods inward stocks can be eliminated in a variety of ways. Suppliers can be asked to supply direct to points of usage – be they in offices or at work centres in the factory. The suppliers may do so from their own finished goods or distribution stores or they might deliver straight from their own production lines. Stockless purchasing systems, as used in the supply of stationery products, provide an example. Clearly, the 'wasteful' costs of operating one storage point can be saved.

Other methods can remove stocks from the balance sheet of the purchaser's firm, but they do not remove the physical stocks themselves. Consignment stocks, financed and replenished by the supplier, might be held in the purchaser's warehouse or held at the work centre on a 'direct line feed' basis. Another solution, used in the automotive industry, is to require groups of suppliers to operate a 'consolidation' warehouse near the purchaser's site and to maintain stocks therein. A third party distribution company might operate this, on behalf of the suppliers. Then, 'just in time' deliveries can be called off to meet trackside needs. It has to be said, however, that stocks in this case are simply pushed back to the suppliers. Total stocks in the chain are not necessarily reduced and, hence, the costs are not removed from the wider system.

Integrated techniques

Another major development, with regard to stock control and purchasing, has been the emergence of the approach to material control which is built into systems, labelled by the generic terms of material requirements planning (MRP 1) or manufacturing resource planning (MRP 2). Some aspects are also to be found within distribution requirements planning (DRP) systems. MRP 1 and MRP 2 systems establish a database in which stock records (part or item master files) and details of product structures (bills of materials) are held. The requirements planning process takes end product demand, projected into the future on the basis of actual orders and/or forecasts, and calculates the times and gross quantities of all items at each level in the product structure. Net requirements, allowing for supplies already held in stock and on order in the pipeline, can be scheduled from internal and external suppliers. As a planning approach, it generates information to assist and instruct both types of suppliers. In principle, the approach attempts to control the flow of supplies to meet planned requirements, rather than simply replenishing stocks as they are consumed. (The validity of this comment depends on the detailed operation of the system with regard to choice of ordering rules and policies with regard to safety stocks.) (*See* Fig 7.3.)

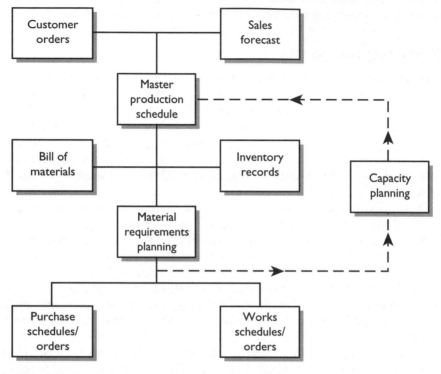

Fig 7.3   MRP system

An important feature of the MRP approach is that it recognises the 'dependent' demand nature of material inputs in the build-up of the end product. The bill of materials indicates a list of all the items necessary to make a particular component or subassembly. Furthermore, the requirements planning process takes into account the fact that the demand for the end product and the demands for all its constituent parts are dependent on or derived from the level of demand in the customer market. The application of MRP tries to control the flows of all the items needed by a build programme. More traditional stock control techniques, on the other hand, are based on the idea of 'independent' demand. Each item under these regimes is regarded as being a unique problem and decisions to control replenishment of each item are not related to the demands of others.

The MRP approach attempts to create an integrated planning system, which can co-ordinate the decisions and activities of the functions distributed along the supply chain – from marketing/sales back through production and stock control to purchasing. There are many software packages on the market, and taking into account developments in both computing and telecommunications

technologies, firms of any size can consider the possibilities of its use. To introduce new or later versions of such systems is a major task, however, and some
firms have been disappointed, simply because they failed to manage such projects in an effective way. Resources are needed, not only for software and
hardware development, but also in developing the knowledge and skills of
users. However, MRP should not be seen as a universally applicable approach.
'Horses for courses' is the best way to sum up the situation and to complete this
necessarily brief account of the approach.[7]

DRP adopts a similar approach with regard to the co-ordination of product
flows through different levels in the supply system, but it focuses on flows of
goods through distribution channels on the downstream side. Planning information with regard to demands for goods can be seen to cascade from
customers to local distribution depots, and from these to a main warehouse
and, finally, back to the factory, taking into account ordering and delivery
requirements between the levels. It can be seen as a front end extension of an
MRP system (*see* Fig 7.4).

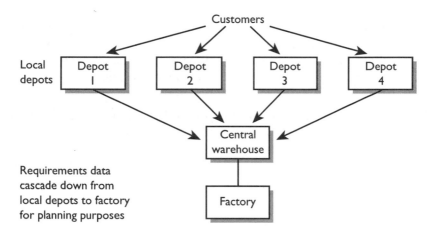

Fig 7.4 Distribution requirements planning

Modern storage techniques

The main emphasis in the discussion of storage and stock control has been concentrated so far on the topic of stock control. It is not the intention of this book
to examine in depth the technological developments that have revolutionised the
physical storekeeping side of the function and the opportunities for effective and
efficient warehouse design. Among these developments can be found a wide
range of mechanical and automated equipment which both increase the efficiency of stock movement in and out of the storage areas and, also, enable better
use of the 'cube' (the cubic area of the store) to be realised. Use of bar-coding and
computers can provide assistance in controlling order picking and also provide

a direct link with stock control systems. Where it is envisaged that the holding of inventory is necessary, strategies need to be worked out with regard to both the structural and infrastructural features that can best cope with the requirements that are anticipated. The interface with other operational areas should also be borne in mind.

Scope for more efficient and effective stores management is open to every type of organisation. It is an activity that needs to be directed by a strategic perspective, so that it can play an effective part in the efficient functioning of the supply chain as a whole. In the past, many companies tended to neglect the development of the function and failed to invest adequate resources in either staff or equipment. More enlightened companies now adopt a different view. Spare parts distribution in the automotive industry and facilities for fast moving consumer goods (fmcg) operations are examples of what can be achieved.

Trends and issues in manufacturing

It has already been seen that some of the strategies needed to reduce levels of stock lead into aspects of manufacturing – either inside the firm or in the suppliers' firms. Thus, those who are involved in the strategic planning of supplies need to be aware of the changes taking place with regard to production management. Much of the progress made in the development of ideas is captured by the 'umbrella' term of just in time (as well as total quality management, discussed in Chapter 6).

> The task of manufacturing management has changed irrevocably as a result of changes developed in Japan and used with devastating effect in Japanese products and services around the world.

The above quotation is taken from the preface of a book by Alan Harrison, which gives a thorough account of JIT.[8]

The meaning of just in time

Several definitions were provided at the beginning of the chapter and these help to capture some of the content of the concept of JIT. However, rather like TQM, it has been so widely used in different ways that it lacks any clear meaning. Any firm can lay claim to being an advocate of it in order to wear the garments of a progressive firm. There are, perhaps, four basic ideas that take in the main usages of the term:

1 JIT as the elimination of inventory in supply chains
2 JIT as a production control system – kanban
3 JIT as a philosophy – the elimination of waste
4 JIT as a human resource management strategy – concern for and involvement of people

Certainly, a reduction in inventory is a key aim for most, if not all, supporters of JIT, and it was a major concern as western visitors to Japan first commented on their findings. Frequent deliveries, of small quantities, to meet immediate demands was seen to be the answer to greater efficiency.

Accounts of Toyota's car production system highlighted the use of kanban tickets as a way of controlling the flow of material on a short-term basis. Such tickets enable a downstream work centre, when it needs replenishment supplies, to call for the movement of a small, fixed quantity of replenishment supplies from an upstream supply point. As a quantity is drawn off, a production kanban authorises the upstream supplier to manufacture a similar quantity as a replacement. It has been described as a 'pull system', as users call off supplies as required. There is direct communication between customer and supplier on the shopfloor. Other planning and control systems, such as MRP, rely on instructions being issued from a remote control point, which in turn depends on the feedback of data to be kept informed of progress. Kanban can respond more quickly to changes. However, other medium- and long-term planning approaches are needed to plan the capacity of facilities at the different points in the supply chain. Kanban can, perhaps, be seen as a fine-tuning mechanism. Instead of cards, various other ways have emerged to operate this pull system. Containers or squares on the floor, which are designed to hold only a fixed quantity, are other ways of transmitting the same type of signal. Computers can also generate instructions. The kanban approach may also, of course, be used with external suppliers.

Reliable delivery, over short distances, and consistent quality are necessary for such a low inventory approach to work. Stable, level schedules are also necessary, as there will only be an ability to respond quickly in the case of small fluctuations in demand.

As a philosophy, JIT is seen to be concerned with the elimination of waste – the reduction of the non-value added activities. This notion complements the idea of continuous improvement, which was seen to be at the heart of the TQM philosophy. Seven sources of waste have been identified. These are defective goods, inventory, unnecessary motion in work methods being used, overproduction – too early and too much, too much movement and handling of goods, waiting time, and process weaknesses. Development programmes can be centred on these sources of waste, with a view to eliminating, or at least reducing them.

To help accomplish JIT goals, different approaches to the management and deployment of people are called for and, once again, there is an overlap with TQM. Ideas such as job enlargement and job enrichment, which have been available in the West for several decades, are akin to the Japanese approach. Workers should be multi-skilled and should be used flexibly, as one of the ways of coping with minor fluctuations in levels of demand. Maintenance, cleaning and training are things that can be done when demand is slack. Workers should also be encouraged to act as problem solvers and to propose changes as part of the process of continuous improvement. The formation of teams, led by team leaders, is also a key part of the human resource management strategy. Chapter 10 deals with these issues in more detail.

Unlike traditional western ideas, JIT embodies the belief that it is not wrong to have idle machines when there is no demand for the outputs from them. Conversely, in the West, incentives to continue production for stock, to absorb overheads, are signalled by such measures as capacity utilisation rates. More rigid demarcation of jobs in many plants has made it difficult to increase flexibility in western firms. However, the changing climate of industrial relations in the UK, influenced both by trade union legislation and by high levels of unemployment, has made it easier for firms to consider more radical changes.

Improving material flow

One framework, which helps to bring order to the multitude of ideas about JIT, is used by Christopher Voss in a paper given at a conference of the British Production and Inventory Control Society (BPICS).[9] He suggested that strategies to improve performance should concentrate on three core areas. These are flow, flexibility and chain of supply. To enable improved performance to be achieved in these areas requires attention to what he called 'enablers' and the use of various tools and techniques. These concepts will now be examined in more depth. It will be seen that improvements can be made without necessarily having to carry out major investment programmes.

1 **Flow.** The redesign and restructuring of factory layouts are basic contributors to the simplification and improvement of product flow. The switch from a process or functional layout (each work centre set up to specialise in a particular type of process) to a cellular or a group technology layout has also produced many benefits. Each cell becomes a self-sufficient unit, with all the processes needed to make a 'family' of parts, components or even complete products. Layouts in the cell may be U-shaped, to allow machine minding to be done by fewer people. Benefits, in terms of much shorter manufacturing times, lower work in progress, lower materials handling costs and simpler scheduling, can be gained. There is also scope for a more flexible use of human resources. Cells form a convenient unit to which authority and responsibility can be delegated. A cell is an easily identifiable unit as a basis for both accountability and reward for performance.

2 **Flexibility.** The second core area is concerned with the creation of a manufacturing structure that can be operated more flexibly. Particular attention is given to the redesign of set-up or changeover procedures, in order to slash times and costs, so that a pattern of frequent, small batches can be built into schedules, while keeping unit costs of production low. Some spare plant capacity might be needed to be able to cope with small fluctuations in demand. A more flexible workforce can also enhance the ability to cope. Automation may also permit machinery to be used more flexibly.

3 **Chain of supply.** An important theme within the JIT 'movement' is the suggestion that improvements should be made not only in one factory, but in other parts of the supply chain as well. Arrangements at the interface between supplier and customer are also significant. Suppliers may be able to respond more quickly and flexibly, and also more efficiently, if they too have

adopted JIT within their own plants. Supplies, delivered dire
of use, in small quantities, on a frequent basis, are required.
planning data, based on different time horizons (operati
strategic) helps to bring about closer co-ordination.
kanban, for short-term scheduling of some items, and Mrᴋ , _
of others and the generation of longer-term planning information, is a w_
of achieving this. EDI can also permit fast communication of data. Level
schedules and rate-based production also enhance the chances of integrating
flows successfully on a JIT basis.

To enable operations to proceed smoothly, various 'enablers' are needed to
eliminate the uncertainties that tend to plague western production and materials
management. Effective management of plant maintenance is necessary to
improve the 'uptime' and reliability of machinery. 'Right first time', the slogan
of quality improvement, applies to both products and processes. Product
designers can assist in achieving more regular material flows, for instance, by
standardising on the use of parts and materials, by reducing the number of parts
and by adopting modular approaches. The adoption of appropriate planning
and control approaches makes the best use of operating facilities. Engineering
support for the manufacturing areas is also important.

Finally, some of the tools and techniques adopted by Japanese companies can
also be identified. 'Housekeeping', to maintain clean, tidy, orderly facilities, is
regarded as an essential discipline. Problems should be made visible and problem solving techniques should be quickly applied to sort them out. Attention to
small details and to the elimination of waste is apparent in Japanese practices,
as is concern for continuous improvement. Steps are taken to prevent things
from being done wrongly (foolproofing).

The discussion of the nature of JIT has revealed a wide range of ideas and
techniques that offer potential for improving performance. Several concluding
points need to be considered. First, firms need to assess their own requirements and tailor a suitable programme both to change the structure of facilities
and to improve the methods of controlling their use. Rather than *ad hoc* piecemeal change, firms should adopt an integrated perspective and give a more
coherent, strategic direction to the reforms. For the supply chain as a whole to
gain a competitive edge, increases in productivity and effectiveness need to be
gained at each level.

Trends and issues in transport and distribution

The pace of change and the increase in opportunities for improved performance are just as great with regard to 'move' activities as with the two other
activities concerned with 'make/transform' and 'store' operations. It is also
recognised that considerations with regard to transport and distribution should
not normally be divorced from questions with regard to the siting and operation
of storage points in supply chains or distribution channels. There are many supporters of what might be called a total logistics view.[10]

rspectives of decision makers with regard to logistics vary, and their differ-
g vantage points tend to shape their interests and objectives. Buyers will be
mainly concerned with arrangements for the inward flow of supplies into their
firms, though it might be left to their suppliers to make appropriate contractual
arrangements. Transport and distribution personnel may have their main responsibilities in the operation of 'own account' logistics facilities to distribute
products made by their companies, though their facilities may also be used for
inward journeys as well. Others may work inside specialist transport and distribution companies and have, as their main interest, the marketing and provision
of logistics services. The complementary role to the latter group is played by
those who are acting as buyers of such third-party services. It may be noted that
fleet management is a topic that will not be dealt with in this book, though it is
clearly both relevant and a key strategic issue for some. The perspective of users
of logistics services, rather than that of providers, will be adopted here.

Logistics decisions

The main strategic logistics considerations, from a user point of view, involve:

1 Identification of the range of logistics services required
2 Choice of transport media
3 Choice of logistics operator
4 Choice of supply chain/distribution channel structure
5 Assessment of materials handling and packaging implications

The interest of buyers in inward logistics

Concern for supply chain management and also the introduction of JIT strategies have heightened the motivation of buyers to become more directly
involved in shaping the arrangements for inward logistics. Traditional purchasing approaches often relied on contracts with suppliers that delegated
responsibility for making delivery arrangements to the latter. The greater
involvement of buyers is manifest in a number of ways. Buyers may place purchase contracts on an 'ex works' basis and take over the task of organising
transport, using their own firms' services or those of third-party distribution
companies. To enable frequent deliveries of small quantity shipments to be
made, less than full lorryloads may be picked up from a group of suppliers
located near each other, on a 'milkround', for delivery to the purchaser's site.
The need for reliable, short leadtime, delivery service is at a premium in order
to support a JIT approach. The opportunity to group and co-ordinate the purchase of inward logistics services is an added reason for increased buyer interest.

Developments in methods of transport

Technological change has affected all transport media, thus altering the relative
importance of each with regard to factors such as flexibility of service, versatility,

speed, capacity, cost, reliability and safety. Changes have affected both specialist and general freight traffic. Within the United Kingdom, road transport now dominates the market for the movement of goods as a result of its general ability to provide an economic, flexible, door-to-door service. Unitisation of loads, through the development and use of containers and pallets, has increased the efficiency of materials handling techniques and has opened up opportunities for intermodal transport arrangements. Roll-on roll-off ferries and the road/rail transit system of the Channel Tunnel are examples of this.

Third-party distribution services

A notable development in recent years has been the emergence and growth of third-party distribution companies. As well as transport firms supplying specific freight services, other companies have developed a more comprehensive range of services that can be provided to customers on a 'third-party basis'. The range includes collection and delivery, the use of transshipment and consolidation warehouses and the provision of an information service to relay orders and to track the flow of goods. Bulk shipments can be received into a distribution centre from manufacturers and consolidated or mixed loads dispatched out to customer locations. Such services can be bought by large users on a dedicated basis, which means that both certain vehicles and stores may be operated solely for particular clients. Vehicles may then provide an advertising service if they are dressed in the livery of a client. Excel Logistics, Salserve (a subsidiary of Christian Salveson) and Lowfield Distribution (part of the Tibbett & Britain Group) are examples of such firms. Buyers are therefore faced with a wider range of possibilities.

There is a world of difference between prevalent past practices, based on 'spot' use of common carrier services, and today's fully integrated, dedicated services that third-party distribution firms can offer. Their position in supply chains opens up the possibility of 'triangular' partnership relationships, as they enter into agreements to integrate distribution operations between manufacturers or suppliers at one level and the purchaser at the customer level. Another type of arrangement involves the third-party distribution provider contracting to handle a significant proportion of both inward and outward movement of goods for a firm, so that efficiencies can be gained by using vehicles to carry loads in both directions. It might also be added that modern information technology provides the enabling mechanisms to track the movement of supplies and to provide both communication and control links between the various parties.

Supply chain or channel structures

Logistics strategies involve the assessment of the most appropriate configuration with regard to the structure of the supply chain or distribution channel. The simplest, but not necessarily the best, is direct delivery from the manufacturer to the purchaser. The insertion of intermediate stocking points introduces the possibility of other patterns, as indicated by the following list:

- Manufacturer → purchaser/user
- Manufacturer → manufacturer's depot → purchaser/user
- Manufacturer → distribution centre → purchaser/user
- Manufacturer → wholesaler → purchaser/user
- Manufacturer → retailer → customer
- Manufacturer → wholesaler → retailer → customer
- Manufacturer → distribution centre → retailer → customer

Comments have already been made on the fact that ownership patterns of points in the chain can also demonstrate variability.

The European dimension

The expansion and development of the European Union and the concept of the Single European Market are helping to transform transport and distribution activities. These changes mean that logistics strategies can both support and stimulate the adoption of business and corporate strategies with a European scope. Opportunities to operate on a European scale are opening up for manufacturers, retailers, wholesalers and transport and distribution companies. Statistics of international trade already underline the importance of the European market for both exports and imports. Developments in eastern Europe and closer relationships with EFTA countries are also widening the area for trading purposes. Some of the factors affecting the European dimension of logistics are as follows:

1 The free movement of goods across the borders of member countries and the abolition of controls have reduced transit times and also costs, because of the time saved and the removal of tariff duties.
2 The common transport policy of the EU is promoting deregulation and is gradually increasing competition between transport operators.
3 Developments in rail and road networks across Europe and across the Channel result in the faster movement of goods.

European distribution networks are being developed either by third parties or by firms themselves to distribute their own goods.

There are, also, other considerations that can impact on strategy for firms already operating on a European basis. Manufacturers may be able to increase plant specialisation and rationalise plant locations to take advantage of economies of scale and scope. The number and location of stockholding positions may need to be reviewed and the chain restructured. Therefore, a number of options arise with regard to pan-European logistics strategies.

European logistics strategies

1 A firm may supply goods directly from a single point of origin to locations in any of the other countries – direct export – using its own transport or by buying in a distribution service.

2 A firm may supply from a single point of origin to its own stockholding points in various locations in Europe. With faster delivery times and the declining influence of national borders, fewer points may now be needed to serve the single market.

3 A firm may supply through independent wholesalers and retailers.

4 A firm may be able to locate manufacturing plants in different parts of Europe and set up a supply network between them.

5 Where products have a European appeal, a retailer may expand into other European countries and expand its distribution arrangements to accommodate common sources of supply.

6 European sourcing policies for a firm become more feasible either to serve a single location or a group of locations spread around the region.

The widest choice of options, with possible room for improvement, is in the hands of the larger multinational firms. Many small and medium sized companies are either only operating within one country or not large enough to play an influential part in the development of logistics structures. Many can only seek out the service providers who can offer a service to match their requirements.

Lean supply and lean production

This general survey of some of the key developments in the three activity areas of 'make/transform', 'store' and 'move' is intended to demonstrate how dynamic each field has become in recent years. Both individually and in combination with each other, they offer prospects for improving performance and achieving the goals of lean supply and lean production. The need to achieve leaner operations, it must be remembered, was a conclusion reached in Part One. However, purchasing and supply management has the responsibility of controlling a wide range of supplies and they cannot all be treated in the same way. The problem of identifying varying characteristics and different categories, as a preliminary task before determining appropriate strategies, will now be examined.

DIFFERENT CATEGORIES OF MATERIAL FLOW

In Chapter 1 it was suggested that a basic distinction could be made between inputs to production, capital equipment, consumables/maintenance, repair and operating supplies (MRO), goods for resale and services. This scheme will be used again in this chapter. However, before coming back to it, consideration will be given to the identification of a range of characteristics, which may help planners to differentiate between different types of problems. It will be seen that some of the differences arise from the underlying nature of the different basic categories that are listed at the beginning of this paragraph.

Characteristics of material flows

1 Relative level of expenditure on the item (Pareto distribution)
   – high, medium, low
2 Type of expenditure
   – capital or revenue
3 Terminal point of the supply chain
   – internal customer or external customer
4 Type of demand
   – dependent or independent
5 Pattern of demand
   – regular, intermittent, 'special' or 'one-off'
6 Volume of demand
   – high, low, medium
7 Life of the product
   – long life in use or for immediate consumption/sale
8 Physical size
   – large, medium, small
9 Health and safety aspects
   – hazardous or dangerous products
   – need for temperature control
   – shelf life of the product
10 Security aspects
   – vulnerability to theft
11 Degree of technological sophistication
   – high or low
12 Degree of significance/essentiality to operations
   – high, medium, low
13 Design aspects
   – special to purchaser's design
   – special to supplier's design
   – proprietary item
   – standard commodity
14 Supply market conditions
   – stable or unstable

It is possible to analyse a 'portfolio' of products so that evaluations of material flows in terms of 'degree of risk' or 'level of priority' can be made. Such assessments are likely to be based on one or more of the above characteristics. The list is not intended to be exhaustive, however. Firms may be aware of other significant features in their operating environments, which may determine their important strategic items.

STRATEGIES FOR DIFFERENT MATERIAL FLOWS

Strategic analysis and planning, in relation to material flows in general, should focus on the development of supply arrangements with regard to:

1 The identification of the pattern of customer service requirements and the pattern of expected demand for a particular product or group of similar products.
2 The establishment of relevant structural features for the supply chain, with respect to the desired 'make/transform', 'move' and 'store' activities, through which materials are to flow. All relevant parties need to be involved in a joint planning exercise to set up the arrangements in the first instance.
3 The selection of a planning and control system, in order that all parties are provided with information, enabling them to plan and control the use of capacity at each point in the chain and to manage the flow of materials as required. Information should be shared by all the involved parties both at the outset and on a continuing basis.
4 The identification of scope for future improvements as part of a development programme.

Further analysis of material flows and control strategies will be based on the basic categories of supplies previously outlined.

Inputs to production

Certain general characteristics of this category can be observed:

1 Demand for inputs of materials, components, subassemblies, etc. is 'dependent' on the demand for the finished product.
2 Expenditure is from revenue.
3 The terminal point of the supply chain is external.
4 Items are used/consumed within a short period of time (hopefully).

From a strategic point of view it is imperative to search for ways of integrating the flow of materials along the total supply chain. Input, throughput and output logistics stages are relevant, in other words. In general, it might be said that the generic approach underlying the varying types of MRP and DRP packages can provide data to link the customer market demand back down the chain of supply. For firms that have a small range of relatively simple products, which have few parts and levels in them, the data problem may be handled easily without the need for such a comprehensive system. Manual processing or simple spreadsheet operations may be sufficient.

However, within the category there will be variations in terms of the other characteristics, and the overall distribution of types of problem may be affected by the mode in which the firm operates.

Variations within different manufacturing firms

Production environments vary depending on whether the firm operates on a basis of jobbing, batch, mass or continuous flow type. The degree of standardisation and frequency of demands for materials will vary in relation to these types.

The range and number of inputs to be purchased will be affected by the basic architecture of the products to be made and the associated patterns of flow through the manufacturing facilities. Four basic types have been identified:

1 **V-shaped flow** – a small number of relatively standard inputs, branching out into a wide range of finished products.
2 **A-shaped flow** – a large number of inputs, flowing into a small range of finished products.
3 **T-shaped flow** – a small range of inputs, flowing through the sequence of operations, but with the potential to be assembled into a wide range of configurations at the final assembly stage.
4 **I-shaped flow** – a wider range of inputs, flowing into standard components or modules, which can then be assembled into a wider spread of end product configurations.

The nature of the manufacturing context also affects the extent to which plans for activities at each stage can be based on forecasts or actual customer orders – leading to 'make for stock' or 'make to customer order' modes of planning and control.

A related question, which may be affected by the same considerations, is concerned with the choice of the stage in the supply chain to hold safety stocks (if any). Holding safety stocks is less expensive when, first, items are close to the bought-in stage (before further value is added in production). Second, costs are lower if the items are standard parts or modules (so that the number of stock items covered by safety stocks is small, but support is available for the assembly of a more varied range of end products).

Some manufacturing planning and control systems recognise the existence of 'bottlenecks', which are seen to be critical resource centres with regard to the potential throughput of the factory. It is important to maximise the volume of throughput that can be scheduled at such a centre and it is also important that no hold-ups occur because of shortages of supplies. The inputs to the bottleneck centre can be regarded as priority items.

Patterns of demand and choice of control system

The choice of control system should take into account the differing patterns of demand. David Jones has described the way that Lucas Engineering and Systems Ltd has analysed these in relation to different types of control system within the context of the automotive industry.[11] The categories are 'runners' (very regular demand), 'strangers' (inconsistent demand) and 'repeaters' (demand falling in between the two others). These three categories can then be divided, on a Pareto basis, into 'the vital few' and 'the trivial many'. Tighter, more sophisticated control is needed to manage the vital ones and a low-cost, simple system for the trivial ones. The following recommendations emerge from the analysis:

1 'Runners/vital few'
   – use kanban or direct line feed
2 'Runners/trivial many'
   – use two-bin (fixed order quantity system) or direct line feed
3 'Repeaters/vital few'
   – use MRP (schedules)
4. 'Repeaters/trivial many'
   – use two-bin or direct line feed
5 'Strangers/vital few'
   – use MRP (discrete orders)
6 'Strangers/trivial many'
   – use 'one-off buy' or direct line feed

Another factor that may be taken into account when identifying candidates for control by the kanban system is the physical size of the item. Large bulky items take up a lot of space and stocks need to be kept low.

However, the above analysis is perhaps more appropriate to the needs of a batch or mass production type of operation. Jobbing industries are concerned with meeting the special needs of customers on a one-off basis. Fewer materials demonstrate regularity or high volume. Many items will need to be supplied on an 'order as required' basis. Project-based control systems may be used to determine the timing of activities in operating plans, using network and critical path analysis techniques.

Inwards logistics arrangements

Logistics arrangements with regard to the inward movement of supplies are most critical for items to be controlled by the kanban system. Frequent deliveries (several times a day for some items), in small quantities, in response to often short leadtimes, are the service features that have to be met on a reliable and dependable basis.

Capital equipment, plant, machinery and buildings

As the label suggests, items covered by this category are treated as capital items, procured under the heading of capital expenditure (though other forms of acquisition may be used, such as leasing or hiring). The terminal point of the supply chain is inside the firm and, thus, generally decisions will not have any direct implications for its customers.

The main characteristics of this category are:

1 Items are covered by capital expenditure (major or minor) – which may involve the application of investment appraisal techniques. Comparisons

with alternative financial arrangements may be carried out as part of the search for the best option.

2 Items have a long life and hence the decision should take into account life cycle costs, such as initial acquisition, maintenance and running costs, as well as allowing for any residual value at the end of its expected life.

The demand for capital requirements may be determined by the implementation of business or corporate strategic plans, which call for the building of new facilities or for major refurbishment or re-equipment schemes in relation to existing facilities. The management of such processes may adopt project planning techniques to identify and control programmes according to critical milestones. In other cases, demand may be related to more piecemeal expansion or replacement programmes, though even in these cases expenditure might be quite high.

For some organisations, the acquisition of capital equipment may be of fundamental and critical importance to their ability to carry out their basic function. Aircraft for airline operators and major weapons systems for the armed forces are examples.

Consumables/MRO items

The main general characteristics of this category are:

1 Items are financed from revenue expenditure
2 The terminal points of the supply chain are internal customers
3 Items are consumed as implied by one of the labels
4 Demand is 'independent'

As demand is generally independent, traditional stock control systems within the fixed order quantity (point) or periodic review systems offer scope for the control of supplies in this category. Demand arises from internal customers and, hence, problems are handled internally. A wide variety of goods can be covered by this category, with wide variations in both patterns of demand and levels of expenditure.

Some items may be classified as strategic, because they possess characteristics such as relatively high expenditure or criticality for the operations of the organisation. For example, the availability of certain types of medical supplies, such as drugs, is a critical requirement. The availability of some spare parts may also be critical with regard to the support of emergency maintenance operations. In the case of medical supplies the pattern of requirements may be regular, whereas the strategic spare item may only be called for very occasionally. Therefore, logistics plans have to be selected to cope with the varying circumstances.

The main strategies in this area may be concerned with minimising the administrative and storage cost components of 'total supply costs', rather than purchase prices, because of the relatively low amount of purchase expenditure on many of these items.

Goods for resale

The main characteristics of this category are:

1 The terminal points of the supply chains involve external customers
2 Demand is 'independent'
3 Product life can be either short or long, but all goods are intended to be sold within a short period of time
4 They are revenue expenditure items

The main task is to pursue the service requirements of the targeted customers, which will often be to meet their demands from stock (held in a warehouse or on display). Quantitative service levels may be set in terms of frequency of meeting demands.

Patterns of demand

A variety of different conditions are possible. Some examples are as follows:

1 Products with short shelf lives or specified sell by/use by dates. These pose particular logistics requirements with regard to speed of replenishment on a frequent (daily or less, in some cases) basis. Often these goods need to be kept in temperature controlled conditions throughout all stages, including all stores and transit points.
2 Consumer products with regular, high-volume demand, which are suitable for regular JIT delivery arrangements.
3 Consumer products with regular, lower-volume demands, which require less frequent replenishment deliveries.
4 Products with short product life cycles. Fashion goods, with short life cycles, provide little time for feedback of sales data for comparison with planning forecasts.
5 Products with seasonal demands. Plans to cope with this type of problem may depend on whether the manufacturing stage can be organised to respond quickly and flexibly to volume changes. If it is necessary that production remains at a more even level, stock level policies can be used to adapt to the changing levels of demand. In other words, stocks can be built up in advance of the peak periods.

Supply chains are driven by forecasts of customer demands, therefore, and a premium can be placed on obtaining rapid feedback with regard to actual sales, so that the flows of replenishment supplies can be adjusted if necessary. Electronic point of sale devices (EPOS) used by retailers have enabled them to monitor trends and to co-ordinate the flow of replenishment supplies more accurately. Fast response on a JIT basis is also required from those manufacturers who are feeding into the distribution chains for fast moving consumer goods. In short, both the planning and control systems and the physical structure of the supply chain are closely integrated to be able to respond effectively and efficiently to demand conditions.

flows

...s with a significant service element are inherently different to goods. ...cannot be stored. The key task is, therefore, to plan the availability of capacity, with regard to labour, equipment and material resources, to be able to meet customer demands and service targets in relation to customer waiting times. Work loads of 'back room' operations may be smoothed, because the service, by definition, does not directly involve customers and there is room for some discretion in scheduling activities. There may be some scope for influencing the pattern of customer flows to generate a more even pattern of demand on the capacity of 'front room' service operations. Staggered times for different groups of workers to use a dinner canteen may reduce queuing problems for a contract caterer, for example.

SUMMARY

To conclude this chapter, it is appropriate to emphasise that every supply chain serves customers, whether they are internal or external. A supply chain management perspective should help planners to realise the importance of integrating the activities at different stages in the chain so that the appropriate level of service is given to the final customer. Successful achievement of this aim can be to the benefit of all participants.

Stalk and Hout argue that every chain needs a 'product champion', a leader who is both prepared and powerful enough to play a significant role in attempting to foster closer integration between the different organisations in the chain.[12] Even inside organisations there may be the need for such an integrating force as well. Improved information flows for both operational and strategic planning purposes need to be provided to the members of the chain. Joint co-operation is required to identify and develop ways to improve processes and to increase the level of synchronisation of activities in each tier of the chain. In the retail field, major retailers seem to have become the champions and generally have taken over the mantle from manufacturers. In the automotive industry it is the car assembly companies that have taken on the dominant role.

It must be the case that if there are leaders, then others must be followers. So, some firms may not be able to take the initiative in shaping arrangements and may have to respond more to the wishes of the more dominant leader. The question may be raised as to whether the dominant force in the chain necessarily uses that power in the best way. Research by Richard Lamming, for instance, suggests that powerful players in the chain have not done so in the past.[13] Arm's-length trading approaches, relying on competitive bidding processes, appear not to be helpful in bringing about close integration. Partnerships between unequal partners may also have drawbacks. Chapter 9 returns to this debate in more detail, after aspects of costing have been examined in Chapter 8.

Alan Harrison claims that, 'In an excellent company, it is possible to meet demand instantaneously, with perfect quality and no waste'.[14] Whether the claim is true or not is perhaps debatable, but it identifies an ideal that all should pursue.

NOTES AND REFERENCES

1 Towill, D.R. 'Supply Chain Dynamics – the Change Engineering Challenge of the Mid-1990s', *Proceedings of the Institution of Mechanical Engineers*, Vol. 206, 1992, p. 233 of pp. 233–45.

2 Forrester, J.W. *Industrial Dynamics*, MIT Press (1961).

3 The Chartered Institute of Purchasing and Supply and Anderson Consulting. *Managing Logistics: Survey Report* (1993).

4 Farmer, D. and Van Amstel, R.P. *Effective Pipeline Management*, Gower (1991).

5 Voss, C. (editor). *Just in Time Manufacture*, IFS Publications (1987).

6 Schonberger, R.J. *Japanese Techniques: Nine Hidden Lessons in Simplicity*, Free Press (1982).

7 For examples of more detailed accounts of MRP 1 and MRP 2, as well as of other systems, *see*:
Vollman, T.E., Berry, W.L. and Whybark, D.C. *Manufacturing Planning and Control Systems*, 3rd Edition, Irwin (1992).
Dobler, D.W., Burt, D.N. and Lee, L. *Purchasing and Materials Management*, 5th Edition, McGraw-Hill (1990), Chapter 20.
Harrison, M. *Operations Management Strategy*, Pitman Publishing (1993), Chapter 7.

8 Harrison, A. *Just-In-Time Manufacturing in Perspective*, Prentice-Hall (1993), p. xi.

9 Voss, C.A. 'Integration of JIT and MRP – The Japanese Experience', in *Proceedings of the 23rd European Conference of Production and Inventory Control*, BPICS (1988), pp. 209–21.

10 *See*, for example:
Fawcett, P., McLeish, R.E. and Ogden, I.D. *Logistics Management*, Pitman Publishing (1992).
Coyle, J.J., Bardi, E.J. and Langley Jr, C.J. *The Management of Business Logistics*, 5th Edition, West Publishing Company (1992).

11 Jones, D. 'The Procurement Control Systems Matrix', *Purchasing and Supply Management*, December 1992, pp. 35–7.

12 Stalk Jr, G.H. and Hout, T.M. *Competing Against Time: How Time-Based Competition is Re-shaping Global Markets*, Free Press (1990).

13 Lamming, R. *Beyond Partnership: Strategies for Innovation and Lean Supply*, Prentice-Hall (1993), Chapter 6.

14 *See* p. 3 of Harrison, A. (1992), as mentioned in note 8 above.

CHAPTER 8

Strategic management of costs and added value

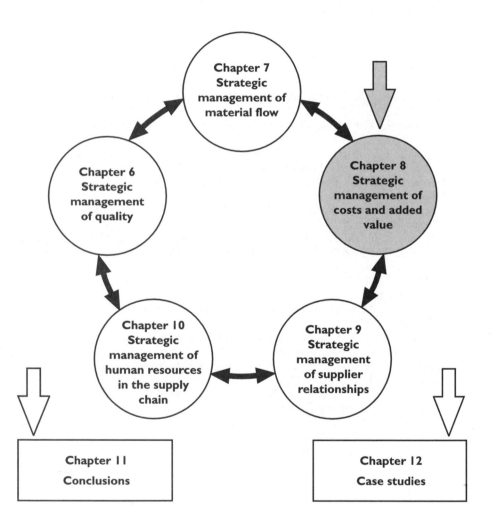

INTRODUCTION

Purchasers may be said to buy a 'package of value', which embodies features of quality, delivery and service and costs. Chapters 6 and 7 examined aspects of quality and material flow, and so attention will now be switched towards concern for costs and the prices purchasers pay. The key interest will be in the strategic management of added value and costs in the supply chain for key products and services. The theme of this chapter will support the general view that effective management of processes in supply chains, which create value for customers and at the same time generate costs, requires a strategic perspective.

It will be helpful to consider several questions about the buying performance of companies, which will draw attention to some of the issues in this chapter. How much 'inefficiency' is being bought in the arrangements made with suppliers? This question is prompted by conclusions from benchmarking studies that European car assembly companies are buying in components at an average 30 per cent cost disadvantage from their suppliers, by comparison with the best Japanese companies! The latter demonstrate the feasibility of achieving both high quality and high productivity in the use of resources.

A second question relates to those with buying power in supply chains and is concerned with how wisely that power is used in pricing agreements. Work by Richard Lamming, for example, suggests that powerful buyers in the automotive industry used their strength to pursue short-term advantages.[1] In the long run, however, tactics that emphasised confrontation and an adversarial approach in negotiations did not lead to improvements in the value package being bought. Problems of quality and delivery performance tended to arise. Thus, if 'product champions' exist in supply chains, how can they manage value creation and exchange processes effectively and efficiently?

Observations of Japanese practices reveal a strong motivation to force costs and prices down, based upon the assumption that the trend of prices in the markets in which their companies sell goods is downwards.[2] The question arises for western companies as to whether they can continue to make money and survive, while both driving prices down and improving the value of benefits offered to customers. How can buyers manage suppliers, so that both the vendor and the purchaser companies can attain these goals simultaneously in a sustainable fashion?

Figure 8.1 identifies the list of issues to be analysed in this chapter.

OBJECTIVES OF THIS CHAPTER

The following objectives will be pursued in this chapter:

1 To examine changing perceptions of value creation in supply chains and the associated costs incurred, including total costs of ownership or supply
2 To assess the value and relevance of different cost and management accounting systems for the management of costs in supply chains

3 To evaluate different contracting processes and the management of supplier costs and prices

4 To assess different policies for the acquisition of capital plant and equipment

---

1 Changing perceptions of 'value creation' and 'costs' in supply chains
  - value and costs in the supply chain
  - price and costs in exchange processes
  - total cost of ownership
  - failure to know the real costs – the problem of overheads
  - cost down/price down approaches
  - innovation and change
  - buyer-supplier relationships
2 Cost and management accounting systems
  - uses of cost data in purchasing and supply management
  - criticisms of traditional costing systems
  - analysing overhead costs
  - departmental structures
  - improving the flow of cost data
3 Contracting processes and the management of costs and prices
  - market-based approaches
  - cost-based approaches
  - target costs
4 Acquisition of capital plant and equipment
  - characteristics of acquiring capital goods
  - methods of investment appraisal

Fig 8.1 Topics in relation to 'costs' and 'values'

CHANGING PERCEPTIONS OF VALUE CREATION AND COSTS IN SUPPLY CHAINS

This first topic, changing perceptions of value creation and costs in supply chains, reinforces the need to step back from traditional views of purchasing and to reflect on the value of more recent developments. Points will be developed in greater detail in later parts of the chapter.

Value and costs in the supply chain

In Part One of this book, the analysis of what firms need to do in order to achieve and sustain competitive advantage revealed the importance of the contribution of suppliers towards the ability of a company to develop and implement effective strategies. The 'lean production' model, for instance, also needs to be supported by 'lean supply' arrangements. Much of the value in a product sold by a company to its customers has been created by the suppliers of parts and components. Strategic purchasing and supply management needs to control and influence performance, not only in terms of quality and delivery objectives, but also in terms of costs. In the automotive industry, for example, approximately 44 per cent of the final cost to the car purchaser stems from the suppliers to the car assembler and only 29 per cent from the manufacturing operations of the assembler.[3] Activities in the supply chain, therefore, need to be assessed with regard to both costs and their contribution to the creation of value. Opportunities also exist to identify other activities that lead to the generation of waste. Identification of wasteful activities, as viewed in the just in time approach, can lead to improvements and reduced cost.

Price and costs in exchange processes

At the interface between the vendor and the purchaser, purchase contracts or exchange agreements affect the way in which costs are shared and can affect significantly the fortunes of both companies. A long-term strategic perspective suggests that both vendor and purchaser need to be successful, and that they share a mutual interest in being able to provide value packages, which meet and satisfy the expectations of customers further down the supply chain. The view that interests are shared, however, runs counter to traditional competitive purchasing perspectives.

Traditional buying practices have tended to focus on purchase prices alone and managerial control systems have reinforced such approaches. Edwards Deming, however, when talking about quality, put forward the principle of 'end the practice of awarding business on the basis of the price tag'.[4] A more holistic, systemic approach recognises that the purchase price is only one element in a framework that includes a wider set of costs in the supply process. 'Total cost of supply' or 'total cost of ownership' are labels attached to such a perspective. It is seen to be more important to pursue the goal of minimising these total costs, than just to obtain the lowest price. It also recognises the complex interdependencies that can exist between activities in different stages of the supply chain. From a strategic purchasing and supply management point of view, options need to be examined and evaluated from this total cost point of view.

Total cost of ownership

A model of total costs can be used to identify the costs of buying requirements from a supplier and as a basis for considering benefits from improving the arrangements. One way of thinking about the 'total cost of ownership' is to consider the following categories, as suggested in a conference paper by Nix, McCarthy and Dale:[5]

1 **'Costs of acquiring' a product.** As well as the profile of the unit purchase cost of the product, other costs of acquisition include costs of specification

evaluation, sourcing, negotiation and selection of supplier, as well as those of expediting, receiving and inspection.

2 **'Costs of possessing' a product.** These are defined as the costs of 'ensuring that a conforming product is available for manufacture'. Under this heading can be included various internal and external failure costs associated with faulty products, the costs of holding stocks of the item and handling and transportation costs.

3 **'Costs of sustaining'.** These costs are associated with activities to ensure that conformance will be maintained in the future. Among these are the costs of supplier audits and certification, and the costs of other preventive measures with regard to supplier education and development.

One difficulty facing companies at the moment is the inadequacy of most accounting systems to supply data in a suitable format to be able to consider total costs. However, developments of computer applications offer the prospect of being able to collect and structure cost information in a way that is more relevant to planners and decision makers.

Failure to know the real costs – the problem of overheads

The continued application of traditional cost accounting systems, it is argued, has failed to take into account the changing profiles of manufacturing costs. As a result, firms may not know the true cost and profit positions of their products. The main changes in cost profiles are the growing significance of overhead and bought-out material costs and the decline of direct labour costs. However, many firms still recover overheads in relation to direct labour costs and this can distort product costings, if overhead activities vary from product to product, and lead to under- or over-costing. More effective management of overhead activities and costs is important both internally in an organisation and in suppliers' organisations. Other approaches, such as activity-based costing (ABC), have been developed as alternatives in order to present costs in what are suggested to be more realistic ways. Managing supplier costs, through sharing cost information ('open book costing'), requires buyers to develop skills and understanding in the analysis of costs and the negotiation of prices in making arrangements with suppliers.

Cost down/price down approaches

Howell and Sakurai have suggested that 'driving costs down is a way of life in Japanese companies' in order to lower prices.[6]

This mentality encourages a proactive approach to cost management. It starts with the recognition that product costs should be managed and avoided at the design and development stage, as product and process characteristics are shaped. There is less scope for taking costs out after the design has been finalised and products have gone into production. Instead of a 'cost-plus' approach, they have introduced a 'target costing' method at the design stage, which directs efforts in the pursuit of improvements that can bring costs down over a period of time. The objective is to ensure that product costs are driven below market prices and that the firm can make money, therefore. It is a dynamic, as opposed to a static perspective. There is a clearer emphasis on the introduction of cost improvements, therefore, and less of a focus on maintaining existing cost positions, as in the West. This same approach can be used by buyers and sellers with regard to progressive arrangements for the supply of requirements and the pursuit of cost reductions. Price reductions can be achieved as a result, without squeezing the seller's margin.

Innovation and change

In an era in which shorter product life cycles and changing process technologies are adding to the competitive nature of markets, innovation plays an increasingly important part in business strategies. This enhances the need for purchasing and supply management to focus attention on introducing changes in supply arrangements, including both the products and services being bought and the activities employed in their provision. It follows that the aim of cost reduction applies not only to existing products and operations, but also to new product and material developments and their supply arrangements. Techniques such as value engineering and early supplier involvement require cost data and a longer-term strategic perspective. It is these 'upstream' activities, associated with new and modified products which will come on stream in the future, which offer the greatest prospects for cost reduction.

Buyer-supplier relationships

The final point to note, in relation to changing perceptions with regard to the management of costs and value creating activities in supply chains, is one that has arisen before. It appears that improvements in cost and price positions, in the same way as enhanced performance in quality and material flow, can best be achieved within the context of long-term partnerships, which permit close collaboration between buyer and seller. Co-operation rather than aggressive competition in supply markets seems to offer better prospects for improving the value of products in supply chains. The debate on this issue deserves a chapter on its own, and is Chapter 9.

Implications of these perceptions

Firms wishing to pursue a strategy of lowest-cost producer status need to pursue cost containment as a competitive driver. They cannot afford to ignore the total costs in supply arrangements and they need to perceive suppliers as a source of competitive advantage with regard to costs and prices. Even firms that pursue a strategy of product differentiation with regard to quality and delivery should pay attention to costs, to ensure that the values of these advantages are not offset by too high a cost in the perceptions of potential customers. Cost containment will also make it more difficult for competitors to copy the other features that give such a firm a competitive edge.

The points that have been raised support the adoption of a proactive role for purchasing and supply management in the control of costs and prices, as far as important products in supply chains are concerned. To carry out such a role in an effective manner requires that those involved have a detailed understanding of both activities and their costs in relation to different supply options. So that opportunities for continuous improvements in performance can be exploited, a relationship needs to exist between teams of buyers and sellers, which provides a climate in which joint problem solving approaches can be cultivated. In essence, a cultural change is needed at the buyer-seller interface, if the standards of world-class performance are to be achieved. Such a proactive approach may also enable non-market organisations to obtain better value for money from their purchasing expenditure with suppliers.

This proactive approach in managing the costs of supply and in pursuing purchasing cost reductions is contrary to traditional top management views, which tended to treat purchasing costs as largely uncontrollable. Instead, the attention of top management was focused on the control of other costs, such as labour, selling and administration costs. Therefore, the potential contribution to profitability from purchasing and supply management was often neglected in firms. In more recent years, however, the visibility of the function has increased, as a result of concern for things like quality and delivery, but also for costs as well.

COST AND MANAGEMENT ACCOUNTING SYSTEMS FOR PURCHASING AND SUPPLY MANAGEMENT

Japanese subcontracting practices may have shown an interest in improving quality and delivery performance, but they also demonstrate a concern for cost improvements, so that downward pressures on prices can be maintained. In order to control costs and to identify what improvement possibilities will produce a rewarding pay-off, persons concerned need to have an understanding of the costs involved. However, costs incurred in making and supplying goods are not just matters of fact which can be easily determined. Costing frameworks, which structure perceptions of cost, involve the application of accepted rules and conventions. The application of such rules and conventions introduces elements of choice and subjective judgement. In a changing business world, in which no traditional approach adopted by the West can be regarded as being sacrosanct, cost accounting practices have been put under the spotlight and different approaches have emerged. Cost analysis is not new to buyers, but it is necessary to review the value and applicability of these developments.

It must also be recognised that accounting systems not only produce costing data to help inform decision makers as they assess the potential consequences of decision alternatives; they also have a motivational effect on the behaviour of such decision makers. The measurement of results and the consequent assessments of performance provide signals to staff as to what are the important factors that they should give attention to. It can also be implied that what is not being measured may often be perceived as being of no or less significance. A regime that emphasises purchase price performance, for example, may encourage buyers to pursue this factor and to neglect other aspects which might bring net benefits from a total cost of ownership point of view. Analysis of price variances in standard costing systems is an example.

Uses of cost data in purchasing and supply management

Before examining the arguments for different accounting approaches, an examination will be made of the different uses of cost information that can be found in purchasing and supply management. The following list illustrates a rich diversity of applications:

1 In negotiations with suppliers, an awareness of actual or estimated costs can assist buyers in a variety of ways. Alternative arrangements can be analysed with regard to their cost implications and cost information may be used in negotiation processes. As 'open book' policies are adopted, so a premium is placed on the analysis, interpretation and credibility of data which is so furnished by suppliers.
2 'Make or buy' investigations need to take into account the expected cost behaviour of both internal and external sourcing possibilities.
3 Involvement in new product development and product modification projects requires cost data in the assessment of design alternatives and of the commercial viability of the product 'bundles' being devised.
4 Cost data can be used to analyse the 'total cost of supply' of alternative purchasing and logistics plans.
5 Firms that have 'intra-firm' trading possibilities use cost data to establish internal transfer prices.
6 Cost information can assist in the comparison of 'home' versus 'foreign' sourcing alternatives, taking into account the different procedures and logistics operations.
7 The construction of material and departmental budgets, naturally, is built up on the basis of cost information.
8 An understanding of overhead costs and their allocation is needed in managing the purchasing and supply management function and in analysing suppliers' costs.
9 Cost data may be used as measures of performance in purchasing and supply management.

Criticisms of traditional costing systems

The traditional approach to costing, in a manufacturing firm, is based on a structure which has the following key headings:

- Direct labour costs
- Direct material costs
- Manufacturing overheads
- Administration and selling costs

A major issue arises in the choice of a suitable basis on which the manufacturing overheads can be absorbed. A common solution to this problem is to allocate overheads as a percentage of direct labour costs and to use a single uniform rate. However, as cost profiles have undergone a transformation in recent years, as direct labour costs have declined, the opinion has grown that the use of this factor as the base is no longer appropriate.

This is but one point in a more general critique of traditional costing approaches, led in particular by the voice of Robert Kaplan.[7] He formed the view that continued use of what he saw as an outdated cost accounting approach was a positive impediment to the improvement and reforms that companies needed to introduce, in order to achieve the standards of performance required in world markets. He wrote:

> There remains, however, a major – and largely unnoticed – obstacle to the lasting success of this revolution in the organisation and technology of manufacturing operations. Most companies still use the same cost accounting and management control systems that were developed decades ago for a competitive environment dramatically different from that of today.[8]

While not disputing the use of traditional accounting systems from the point of view of inventory valuation and the preparation of financial statements, he argued that the methods of collecting and classifying cost information for such uses were less than helpful for other purposes. In particular, he argued that they were not suitable for measuring individual product costs and profits.

Analysing overhead costs

The use of direct labour as a basis for the recovery of overheads loses justification as this factor declines within the total cost profile. As this base falls as a proportion of total cost and as the converse occurs in the proportion taken by overheads, so the percentage recovery rate becomes larger. Its use also puts pressure on managers to reduce the amount of direct labour further, in order to reduce the overhead charge, and this might be detrimental to the process in which the direct labour is employed.

Another underlying assumption is that overheads are related to volume and that they do not vary for different products made by the firm. The suggestion of the critics, however, is that high-volume, standardised products consume less overhead resources than low-volume, specialised items. Thus, the adoption of a single rate may mean that high-volume products actually subsidise low-volume ones. Firms may form false conclusions with regard to the profitability of particular products and might, as a result, take wrong decisions in relation to product ranges in their marketing portfolio and in strategies with regard to make or buy issues.

A further criticism in the traditional treatment of overheads is that it does not stimulate adequate interest in overhead activities and the costs associated with them. In many firms, the real cost problems are in the rise of overheads, but not all such firms have attempted to understand them better or to identify the causes of their increase. Effective attacks, therefore, have not been mounted on what has been called 'the hidden factory'.[9]

Departmental structures

Traditional cost structures tend to reflect the functional or departmental divisions in organisations for the collection of costs and the operation of budgetary control systems. These divisions cut across the sequential flow of supply chain activities and do not reflect their interdependent nature. As a result the total process costs of the wider system are not easily discovered. A further weakness is that the consequences of a decision taken in one department, which affect performance elsewhere, may not be properly monitored. A narrow perspective of what appears, from the vantage point of one department, to be optimal and the right decision may not be in the best interests of the wider system as a whole.

The application of many of the techniques, encompassed by the philosophies of total quality management and just in time, requires a wider, systemic perspective if their benefits are to be fully appreciated. As firms encourage the adoption of cross-functional team approaches and lower the barriers between departments in order to solve problems, so there is a demand for accounting data that provide information on the performance of the wider supply chain. Few firms have as yet managed to produce these.

Improving the flow of cost data

While there might be agreement on some of the criticisms that have been levelled at the traditional cost accounting approaches and which have now been discussed, there is less unanimity as to how to overcome them. Broadly the solutions fall into two groups. On the one hand, there are those who believe that there is scope for a more sophisticated application of the traditional principles which already exist. Others, however, look for a more radical treatment and propose new approaches, such as activity-based costing.

Overhead recovery rates

Those who continue to support traditional principles point out that it is possible to use different overhead recovery rates for different work centres. They also argue that different bases on which to allocate overheads are known and are already being used by some firms. Thus, material costs or machine hours might provide a basis that may reflect more accurately the pattern of overhead activities and provide a more realistic picture of the resources they consume. Malcolm Morgan suggests that many companies in Germany and elsewhere in

Europe may already have implemented more suitable allocation methods along these lines.[10] Peter Primrose also supports the view that the problems lie in the practice and not in the principles themselves.[11]

Activity-based costing (ABC)

Activity-based costing (ABC) is one approach in which 'the beans are counted differently'.[12] As the name of the approach suggests, the underlying basis lies in the identification of activities that are linked to the operations involved in designing, obtaining supplies, producing, marketing and delivering products. It is these activities that consume resources and the costs of them need to be established. Some activities can be directly linked to the production of particular products or services, but other overhead activities are needed to support these direct activities. The objective is to trace as many of these indirect activities as possible to the particular products or services that consume them and to avoid the more arbitrary allocation of traditional approaches.

The ABC approach also encourages an analysis of the causes of these support costs – the cost drivers. In the purchasing area, for example, transactions, such as the processing of requisitions and the issue of purchase orders, incur costs. Cost centres or cost pools can be set up for each cost driver and it is then possible to identify rates for each transaction. Transactions can then be linked to specific products that have made demands for them.

Further insights into the nature of overhead activities and costs are provided by the recognition that they can arise at different levels. While some arise at the unit level, others, such as set-up, materials handling and scheduling activities, are related to batches. At a product level, there are others. Activities to do with product design and engineering efforts that develop product modifications are examples of these.

It follows from these observations that the use of standard parts, the reduction in the total number of parts and components and the reduction of suppliers can reduce the number of transactions required. Processes can be examined with a view to improving methods, thereby reducing costs, or, indeed, with a view to eliminating activities that do not add value to products. In other words, a clearer understanding of costs can support the search for improvements. An evaluation of the potential benefits of a stockless purchasing system, for the supply of stationery requirements, for example, can take into account not only purchase costs, but also costs of the total supply process.

A number of advantages have been identified for the use of the ABC approach and these may be of assistance to personnel working in purchasing and supply management. According to Innes and Falconer,[13] these embrace the following:

1 A more detailed analysis of overheads is produced and a clearer relationship to specific products can be made.

2 Costing data for product profitability analysis and make-or-buy studies may show a more accurate picture of positions than that produced by traditional costing approaches.

3 Opportunities can be identified to introduce improvement programmes that lead to the redesign or elimination of activities. Business re-engineering projects can be triggered off, therefore.
4 Data covering activities and their effects in wider systems, which transcend both internal departmental boundaries and external organisational boundaries, can be produced.

In summary, therefore, it might be said that the introduction of the ABC approach, as a substitute for traditional costing approaches or as a basis for a particular project, can help, for instance, in negotiations with suppliers, in carrying out value analysis/value engineering studies and in total cost of ownership studies.

CONTRACTING PROCESSES AND THE MANAGEMENT OF COSTS AND PRICES

Some might argue that there is no need to collect cost data when trying to establish contract prices with suppliers and that it is simply a waste of time and effort. Supporters of this viewpoint rely on the operation of market forces as the key influence and use competitive tendering and requests for quotations as the mechanism that allows such forces to take effect. In this section, a comparison will be made between strategies that are market based and those that are cost based.

Market-based approaches

The underlying theory of seeking competitive tenders or quotations, as the method of establishing prices in purchasing, is that potential suppliers will prepare their bids, knowing that they are competing against others for the business. All other things being equal, the lowest bid will normally be selected. Government initiatives in the United Kingdom, such as compulsory competitive tendering (CCT) and the introduction of the 'internal market' for the National Health Service, have extended this approach, with a view to increasing the value for money that can be obtained from resources allocated to public sector organisations. Procurement directives of the European Community are also designed to ensure fair competition and to prevent national discriminatory practices in purchasing processes being operated by public sector organisations and by specified types of utility companies. Stronger measures have been introduced, as part of the programme to develop the Single Market, to try and ensure that organisations comply with these directives. It remains to be seen whether these are effective in overcoming, for instance, pressures placed on purchasing units to award business to protect jobs in their own countries.

EC directives covering the public sector include:

1 The Supplies Directive
2 The Works Directive

3 The Services Directive
4 The Compliance Directive

EC Directives covering the utilities include:

1 The Utilities Directive
2 The Utilities Service Directive
3 Remedies in the Utilities Directive

As bids are being assessed in the competitive bidding process, buyers may also bring into the analysis other information, such as historical price data and price trend data, based on selected price indices. An examination of the current conditions with regard to supply and demand may also throw further light on the bids which have been received. Nevertheless, the main yardstick in forming judgements will usually be the bids received from suppliers. It is possible, however, to set out a wider range of factors, together with their relative weightings, which are to be used in the evaluation of bids. Therefore, aspects such as quality and delivery performance can be taken into account.

A strict operation of tendering procedures would appear to rule out detailed discussions with individual suppliers in the preparation of tenders and to require clear, unambiguous specifications of what is wanted. In Chapter 9 this question of whether the competitive bidding model is a constraint, which precludes the formation of close co-operative relationships, will be discussed. Do competitive bidding procedures reduce opportunities to foster investigations into improving the effectiveness and efficiency of supply arrangements? Nevertheless, it can be said that the competitive bidding process works more effectively with more widely available, standardised products than with those specially tailored to the specific needs of one customer.

Cost-based approaches

An alternative approach to that of 'testing the market' by securing competitive bids is to focus on the costs involved in making and supplying the requirement being sourced. In the private sector particularly, but also in some cases in the public sector, it may be possible to supplement bidding processes with negotiations, with one or more of the suppliers, before the final selection is made. Such negotiations may consider the costs likely to be incurred by the supplier. Within a partnership arrangement, however, the decision to source from a particular supplier may already have been taken before the details have been discussed. In such cases, cost analysis may, therefore, be the main instrument through which the contract price is determined.

Cost analysis

The approach of cost analysis, when first applied, made use of traditional costing models to guide investigations of the various cost elements. Buyers and/or cost analysts within the buyer's organisation first prepared estimates on the basis of the direct costs of material and labour that were thought to be incurred by a supplier in the production of the product. Other costs, for tooling (unless contracted for separately) and delivery, might also be added, before building in allowances for overheads and administration and a profit margin. This 'cost plus' framework and the data based upon it could then be used as a reference base in negotiations with the supplier. The size of the profit margin in such a model might be varied, depending on the degree of risk assumed to be involved in the contract. It can be seen that there may also be problems of accurately identifying appropriate levels of overhead expenses.

More powerful buyers found that it was possible to insist that suppliers provide cost data, and the use of this 'open book' approach was given an added stimulus by observations of Japanese practices. It may still be useful, however, to gather independent evidence, at least until confidence has been gained in the integrity of the supplier.

The principle of relating prices to costs is, thus, different to that of allowing the market to shape prices. There is a danger that the adoption of the principle encourages suppliers to look for price increases, when there are movements in the prices of materials or wage rates. Whether a supplier has to wait for the renewal of a contract may be determined by the terms of the contract. Contracts with price escalation or contract price adjustment clauses (as opposed to fixed price contracts) might have automatic adjustments, related to agreed price indices, built in. Neither of these latter types of contract, however, provides any stimulus for the supplier to seek improvements in cost performance that will benefit the buyer.

However, there are several pricing approaches that can encourage a more dynamic outlook:

1 **Incentive agreements.** Incentive contracts can be used to influence supplier behaviour in searching for cost improvements during the operation of the contract. A price can be determined initially on the basis of the expected costs of the inputs required in the production of the product being purchased. If the supplier is able to create improvements in operations, then an agreed formula can be brought into use, to reward the supplier, on the one hand, by an increased profit margin and to pass on some of the benefit, on the other hand, to the buyer in the form of lower prices.

2 **Learning curves.** In the aircraft industry, in particular, it was recognised that, as repeat orders were handled over a period of time, learning effects on the part of workers could lead to shorter manufacturing times per unit and, as a result, a reduction in unit cost. It follows from this perception that the unit price might start out at a high level, when a new part is purchased for the first time, and then fall with subsequent orders. As described, for instance, in Baily and Farmer and in Dobler, Burt and Lee,[14] this learning rate can be expressed quantitatively and can be built into purchase agreements. Other improvements in methods and processes used, or in product design, can contribute to 'experience' effects and similar reductions in unit cost.

3 **Challenging requests for price increases.** Buyers can take the initiative when challenging requests from suppliers for price increases. Suppliers should be asked what steps they are taking to reduce material inputs and costs and to increase productivity in the use of labour. Also, the technique of value analysis may be used to increase the value/cost relationship of the products made by the supplier. In other words, suppliers should be expected to offset price increases by operating more efficiently and should not simply expect to recover all increases by passing them on to the customer.

There is scope, therefore, for buyers not only to control costs and prices of supplies, but also to adopt proactive methods in seeking improvements that can lead to cost reductions and savings. There is clearly a cost involved in making the effort to collect and understand cost data and to spend time working with suppliers. It can be concluded, therefore, that strategic items or groups of similar items, which offer a worthwhile return for effort, need to be identified, and efforts should be concentrated on these.

Target costs

Richard Lamming argues that target costing is an important practice used by the Japanese in their partnership arrangements between buyers and suppliers, and that it is an important ingredient in achieving lean supply conditions.[15] The idea is that both parties should work closely together to identify opportunities for cost reductions and progressively seek to drive costs and prices downwards. It is a vision of what costs and prices might be, rather than existing costs, which provides the motivating force. To turn the vision into reality requires the application of appropriate tools and techniques which are embodied in the philosophies of total quality management and just in time.

Long-term agreements between buyers and suppliers provide a framework within which improvement efforts can take place. The Rover Group, which benefited from its previous link to Honda, is an example of a company in the United Kingdom that adopts a proactive approach to cost reduction where suppliers are concerned. The group's policy is to encourage 'best practice' with its suppliers.

> The whole philosophy of best practice is allied to 'continuous improvement'. It is a technique that examines the way we go about things, and sets about eliminating waste. There is no magic formula, no hidden agenda, it is just a common sense logical approach to improving efficiency and utilisation and hence reducing cost.[16]

Suppliers are asked initially to supply a Quotation Analysis Sheet, which provides information on the materials and process costs in making the product. Rover Group purchasing teams then work with their suppliers to look for ideas for improvements, and agree on action plans. The objective is to introduce savings before production starts and these will be reflected in the initial unit price. Further savings at a later stage, unless they are direct material savings, are shared on an agreed basis. This example demonstrates the advantage of buyer and seller companies working closely together for mutual benefit, with, it is claimed, the following outcome:

You the supplier, become more competitive, Rover Group becomes more competitive.

THE ACQUISITION OF CAPITAL PLANT AND EQUIPMENT

The interest in accounting approaches and techniques in this chapter has, so far, concentrated on costing aspects with regard to the management of purchasing, and supply arrangements of strategic goods in particular. The discussions addressed, if implicitly rather than explicitly, the supply of goods for either production or consumption purposes. The acquisition of capital goods opens up different considerations and different accounting conventions. Major capital investment projects may be evaluated and then implemented as part of business and corporate strategic processes. Purchasing and supply management personnel may be involved in such projects within their own companies, but they may also work with and advise suppliers on schemes to be carried out within supplier businesses. In either case, supplies personnel need to be conversant with appropriate accounting knowledge and techniques. Purchasing departments also need to develop policies to guide the acquisition of capital items of a more minor kind as well.

Characteristics of acquiring capital goods

The acquisition of capital goods differs in a number of respects to the procurement of other types of supplies. The following points bring out some of these differences:

1 The purchase of capital goods involves the investment of money in fixed assets and commits funds on a long-term basis.
2 Capital goods are used over a long period of time and their benefits can be evaluated over what might be expected to be their normal working life, though there may be some residual value left as they are replaced.
3 To use and maintain capital goods in working order involves additional costs, which may exceed the initial acquisition cost. Such 'life cycle' costs should be taken into account in acquiring them and in appraising the economic benefits to be gained from the financial investment.
4 The scale of investment can be very high on major development projects, such as the construction and provision of machinery and equipment of a new operating facility, or a new store or factory. Some organisations may open and operate a large number of similar types of facilities and there may be opportunities to establish specialist teams to work on a series of projects. Major retailers, for example, may have an ongoing programme of building and developing new stores.

5 Other methods of financing the acquisition rather than outright purchase, such as leasing or hiring, can be used, and these can have different tax, cash-flow and legal implications.

6 Analysis of the financial returns to be gained from capital investments requires the choice and application of a method of appraisal.

7 Estimates of future revenue and expenditure flows used in techniques of capital appraisal involve risk and uncertainty.

8 As well as appraising projects from the point of view of the expected financial return to be obtained from the investment, there can be other benefits in terms of other dimensions of performance. Gains may be made in quality and delivery performance, for instance. The ability to respond more flexibly and quickly to customer demands are further benefits that might be sought. The question arises as to whether these benefits can be quantified in terms of extra sales volume. If the answer is in the affirmative, then they can be treated in a conventional way by examining their effect in terms of profitability and return on capital. Others argue that these benefits are 'intangibles' and cannot be appraised in this normal way. Investment decisions, if this latter view is accepted, seem to require an 'act of faith' rather than an analytical approach. This debate is one that has been raised especially in connection with projects that involve investment in advanced manufacturing technology (AMT).[17]

9 Assessment of quality and performance in connection with capital items raises concern for features such as reliability, maintainability and durability.

10 Additional requirements in the 'package' to be acquired might include:
   – installation and commissioning services
   – maintenance services
   – training of operators
   – supply of spares
   – the provision of technical data about spare parts lists and specifications.

11 The expected rate of obsolescence is a factor that might affect the analysis of options for the speed of payback and the method of acquisition.

12 Project management techniques may be used to organise teams and to schedule activities for capital investment plans. Purchasing and supply management personnel may be included and their acquisition tasks will be built into the overall programme. Indeed, some of these tasks are likely to be on the 'critical path' and will help to determine the total leadtime of the project.

Methods of investment appraisal

Decision makers are faced with making a choice as to which of several investment appraisal methods to employ in analysing and comparing investment options. A key difference in the techniques to be described is that two take account of the time value of money and two do not. The 'payback period' and the 'return on capital employed (ROCE)' approaches do not, but it is embodied in the more recent approaches of the 'discounted cash flow (DCF) yield or internal rate of return' and the 'net present value (NPV)'.

The DCF and NPV approaches accept the notion that the real value of money received today is worth more than money received at some point of time in the future. Money that a firm possesses today could be invested and earn a rate of interest and, thus, increase in amount as time passes. The principle of compound interest is involved in this notion. The reverse process is to consider what a sum of money, received in the future, is worth today and then to use the opposite to the principle of compound interest, which is 'discounting'. Discount tables can be used when applying this approach.

Payback period

This approach measures the number of years a project takes to generate sufficient net income to cover its capital cost. If a choice has to be made between competing projects, this method will favour the one with the shortest payback period. Guidelines for selection might also set a maximum acceptable period and anything over this would be automatically rejected. This maximum could be varied in line with different degrees of risk associated with the project.

This approach ignores differences in the timing of earnings prior to the payback date and does not take into account the changing value of money in different time periods. It also ignores earnings after the payback period.

Return on capital employed (ROCE)

The ROCE method calculates the average annual net earnings throughout the estimated life of the project and it is expressed as a percentage of capital employed. Choice between competing projects would be based on the alternative that offered the highest rate of return. The rate of return can also be compared to the cost of capital. Some firms may wish to set a minimum ROCE rate which is acceptable – sometimes referred to as the 'hurdle rate'. It might also be pointed out that some critics argue that firms in the United Kingdom and, perhaps, in the United States as well, are expected to earn a higher rate of return than firms in Japan and Germany. The financial environments in the latter countries are said to be different and to demand a lower rate of return. If the argument of the critics is accepted, then some good projects might be rejected in the former countries.

The ROCE method does not take into account the timing of cashflows and it ignores variations in the earnings rates in different periods.

Discounted cashflow yield or rate of return

The DCF yield or rate of return is the rate of interest, when used as a discount factor, which makes the present value of the expected net inflows and outlays exactly equal. Projects that give a yield that is higher than the cost of the finance or of the funds may be accepted. If a choice has to be made between competing schemes, then it can be based on a comparison of the yields and the one with the highest would be preferred. This approach does reflect the timing of cashflows.

Net present value (NPV)

A minimum acceptable rate of return is selected and this rate is used to discount the net cash inflows. If the sum of the present values of the cash inflows exceed the cost of the investment, then the project could be accepted. The choice of the interest rate is clearly crucial in this method. The method does reflect the timing of the cashflows.

It can be seen, in conclusion, that personnel involved in the acquisition of capital requirements have to cope with different circumstances and apply different knowledge and skills, compared with those in other fields in purchasing and supply management. Managing the acquisition of capital items is an important aspect in projects which involve capital expansion or major re-equipment programmes and which are concerned with the implementation of strategic plans.

SUMMARY

In this chapter the main message has been to say that the development of strategic plans for the supply of key requirements has to consider carefully the cost implications, along with other aspects of value relating to quality and delivery etc. A knowledge of costing processes and the costs of all relevant activities in the supply chain is necessary if costs are to be managed effectively. Processes of establishing prices for strategic purchases are increasingly becoming cost based or target based, and knowledge plays a vital part in price negotiations.

It is also clear from discussions in this chapter, as well as in Chapter 6, on managing quality, that the maximum scope for exercising leverage on costs is at the design or pre-manufacturing stage. The involvement of buyers in 'upstream' activities and, also, the inclusion of suppliers' representatives in product design and development processes enables a thorough investigation to be made of ideas that can contribute to the formation of the most effective and efficient supply plans. Such studies can embrace total cost considerations.

Proactive supply strategies can make a significant contribution to the competitive edge of companies and to the ability of all organisations to obtain value for money. Cost is an important dimension of performance in supply chains and it is a factor that needs to be managed on an integrated basis. The level of effectiveness in achieving this depends partly on the relationships that exist between buyers and other functions in the same firm. Success also depends on the relationships between buyers and vendors and on the 'modus operandi' that are developed to implement agreed strategies.

NOTES AND REFERENCES

1 Lamming, R. *Beyond Partnership: Strategies for Innovation and Lean Supply*, Prentice-Hall (1993), Chapter 6.

2 Howell, R.A. and Sakurai, M. 'Management Accounting (and Other) Lessons from the Japanese', *Management Accounting (USA)*, December 1992, pp. 28–34.

3 Houlihan, J. 'Exploiting the Industrial Supply Chain', in Mortimer, J. (editor). *Logistics in Manufacturing*, IFS Publications (1988).

4 *See* a listing of the 14 points for management, proposed by W. Edwards Deming, one of the quality 'gurus', on p. 444 of Oakland, J.S. *Total Quality Management*, 2nd Edition, Butterworth-Heinemann (1993). The quotation is point four in this list.

5 Nix, A., McCarthy, P. and Dale, B.G. 'The Key Issues in the Development and Use of Total Cost of Ownership Model', 2nd Conference of the Purchasing and Education Research Group (1992).

6 *See* p. 30 of Howell, R.A. and Sakurai, M. (1992), as mentioned in note 2 above.

7 Presentations of Kaplan's views can be found in, for example, the following references:
Johnson, H.J. and Kaplan, R.S. *Relevance Lost: The Rise and Fall of Management Accounting*, Harvard Business School Press (1987).
Kaplan, R.S. 'Yesterday's Accounting Undermines Production', *Harvard Business Review*, July–August 1984, pp. 95–101.
Kaplan, R.S. 'One System Isn't Enough', *Harvard Business Review*, January–February 1988, pp. 61–6.

8 *See* p. 95 of Kaplan, R.S. (1984), as mentioned in note 7 above.

9 Miller, J.G. and Vollman, T.E. 'The Hidden Factory', *Harvard Business Review*, September–October 1985, pp. 142–50.

10 Morgan, M. 'Is ABC really a need, not an option?', *Management Accounting (UK)*, September 1993, pp. 26–7.

11 Primrose, P. 'Is Anything Really Wrong with Cost Management?', *Logistics Supplement* of *Purchasing and Supply Management*, June 1993, pp. 21–3.

12 This phrase is taken from:
Drucker, P. 'The Emerging Theory of Manufacturing', *Harvard Business Review*, May–June 1990, pp. 94–102.

13 Innes, J. and Falconer, M. 'Managing with Activity Based Costing', *Professional Engineering*, July–August 1991, pp. 20–1.

14 Baily, P., Farmer, D., Jessop, D. and Jones, D. *Purchasing, Principles and Management*, 7th Edition, Pitman Publishing (1994), Chapter 9, pp. 157–8.
Dobler, D.W., Burt, D.N. and Lee, L. *Purchasing and Materials Management*, 5th Edition, McGraw-Hill (1990), Chapter 13, pp. 267–75.

15 *See* pp. 199–201 of Lamming, R. (1993), as mentioned in note 1 above.

16 This and the next quotation are taken from p. 3 of a Rover Group document, entitled 'Best Practice with Suppliers . . . A Supplier's Guide'.

17 Harrison, M. *Advanced Manufacturing Technology Management*, Pitman Publishing (1990), Chapters 9 and 10.
Primrose, P. 'Is Anything Really Wrong with Cost Management?', *Logistics Supplement* of *Purchasing and Supply Management*, February 1993, pp. 19–21.

CHAPTER 9

Strategic management of supplier relationships

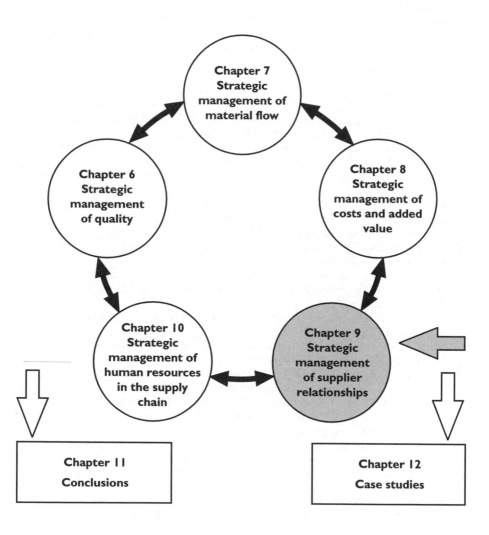

INTRODUCTION

Never before in the history of man's industrial endeavours, has the value of building effective and responsive relationships between suppliers and customers been more crucial to the survival of free-market enterprise than today.[1]

This might appear to be a somewhat exaggerated claim to make, referring as it does to the free-market enterprise approach as a whole, but many might support such a claim at the level of individual firms. A more measured statement, concerning relationships between suppliers and customers, was made by Sir Derek Hornby, Director General, Partnership Sourcing Ltd:

> Over the past decade the best UK enterprises have adopted the practice of continuous improvement. Partnership sourcing builds on previous innovations such as total quality management, just in time and electronic data interchange to help businesses to become more competitive in global markets . . . Like most good ideas the concept (i.e. partnership sourcing) is simple: that customers and suppliers working together as a team can drive down total cost, improve quality and speed products to market far more effectively than the same people working as adversaries.[2]

Interest in partnership relationships has been stimulated by the effect of Japanese imports and Japanese transplant firms and the attention given to ideas that Japanese firms were perceived to be adopting. The revolutionary nature of changes in the relationships between suppliers and customers is seen graphically in the following quotation relating to automotive industry:

> Changes in the relationship between motor manufacturers and their suppliers are likely to have a particularly profound effect on the automotive industry in the UK and the rest of Europe. According to Hoffman and Kaplinsky,[3] altered contractual relations represent the most thorough-going organisational change the industry has yet seen since Sloan's reforms in GM (General Motors) in the early 1920s.[4]

These statements underline the significance of the changing approaches towards buyer-supplier relationships and an aim of this chapter will be to examine a range of issues and questions that arise with regard to the strategic management of this interface. Co-makership is another term that is broadly synonymous with partnership, and the kind of relationship, labelled by either of these terms, is profoundly different to traditional practices. Practitioners, whether acting as buyers or sellers, need to adopt a radically different perspective and a different set of skills and techniques in implementing the partnership approach.

Figure 9.1 provides a list of topics to be discussed in this chapter.

OBJECTIVES OF THIS CHAPTER

An indication of the main content of this chapter has been given already, but the more specific objectives are as follows:

1 To assess the strategic features of buyer-supplier relationships
2 To examine a range of models of buyer-supplier relationships

3 To study aspects of managing buyer-supplier relationships
4 To consider methods of assessing and selecting suppliers
5 To investigate the content and style of agreements
6 To analyse some strategic sourcing issues

---

1 Strategic features of buyer-supplier relationships
- long-term relationships
- interactive nature
- adversarial versus partnership approaches

2 Models of buyer-supplier relationships
- control strategies
- types of exchange situation
- life cycle models

3 Managing buyer-supplier relationships
- the approach of Partnership Sourcing Ltd
- interactive nature
- portfolios
- competitive tendering and partnerships in the public sector

4 Assessing and selecting suppliers
- the process of assessment
- assessment and supplier development
- selection criteria
- 'best customers'

5 Content and style of agreements
- partnership agreements

6 Strategic sourcing issues
- single versus multi-sourcing
- rationalisation of the supply base
- tiers in the supply chain
- using foreign sources of supply
- reciprocity and countertrade

Fig 9.1 Supplier relationship topics

STRATEGIC FEATURES OF BUYER-SUPPLIER RELATIONSHIPS

It is sometimes said that 'you get the suppliers you deserve'. The message contained within this saying is that supplier performance, in part at least, reflects both the way customers treat their suppliers and the expectations customers have of them. It can be argued that many companies in Europe and North America failed to get the best supplier performance because of both these factors. This is being revealed more clearly in recent years as awareness of Japanese achievements become more widespread. Even in cases where buyers had power to exercise considerable influence over suppliers, it seems that it was not necessarily used to best advantage. Richard Lamming, for example, describes how pressures to secure quick price reductions in the automotive industry led to car assemblers squeezing the margins of component suppliers and driving some of them into liquidation.[5] There is a danger that conditions of recession in the 1990s are bringing back similar short-term pressures and consequent harmful long-term effects in supply performance.

Business Week, for example, reported that General Motors in America used Draconian and arbitrary methods to achieve price cuts in its contracts with suppliers.[6] Though significant savings were made in the short term, the drawbacks of policies adopted only became apparent with the passage of time. Bringing new suppliers on stream quickly, in response to lower bids, produced quality problems and production delays. The practice of passing on technical information concerning proprietary parts to competitors has generated a lack of trust on the part of suppliers and a reluctance to co-operate on new technological projects.

Long-term relationships

Interest in partnerships is based upon a long-term perspective of buyer-supplier relationships and it implies, therefore, the adoption of a strategic role and approach for purchasing and supply management. This is in contrast with traditional purchasing practices which emphasised the short-term, transactional or clerical nature of purchasing work. Strategic perceptions of the supply task are shaped by concern for issues such as the configuration and co-ordination of activities in the supply chain. The selection of suppliers and management of the supply base, together with the management of relationships between buyers and suppliers, also figures on the strategic agenda.

The continued contact between buyer and supplier organisations in a long-term relationship creates an enabling mechanism through which they can work together and develop arrangements for the supply of requirements tailored to the needs of the purchaser. Such arrangements may involve, in effect, the procurement of design and manufacturing services, the output of which happens to be flows of particular products from time to time, as required. The relationship should involve joint planning activities that cover different time horizons. A long-term strategic perspective is needed as a framework for medium-term, tactical and short-term operational planning processes.

The interactive nature of relationships

While the partnership might provide a vehicle through which supplies of goods and services can be planned and controlled and through which innovations can be fostered to enhance future performance, the relationship has to be perceived from the point of view of its social and cultural nature, as well as its technical and commercial facets. Communications can take place between a variety of representatives from different functions of both buyer and seller organisations. Each person brings to the relationship different personal characteristics, experiences and knowledge. Participants' interpretations of requirements and reactions to other people will be made in the light of the values and intentions that they have formed. Previous experiences and the evaluation of the outcomes of earlier interactions will also affect the pattern of development of the relationship. The dynamics of the interactions will also involve forces of both common and conflicting interests and power-dependence relationships. As the relationship progresses, so expectations and behavioural patterns will be formed. The interpersonal nature of the relationships places a premium on the need for people to develop the appropriate skills in working with and through other people.

The 'Interaction Model', as developed by the Industrial Marketing & Purchasing Group, indicates the complexity involved in analysing and understanding buyer-supplier relationships.[7] It is suggested that there are four elements in the exchange process as parties in the relationship make contact. These are said to be product or service exchange, information exchange, financial exchange and social exchange. In this model there are four sets of variables:

1 Variables describing the 'parties' involved, both as organisations and as individuals
2 Variables describing the 'elements and processes of interaction'
3 Variables describing the 'environment' within which the interaction takes place
4 Variables describing the 'atmosphere' affecting and affected by the interaction[8]

Other references to behavioural aspects of buyer-supplier relationships were introduced in Chapter 1.[9]

The metaphor of a life cycle, which is commonly used in relation to products, can also be used to assist in understanding the task of managing relationships. The relationship between a buyer and a vendor can be seen to have stages between initially starting it through to a possible terminal point at which it might cease. This aspect will be developed in more detail in a later section of this chapter. Strategies for managing relationships can identify different actions for each stage.

Adversarial versus partnership approaches

The partnership model for buyer-supplier relationships is often contrasted with that of the adversarial model. The latter is characterised as being of an 'arm's length nature', which relies on formal paperwork communications rather than personal contact. It is seen essentially as a short-term, competitive sourcing approach, which can lead to frequent changes of suppliers. Outcomes of adversarial or competitive behaviour are perceived in terms of 'win-lose' results, whereas the partnership model is held up as possessing the possibility of a 'win-win' outcome – both sides winning simultaneously, through the adoption of problem-solving approaches, for example, to resolve any difficulties. The characteristics associated with the two models might be summarised as indicated in Figs 9.2 and 9.3.

1	Arm's length, formal communication approach
2	Adversarial attitudes
3	Lack of trust
4	Aggressive, 'win-lose' approach in negotiations – price focus
5	Emphasis on individual transactions and short-term contracts
6	Little direct contact and involvement in design activities
7	Reluctance to share information
8	Reliance on goods inward inspection and defect rectification

Fig 9.2 The adversarial model

1	A high frequency of both formal and informal communications
2	Co-operative attitudes
3	A trusting relationship
4	Problem-solving, 'win-win' negotiating styles, with an emphasis on managing total costs
5	Long-term business agreements
6	Open sharing of information by multi-functional teams
7	Vendor certification and defect prevention approaches

Fig 9.3 The partnership model

However, comparison of the two contrasting models in Fig 9.2 and Fig 9.3 oversimplifies the range of possible sourcing relationships, and the next section will examine this issue in more detail. For the moment, the main implication of recognising this diversity is that purchasing and supply management can involve managing a portfolio of different types of relationship. Personnel in the function need to be flexible in their choice and in their approaches to suppliers. Choice of negotiating style, for instance, should be contingent on the particular sourcing strategy being adopted in relation to a particular supplier.

A detailed comparative study of relationships, conducted by Sako,[10] throws further light on to this complex topic. This investigation into inter-firm relationships in Britain and Japan suggested that they could be represented as a continuum between two ideal types:

1 Arm's-length contractual relation (ACR), and
2 Obligational contractual relation (OCR).

The features of these two types bear some resemblance to the points listed in Figs 9.2 and 9.3. However, the work is significant for its analysis of the concept of 'trust' in the context of buyer-seller relationships.

Trust

Trust is a state of mind, an expectation held by one trading partner about another, that the other behaves or responds in a predictable and mutually acceptable manner.[11]

Mari Sako went on to suggest that there are three types of trust, namely:

1 **'Contractual trust'** – both parties keep their promises
2 **'Competence trust'** – both partners can perform their role competently
3 **'Goodwill trust'** – mutual expectation of open commitment to each other or the willingness to do more than is formally expected.

She argued that contractual trust and competence trust are present in both ACR and OCR relations, but it is the presence of goodwill trust that is significant for an OCR type of relationship. As a final comment on this work it should be pointed out that the empirical research was carried out in relation to a theoretical discussion which analysed ideas of transaction cost economics, relational contract theory, sociological approaches to networks and networks in management strategy.

As firms develop a strategic role for purchasing and supply management, so the implementation of that role is likely to lead to closer working relationships between buyer and supplier organisations and their representatives. The way in which these relationships are managed on an interpersonal basis can be expected to have a material effect on the results obtained. Co-operation between the parties within a partnership model, it is suggested, will produce greater benefits than the traditional adversarial model.

MODELS OF BUYER-SUPPLIER RELATIONSHIPS

It was suggested in the previous section that the apparent choice between an adversarial model and a partnership model is an oversimplification of the possibilities. At best, they should be regarded as 'ideal types', in which each is characterised by certain sets of features. They may provide some normative direction for practitioners in establishing and managing relationships. Such 'ideal types' may also give some guidance in analysing a particular relationship, but they do not give a complete account of what might be observed in reality.

It can be stated, however, that the guidelines set out in *Making Partnership Sourcing Happen* are more extensive and, therefore, more helpful, than most simple presentations of the models. It might also be pointed out that Douglas MacBeth and his colleagues have developed a set of management aids to audit buyer/supplier relationships and to develop action plans to improve them.[12]

Another important study of customer-vendor relationships is that of Richard Lamming, which was carried out in the automotive industry.[13] In his work, he used a list of nine factors to analyse the relationships, as given in Fig 9.4.

I	The nature of competition in the components supply market
2	The basis on which sourcing decisions are made
3	The role played by data and information transfer, and the approach towards managing it jointly
4	The attitude to capacity planning and the approach to managing it jointly
5	Delivery practices
6	The manner in which price changes are dealt with
7	The attitude towards product quality and the approach towards managing it
8	The role of research and development (products and services) in the relationship, and the approach towards managing it
9	The level of the pressure in the relationship

Fig 9.4   Factors in Lamming's approach

The use of the framework in Fig 9.4 as a guide for investigations led to the emergence of a four-phase model of customer-supplier relations. This illustrated the nature of transitions in relationships in the automotive industry since 1975. The phases are: traditional, stress, resolved and partnership/Japanese.[14] Subsequently, a fifth phase has been proposed – the lean supply model. This, it is suggested, is the way in which relationships should be developed. A key difference between this and the fourth phase concerns the power-dependence relationship between the component suppliers and the car assembly companies. The partnership phase is one in which power lies in the hands of buyers, and although co-operation is sought and obtained from suppliers, Richard Lamming argues that it is not collaboration between equals.

A study undertaken by the National Economic Development Council (NEDC) also revealed that the extent to which the normative partnership model had been adopted varies.[15] It pointed out that large customers can exercise significant influence on the type of relationship they wanted. This study produced a classification of buyer-supplier relations in engineering as:

1 Co-operative
2 Trying to become so
3 Restricted in co-operation
4 Competitive.

Control strategies

A picture that is emerging from the discussions is that the basic notion of a partnership in the context of buyer-supplier relationships tends to imply equality of power between the parties. In supply chains such as the automotive industry, it has been demonstrated that the balance of power may be tipped in the direction of the car assemblers. Al Rainnie made a similar point when studying small firms and the demands of customers for just in time deliveries.[16] The supposed co-operative relationships, based on trust and mutual concern, were found to be lacking.

Peter Ring and Andrew Van de Ven suggest that there are different forms of transaction and that they are different in terms of several distinguishing characteristics.[17] They identify four forms of transaction (*see* Fig 9.5).

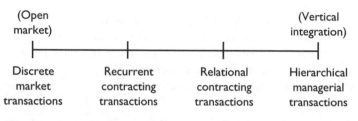

Fig 9.5 Types of transaction

A way forward in considering relationships is, thus, to identify different exchange situations. These may be regarded as a spectrum of possibilities (as in Fig 9.5), between the one extreme of open market transactions and the other extreme of direct hierarchical or managerial control of internal operations (i.e. vertical integration). In between are various forms of partnership, sometimes referred to as relational or obligational contracting.[18]

Open market forces are constrained or suspended by such bilateral agreements. It is also worth considering vertical integration as having two sub-categories, because there are different relationship problems between the situation of intra-firm trading and the direct internal operations of the same organisational unit. Intra-firm trading involves two quasi-independent units – divisions or subsidiary companies. Relationships between the supplier and customer divisions may vary depending on how far the supplier unit is expected to compete with external vendors to win the business. A supply source managed as a joint venture, with shared equity, adds great permanency to a partnership relationship and comes closer to a position of vertical integration.

Types of exchange situation

The following list indicates the range of exchange situations. Each should be regarded as an 'ideal type', in the sense described earlier in the chapter:

1 Market/competitive – single transactions
2 Market/competitive – period contracts
3 Partnership – supplier dominant/buyer dependent
4 Partnership – equal balance of power

5 Partnership – buyer dominant/supplier dependent
6 Joint venture – a partnership cemented by joint ownership
7 Hierarchy – intra-firm trading
8 Hierarchy – direct internal control

Market/competitive situations

In both of the market/competitive situations, contact between buyer and supplier is limited and tends to be on a formal basis, using documents as the main form of communication. Period contracts co-ordinate repeat business and secure special terms, such as special prices, discounts or rebates, based on the total trade expected during the stated period. Standing orders, blanket contracts, systems contracts and group contracts are typical of the mechanisms which might be used to formalise the arrangements. However, the length of time in the agreements will tend to be no more than a year and renewal procedures will be implemented as the expiry date of the old contract approaches. A change of supplier after each order or contract is possible as there is no clear intention necessarily to prolong the relationship. Goods and services being purchased are likely to be standardised and with limited differentiation between the products offered by competing suppliers. In both cases, buyers will tend to rely on securing bids or quotations from competing suppliers in the process of developing agreements.

Especially in the private sector, buyers may also enter into negotiations with one or more of the potential suppliers. Thus, relationships in such cases will be strengthened because of an increase in contacts between the parties not only in forming contracts, but also during the implementation of the agreements.

The practice of using period contracts, therefore, can lead to close working relationships between buyer and seller organisations. Indeed, trading links may continue year after year and may appear to take on some of the characteristics of a partnership. However, two aspects may be missing. First, there is no long-term commitment on the part of the parties involved and, second, the communication between them is more limited and does not involve the close multi-functional interactions, typical of a full partnership arrangement.

Partnerships

A definition of a partnership that provides a clear distinction is provided by Partnership Sourcing Ltd:[19]

> Partnership sourcing is a commitment by both customers and suppliers, regardless of size, to a long-term relationship based on clear, mutually-agreed objectives to strive for world-class capability and competitiveness.

It can be claimed that the commitment to a partnership transcends any single agreement for the supply of a particular product and contains the will to develop a variety of business arrangements in the future. Generally, the goods or services to be exchanged, as well as the logistics arrangements, will be specially tailored to meet the needs of the immediate customer and of the supply chain as a whole. Both parties invest resources in meeting the specific needs of the partnership as a concrete demonstration of their commitment.

In taking note of power-dependency relationships, it is possible to distinguish the three types of partnership situation, although some people might like to dispute whether the relationship can be a genuine partnership, if it is dominated by one of the parties. It depends, perhaps, on how the dominant partner chooses to use that power and how far trust and mutual interests are pursued.

This discussion of control strategies and the relationships associated with them can be brought to a close by focusing on the possible purchasing strategies. Campbell, for instance, differentiates between three purchasing strategies.[20] These are competitive, co-operative and command. Some suppliers might say that the rhetoric of a co-operative approach is used to disguise a command strategy!

Life cycle models of buyer-supplier relationships

A life cycle perspective of buyer-supplier relationships recognises that they develop and change over time. If this premise is accepted, then management of the relationship may also need to be varied at different stages in the life cycle.

David Ford considered that relationship development between buyer and seller can be examined from the point of view of five stages.[21] As the relationship progresses, so experiences of each other's performance help to reduce uncertainty and social exchanges increase trust between the parties. Also, norms, values and working methods are brought closer in line with each other as time passes and as each makes adaptations to the other. He identified these stages as being the following:

1 Pre-relationship stage
2 Early stage
3 Development stage
4 Long-term stage
5 Final stage

It should be noted that the fifth stage is not meant as the ending of the relationship. On the contrary, it is the relationship in its most developed form. In the scheme proposed by Dwyer, Schurr and Oh, however, the life cycle is brought to a close in the last phase.[22] Their scheme is shown in Fig 9.6.

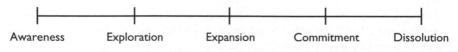

Awareness   Exploration   Expansion   Commitment   Dissolution

Fig 9.6 Relationship life cycle

The nature of buyer-supplier relationships and the behaviour of partnerships are far more complex in practice than some of the simpler prescriptive models indicate. However, the level of knowledge about managing relationships and the awareness of the skills and techniques required are both increasing. Rosabeth Kanter[23] draws a comparison with courting and getting engaged, where two people are concerned.

MANAGING BUYER-SUPPLIER RELATIONSHIPS

Making Partnership Sourcing Happen provides useful guidelines for both buyers and suppliers.[24] It is worth noting that initiatives in establishing partnership relationships may be taken, of course, by suppliers as part of their marketing strategies. Martin Christopher, Adrian Payne and David Ballantyne suggest how marketing is evolving from a transaction-oriented approach into relationship marketing.[25] Relationship marketing is characterised in their book by features that complement those normally presented in purchasing literature:

1 Focus on customer retention
2 Orientation on product benefits
3 Long time scale
4 High customer service emphasis
5 High customer commitment
6 High customer contact
7 Quality is the concern of all[26]

Buyers, therefore, may find themselves in a position in which they have to respond to overtures from suppliers. However, the perspective adopted in what is to follow is that of the purchaser taking the strategic initiative.

The approach recommended by Partnership Sourcing Ltd

The scheme recommended for customers in *Making Partnership Sourcing Happen* is as below.

1 **Which markets and which products/services?** The initial task in answering this first question involves the strategic analysis of the procurement requirements needed to match the product and marketing strategies of the business. Then the key products and services need to be identified as candidates for partnership sourcing. The main criteria influencing selection should be: high expenditure items ('A' class in a Pareto distribution), high risk, complexity in terms of design, production and innovation.
2 **Sell the idea.** It may be necessary to sell the idea of a partnership both internally and to the potential partners. The support of internal functions needs to be enlisted. As regards promoting the policy with the suppliers, buyers need to be able to appreciate and point out the benefits to be gained from a long-term association. Among the benefits for them is the promise of future business that enables plans to be drawn up and investments to be made. The

fruits of collaboration with regard to product development, cost reduction programmes and other improvement activities contribute to the success of the partner firm.

3 **Choose your first partners.** The recommended steps are set out in the context of developing a partnership policy for the first time, but most of the points also apply to implementing the policy as an ongoing programme. Potential suppliers of the key products that have been targeted need to be identified. Criteria by which to assess them have to be drawn up and applied. The extent to which the firms are willing and able to put into practice the partnership philosophy must also be evaluated.

4 **Define what you both want from the partnership.** Tangible objectives need to be jointly agreed to establish a clear purpose for the partnership. Specific objectives are likely to differ for each situation, depending on what are perceived to be the priority issues. Product development, cost reduction, improvements in logistical arrangements and a lower defect rate are some of the possible items for consideration. Partners are advised to show their commitment to the arrangement by entering into a simple formal agreement. However, as the relationship starts to take shape, other less tangible objectives, such as establishing trust and teamwork, will also require attention. Norms and values emerge from the interactions as the methods and style of working together begin to crystallise and confidence grows in sharing information.

5 **Refine and develop.** As a partnership programme is introduced by an organisation for the first time, the first few projects with suppliers act as learning vehicles. Reviews can be undertaken so that lessons learnt can help to refine approaches for a more general application of the policy.

Attention should be paid to a cautionary note about the partnership approach: 'Some of the difficulty with the philosophy is that there are no precise and universal rules. A partnership should be tailormade for each partner and/or commodity or service purchased'.[27] The progress in the development of a particular partnership needs to be regularly monitored by those involved, often a multi-functional buying team in the customer company.

The interactive nature of partnerships

The extent to which the proposed strategy of the party taking the initiative in trying to set up a partnership is implemented is partly in the hands of the other party. Steps to promote and develop the relationship, together with the negotiation approaches employed, need to be adapted to the responses of the other party.

Suppliers accustomed to traditional adversarial attitudes and negotiating stances may be suspicious and reluctant to change, at least at first. There do appear to be grounds for this apprehension, in the light of some experiences, in which a dominant party has used an apparent partnership policy as a smokescreen for more exploitative and dictatorial approaches. Some suppliers may retain fundamental objections to the more open methods of the partnership philosophy and prefer not to change their ways. Japanese transplant firms in the United Kingdom, for example, have found that some indigenous suppliers have refused to adapt and co-operate with their methods.[28]

Not all firms, therefore, will prove to be good candidates for a partnership arrangement. Buyers will need to decide whether there are more favourable alternatives or whether they will need to continue on a more traditional basis. The relative strength of a buyer's negotiating position in the supply market, together with the negotiating ability of the buyer, will determine whether resistance of a reluctant supplier can be overcome and a genuine conversion effected. Successful partnerships, of course, are likely to occur when both sides commit 'hearts and minds', as well as their formal pronouncements, to making them work. There is a danger that some suppliers may feel obliged to put on a front, to appear to accept the policy, but without genuine conviction.

Portfolios

The development of collaborative approaches between buyers and sellers is clearly occupying an important place in current programmes of change in relation to purchasing and supply management. There is no shortage of advocates, as is evident from further references.[29] Before we discuss portfolios as they concern relationships, two comments can be made. First, the depth and intensity of the relationship has been found to vary in empirical studies,[30] suggesting that there is a weakness in relying on any one single model of a 'partnership' as an account of behaviour. Second, a contingent approach to the selection of different patterns or types of relationships has emerged in the prescriptive literature. In other words, approaches which reflect more traditional adversarial relations may still be useful.

Cox,[31] for example, suggests that relationship strategies need to be based upon a 'portfolio' approach, with different approaches being selected for different situations. His justification is based partly on considerations of competences or capabilities, ideas reminiscent of discussions regarding business strategies, as a whole, and 'make or buy' studies, in particular. The depth of the buyer-supplier relationship, thus, might vary in relation to the level of reliance by the buyer on the supplier for the provision and development of specialist expertise. Within the proposed model, 'competitive leverage' might be exerted, in traditional fashion, where there is a market characterised by the presence of many alternative suppliers with similar levels of capability. Close collaboration, extending even to shared ownership, on the other hand, should be reserved for the development of significant 'complementary competences'.

Developments in the public sector in the United Kingdom, emphasising competitive tendering or market testing and the creation of internal markets, would appear to reinforce a philosophy of 'competitive leverage'. The next section will examine the debate as to whether there is, or should be, scope for fostering closer collaboration in the pursuit of value for money in this environment.

Competitive tendering and partnerships in the public sector

The concept of the buyer-supplier partnership is offered as a vehicle through which the procurement of supplies can be managed more effectively and efficiently. It would also appear to be an approach that is prohibited by a strict application of competitive tendering rules as required by the European Community directives and other public sector policy statements at local and central government level. Thus, concern for the prevention of unfair discriminatory practices and a predisposition for the encouragement of competition promote the desirability of operating clearly specified tendering procedures. A wish to meet requirements for accountability and the prevention of corruption and a need to satisfy the scrutiny of various auditing bodies add further support for such an arm's length trading approach. However, as stated in Chapter 1, value for money is also upheld as a goal for public sector procurement. In the light of the arguments advanced to support the partnership approach, the question has to be raised as to whether the competitive tendering approach offers the best way of achieving the value for money goal. Paradoxically, legislators are introducing measures to increase the use of competitive tendering in the public sector, influenced by the belief that competition is a key principle of the private sector, just as firms in the private sector are promoting the benefits of co-operation and collaboration.

Disadvantages of competitive bidding

In so far as short-term contracts and frequent switching of suppliers are the outcomes of competitive bidding procedures in the public sector, there can arise a number of disadvantages as a consequence. It can take time for both buyer and seller organisations to familiarise themselves with the details of each other's methods and requirements at the beginning of the contract period. Sellers have no real incentive to improve performance during the operation of contracts and, indeed, may let it deteriorate towards the end, if there is perceived to be a strong probability of not retaining the business. Perhaps of greater importance than these switching problems is the suggestion that the tendering procedures are too rigid in preventing discussions with suppliers to find the right solutions and in requiring specifications to be drawn up in advance. Further criticisms are associated with the administrative costs of operating the process and the length of time involved to complete arrangements. To sum up these points, it can be said that the competitive bidding approach seems to rule out the possibility of close co-operation between buyer and seller and, therefore, to lose the potential for improvement gains and better value for money, which the partnership relationship appears to offer.

Reservations about partnerships

Critics of the partnership approach for public sector organisations are concerned that the forces of competition will be reduced and complacency, inertia and inefficiency will arise. Especially in cases where the partnership is seen as involving single sourcing, open relationships and a long-term agreement, dependency and lack of security of supplies will possibly increase. Furthermore, the possibilities of increased scope for corruption and the influence of political interests on decisions, which are thought to accompany partnership relationships, might have a deleterious effect on the way in which public money is spent.

A mixed model

Andrew Erridge, having analysed the competitive bidding and partnership models, from the point of view of public procurement, suggested that there is middle ground between the two extremes – a mixed model.[32]

> Thus competition would be used, as required by EC Directives, to select suppliers, who would be subject to pre-tender evaluation. Non-discriminatory selection criteria could be developed emphasising the compatibility of potential suppliers with the contracting organisation, for instance the potential for EDI links, as well as a balanced mix of value for money criteria using the 'most economically advantageous offer' formula. During the period of the contract, partnership could be effectively developed, with an emphasis on continuously improving the quality of the goods or services delivered to internal or external customers.

ASSESSING AND SELECTING SUPPLIERS

> Standard criteria of quality, price, and delivery are necessary-but-not-sufficient conditions for consideration.[33]

This quotation by Robert Spekman captures the essence of the problem with regard to the selection of suppliers as long-term partners. The standard criteria are appropriate for short-term, transactional purchasing, but they are inadequate when searching for partners. For the latter purpose, factors that determine long-term future performance and the potential for innovation and improvement need to be identified. Less tangible issues such as commitment, openness and trust are also involved if the partnership is to succeed. The propensity of firms to develop and apply these attributes is not easy to assess.

The process of assessment

The process of assessing suppliers may generally have three elements. First, potential suppliers may be asked by the buyer to complete a self-assessment document. This can be designed to include questions that will provide much of the basic information that is being sought. A follow-up visit by a buying team can both check out the honesty and realism of the information provided and carry out its own investigations. Finally, the total findings need to be evaluated and a decision made with regard to selection or rejection as a partner. Most schemes in practice attempt to quantify findings through the introduction of rating scales for the factors being assessed to make the process as objective as possible. In addition, weightings can be applied to reflect evaluations of the relative importance of the factors.

Assessment and supplier development

In the cases of those suppliers who subsequently become partners, further assessments on an intermittent basis can map out progress being made and can track the effects of improvement programmes. Supplier development, in other words, can be closely linked to the process of regular assessment. Areas requiring improvement can be identified, action plans drawn up and progress monitored. The linking of assessment systems to development programmes underlines the dynamic nature of partnerships and emphasises that the overriding concern is (or should be) for progressive improvement of performance. Opportunities for improvement and appropriate techniques can be based on ideas discussed in Chapters 6, 7 and 8.

Selection criteria

Lisa Ellram has developed, as a result of empirical research, a list of issues that are seen to be relevant to strategic supplier selection.[34] Her views reinforce the viewpoint that long-term considerations need to embrace a wider range of attributes than short-term performance. She suggests that the following list of issues provides a focus for questionnaire designers:

1 **Financial issues**
   - economic performance
   - financial stability
2 **Organisational culture and strategy issues**
   - feeling of trust
   - management attitude/outlook for the future
   - strategic fit
   - top management compatibility
   - compatibility across levels and functions of buyer and supplier firms
   - supplier's organisational structure and personnel
3 **Technology issues**
   - assessment of current manufacturing facilities/capabilities
   - assessment of future manufacturing capabilities
   - supplier's design capabilities
   - supplier's speed in development
4 **Other factors**
   - safety record of the supplier
   - business references
   - supplier's customer base

Marybeth Pallas reported that General Motors had identified five critical areas which the GM visiting teams investigate and there is some correlation with the above list.[35] The five areas were:

1   Organisational effectiveness and commitment
2   Planning systems and documentation
3   Cost awareness, monitoring and reduction
4   Scheduling and delivery compliance
5   Technology capabilities and R&D

A third list for consideration is that suggested by Partnership Sourcing Ltd,[36] as follows:

1   Total quality management policy
2   BS 5750/ISO 9000 certification or equivalent
3   Implementing latest techniques, e.g. just in time, electronic data interchange, etc.
4   In-house design capability
5   Ability to supply locally or world-wide as appropriate
6   Consistent delivery performance, service standards and product quality
7   Attitude to total acquisition cost
8   Willingness to change, flexible attitude of management and workforce
9   Innovative suppliers of services

A recent survey, carried out and reported by *Purchasing* in the United States, indicated that 83 per cent of the largest purchasing organisations carried out formal supplier site audits and others were preparing to do so.[37] The main purposes were said to be to facilitate communication with suppliers, identify candidates for certification and partnership and drive product/process improvement within the supply base. Concern was expressed about the duplication of efforts by buyers and the time and expense incurred by vendors in hosting customer visits. However, proprietary systems of audit developed by buyer organisations were believed to be more comprehensive than any more general third-party assessments, and, therefore, their use seemed to be both justified and necessary. Furthermore, audits in the context of forming partnerships are intended to support more than just approval activities.

Before leaving the topic of assessment, it is worth pointing out that efforts are being made to develop computer-based, decision support systems to aid the supplier selection process. Paul Cousins at Bath University has developed a Vendor Selection Model.[38] Charles Weber and Lisa Ellram, also, give an account of a multi-programming approach for supplier selection.[39] Such tools can aid the buyer's judgement and enable the analysis of possibilities to be conducted on a more flexible basis – by trying out different factor weightings, for example.

'Best customers'

It should be remembered that setting up a partnership is not necessarily a one-sided decision taken by buyers. Suppliers will also make assessments of their customers and make decisions of who their preferred customers are, with whom they wish to establish partnerships. Good customer practices play a part in creating customer supplier integration. Customer companies can develop and use survey instruments to gather information from suppliers in order to assess the attitudes and treatment they receive.

An American survey, reported by Patricia Moody, cited 'buying by price, rather than total value . . . as a trust destroyer'.[40] An effective buying organisation, as a partner, needs to be trusted by suppliers. Methods of involving suppliers and sharing of information with regard to requirements and schedules help to establish the climate. The manner of responses to supplier proposals for improvements and cost reduction ideas and feedback on performance also help to shape supplier perceptions of the degree of professionalism on the buying side. Consistency in approach and in the processes used help to forge a foundation of trust and sincerity. It might also be said that a customer's record with regard to payment in relation to agreed terms will affect the supplier's evaluation of the customer.

CONTENT AND STYLE OF AGREEMENTS

The traditional transaction-based model of purchasing uses a strict legalistic approach in the formation of orders and contracts. Terms and conditions are set out in detail in order to provide a clear statement of the requirements that the supplier is expected to meet in providing the goods or services that form the subject of the agreement. The rights and duties of both parties are expressly stated to ensure performance and to provide redress for injured parties if terms are not adhered to. Such a formal approach is more suited to an adversarial approach and relies on legal sanctions or the threat of legal sanctions to ensure compliance and to curb opportunistic or exploitative behaviour by one or both of the parties. It can be argued that the desire of the buyer to operate through legally binding contracts is a sign of a lack of trust in the seller. As such it appears to be out of harmony with the spirit of the partnership approach. On a more practical level, the legalistic approach is inappropriate for the implementation of the partnership approach, because the exact nature of goods or services to be provided in several years' time might not be known.

Partnership agreements

Although traditional legal contracts might not be desirable, it may nevertheless be sound practice to develop a simpler form of agreement that helps to cement the partnership relationship. Such an agreement can provide a clear sense of purpose by setting out a mutually agreed set of objectives and it can establish principles to guide the way both parties might be expected to operate in conjunction with each other. It can provide an outline of the contributions both parties are expected to make to the functioning of the partnership. Aspects with regard to confidentiality of information, exclusivity in the use of designs and special tooling and the basis for special capital investment undertaken by the supplier can be covered. A 'divorce clause' may also be framed to cover for the eventuality of the termination of the agreement. Essentially, however, the framework agreement, which establishes a basis for long-term co-operation, should be flexible enough for more specific objectives and plans to be developed to cover shorter-term periods of joint activity. Long-term contracts may be made from time to time to cover the specific agreement of plans for particular products. Sometimes an agreement may be based on buying the part for the period of the life of the product.

The goals for a partnership agreement might include a selection from the following:

1 Improved product quality – design and conformance aspects
2 Development of technical support capabilities in product and process engineering
3 Inventory reductions
4 Improved transport and distribution arrangements
5 Management of cost reduction activities
6 Improved administrative processes to reduce cost and time
7 Development of EDI systems

Additional aspects with regard to the adoption of partnership strategies will be dealt with in the next section, on strategic sourcing issues. The controversial topic of single versus multi-sourcing, as well as others, such as reduction of the supply base and tiering of the supply chain, will be addressed.

STRATEGIC SOURCING ISSUES

Two of the most important strategic sourcing issues from a purchasing and supply management point of view have been dealt with at some length already – 'make or buy' and 'buyer-seller relationships'. There are several others worthy of discussion. 'Make in' is clearly one sourcing strategy, but the focus of this section will be on external sourcing issues. The first is that of single versus dual or multiple sourcing – an evergreen topic, which has developed new facets as a result of the interest in partnerships and Japanese supply policies.

Single versus multi-sourcing

The traditional debate in western purchasing literature concerning the choice of single versus multi-sourcing options tended to focus, implicitly or explicitly, on short-term possibilities only. The balance of arguments perhaps favoured a multi-sourcing approach, if the volumes being purchased were big enough. As the partnership approach gained support, so claims that single sourcing offered the best prospects gained a hearing. Thus, as Ramsey and Wilson have pointed out, the literature tends to suggest that choice lies between short-term multi-sourcing, accompanied by adversarial relationships, and long-term single sourcing, associated with co-operative relationships.[41] However, Ramsey and Wilson argue that these western and eastern options are an oversimplification of the possibilities.

Part of the current impoverishment of thought in this area springs from the way sourcing and contracting strategies have become entangled in the Western and Eastern caricatures.[42]

Many advocates of long-term single sourcing have joined the bandwagon of supporters for this strategy, as a result of ideas gleaned in Japan, without fully evaluating the merits of doing so. Although the long-term single sourcing model is to be found in use in Japan, so also are long-term multi-sourcing arrangements.

Further treatment of this debate will first look at the advantages and disadvantages of the choices in the short term, and then take into account the 'pros and cons' of the long-term single versus multi-sourcing possibilities. It is assumed that buyers have a choice in both cases and that a sole sourcing situation, defined as only one possible supplier being available, does not exist.

Analysis of the short-term single sourcing option

The supposed advantages of single sourcing can be summarised as being:

1 Lower costs and prices, because of economies of scale arising from the allocation of the buyer's total requirements to the one supplier, one set of tooling costs and lower administration costs.
2 Improved communication and greater certainty for the supplier of the volume of business to be transacted.

Disadvantages, on the other hand, might be:

1 Lack of security of supply – 'all the eggs in one basket'.
2 The reduction of competitive pressure.

Analysis of the short-term multi-sourcing approach

Not surprisingly, the arguments here tend to counter the ones relevant to the alternative choice, and are as follows:

1 Increased security of supply – a point valued particularly in an earlier era of more turbulent industrial relations in the United Kingdom, when supplies from some industries were affected by 'wild cat' strikes, occurring with very little or no prior notice.
2 It is apparent that competitive pressures can be leveraged by varying the amount of business flowing to each of the contracted suppliers.
3 Contact with several suppliers enables buyers to compare performance and to keep in touch with developments in more than one supplier firm.

However, these advantages might be offset by the following disadvantages:

1 Loss of economies of scale, because of lower volumes of business received by each supplier. Extra tooling costs and administrative expenses arise through dealing with more suppliers.

2 Suppliers have increased uncertainty regarding expected levels of business, thus making planning more difficult.

3 Suppliers may be less willing to communicate about developments for fear of information being passed on to competitors.

Long-term single versus multi-sourcing options

Attention will first be turned towards the long-term, single sourcing strategy.

Long-term single sourcing

Many of the arguments for long-term single sourcing are the same as those advanced in support of co-operative, partnership relationships. Some are also arguments picked up from the analysis of the short-term debate and extended over a longer period of time.

The benefits of single sourcing over the long term have been summed up by the British Deming Association as being improved quality and lower costs.[43] Factors contributing to these outcomes were depicted as:

1 Reduced product variation. A single source of supply can improve processes and reduce variability. Products received from different production facilities, on the other hand, might be within the specification, but result in wider variation and less consistency.

2 Better planning and control arising from improved communications can permit improved logistics operations and less inventory.

3 Collaboration between buyer and supplier can trigger product and process innovations and provide a climate in which suppliers are prepared to make the necessary investments in fixed assets and people.

4 Working with the supplier on a long-term basis can reduce administrative costs and develop a closer understanding of the supplier's business.

Long-term multi-sourcing

Ramsey and Wilson argue that the main weakness of multi-sourcing is the uncertainty and lack of security induced in suppliers and the consequent difficulties of planning how to meet requirements. They suggest, therefore, that the award of long-term contracts, even on a multi-sourcing basis, 'bring certainty and a concomitant increase in supplier responsiveness and may be used to reward desirable performance and behaviour.[44]

The long-term nature of an agreement may, therefore, be more significant in encouraging a progressive relationship than the adoption of a single sourcing approach. The counter-argument is that some suppliers may resent and be cautious of working on the same products as competitors.

A mixed approach

Another solution is for buyers to manage groups of similar products with a mixed strategy. Particular parts within the group may be single sourced to gain the economies of scale and to reap the advantages of reduced product variation. However, a number of preferred suppliers may be used on a long-term basis and given some of the parts within the group total. This way may allow an element of credible, long-term competitive pressure to be retained, but at the same time provide a basis for co-operative efforts to be fostered. Buyers may also maintain contact with a wider range of developments and standards of performance.

As yet no simple rules exist to guide the selection of sourcing strategy with regard to single or multi-sourcing. There are many variables that can affect the circumstances in which firms operate and each case has to be treated on its merits.

Rationalisation of the supply base

The adoption of the partnership approach, aided in part by the frequent simultaneous acceptance of a long-term single sourcing policy, has led to many firms reducing the size of their supply base – at least for their strategic supplies. This is a process sometimes referred to as rationalisation of the supply base. We have already outlined the various general benefits of closer co-operation, and here highlight the impact of this process on the workload of the buying firm. There are fewer suppliers with whom arrangements and interactions have to be managed. Efforts can be concentrated on increasing the depth of knowledge of these preferred suppliers and on improving the quality of the supply arrangements. A more intensively used network of communications will tend to come into existence between different functions of supplier and customer organisations. This can make it difficult, however, for both parties to maintain a coherent team approach.

Another outcome of a reduced supplier base is of greater concern to suppliers. If a supplier fails to become a preferred supplier of a major customer, then business could be lost on a long-term basis.

Tiers in the supply chain

A sourcing issue that is gaining prominence in discussions of supply chain strategies is that of the structure of chains and the number of levels or tiers in it. Decisions to out-source parts and components and to buy assembled systems or complete subassemblies (rather than buying the parts and retaining assembly in-house) introduce another level into the supply chain. This approach helps to reduce further the size of the customer's immediate supply base. The role of the first-tier supplier is likely to change, as such a move is likely to place the main responsibility for investment in product and process developments on the supplier at this level. Each first-tier supplier will also have immediate responsibility for co-ordinating the required supply of inputs from the second-tier suppliers.

In so far as the customer company at the head of the chain can influence developments of its suppliers, views need to be developed regarding desired relationships both vertically and horizontally in the chain. The customer may still wish to retain influence through the first-tier suppliers on the operations and developments of the second tier and so on up the chain on the supply side. There is evidence to show how, for example, the automotive assembly companies have taken the initiative in stimulating quality improvement programmes at different levels. First-tier suppliers take on the main burden of co-ordinating the activities of second-tier suppliers, however. Second- and third-tier suppliers may often be small firms operating with lower wages and lower overheads. Stable linkages in the supply chain allow the introduction of flexibility of supply in line with demand, and improvement efforts can filter through the network (*see* Fig 9.7).

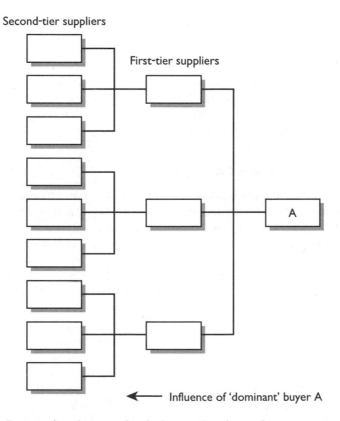

Fig 9.7 Influence in the supply chain – a dominant buyer

The horizontal dimension or, perhaps more appropriately, a diagonal one, raises the question of how far the customer firm wants its suppliers to work with the supply chains of its own competitors. Should the purchasing policy of the customer firm attempt to retain exclusivity of supply and foster these external resources for its own competitive advantage? The answer partly depends on the size and relative power of the first-tier suppliers, in particular. The amount of investment needed by the supplier to carry out research and development of new products and processes may also affect the situation. In some areas the amounts needed are so high that they are only feasible if the costs can be recouped from supplying output to a number of competing customers. On the other hand, key suppliers might be able to establish separate facilities or product lines, with each dedicated to the requirements of particular customers. The pure model, of co-operation within the supply chains of the end product manufacturer and rivalry between the competing chains of different end product manufacturers, may be only partly achievable and, indeed, only partly desirable.

In Japan there are additional ways through which networks of subcontracting suppliers can receive support. Peter Hines, for example, describes his findings about the operation of supplier associations ('kyoryoku kai') on a visit to Japan.[45] Toyota was the first company to develop one and the idea has now spread to others. He also reports how Llanelli Radiators adapted the idea of a supplier association to enable its supply chain to speed up developments and the diffusion of ideas through joint co-operative efforts.[46]

Another difference in the structuring of supply chains in Japan is that of the 'keiretsu', large business groups, such as Mitsui, Mitsubishi and Sumitomo. Relationships within them are given a tighter format through equity shareholdings, loans and intra-group trade.

Using foreign sources of supply

A region like the United Kingdom has of necessity to purchase certain natural raw materials and food products from overseas, because they are non-existent within its boundaries. For other products, naturally grown or manufactured, other reasons such as better prices, quality or delivery might be the main motivation for using foreign sources. More recently, additional considerations, such as the need to establish regional and global supply arrangements and the wish to source parts in countries to which the finished product is to be exported, have come into the reckoning.

The formation of policy guidelines to aid purchasing decisions in this area need to take into account the following issues, which may add to either higher costs or greater uncertainty (or both) by comparison with sourcing from within national markets. Clearly, the emergence and continued development of the Single Market in Europe is helping to remove or reduce some of these impediments. Among the factors are to be found the following:

1 **Communication problems**
   - different languages can cause communication and contractual difficulties;
   - longer distances affect the feasibility of personnel visits and make close co-operation more difficult;
   - different time zones affect direct telephone contacts;
   - the operation of different standards in different countries.
2 **Logistics problems**
   - more complex transport and distribution arrangements increase costs and add to uncertainty regarding delivery;

- longer distances may reduce the feasibility of operating on a just in time basis;
- problems in acquiring spares and replacements.

3 **Procedures and regulations**
- need to comply with import procedures and import licences for entry of goods into the country;
- need to apply appropriate rules on tariffs, levies, quotas and value-added taxes and take them into account when calculating total costs.

4 **Exchange rates**
- especially in an era of fluctuating exchange rates, the cost of the purchases may be unclear. Policies for sharing, carrying or avoiding such risks need to be established.

The degree to which firms have developed the expertise among personnel in purchasing and supply management to cope with these issues effectively and efficiently varies. Likewise, the extent to which support services exist to provide assistance, such as shipping departments, also differs.

Reciprocity and countertrade

Another issue that may affect sourcing considerations is the possibility that the firm's own customer may be in a position to supply goods or services as inputs into the firm's operations somewhere. The potential of a two-way flow of business needs to be analysed to assess the costs and benefits arising from such a pattern. In the case of foreign trade, further complications to this basic position can arise and several types of countertrade arrangements have come into existence. Problems in obtaining 'hard' currency to pay for imported goods have been the major factor in causing these developments. From a purchasing and supply management point of view, the main difficulty with these issues is that freedom of choice in selecting suppliers might be constrained by sales and marketing wishes to win sales contracts tied to reciprocal purchasing deals.

Basic reciprocity

Trading within an area that shares a common currency naturally takes away the main problem, which might be resolved through a countertrade arrangement. Thus, the analysis of this basic reciprocal trading question is more straightforward. It can be based on the assessment of the following three questions:

1 How necessary is it to have a reciprocal agreement with the customer in order to win the sales contract?
2 What are the benefits to the company of winning the sales contract?
3 What are the costs to the company of using this customer as a supplier, as opposed to exercising a free choice? In other words, are there any performance disadvantages, in relation to quality, delivery, price and innovation, for example, in using this supplier rather than the 'best' in the market?

The outcome of the analysis should be judged primarily on the criterion of what is best for the company. The interests of either the purchasing or the marketing/sales function in isolation should not be allowed to dominate the decision.

Countertrade

Customers' main motivation in buying goods or services tied to countertrade arrangements is to limit or eliminate the difficulty of acquiring 'hard' currency. Suppliers may wish to insist on the use of 'hard' currency in a normal one-way supply arrangement. The main forms of countertrade may be identified as follows:

1 **Barter** – swapping goods in a single contract, with no money exchanged (in the simplest case).
2 **Buyback** – in return, for example, for providing plant and equipment, the seller receives manufactured products from these facilities at a later date, or over a period of time, as the payment.
3 **Counterpurchase** – the seller, as a condition of the sale, undertakes to purchase goods or services from the country concerned, while receiving cash for the product being sold. There are two separate contracts in this case.
4 **Switch trading** – this method involves triangular trading between three countries to overcome the problem of imbalances of money flows between the countries involved.

From the point of view of purchasing and supply management, the same problem might exist as in simple reciprocal trading situations. Where the goods or services being received are for consumption in the purchaser's own business, there may be disadvantages by comparison with using other suppliers. In many cases, however, the goods being received in exchange for the goods being sold have to be sold to other customers in order to realise their value. Thus, there can be problems in making price agreements and in finding customers for these sales. Brokers might be used in setting up the arrangements. The timing of when the benefits will be received also has to be taken into account.

Firms should draw up policy guidelines on how the firm as a whole should handle basic reciprocal trading situations and the more complex countertrade variations. In particular, details should also cover the part that purchasing and supply management is expected to play and what procedures should be adopted.

SUMMARY

There can be no doubt that a major shift in thinking, with regard to both the nature and the management of buyer-supplier relationships, has occurred in the last part of the twentieth century. Changing world competitive conditions and the demand for enhanced standards of performance with respect to quality, delivery and costs of supply have led to visitors from the West travelling around the world in search of new ideas. Observations of Japanese ideas and practice have helped to widen the range of possible strategies available for selection. Emulation of Japanese practices by many leading western companies has brought about a degree of convergence. Japanese investment in operations in western countries has also been accompanied by Japanese sourcing policies and these are also influencing supplier developments. Often the policies are put into practice by indigenous employees who have been trained to do so. They act as role models and demonstrate that Japanese methods can be transferred into other countries, which do not share the same general cultural background.

The introduction of the partnership approach to buyer-supplier relationships has profound implications for personnel on both sides of the interface. The adoption of different attitudes towards each other and the application of different sets of skills and techniques are required. The link is increasingly being managed, too, by multi-functional teams. Underpinning the successful introduction of this approach, therefore, is a different set of cultural norms and values, compared to the traditional adversarial stance of those involved in short-term, opportunistic transactions. Programmes devised to implement partnering strategies, thus, must not only involve conventional training and development aspects, but also focus on the management of change processes. Such human resource issues, relevant to both buyer and vendor companies, will be investigated in Chapter 10.

Further effects of the introduction of partnership or co-makership strategies by purchasers can be seen on the profile of the supplier base and on the structure of supply chains. The number of suppliers is being reduced deliberately by many firms, as the potential for developing and implementing improvement programmes with a limited number of the best suppliers is felt to be superior. Opportunities to develop the performance of the supply chain in meeting the final customers' requirements are seen to offer mutual benefits to all participants. Partnership relationships are seen as the ideal way by which philosophies of just in time and total quality management can be diffused and implemented throughout the network of suppliers.

It is easy, therefore, to paint a rosy picture of the prospects of partnerships and to be carried along by the enthusiasm of presentations about them. The reality of the implementation of the approach does not always fit this picture, however. Often there is a dominant partner who can exploit a power base and rule with an iron fist, covered by the velvet glove of the rhetoric of the partnership ideal.

In answer to the question, 'How many purchasing departments have true religion about partnering with "world-class" suppliers and how many are gargling mouthwash?', a survey conducted by *Purchasing* said that 'there probably are as many garglers as there are true believers'.[47]

NOTES AND REFERENCES

1 Pender, R. 'Partnering for Profit', *Total Quality Management*, October 1993, pp. 13–16.

2 *See* the Introduction by Sir Derek Hornby on p. 1 of:
Partnership Sourcing Ltd. *Making Partnership Sourcing Happen* (1992). Partnership Sourcing Ltd was established to promote the concepts, application and benefits of partnership sourcing. The project evolved through collaboration between the Department of Trade and Industry and the Confederation of British Industry.

3 Hoffmann and Kaplinsky, R. *Driving Force*, Westview Press (1984).

4 Turnbull, P., Delbridge, R. and Wilkinson, B. 'Winners and Losers – The Tiering of Component Suppliers in the Automotive Industry', *Journal of General Management*, Autumn 1993, pp. 48–63.

5 Lamming, R. *Beyond Partnership: Strategies for Innovation and Lean Supply*, Prentice-Hall (1993). *See*, in particular, the account of the 'stress model' given in Chapter 6.

6 'Can Jack Smith Fix GM?', *Business Week*, 1 November 1993, pp. 60–5.

7 Ford, D. (editor). *Understanding Business Markets: Interaction, Relationships and Networks*, Academic Press (1990).
Hakansson, H. (editor). *International Marketing and Purchasing of Industrial Goods: An Interaction Approach*, John Wiley (1982).

8 This list is taken from p. 12 of Ford, D. (1990), as mentioned in note 7 above.

9 *See* note 18 of Chapter 1.

10 Sako, M. *Prices, Quality and Trust*, Cambridge University Press (1992). Table 1 on pp. 11–12 provides a summary of the features of both ACR and OCR approaches. The following article also provides a helpful synopsis: Hunter, L., Beaumont, P. and Sinclair, D. 'A Partnership Route to Human Resource Management', *Journal of Management Studies*, Vol. 32, No. 2, 1996, pp. 235–57.

11 This quotation, together with an account of the three types of trust, is given on pp. 37–8 of Sako (1992), listed in note 10 above.

12 The following references are helpful in building up an understanding of their approach:
Macbeth, D., Ferguson, N., Neil, G.C. and Baxter, L.F. 'Not Purchasing but Supply Chain Management', *Purchasing and Supply Management*, November 1989, pp. 30–2.
Macbeth, D., Baxter, L., Ferguson, N. and Neil, G. *The Customer-Supplier Relationship Audit*, IFS Ltd (1990).

13 *See* especially Chapter 6 of Lamming, R. (1993), as mentioned in note 5 above.

14 Table 6.3 on p. 152 sets out the four-phase model in relation to the nine relationship factors. *See* p. 52 of Lamming, R. (1993), as mentioned in note 5 above.

15 NEDC. 'Developing Suppliers in Engineering', National Economic Development Office (1990).

16 Rainnie, A. 'Just in Time, Subcontracting and the Small Firm', *Work, Employment and Society*, Vol. 5, No. 3, 1991, pp. 351–75.

17 Ring, P.S. and Van de Ven, A.H. 'Structuring Co-operative Relationships Between Organizations', *Strategic Management Journal*, Vol. 13, 1992, pp. 483–98.

18 *See*, for example:
Williamson, O.E. *Markets and Hierarchies*, Free Press (1975).
Williamson, O.E. 'Transaction Cost Economics: The Governance of Contractual Relations', *Journal of Law and Economics*, Vol. 22, October 1979, pp. 223–61.

19 *See* p. 4 of Partnership Sourcing Ltd (1992), as mentioned in note 2 above.

20 Campbell, N. 'An Interaction Approach to Organizational Buying Behaviour', *Journal of Business Research*, Vol. 13, 1985, pp. 35–48.

This article also appears in Ford, D. (editor) (1990), as mentioned in note 7 above, pp. 265–78.

21 Ford, D. 'The Development of Buyer-Seller Relationships in Industrial Markets', *European Journal of Marketing*, Vol. 14, No. 5/6, 1980, pp. 339–54.
This article is also printed in Ford, D. (editor) (1990), as mentioned in note 7 above, pp. 42–57.

22 Dwyer, F.R., Schurr, P.H. and Oh, S. 'Developing Buyer-Seller Relationships', *Journal of Marketing*, Vol. 51, April 1987, pp. 11–27.

23 *See*: Kanter, R.M. 'Collaborative Advantage', *Harvard Business Review*, July–August 1994, pp. 96–108.

24 *See* note 2 above.

25 Christopher, M., Payne, A. and Ballantyne, D. *Relationship Marketing: Bringing Quality, Customer Service and Marketing Together*, Butterworth-Heinemann (1993).

26 Christopher, M., Payne, A. and Ballantyne, D. (1993), as mentioned in note 25 above, p. 9.

27 *See* p. 30 of Partnership Sourcing Ltd (1992), as mentioned in note 2 above.

28 Trevor, M. and Christie, I. *Manufacturers and Suppliers in Great Britain and Japan*, Policy Studies Institute (1988). Comments on the reluctance of some British suppliers to adapt in the 1980s.
Morris, J. and Imrie, R. *Transforming Buyer-Supplier Relations*, Macmillan (1992) includes other examples.

29 For example, *see*: Merli, G. *Co-Makership: The New Supply Strategy for Manufacturers*, Productivity Press (1991) and Moody, P. *Breakthrough Partnering*, Oliver Wight (1993).

30 Wells, P. and Rawlinson, M. *The New European Automobile Industry*, St Martin's Press (1994).

31 Cox, C., Hughes, J. and Ralf, M. 'Influencing the Strategic Agenda', *Purchasing and Supply Management*, September 1996, pp. 36–41.
Cox, C., Hughes, J. and Ralf, M. 'Developing Purchasing Leadership: Competing on Competence', *Purchasing and Supply Management*, October 1995, pp. 37–42.
Cox, A. 'Relational Competence and Strategic Procurement Management', *European Journal of Purchasing and Supply Management*, Vol. 2, No. 1, 1996, pp. 57–70.

32 Erridge, A. 'Competitive and Partnership Models and Public Procurement', Conference Paper at the Purchasing and Supply Education Research Group 2nd Conference (1993).

33 Spekman, R.E. 'Strategic Supplier Selection: Understanding Long-Term Buyer Relationships', *Business Horizons*, July–August 1988, pp. 75–81.

34 Ellram, L.M. 'The Supplier Selection Decision in Strategic Partnerships', *Journal of Purchasing and Materials Management*, Fall 1990, pp. 8–14. Table III on p. 12 provides a list of selection criteria.

35 Pallas, M. 'GM's Evaluation Procedure', on p. 130 of Burt, D.N. 'Managing Suppliers Up to Speed', *Harvard Business Review*, July–August 1989, pp. 127–35.

36 *See* p. 10 of Partnership Sourcing Ltd (1992), as mentioned in note 2 above.

37 Porter, A.M. 'Audits Under Fire', *Purchasing*, 5 November 1992, pp. 50–5.

38 Cousins. P. 'Choosing the Right Partner', *Purchasing and Supply Management*, March 1992, pp. 21–3.

39 Weber, C.A. and Ellram, L.M. 'Supplier Selection Using Multi-Objective Programming: A Decision Support System Approach', *International Journal of Physical Distribution and Logistics Management*, Vol. 22, No. 2, 1992, pp. 3–14.

40 Moody, P.E. 'Customer Supplier Integration: Why Being an Excellent Customer Counts', *Business Horizons*, July–August 1992, pp. 52–7.

41 Ramsey, J. 'Selection of Sourcing Strategies', *Purchasing and Supply Management*, May 1990, pp. 19–23.
   Ramsey, J. and Wilson, I. 'Sourcing/Contracting Strategy Selection', *International Journal of Operations and Production Management*, Vol. 10, No. 8, 1990, pp. 19–28.
42 *See* p. 20 of Ramsey, J. and Wilson. I. (1990), as mentioned in note 41 above.
43 The British Deming Association. 'Single Sourcing', *Total Quality Management*, February 1990, pp. 33–5.
44 *See* p. 26 of Ramsey, J. and Wilson, I. (1990), as mentioned in note 41 above.
45 Hines, P. 'Studies in the East', *Logistics* (supplement to *Purchasing and Supply Management*), February 1992, pp. 22–5.
46 Hines, P. 'Lessons from the West', *Logistics* (supplement to *Purchasing and Supply Management*), May 1992, pp. 13–15.
47 Morgan, J.P. and Cayer. S. 'True Believers?', *Purchasing*, 13 August 1992, pp. 49–57.

CHAPTER 10

Strategic management of human resources in the supply chain

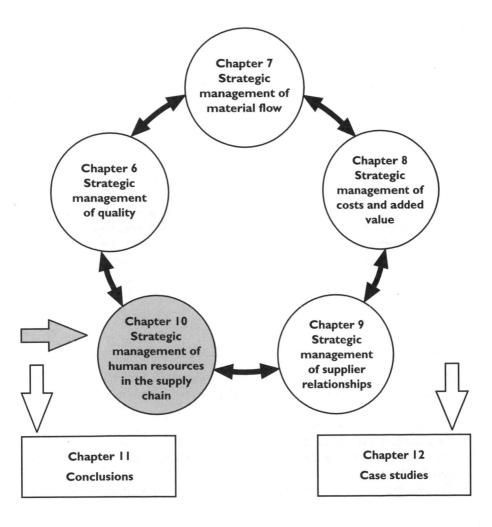

INTRODUCTION

People are the most important asset of an organisation, and increasingly so.[1]

Readers might argue about putting people at the top of the list and might debate the merits of other assets such as finance, buildings and capital equipment. Sue Cartwright argues that organisations are human creations and that they consist of 'individuals who produce the product, make the decisions, conceive the strategies, etc.'.[2]

Earlier chapters have focused mainly on strategic ideas and techniques, but it is now appropriate to concentrate attention on the management and development of human assets in the supply chain. In the context of the supply chain, however, discussions will not be confined within the boundaries of a single organisation – interpreted in the normal sense of an entity, such as a firm or company – as is generally the case. Because of the linkages between supplier and customer firms in the supply chain, a broader perspective will be adopted. In so far as purchasing and supply management is concerned with the development of supplier firms, then human resource issues within those firms may have to be taken into account as well. Also, it may be argued that at the interface between the companies, there may be an organisational structure in the form of a joint partnership team, which transcends the normal legal boundaries of firms. Nevertheless, the management and deployment of the human resources within such a team are important to the effectiveness of the partnership. Aspects of managing human resources can, therefore, be considered from a number of different standpoints in the context of supply chains. Figure 10.1 lists the topics for discussion in relation to the management of human resources in the supply chain.

OBJECTIVES OF THIS CHAPTER

In this chapter the following objectives will be addressed:

1 To link the management of human assets to learning and change processes
2 To identify the factors affecting the behaviour of people in a business context
3 To consider the impact of structural factors
4 To analyse management styles
5 To address aspects of staff recruitment, training, performance appraisal and development
6 To investigate ways of managing change and overcoming obstacles to change

1   Learning and change
2   Factors affecting the behaviour of people in business
    ● the 7-S Framework
    ● the 'cultural web'
3   Organisational structures
    ● classical and scientific management traditions
    ● the human relations tradition
    ● the contingency approach
    ● 'just in time' and 'total quality management'
    ● co-ordination in organisations
    ● organisational trends
4   Management styles
5   Staff recruitment, training, performance appraisal and development
    ● knowledge and skill requirements
    ● interpersonal skills
6   The management of change
    ● force-field analysis and resistance to change
    ● problems with introducing buyer-supplier partnerships

Fig 10.1   Topics for management of human resources in the supply chain

LEARNING AND CHANGE

Knowledge, which accumulates in the organisation as a result of learning from research and from experience, is also seen by some to be the most valuable asset of the firm. Knowledge relating to the activities of the business helps a firm to maintain a sustainable competitive advantage, long after the value of any particular capital assets has diminished. Yet learning and the creation of knowledge, and the subsequent application of it are essentially the achievements of people. The argument, therefore, leads back to human assets again.

Buyer-supplier partnerships may be seen as having a key effect on the rates of learning in both organisations. The extent to which learning is achieved will be reflected in the progress made with regard to improvements in product designs, in standards of manufacturing performance and in the levels of supply service achieved. The emergence of the partnership idea represents a significant challenge to traditional orthodox thinking in the West about market behaviour and the desired nature of buyer-supplier relationships. The theory of partnerships suggests that they are more effective vehicles for the generation of improvements, which will be for the mutual benefit of both parties, compared with more traditional approaches.

In commenting on the need for a renaissance in manufacturing industry in the United States, the following statement was made by Abernathy, Clark and Kantrow:

What is needed is a view of production as an enterprise of unlimited potential, an enterprise in which current arrangements are but the starting point for continuous organisational learning.[3]

The importance of learning should not be underestimated, particularly in times of a more rapidly changing environment. Ideas concerning the management of human resources need to include ways of ensuring that learning takes place and that the fruits of it are implemented in commercially viable innovations. In a dynamic or turbulent environment the management of change becomes a vital priority. There are different implications with regard to the management of human resources in such circumstances, compared with a more stable, unchanging situation. However, forces present in today's world, such as heightened competition in world markets, shorter product life cycles, more varied customer demands and rapidly changing technologies, make it less likely that firms can remain isolated from them – at least in the long run. Slower, incremental change may be an adequate strategy in some circumstances, but other firms may need more radical step changes in order to cope with the circumstances of their environment.

It was argued in Part One of this book that more fundamental long-term changes are taking place which affect the behaviour of organisations and the way in which they are structured and managed. The transition from the model of mass production to lean production, through the application of just in time (JIT) and total quality management (TQM) philosophies, is illustrative of such a shift. As a result, what is expected of people within organisations is changing. It may be imperative, therefore, for firms, or rather people in them, to break the inertia of taken for granted ways of thinking and to reassess organisational and human resource strategies. The purchasing and supply management area is certainly not immune from these forces. Indeed, it can be claimed that personnel within the function not only may need to change their own behaviour, but also are change agents with regard to the behaviour of other people and other organisations in the supply chain.

FACTORS AFFECTING THE BEHAVIOUR OF PEOPLE IN BUSINESSES

The first few paragraphs have set out the basic character of the environment in which the strategic management of human assets in the supply chain need to be considered. The main factors, which will need to be considered in more detail, revolve around those that have an impact on what people do and the level of ability they apply. Business and corporate strategies should set the general direction for the development of the firm and its human assets, and functional strategies have a similar purpose at the functional level. In purchasing and supply management, the selection of product and commodity group strategies will also carry implications for the development and use of human assets. People can contribute to both the formulation and implementation of these strategies.

Decisions, with regard to the division of work and the grouping of people into units, provide the skeletal features of the organisational structure and these have a significant effect on the nature of work that people are required to do.

The 7-S Framework

Much emphasis has been given to the importance of strategy and structure as key factors in the management of businesses. However, in the 1970s, as western countries slowly became aware of both the standards of performance and the nature of management practices in Japanese companies, attention was drawn to other factors. In particular, ideas developed by the management consultancy firm of McKinsey & Company received publicity. A wider range of variables were believed to be important and the so-called '7-S Framework' was created. It was developed, mainly by Peters and Waterman, who wrote the book *In Search of Excellence*.[4] The five additional S factors, which were added to Strategy and Structure, are Systems, Style of management, Super-ordinate goals, Skills and Staff. 'Super-ordinate goals' refer to the shared values of the firm with regard to goals and guiding concepts – what might today be included in descriptions of cultural factors.

Strategy, structure and systems are sometimes called the 'hard' factors and are broadly familiar to traditional management thinking. The other variables of staffing policy, skills, shared values and style of management, the 'soft' factors, can also be seen to play an influential part not only, of course, in determining the results of the business, but also in affecting people employed in the organisation.

The relevance of business culture to both the performance of the firm and the behaviour of people has been given added weight in recent years, and cultural issues in business have spawned a large output of literature. The view has emerged that successful change – as, for instance, in the introduction of JIT and TQM philosophies – can only be achieved successfully if attention is given to appropriate modification of the associated cultural values. Values, once accepted and absorbed by a person, exercise a form of internal control on actions and they win support and commitment for the forms of behaviour that are appropriate to them. External controlling influences like procedures and policy statements might have an effect on what is done, but they might not win the same level of commitment and conviction.

The 'cultural web'

> Managing strategic change is, in the end, to do with achieving a change in the culture of the organisation, that is, a change in the recipe and the aspects of the cultural web that preserve and reinforce that recipe. It is unrealistic to suppose that strategic change can be implemented if the current beliefs and assumptions and ways of doing things remain the same.[5]

In a later edition of the book, Johnson and Scholes use the word 'paradigm' instead of 'recipe', when referring to the cultural web of the organisation.[6] The paradigm embodies deep rooted beliefs and assumptions about the way to do things, which are normally taken for granted and not often talked about. In the 'cultural web',[7] the authors list the following factors:

1 'Rituals' and 'routines' – 'the way things are done around here'.
2 'Stories' – accounts of past events and personalities which contribute to the history and character of the organisation.
3 'Power structure' – identification of those individuals and groups who are seen to hold and exercise power in the organisation.
4 'Control systems' – the performance measurements in operation that signal things that matter and which may be linked to reward systems.
5 'Organisational structure – this identifies positions in the hierarchy and helps to influence relationships between people and groups. There is usually a link to the power structure.
6 'Symbols' – features, such as titles, styles of office furniture and cars are further frames of reference with regard to status and relationships.

It may also be observed that some of the S factors in the McKinsey framework are depicted as part of the cultural web in the Johnson and Scholes model. The concept of culture is to some extent an elusive one and it is capable of being treated by commentators in different ways.

Factors in the cultural web help to account for the social and political forces in an organisation. They also affect career opportunities and have implications for staff development. The factors in the web also guide and constrain decision-making processes, including strategic decision-making activities. They can affect performance outcomes at all levels, therefore. On an interorganisational level, there could, of course be a conflict between some elements in several cultural webs, as people from two or more companies come together.

Nevertheless, it can be argued that those making strategic changes in purchasing and supply management need to address the various S factors or the items in the cultural web which have been identified. If the function is being repositioned and is moving from an essentially clerical mode to a strategic mode, then it may be stressed that changes in local cultural values relevant to this sphere of operation need to be addressed as well. The implication is that programmes for staff and organisational development, therefore, should cover more than just procedures, skills and techniques. Similarly, the successful implementation of the partnership approach depends on bringing about appropriate modifications in the 'soft' factors.

ORGANISATIONAL STRUCTURES

Ideas of how to manage organisations and how to structure them have evolved during the course of this century, and several schools of thought have emerged. It will not be possible to provide an in-depth critique of these here. Nevertheless, it is useful to give a broad overview, in order to recognise the main strands of thought that act as frames of reference in the formation of perceptions and in the shaping of taken for granted assumptions.

Classical and scientific management traditions

Ideas associated with the classical and scientific management tradition give a lot of attention to organisational issues and they have had, and continue to have, an influence today. An organisational chart is typically used to illustrate the basic divisions of personnel and their relationships within groups and within the organisation as a whole. In this image of the organisation, divisions on the basis of functional specialisation and vertical relationships between the different levels in the structure tend to be given prominence. Further divisions, based on geographical and product factors, might also be reflected in the structures of more complex companies. The idea of separate product divisions, acting as separate profit centres, was developed to cope with the problems of managing multi-product companies. Additional principles of organisation associated with this classical school embrace concepts of authority and responsibility and recommend how these should be delegated and defined in relation to positions in the structure. The structure is seen to be hierarchical, with authority located at the top, and it is sometimes described as being mechanistic in nature. Jobs are carefully defined and people are expected to fit into them. This picture conforms to the type of organisation that is sometimes characterised as being bureaucratic.

The scientific approach, implemented partly through such specialist units as Work Study, Operations Research and Organisation and Methods, tended to further separate the tasks of deciding how best to do things and the tasks of following instructions in doing the jobs. F.W. Taylor is usually seen as the 'father' of this approach. The model, which emerges from the combination of these classical and scientific management traditions, is now sometimes described as the 'Fordist' approach. Car plants, such as Highland Park in the United States, built by Henry Ford I in the early part of this century, are held up as examples in which the principle of the division of labour has been taken to an extreme and in which methods are specified and carried out in a standardised fashion. Workers are simply extensions of their machines!

The human relations tradition

Parallel with the development of the traditions just described, but to a great extent separate from them, was the emergence of the human relations tradition, which focused more on the human characteristics of people, the recognition of social factors in work environments and the existence of informal systems. When attempts were made to combine the traditions, a different image of the organisation began to emerge, which Burns and Stalker referred to as an 'organic' system.[8] This latter approach allows the organisation to adapt to changes and to allow more freedom to people to apply their expertise in solving problems, which might not have arisen before and which could not be anticipated by organisational designers operating in the classical tradition.

Within the organic model, greater recognition is given to the aspirations of personnel and to the need to create an environment in which people can develop their capabilities to their full potential. A more optimistic view is taken of the potential contribution that people can make to the fortunes of the firm if the right climate is created. Ideas of job enrichment, job enlargement and job rotation are intended to allow this potential to be exploited. The role of managers and supervisors and the styles of management they need to adopt are also seen to need modification in this organic system. This point will be developed further at a later point in the chapter. Nevertheless, the positions people are expected to fill still remained stratified within this revised model.

The contingency approach

The emergence of contrasting models strengthened the conviction that there is no one universal best way to solve the organisational problems. Scope for choice became apparent. To help guide firms in making their choice, it was suggested that a key factor to take into account is the nature of the environment in which the firm is located. This contingency approach suggested that the mechanistic model is more appropriate to a static environment, in which there is little change with regard to market conditions and product and process technologies. Operating rules and procedures, as well as decision models, can be devised to cope with the types of problems which are anticipated and whose characteristics were well known.

On the other hand, if the environment of the firm becomes more unstable, then the organic model should be selected, as it would be more capable of adapting to the changing circumstances. A more competitive market might arise because of the appearance of new products and/or suppliers. The rate of technological change might gather pace, requiring the firm to develop new methods and techniques. A small group of designers, at the top of the classical organisation pyramid, would not be close enough to these problems to be able to produce a rigidly specified 'blueprint' to guide everyone, it was argued.

'Just in time' and 'total quality management'

The philosophies of JIT and TQM share many ideas, but there is one major common feature relevant to the current discussion. Both are concerned with enhancing the contribution that people can make to the improvement of the performance of the firm in general, and in raising the quality of work, in particular. An aspect of the Toyota system, to which western observers did not give as much importance initially as they gave to the prospects of reducing inventory by the adoption of the kanban technique, was this concern for people. These philosophies are to some extent compatible with the human relations tradition and, arguably, add to it. Ideas and techniques, with regard to problem solving and to their application by people closely involved in the work area to be improved, are in line with a more flexible, organic organisational model.

The two philosophies also share the ideas that change becomes the norm and that there is a need for continuous improvement. It follows, therefore, that they are less in harmony with a rigid mechanistic organisational structure. They perhaps take it for granted that environments are sufficiently dynamic to make it necessary to pursue improvements all the time.

Both JIT and TQM highlight the need to concentrate on processes as the focus of attention for introducing improvements. There are two implications of this. First, faults in the design of processes are seen to be the main source of quality problems and not people themselves. This is a view taken by Deming, for example, in *Out of the Crisis.*[9] Second, investigations into the causes of problems with processes involve more than one person and, frequently, the processes under examination cross functional boundaries. Thus, problem-solving activities often require teams. This is particularly true of processes relating to purchasing and supply management. Both philosophies reinforce the importance and value of teams or groups as an organisational concept.

Co-ordination in organisations

One problem of applying the principle of specialisation, as a way of dividing up the total task of the organisation as a whole into smaller and more manageable fields of activity, was well known before the advent of TQM and JIT. Co-ordination between different functions or departments is difficult to achieve, especially in times of change. In a stable environment the problems can be more easily handled by the adoption of standard procedures. Transmission of documents suffices as the normal way of communicating most information and as a method of allowing a series of actions to be taken sequentially by different departments. These mechanisms, however, become less effective as conditions become more variable.

Difficulties of achieving integration

In more dynamic environments the emergence of a larger number of new problems and the recognition of the need to introduce changes, with regard to products, markets served and production processes used, reveal the limitations of the functional organisation. Rigidly defined departmental boundaries, concerning areas of authority and spheres of operation, reduce the ability of the organisation to make the necessary adaptations. Buck passing and the 'not my problem' syndrome illustrate the difficulties that can arise in a bureaucratic organisation confronted by the demands of a changing world. Functional separation can often be accentuated by political power struggles and by the 'empire building' behaviour of some functional managers. Thus, the interests of the organisation as a whole can become submerged by departments pursuing their own sectional objectives and interests. Horizontal integration is hard to achieve, therefore, when the organisation emphasises control mainly through vertical relationships. It can be claimed, however, that these difficulties arise more in larger organisations. Contact, often on a more informal basis, is easier to achieve in smaller organisations and problems affecting several people can more easily be aired and resolved.

A number of devices might be used to attempt to resolve these difficulties. These will be briefly outlined, after they have been listed below:

1 Management meetings
2 Committees
3 Redrawing of the organisational structure
4 Integrated computer systems
5 'Line' and 'staff' distinctions

Interdepartmental management meetings and bilateral contact between heads of different functions offer opportunities to discuss common solutions to problems and to overcome conflicts, but such channels cannot be used too often. To increase contact on a more regular basis and at a lower level, multi-functional committees might be convened. Doubts regarding the efficacy of this approach, however, have grown in the minds of people who have experienced delaying tactics, conflict and lack of effective action. Nevertheless, the adoption of materials committees, for example, permits joint discussion of issues relevant to purchasing and supply management. Redesigning the functional structure of a company might also bring about closer integration of units whose work flows are linked. A materials management or logistics structure is based upon this method of achieving integrated management and control of the flow of supplies. The development of integrated computer systems has made a contribution through the creation of shared databases and the speedier communication and updating of information. Distinctions between 'line' and 'staff' relationships help to increase co-ordination without jeopardising the unity of command principle.

However, while these mechanisms may provide some amelioration of the difficulties of achieving co-ordination between departments within the predominantly mechanistic organisation, other more radical solutions have appeared. Collaboration and co-operation between departments (and even between different sections within the same department) can be strengthened by other mechanisms that adopt a more holistic perspective and a wider set of goals. These pose more of a challenge to the dominance of the functional divisions in the traditional model.

Creating multi-functional structures or groups

Personnel concerned with activities in supply chains may find themselves operating in a variety of structures. A range of possibilities for enhancing the degree of co-ordination between different specialisms is identified below:

1 Task forces
2 Teams
3 Matrix structures

Task forces might be set up, consisting of members from a variety of different functions, to tackle particular problems that are seen to affect the interests of several functions. The main objectives of such task forces will be to define and identify the causes of a perceived problem. The application of problem-solving tools and techniques then allow solutions to be discovered and action plans devised and implemented.

Teams allow groups of people to work together on a more permanent basis, either full time or part time. In purchasing and supply management, the formation of value analysis/value engineering teams and buying teams to work with suppliers within partnership arrangements is an example that comes to mind.

• In many manufacturing firms, the teamwork concept has been developed in recent years. More self-sufficient teams have been created as organisational units and given more authority and responsibility to control their own work environment. More power has been devolved to teams in cellular manufacturing layouts, for instance. Within the parameters of overall output targets, more scope has been given to the teams to make decisions with regard to the allocation of work to individuals and the pace of work. Responsibility for controlling quality, improving performance and carrying out other support activities such as maintenance, process engineering and material control may also be granted to a multi-skilled team. Above all, the team can be seen as a convenient unit that can be held accountable for its own performance. Even on production lines, ways are being developed to gain the advantages of teamwork and the application of ideas such as job enlargement and job enrichment.

A special kind of team is the quality circle. The circle is a voluntary group that meets regularly to solve problems and put into operation the ideal of continuous improvements. Success with this approach has been variable. Its continuing survival and operation in an organisation may depend, partly, on the extent to which it is just one part of an overall strategy and, partly, on the existence of a conducive cultural climate.

Skills requirements to enable staff to work successfully in teams will be outlined later in the chapter.

Another movement to break away from a strict functional structure can be observed in the development and application of matrix structures. Project teams can be established to achieve common purposes or project tasks, such as carrying out major contracts for particular customers. Multi-functional skills can be assembled to carry out the project, though there are variations in the way that the matrix concept can be applied. Differences lie in the relative importance attached to project roles, on the one hand, and to functional roles, on the other hand. A project leader, though holding the budget for the project, may simply act as a co-ordinator of staff who remain attached to their own functional departments. At the other extreme is the situation in which staff are seconded from their departments to the project team for its duration and are responsible to the project leader. In this case the objectives of the project will have a more prominent focus than those of any individual function. A middle path is when staff have dual responsibilities to both departmental and project leaders. A project-based structure lends itself to the adoption of project planning techniques, such as network and critical path analysis. Tensions between functional and project goals, however, may be difficult to eliminate and there is a danger that priorities will remain unclear. The resultant ambiguity might allow the project to drift in terms of performance.

Organisational trends

The brief outline of organisational structures demonstrates the range of possibilities that can be found in practice. Personnel may find themselves in varying situations with regard to their own organisation and with regard to those of others in the supply chain. Environmental pressures for change and demands for higher standards of performance by customers are contributing to the search for more effective and efficient ways of combining the expertise of specialists to satisfy and exceed the expectations of the end product customers. Current trends indicate that many firms are attempting to reduce the levels of management and to push more responsibility down to the lowest levels where competence can be fostered. Personnel are expected to own and manage their own change processes. The adoption of single status employment policies, as well as the use of labels such as 'associates' and the wearing of uniforms by all, is in keeping with these developments. At the same time, mechanisms that encourage co-operation and closer collaboration between the functions and between different organisations, rather than conflict and competition, are being introduced. These trends have significant implications for both management and supervisory styles and for the development of careers for staff.

MANAGEMENT STYLES

A contingency perspective suggests that there should be a fit between the approach to organisational design and the nature of the environment in which an organisation has to operate. An extension of this perspective is to consider varying the style of management with the nature of the organisation. A style appropriate for a stable bureaucratic context may not provide the right leadership and support for a business that has to undergo a major transformation, in order to meet the needs of a new world it has to confront. Other firms may have to become more flexible and make progress on a more incremental basis, with managers supporting processes of continuous improvement.

The underlying problem of identifying appropriate management styles is connected with the issue of how far organisations should be managed and controlled by 'top-down' approaches and how far 'bottom-up' influences should be allowed to influence decision making with regard to how jobs and processes are conducted. Current fashions for the implementation of TQM and JIT are adding to the empowerment of people by increasing their participation in problem-solving practices, whereas classical management principles gave weight to the downward flow of direction from the top. There does appear to be a potential conflict between the more extreme attitudes and behaviour of this 'command and control' approach and those required to gain the commitment and the involvement of employees for continuous improvement practices. Yet, a coherent sense of purpose and a clear direction to give guidance to the efforts of those at the 'chalk face' would still seem to be necessary.

The idea of styles of management may be depicted briefly here by considering a small number of contrasting characteristics. An obvious starting point is to compare autocratic versus democratic approaches, with particular reference to manager-subordinate relationships. An autocratic manager relies on a position of authority and power to hand out instructions to subordinates and to closely monitor and control resultant behaviour. A democratic manager, on the other hand, gives opportunities to subordinates to participate in decision making, by consulting and seeking their views, and creates an environment in which their creativity and ingenuity can be released.

'The trend towards devolving decision making to the employees closest to the customer is beginning to turn traditional concepts of delegation on their head.'[10] (Customers might be either inside or outside the company in the general concept of customer-supplier chains, as embodied within TQM perspectives.)

Another difference is in terms of strategic leadership. A person may show entrepreneurial flair, by being creative in developing a sense of vision and in seeking out opportunities and mapping out strategies for the firm. On the other hand, others may be more conservative and be content to maintain the *status quo* and to direct the firm along well trodden paths. The first is more likely to be willing to take risks, while the latter prefers risk avoidance strategies.

In short, some managers may be more suited to the mechanistic organisation in a stable environment and others to the organic organisation in a more dynamic environment. This might be illustrated diagrammatically, by showing the conventional pyramid for the former and by inverting it for the latter (*see* Fig 10.2). A democratic style of management in an organisation that is aiming to foster a more participative approach on the part of its employees puts a greater emphasis on interpersonal and team-building skills. The development of appropriate skills is a topic that will be picked up in the next section.

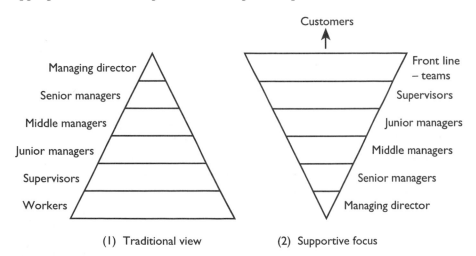

Fig 10.2 Hierarchical and supportive models

STAFF RECRUITMENT, TRAINING, PERFORMANCE APPRAISAL AND DEVELOPMENT

The context in which staff are to be employed has been discussed in relation to organisational and managerial factors. It is now appropriate to switch to the subject of staff themselves and to consider aspects relating to the cultivation of suitable knowledge and skills, relevant to purchasing and supply chain management. The topic needs to be considered from two points of view. At one level there are issues confronting those in managerial and supervisory positions, with direct responsibility for recruitment, training and development of staff within the firm. The other perspective applies to those involved in formulating and implementing product and commodity group strategies. The latter concerns people, who may lead buying teams and who may work within partnerships with suppliers, and who, therefore, may be concerned with personnel strategies in doing so.

Knowledge and skill requirements in purchasing and supply management

It is obvious that people with desired capabilities can either be recruited from outside the firm or, alternatively, be cultivated within the firm, through training and development programmes. The desired capabilities, which reflect both knowledge and skill components, first need to be identified, however. The determining factor, which should influence managers in finding a fit between staff capabilities and the needs of the organisation, is the strategic approach taken by the firm with regard to purchasing and supply management. The direction of development of this functional strategy itself, of course, should be linked to the strategic needs of the business and company, as explained in Part One.

Changing requirements

It was argued by Saunders, Gore, Jones and Salt that a change in the role of purchasing and supply, through the adoption of a strategic stance, makes different demands on both managers and staff.[11] The tasks of managing suppliers through partnerships and of participating in strategic planning processes require different capabilities, compared with short-term transactional, purchasing and supply activities. Paul Cousins made a similar point.

> With the ever increasing popularity of the purchasing partnership philosophy, organisations will have to take a closer look at the educational levels of procurement staff. With purchasing's perceived movement from a clerical service department to that of a strategic business function, the calibre of staff in terms of training, education and skills must increase in order to fulfil procurement's strategic potential.[12]

Research by Paul Cousins suggests that a change in recruitment policy may be, and has been, necessary as the transition to the strategic role is carried out in purchasing. The level of professionalism in the function has increased, with a higher predominance of staff with the Chartered Institute of Purchasing and Supply professional qualification and/or a degree base. In some cases staff have worked their way up through the organisation and have gained both experience and qualifications *en route*. Others have gained qualifications before entry into the function. Career opportunities at both staff and managerial levels have been expanded and the ceilings have been raised for those who meet the challenge. Some, however, may not show the desire or the ability to change from the more traditional role and may be more suited to tasks of a more clerical and routine nature. Staffing policies may need to take into account different levels of grade and ability for different kinds of work. Higher calibre staff, with a wider range of skills and knowledge, will need to be involved in strategic purchasing and supply management, where they can have the most rewarding effect.

Developing knowledge and skills

It can be argued that capabilities to do the required jobs are the essential features to be looked for and developed. There are two basic elements that may be seen to be involved in the concept of capability, which will be discussed here – knowledge and skills. Personnel policies need to address these elements when considering staffing issues.

Relevant knowledge may be divided into several areas:

1 General knowledge of business and management, including strategic management.
2 Specific knowledge relating to purchasing and supply management.
3 Technical knowledge relating to products and processes of a particular business.

Knowledge of the field in question, in which people work, allows them to interpret and build up perceptions of the part of the world they occupy and it identifies a range of possible techniques and courses of action (recipes). It is possible to differentiate between knowledge that is of a more general kind, though possibly still concerned with business, and knowledge that is specific to a particular functional area. From a practitioner's point of view, however, simply possessing knowledge is less important than making use of it and 'putting it to work'. This moves attention to the skills of doing jobs and to demonstrating competences that tasks can be carried out in organisations.

Skills in applying that knowledge are partly specific to the technical field that has been studied or experienced, but there are also more general skills that enable people to negotiate their way in the business context in which they are working.

A list of general skills includes those of:

1 Communication
2 Working in groups
3 Numeracy

4 Information processing
5 Information gathering
6 Problem solving

The skill of problem solving is usually listed in the range, though some prefer to see this as a skill that embodies the others, especially if solutions to the problems are not only discovered, but also implemented.

It is usually claimed that traditional educational schemes have given more emphasis to imparting knowledge to recipients. Courses, which focus more directly on business in general and/or purchasing and supply management in particular, provide underpinning knowledge relevant to the work of the function. More undergraduate and postgraduate programmes relevant to purchasing and supply management are being introduced into university curricula than was previously the case. Even with such 'academic' programmes, there are trends which are reinforcing the view that programmes should not neglect either the specific or the general skills of applying ideas and techniques. Degree programmes are being influenced to develop this approach by such initiatives as Enterprise in Higher Education, promoted by the Department of Employment in the United Kingdom. Sandwich degree courses, with industrial placements forming an integral part of the student learning experience, have always supported the vocational aims of education. BTEC (Business and Technician Education Council) programmes took an early lead in attempting to promote the development of courses that focused knowledge in a more integrated fashion relevant to business problems and which also required the development and assessment of skills, deemed to be appropriate for particular courses.

Concern for the lack of formal development and training of managers in the United Kingdom, as demonstrated in the well-known report of Constable and McCormick and that of Handy, sparked off ideas to improve the situation. The Management Charter Initiative gave attention to the development of standards of 'management competence'. Competence statements have been written, which are concerned with purposes and express outcomes of what people should be able to achieve. Performance criteria are established to judge whether the person is able to demonstrate a particular competence and range indicators are defined to identify contexts or situations in which such an ability should be practised.

A similar approach to that found in relation to management, which identifies and sets out required lists of competences that need to be assessed, has been adopted by the National Council for Vocational Qualifications (NCVQ) and the Scottish Vocational Education Council (SCOTVEC). Thus, National Vocational Qualifications (NVQs) and Scottish Vocational Qualifications (SVQs) are now adding to the development and assessment of skills for business. Further work can be expected to extend the range and level of qualifications that will become available by these schemes. In particular, attention can be drawn to the existence of national vocational qualifications for purchasing and supply. Training and development programmes in firms can take account of this route.

NVQs and SVQs seem to give a heavy emphasis to the application of skills, but, nevertheless, there is recognition of the need to develop underpinning knowledge as well. Thus, although there appears to be a wide difference between the 'competences' route and more conventional courses, the gap may not be so great.

One of the problems in purchasing and supply chain management lies in the need to bring into the arena a wide range of technical and commercial knowledge and skills. The composition of a buying team, with representatives from several functions, is one solution to this problem. However, those involved specifically with staffing the purchasing function should consider what level of technical knowledge, relevant to the products and associated process technologies, buyers need to have acquired in order to function effectively. Buyers, normally, might be expected to have primarily developed business and commercial expertise. Natural common sense and ability and an enquiring mind can be sufficient for able purchasing and supply staff to build up adequate technical knowledge of the products and processes they come into contact with. Some companies have found it useful to draft in staff who are qualified formally in an appropriate discipline.

Staff in strategic purchasing and supply management require the ability to think and plan strategically in order to manage strategic supplies and to manage their supply base. Breadth of vision in forming ideas and an analytical mind in understanding developing situations are attributes not normally found or required in those concerned with a more immediate, clerical purchasing role. They also need a broad understanding of all aspects of supply chain management to be able to appreciate the interconnections between the activities at different stages and to form a total supply plan. To function effectively and credibly in commodity or buying teams, they also need to be able to establish communication bridges to other functions. Horizontal movement to gain experience in different aspects of purchasing and supply management may also be beneficial as part of a career development path.

Interpersonal skills

In organisational environments that are emerging to cope with more rapidly changing conditions and which are being developed to raise standards of performance, more emphasis is being placed on the development and use of interpersonal skills. Those in managerial and supervisory positions need to be both more sensitive and supportive in dealing with their staff. Those, either working in teams or leading them, also need to use interpersonal skills to relate to and co-operate with other members, in order to maximise performance.

Supportive managerial skills

Traditional managerial functions, identified by classical writers, typically embraced planning, organising, staffing, directing and controlling. A more supportive, democratic style also puts emphasis on social and leadership skills.

Social skills involve being able to relate to people, to generate enthusiasm and to motivate people. Ability to influence the formation of values and to use negotiating skills to gain co-operation are important. In situations in which personnel are encouraged to adopt their own improvement programmes, managers and supervisors need to help them to do so. Skills such as listening, encouraging and counselling facilitate staff in setting and achieving goals with regard to their own self-development, as well as improving the performance of their work.

Performance appraisal, while still retaining aspects of performance monitoring with regard to traditional measurements of work performance, can also allow joint exploration of skill and knowledge requirements to foster personal development, taking note of both job and career ambitions. A participative management strategy encourages self-analysis to recognise deficiencies and needs to support learning and development processes. Personal development files might be kept to assist this process.

Teamwork

As firms place more importance on people working in and leading groups as they go about their work, as opposed to traditional practices, which tended to give more weight to individual performance, so different behaviours of both members and leaders may be required. Members need to share common goals and to work with colleagues in achieving them. Participation in decision-making processes is designed to allow each to make a contribution and to increase commitment to supporting the outcomes. Individual potential can be enhanced by receiving support and encouragement from others. In multi-functional teams, the expertise of the team as a whole can be brought to focus on problems and to tease out the full implications and possibilities of ideas that affect their activities jointly. Tolerance in listening to and understanding other people's points of view is necessary if co-operation and trust are to be established. Clearly, influencing, negotiating and facilitating skills, discussed earlier in the context of a supportive management style, can help to forge an effective team. Team-building courses can help to prepare people to function more effectively in teams.

Personalities of members may vary, leaving people to take on different roles in the team. Analysts, such as Belbin, have identified some of these and suggest that an appropriate mix should be taken into account in forming teams.[13] Presiding over the group as leader, developing and shaping ideas, monitoring and evaluating ideas, team building and uniting and making contacts are examples of the roles to which people might be predisposed. In practice, however, it may be difficult to achieve such ideals, when other factors of position, expertise and availability are considered.

THE MANAGEMENT OF CHANGE

The final topic for this chapter is that of managing change, with particular reference to purchasing and supply management. Obstacles to the successful introduction of partnership sourcing will also be considered. In a sense all organisations are in a perpetual state of change, but the pace can vary quite significantly. Changes may be introduced as a result of carefully thought out strategies to give them purposeful direction. Alternatively, they may be the result of *ad hoc* adjustments or reactions to surprise contingencies as they arise. Managers should use rational processes as far as possible to attempt to control the direction and implementation of changes and to anticipate and overcome potential resistance. It has been made evident that strategies can involve changes in a variety of ways. Modifications to the product range, the introduction of new manufacturing and delivery processes or information systems, and changes in purchasing and supply management strategies, are but a few of the possibilities that can have major implications with regard to human resources. In the case of relationships with suppliers, buyers may wish to bring about changes in arrangements, which may have serious implications for the way the supplier operates.

Force-field analysis and resistance to change

Force-field analysis, an approach developed by Kurt Lewin,[14] is one way of introducing a formal examination of the issues affecting the introduction and implementation of desired changes. The underlying theory is that there are some forces acting for change and others that oppose the movement to the desired new state. All the various forces need to be identified in a situation and an assessment made of their relative significance. Some may be critical, either as driving forces for the change, or as resisting pressures. Ways of overcoming or reducing the weight of these restraining forces need to be found. A change strategy that attempts just to increase the power of the forces in favour of change might simply cause resistance to grow as a consequence.

The analysis of the forces calls on the need for the analyst to be able to look at the situation objectively and to understand the implications from the point of view of other involved parties. It should not be taken for granted that they all share the analyst's perceptions and preferences. It may not be the change itself that builds up resistance, but the implications and meaning that it may have for people. Typical points are:

1 Threats of redundancy
2 Threats to status and power
3 Fear of the unknown
4 Belief in inability to learn new ways
5 Established routines will be disrupted – forces of inertia

Ways of overcoming resistance to change

A number of ways may be used to overcome resistance to change and to 'unfreeze' old patterns of behaviour and belief:

1 Communication and education to help people appreciate the need and logic behind the proposed change.
2 Involvement of people in the analysis of the need for change and in the design and implementation of new ways to create 'ownership' of the change process.
3 Negotiation, a process that buyers should feel comfortable with, to look for solutions that enable fears to be overcome and benefits or rewards to be received by the interested parties.
4 Coercive threats, which may obtain compliance, but which may not gain long-term commitment.
5 Support through training and counselling.
6 Pilot programmes and examples of the new approach demonstrate the results and may show that the vision of the new alternative works. Dissatisfaction with the old approach will then be strengthened.

Fundamental changes may naturally cause strong forces for resistance, and steps need to be taken carefully, and at the right speed, to overcome them. This is especially true if the change goes to the heart of the main cultural values of the organisation. Nevertheless, major changes have been made successfully by firms, for instance, which have attempted to adopt Japanese best practices. It is clear that failed firms that have been bought out by Japanese companies, such as in the electronics industry, and new Japanese transplant firms, such as Nissan and Toyota, have succeeded in importing many of these practices and adapting them to a western environment. Others, not under Japanese ownership, however, have managed to transform themselves as well.

Commitment and understanding by those leading the process needs to be visible and genuine. Following fashions and 'flavours of the month' without conviction may simply generate cynicism. This may be a reason why some companies have become disenchanted with TQM. Also, some suppliers have conformed with customer wishes and have been successful in obtaining registration in accordance with BS 5750. However, their basic attitudes have not changed and they have not attempted to pursue more radical improvements.

Problems with introducing buyer-supplier partnerships

There has been much talk and promotion of the value of buyer-supplier partnerships and of how to introduce them, as was evident in Chapter 9. The main forces in favour of this approach relate to the perceived higher standards of performance obtained, via this approach, by the best Japanese companies. The vision held by its supporters is that a co-operative relationship, as opposed to an adversarial one, will be a more productive long-term alternative in terms of improvements in supply performance. Yet there are still frequent complaints from suppliers that genuine partnerships are not being sought by buyers, in spite of claims that they are doing so. How far this is 'sour grapes' on the part of suppliers who have been rejected, as opposed to those who have gained acceptance as preferred suppliers, is not always clear. Other buyers have simply not tried to introduce them and continue to use traditional competitive approaches.

Barriers to progress

What are some of the forces at work in customer companies which resist the introduction and operation of genuine partnerships and restrain movement towards the lean supply model, as depicted by Richard Lamming?[15]

MacBeth, Murphy, Ferguson and Neil suggest that there are several obstacles, which act as barriers to progress.[16] These obstacles are:

1 **Social.** People's reluctance to change existing relations and, in some cases, to become more circumspect in their wielding of power contribute to social inertia.
2 **Attitudinal.** Traditional attitudes, characterised as a reluctance to take risks by becoming too dependent on one supplier and an unwillingness to trust the supplier, provide resistance to the adoption of the partnership approach. Many may also have a predisposition to act as individuals, rather than as a member of a team.
3 **Organisational/managerial.** Lack of full awareness and comprehension of the partnership approach, because of inadequate training, together with the impact of short-term pressures for price reductions are examples of this type of barrier.
4 **Structural.** When purchasing is still perceived as being concerned with operational problems, such a role is not conducive to strategic thinking. Traditional structures, with strong functional boundaries and sequential work flows, are impediments to the introduction of multi-functional buying teams and concurrent engineering practices.
5 **Procedural.** The problem covered by this category is that of a lack of a coherent policy to introduce and support the change to collaborative approaches.

This list identifies potential difficulties in introducing a partnership strategy. Designers of change programmes need to be sensitive to their possible existence in their own organisations and should devise means of reducing their impact.

Forging effective relationships

As buying teams identify particular supplier firms as potential partners, they need to make a similar assessment of the forces at work in those firms. On the one hand, there will be forces that encourage collaborative involvement, and, on the other, forces that might build up resistance to such overtures or which might hold back full commitment. Of course, lack of trust in the customer company, because of previous patterns of behaviour, may be one of the major obstacles. The effects of adversarial treatment and of apparently single minded pursuit of self-interest on the part of the buying company cannot be overcome quickly.

Trust arises gradually, as confidence in the consistency and predictability of the new patterns of treatment grows. If this theory is correct, then buying teams need to take steps to operate in a consistent fashion and to display a common set of attitudes.

Both sides have to invest time and effort in forging an effective partnership. Suppliers may also be expected to make a monetary investment in facilities, such as tools and equipment, in design and development activities and in special logistical arrangements. Suppliers may be asked to make changes of an even more fundamental kind. Changes to the basic cultures of their companies and to their human resource strategies may be necessary, if JIT and TQM philosophies are to be taken on board. Expectations that they will receive a return on their investments have to be built up, therefore. Partnership agreements and long-term contracts may help to ensure that there will be continuing business in the long term. Symbolic awards may also help to cement the relationship and reward excellent performance by promoting the image of the supplier in the wider world and helping to win further business.

The buying firm will also make an investment in terms of the expenses incurred by the buying team in working with the supplier and in developing arrangements. In some cases, there may be a direct financial investment to assist with capital expansion, product development and the purchase of special tools. The main reward lies in securing improved supplier performance.

A successful partnership can be said to make learning and change a way of life. The results can be observed in terms of what the partnership achieves as it pursues the goal of continuous improvement. A partnership for progress might be the ideal that both contributing parties can share. Complacency and inertia are twin dangers which some believe may arise, if market forces are suspended by such bilateral agreements. Compared with the more permanent linkage of vertical integration, it is easier for either side to terminate a partnership, however. But, a rush to the 'divorce court' at the first sign of trouble is more typical of short-term transactional purchasing and should be resisted. A partnership should provide a framework in which problems can be studied and solutions discovered for them.

It might be said that the methods of partnership sourcing, still relatively new in the West, are on trial, and it remains to be seen whether firms can manage to establish loyal supplier bases that provide them with a source of sustainable competitive advantage in the long term. A pertinent question, asked by Phil Southey, is whether stronger 'bonding mechanisms' are needed to overcome the temptations of short-term, self-interest.[17] Possibilities such as inter-linked directorships, cross-shareholding and supplier associations might be considered as offering stronger glue.

SUMMARY

'Investment in People', a phrase promoted by the UK government in one of its campaigns, is a theme running through this chapter. Human resources employed in the supply chain are a (the?) major input into all the processes that create value for customers, as goods and services are produced and passed on at each stage in the chain. Sometimes they may add to the creation of waste, though if the views of Deming are accepted, the source of such waste usually lies in poorly designed processes and not bad workmanship itself.[18] There is scope for business process re-engineering in such cases. He also argues that, if people are given the right opportunity, they can be the major contributors to the elimination of waste.

Strategies and techniques used in supply chain management are bound up with issues of how best to develop and use human resources. Ideas with regard to the management of human assets are relevant to strategic purchasing and supply management in several ways. If it is appropriate to describe the role of this function as 'managing suppliers' or 'managing the outside factory', and a case has been made out for doing so, then human resources are clearly part of the problem. Strategic management of the function itself raises questions relevant to the staffing of it. Managing relationships of both an interfunctional and interorganisational kind is a third reason why human resource matters should not be ignored.

Innovation, the application of new ideas, which can affect all aspects of business, may be said to be the key to survival in the long run. Innovation is an important strategic objective in purchasing and supply management, because it is through innovation that standards of performance will be raised. The way in which human resources are managed and deployed is an important variable in the speed and effectiveness of the processes of innovation. This chapter has explored some of the major issues of managing them at a strategic level and has also considered aspects of managing the processes of change. For some companies, successful strategic purchasing and supply chain management may mean changing the cultural environment in which a network of buyers and sellers operate.

NOTES AND REFERENCES

1 Cartwright, S. 'People – The Most Fundamental Asset of an Organisation', *Business Studies*, October 1992, pp. 14–17.
2 *See* p. 14 of Cartwright, S. (1992), as mentioned in note 1 above.
3 Abernathy, W.J., Clark, K.B. and Kantrow, A.M. *The New Industrial Renaissance*, Harvard University Press (1983), p. 124. This quotation was also included in:
  Lessem, R. *Total Quality Learning: Building a Learning Organisation*, Blackwell (1991).
4 Peters, T.J. and Waterman, R.H. *In Search of Excellence*, Harper & Row (1982).
5 Johnson, G. and Scholes, K. *Exploring Corporate Strategy: Text and Cases*, 2nd Edition, Prentice-Hall (1988), p. 307.

6 Johnson, G. and Scholes, K. *Exploring Corporate Strategy: Text and Cases*, 3rd Edition, Prentice-Hall (1993), p. 61.

7 *See* pp. 60 and 61 of Johnson, G. and Scholes, K. (1993), as mentioned in note 6 above.

8 Burns, T. and Stalker, G.M. *The Management of Innovation*, Tavistock Publications (1961). These authors made a distinction between 'mechanistic' and 'organic' systems.

9 Deming, W.E. *Out of the Crisis*, Massachusetts Institute of Technology (1986).

10 Oates, D. 'Flat Pyramids: The Wave of the Future', *The Sunday Times*, Section 5, 28 March 1993, p. 2.

11 Saunders, M.J., Gore, M., Jones, C. and Salt, D. 'Strategic and Policy Considerations', *Purchasing and Supply Management*, April 1988, pp. 34–5.

12 Cousins, P. 'Purchasing Partnerships: A Professional Approach', *Purchasing and Supply Management*, December 1992, pp. 33–5.

13 Belbin, R.M. *Management Teams – Why They Succeed or Fail*, Heinemann (1981).

14 Lewin, K. *Field Theory in Social Sciences*, Harper & Row (1951).

15 Lamming, R. *Beyond Partnership: Strategies for Innovation and Lean Supply*, Prentice-Hall (1993), Chapter 7.

16 MacBeth, D.K., Murphy, M.D., Ferguson, N. and Neil, G.C. 'Partnering Relationships: Barriers to Progress', Conference Paper at the Purchasing and Supply Education Research Group 2nd Conference (1993).

17 Southey, P. 'Pitfalls to Partnering in the UK', Conference Paper at the Purchasing and Supply Education Research Group 2nd Conference (1993).

18 *See* Deming, W.E. (1986), as mentioned in note 9 above.

CHAPTER 11

Conclusions

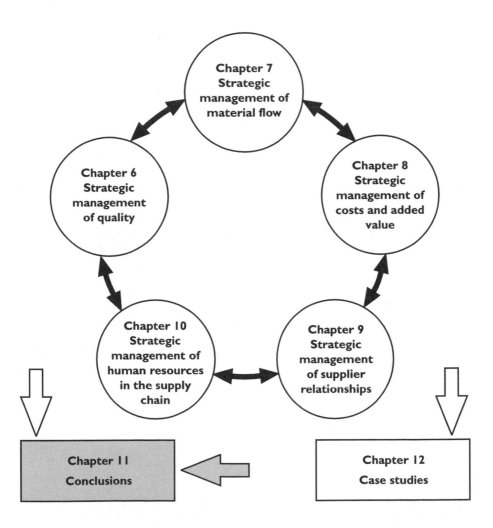

INTRODUCTION

> Time and again it can be seen that factories which supply demanding customers – in the motor industry, for example, or among the big supermarket chains – are obliged to work extremely hard to deliver what and how and when their customers want. High productivity, deliveries spot on time, exacting quality standards – these are essential qualifications for any plant that supplies (and means to go on supplying) Ford, Rover, Nissan, Sainsbury, Tesco, Marks & Spencer, and so on.[1]

The above quotation is testimony to the proactive stance that firms can adopt towards their suppliers and to influence the standards of performance for the supplies that they receive. The article concerned gives an account of 'The Best Factory Awards' for 1993, organised by *Management Today*, in association with Cranfield School of Management. The various winners demonstrate a range of factors that enable them to satisfy their customers and to be successful as businesses at the same time.

A vision for strategic purchasing and supply chain management is that customers and suppliers can work together in improving performance to the benefit of all in the supply chain. This can be just as applicable for firms in the public sector as it is for those in the private sector. This is a central message running through this book and ideas have been examined to see how the vision can be turned into reality. The purpose of this chapter will be to summarise the main developments in ideas about the significance of the role of strategic purchasing and supply chain management and about how this approach may be put into practice. (*See* Fig 11.1.)

1	The significance of purchasing and supply chain management
2	The impact of Japanese 'best practices'
3	Developments in strategic purchasing and supply chain management practice

---

Fig 11.1 Concluding topics

OBJECTIVES OF THIS CHAPTER

The main objectives of the chapter are:

1 To emphasise the significance of purchasing and supply chain management in achieving competitive edge and value for money goals
2 To highlight the impact of Japanese 'best practices' on traditional approaches and the need to improve performance
3 To summarise the main developments in strategic purchasing and supply chain management practice

THE SIGNIFICANCE OF PURCHASING AND SUPPLY CHAIN MANAGEMENT

An assessment of the significance of purchasing and supply chain management can be stated quite simply. The performance of activities in this area can have a major impact on the total performance of the organisation as a whole. Quality, delivery and cost aspects of supply performance affect the ability of organisations to meet the demands of their environments. Ability to meet customer and financial goals, in particular, can be influenced significantly by the degree of effectiveness and efficiency achieved in managing operations in the supply chain. There are variations in the level of impact, depending on the nature and operating circumstances of particular organisations, but in none will the effects be negligible.

The overall theme of this book can be expressed in just a few sentences. Changes in the environment of organisations are placing demands on them to raise their standards of performance. If they are in the market sector they need to stave off and beat the challenges of competitors. If, on the other hand, they are public sector organisations in the non-market sector, they need to comply with the wishes of their paymasters. For some, the pace of change has been so great that they have had to carry out a fundamental reappraisal of their business and corporate strategies and they have had to undergo a major transformation in order to cope. For others, the challenge still has to be confronted. Strategies for purchasing and supply chain management form an integral part of business and corporate strategies and they need to complement and be in harmony with the other functional strategies of the organisation. Rather than just playing a supporting role, strategies with regard to purchasing and supply management can produce capabilities that open up new opportunities for strategy formation at business and corporate levels.

For many, the contribution from the supply chain has been growing as a result of decisions to purchase a higher proportion of goods and services from external, as opposed to internal, sources. As a result, the very character of some organisations is changing.

Local government or local authorities are becoming less in-house 'providers' of services and more 'enablers'. The range of services, which are required to be 'market tested' and which may end up being contracted out to the market-place, is growing. Local authorities, thus, are having to develop purchasing units to carry out this work and to look after the interests of the clients receiving the services. As well as the organisational and staffing implications of such changes, there is also a change of emphasis to a more commercial and entrepreneurial approach.

Outsourcing in the private sector places a greater reliance on suppliers not only to supply more goods, but also to provide other services, such as product design and development. This means that purchasing and supply management can provide added value as well as cost reductions. Competitiveness of the firm can be enhanced through quality improvements, logistics efficiencies and the compression of leadtimes. Multi-functional teams in the buying firm, perhaps led by purchasing, can provide an effective mechanism and put into practice the 'role of evaluator, creator, and manager of interfirm supply links'.[2] Commodity management strategies can shape the structure of the supply chain and can influence the development of mechanisms of co-ordination. 'Champions' in the supply chain may radically affect the way in which other links are managed and operated, in order to produce the desired standards of performance.

THE IMPACT OF JAPANESE 'BEST PRACTICES'

Though many books and articles have been published about Japanese business practices, one book in particular, *The Machine That Changed The World*, has perhaps done more to highlight the huge gap in performance between the best performers in Japan and the others elsewhere in the world.[3] There should be no illusions about the nature of the challenge if firms are to approach world-class standards of performance. Quantum leaps, and not just small increments, in performance improvements have been made by the leaders. Purchasing and supply chain management practices have played a part in the superiority of these companies and they need to be emulated by others as they try to catch up.

Japanese transplant firms, either through the development of 'greenfield' sites or through the transformation of factories that have been bought out, have demonstrated that similar standards can be achieved in other countries. Wherever investments have been made, they have helped to spread ideas and have encouraged suppliers to learn and to adapt, in order to raise their standards to a level where they might be accepted as suppliers. By following the example of such role models, other firms have been able to raise significantly their own performance levels. Traditional methods of managing and operating businesses are being put under the microscope and, in many cases, they are being found wanting. The pursuit of lean production standards, through TQM and JIT approaches, means that the cultural foundations of companies are being transformed. Yet, reforms inside a company on its own appear to be insufficient. Unless lean production is accompanied by lean supply, the full scope of improvement opportunities cannot be exploited and a firm may fail to meet or exceed the standards of competitors in meeting customer requirements. Co-operation, or at least heavily modified views of competition, may offer the best way forward.

Businesses of all kinds in western countries stand at the crossroads, though some have already decided which way to turn and are well down the road in implementing the necessary changes. For some the window of opportunity for reform may soon be coming to an end. Others left it too late and have not survived. Further research reports suggest that there is still a lot to be done by many companies.[4] Gaps in performance between the best Japanese and the other component supplier firms in the automotive industry are as significant as the gap affecting the automotive assembly companies, for instance.

Evidence in the research, based on benchmarking methods, suggests that the world best performers are able to achieve high productivity and high quality simultaneously. Others have apparently been able to achieve similar standards on one of the dimensions, but not both together. Furthermore, the best have achieved faster throughput as well. It was suggested that among the contributing factors within the firms was the ability of team leaders and an environment that supported shop-floor problem-solving approaches. Significantly less time was spent on rework and less inventory was carried throughout compared to other factories. Generally, steps in the production process were more integrated and suffered fewer interruptions in material flow.

High-performance Japanese companies, such as Toyota, have set the standards, therefore, for others to follow. Improvements have been achieved, though, by processes of adaptation to conditions within their own contexts, rather than simple emulation. However, in the 1990s, Japanese firms have had to cope with their own economic difficulties. There has been a slowing down in the growth of home demand and a continuing high rate of exchange of the yen. Reservations, about such factors as 'lifetime employment' and too high a variety of product offerings, have led to changes and a concern among some to seek savings in a western 'cost-cutting' fashion. Nevertheless, the business ideas of other countries have been affected radically by Japanese practices, especially, with regard to ideas about supply chain management. The speed and effectiveness with which they have been implemented has varied, however.

Differences were also revealed in supply chain performance. The best had established a pattern of more frequent deliveries, with lower defect rates and greater schedule stability. Arrangements for communication of information and the operation of joint problem-solving approaches assisted these achievements, as did the functioning of supplier clubs or associations. Integrated control of the supply chain seems to be an important factor, therefore, in separating the best from the rest.

DEVELOPMENTS IN STRATEGIC PURCHASING AND SUPPLY CHAIN MANAGEMENT PRACTICE

There is firm evidence that there is a need for organisations to manage their supply chains more effectively and efficiently if they are to meet their strategic business goals. Several questions follow on from this point and these will now be considered.

First, to what extent have firms identified the need to give greater recognition to purchasing and supply chain management?

> The perceived increase in focus on purchasing and supply chain management over the last few years may simply be a pipedream, with managing directors remaining stunningly oblivious to the benefits which effective practice can bring.[5]

A survey, carried out by the Chartered Institute of Purchasing and Supply, revealed that many managing directors in a wide cross-section of firms did not know what percentage of costs was spent on buying in goods and services. Furthermore, they also had no awareness of the potential savings that could be made through improved performance and were taking no action to improve the function.

Another report, by Booz, Allen and Hamilton, stated that 'Those purchasing managers who are striving to build strategic sourcing capabilities are frustrated by resistance, inertia, and a lack of skills within their own organisation'.[6] The report continues, 'Because suppliers generally represent 50 per cent or more of your costs, control many of the capabilities critical to your performance, and interact with most functions in your organisation, managing them must be treated as a central strategic function of your senior management'.

While the automotive industry, together with the electronics industry, has led the way, there is further evidence of the difficulties of introducing change fast enough to keep pace with the best, even in that industry. The *Worldwide Manufacturing Competitiveness Study – The Second Lean Enterprise Report*[7] – indicated that the sample of component suppliers in the car industry that were studied performed poorly by comparison with leading countries as far as supply chain control was concerned. A report, prepared by Richard Lamming for the Department of Trade and Industry and the Society of Motor Manufacturers and Traders, likewise indicated that faster progress was needed. In particular, the report suggested that 'the necessary levels of inter-firm trust are not present in the industry for lean supply – and therefore comprehensive lean production – to become a reality'.[8] There is a tendency for those in a dominant position in a supply chain to resort to the use of adversarial pressures. Other industries in the United Kingdom, nevertheless, have undertaken initiatives to restructure their supply chains and inter-firm relationships, with a view to enhancing performance. These include aerospace, building and North Sea oil industries.

A number of writers have emphasised the need for collective efforts to improve performance. Moody talked of creating a 'collective enterprise advantage'.[9] Vollmann *et al.*[10] suggested that by 'managing a business as effectively as possible and matching the competencies with others it can attain "virtual integration" that can bring competitive advantages'. In the United States, Harrison[11] has argued that the vertical integration of giant corporations has been replaced by networks in which larger businesses retain influence and control over smaller firms via supply chain management practices. His studies have led him to believe that it is 'large firm-led production networks' which are the generators of growth and employment, not small firms in charge of their own destiny. The final example, however, brings back into the picture two of the authors of *The Machine That Changed The World*.[12] The subsequent publications of Womack and Jones[13] continue to emphasise the idea of 'lean thinking' and the importance of managing the creation of value effectively throughout the 'value stream'.

There is clearly a lot to be done by many companies to gain strategic control of their supply chains. Heads of the function need to be able to provide a bridge at business and corporate level to be able to integrate the functional strategy with the overall business and corporate strategies. Appropriate knowledge and skills are required to articulate the needs of the function and to address how these affect and are affected by the wider strategic concerns of the firm. At the same time senior managers outside the function need to alter their perceptions of the scope and potential of purchasing and supply chain management. The following quotation underlines this point:

> The need to develop, maintain and manage a supply base which performs at world-class levels must not only be of interest to functional purchasing management. Indeed, executive management must begin to link closely corporate/business unit, product and purchasing strategy.[14]

Companies that lag behind must first of all discover and recognise that a gap exists. The technique of benchmarking is one useful approach that might be adopted. Comparisons of performance with regard to standards achieved and procedures used can be based on both competitor and non-competitor firms. Much can be learnt from others working not only in the same industry, but also in completely different circumstances. Once the gaps have been identified, action plans can be drawn up and implemented. Full commitment is a requirement of successful implementation. Companies that have tried to do too many things at once, in a 'half-hearted' way, when trying to implement TQM and JIT, have ended up being disappointed.

The Booz, Allen and Hamilton report suggested that the research data indicated that the prize for those who did apply best sourcing strategies was higher profitability.

Practical measures to improve the situation can be taken to strengthen the involvement of purchasing and supply management in strategic planning processes. The following points might form the core of such a programme.

1 Representation of the function at board level and in senior management teams will enhance the functional link with wider strategic considerations and ensure a more balanced appraisal of the opportunities and threats on the supply side. A diagnosis of the strengths and weaknesses of the firm's current supply chain position can provide a stepping stone to the formation of strategies that are integrated with those of other functions and support business and corporate requirements.

2 Plans should be prepared to reposition the purchasing and supply management function so that it can take on a strategic role and to redesign its organisational structure, if required.

3 There should be an allocation of adequate resources to the function to recruit, train and develop staff with appropriate strategic skills to formulate and apply commodity strategies.

4 Strategies for the purchasing and supply management function should be developed to fit in with business and corporate strategies. Priorities for the supply chain need to parallel those of the product strategy of the business as a whole, which, in turn, should focus on the requirements of targeted customers.

5 Arrangements for multi-functional co-operation within the firm as a whole should be devised.

6 Commodity strategies need to be developed by the buying teams. Current supply chain conditions should be analysed and future developments need to be studied. Porter's approach to the analysis of competitive conditions, identified in Chapter 3, may be adopted for this purpose. Strengths and weaknesses should be assessed relative to these expectations.

SUMMARY

For most organisations there are opportunities not to be missed. According to Monczka, Trent and Callahan:

> The challenge for most firms is to maximise supplier performance contributions and capability improvements at levels better than competitors. A firm which can accomplish this is in a position to achieve competitive advantages through its purchasing and sourcing processes.[15]

Organisations in the public sector also need to find new ways of navigating in a changing world and to learn how to develop supply chains that enable them to maximise the value for money they can obtain, thus enabling the best use to be made of resources.

All organisations can share the aim of creating and maintaining a competent network of suppliers. This requires the establishment of an appropriate 'cultural web' throughout what has been called 'the extended enterprise'.[16] The search for continuous improvement by the joint learning efforts of all in the network is a top priority in a world in which standards of performance are continually rising.

NOTES AND REFERENCES

1 Wheatley, M. 'The Stamp of World Class', *Management Today*, November 1993, pp. 88–127.
2 Cavinato, J.L. 'Identifying Interfirm Cost Advantages for Supply Chain Competitiveness', *International Journal of Purchasing and Materials Management*, Fall 1991, pp. 10–15.
3 Womack, J.P., Jones, D.T. and Roos, D. *The Machine that Changed the World: The Triumph of Lean Production*, Rawson Associates: Macmillan (1990).
4 *See*, for example, the 'Made in Britain' project report by the London Business School and IBM. An account of this was given by:
   Hanson, P. 'Measuring Up', *Manufacturing Engineer*, August 1993, pp. 185–7.
   See also the report of 'The Lean Enterprise Benchmarking Project' by Anderson Consulting, Cardiff Business School and University of Cambridge, *In Search of World Class Manufacturing Practice* (1993).
5 Nolan, A. 'Firms Miss Out', *Procurement Weekly*, 17 September 1993. An account of a survey undertaken by the Chartered Institute of Purchasing and Supply is given in this article.
6 Nolan, A. 'Purchasing Needs High Level Support', *Procurement Weekly*, 27 August 1993. This article reports some of the findings of a report by Booz, Allen and Hamilton, *Strategic Sourcing in Europe*.

7 Andersen Consulting. *Worldwide Manufacturing Competitiveness Study – The Second Lean Enterprise Report*, (1995).

8 The quotation can be found on p. 5 of the report: Lamming, R. *A Review of the Relationships Between Vehicle Manufacturers and Suppliers*, DTI, (1994).

9 Moody, P. *Breakthrough Partnering*, Oliver Wight (1993).

10 Vollmann, T.E., Cordon, C. and Raabe, H. 'Supply Chain Management', *Financial Times – Mastering Management Series*, No. 8 (1996), pp. 13–14.

11 Harrison, B. *Lean and Mean: The Changing Landscape of Corporate Power in the Age of Flexibility*, Basic Books (1994).

12 *See* Womack, J.P., Jones, D.T. and Roos, D. (1990), mentioned in note 3 above.

13 *See*:
Womack, J.P. and Jones, D.T. *Lean Thinking: Banish Waste and Create Wealth in Your Corporation*, Simon & Schuster (1996a) and Womack, J.P. and Jones, D.T. 'Beyond Toyota: How to Root out Waste and Pursue Perfection', *Harvard Business Review*, September–October 1996, pp. 148–58 (1996b).

14 Monczka, R.M., Trent, R.J. and Callahan, T.J. 'Supply Base Strategies To Maximize Supplier Performance', *International Journal of Physical Distribution and Logistics Management*, Vol. 23, No. 4, 1993, pp. 42–54.

15 *See* p. 52 of Monczka, R.M., Trent, R.J. and Callahan, T.J. (1993), as mentioned in note 14 above.

16 *See* note 6 above for the reference in which this phrase was reported.

CHAPTER 12

Case studies

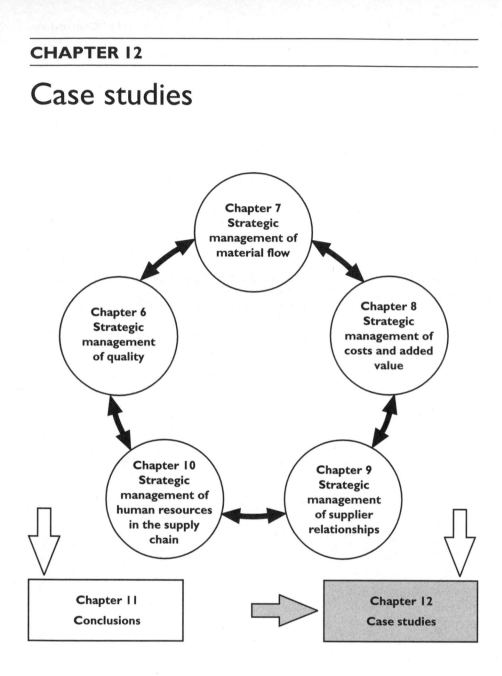

INTRODUCTION

The case studies contained in this chapter are intended to provide examples of a wide range of important strategic issues relating to purchasing and supply chain management. They demonstrate the strategic actions which a cross-section of firms is taking. The key topics for each case study are listed to give an indication of the main content. The names in some of the cases are not the real names of the companies from which some of the material has been drawn.

The cases are as follows:

1 Power tools manufacturer
2 Bankco PLC
3 B & Q
4 Armoured Vehicle Company
5 OEM Manufacturer
6 Fenster Systeme GMBH
7 General Motors
8 Safeco
9 The National Health Service.

Study tasks are provided for each of the cases.

The topics covered by the case studies are summarised in Fig 12.1.

Topic	Case Studies								
	1	2	3	4	5	6	7	8	9
Tiers in the supply chain						✓			
Rationalisation of suppliers				✓					
Sourcing issues					✓				
Buying power								✓	
Information technology								✓	
Technological change		✓							
Environmental issues			✓						
Supplier environmental audit			✓						
Changing markets				✓					
Strategies for survival							✓		
Support for corporate strategy	✓								
Changing role of purchasing in services		✓							
Competitive and co-operative strategies							✓		
Integrated logistics								✓	
Central co-ordination of purchasing	✓						✓		
Organisational structure									✓
Purchasing and supply as an agency									✓
Purchaser/provider functions									✓
Buying alliances								✓	
Make or buy					✓				
Staffing issues		✓							
Just in Time and Total Quality Management	✓								
Quality improvement				✓		✓			
Just in Time delivery						✓			
Long-term contracts	✓								

Fig 12.1   Topics covered in case studies

CASE 1: POWER TOOLS MANUFACTURER

TOPICS

1 Central co-ordination of purchasing
2 JIT/TQM in the supply chain
3 Long-term contracts
4 Support for corporate strategy

The power tools manufacturer ETM is part of a world-wide group that manufactures a wide range of power tools. It has a European organisation under the control of a general manager and it has manufacturing sites in four European countries. The company has made significant progress over the last ten years and has more than doubled sales turnover. The manufacturing operations are concerned with three core processes. These are the machining of key parts, motor windings and assembly of finished products. The result of this manufacturing strategy is that there is a high bought-out content – approximately 65 per cent of product cost. Purchasing and supply management has a key role in the company, therefore, and it has the goal of meeting and beating its competitors with regard to its performance in managing its supply operations.

The firm has recognised that it is operating in conditions that are becoming more demanding, as customers expect greater flexibility and a fast response service. The development of the Single European Market has led to more of these customers operating on a multinational basis. As well as an increased customer focus, the firm wishes to continue to raise the level of quality and to maintain a leading position with regard to product innovation. A policy of cost reduction is another goal being pursued throughout its factories. An increase in earnings per share, not surprisingly, is the main financial goal that has been targeted.

In order to co-ordinate purchasing on a European basis, there is a group purchasing team. Each factory, however, has its own supply team to look after its local needs. The main purpose of the group operation is to gain leverage in its sourcing arrangements for common items. This team also liaises with the parent North American body for the development of global sourcing arrangements and global pricing policies.

To support the corporate goals, three main aims have been established for purchasing and supply management. First, an improvement in supplier quality is sought through policies of upgrading the supply base and an emphasis on preventative quality control techniques. Second, an improvement in the flexibility of service from suppliers is being aimed at. Cost reduction, the third goal, is to continue to be 'a way of life'.

The purchasing and supply management function had already been both active and successful in pursuing higher standards of supplier performance in recent years. Reject rates had fallen substantially. The supply base had been pruned from around 500 suppliers to less than 300, as the policy of dealing with fewer and better suppliers on a long-term basis had begun to take effect. Concern for total acquisition costs had replaced the former emphasis on purchase price.

However, ETM was not content to stand still, and, at the factory level, further cost reductions of between 15 to 20 per cent have now been set as the target. Inventory turnover rates are to be increased from 20 to 45 times, within two years. Savings in the use of space, further quality improvements and an increase in service flexibility are also listed for attention.

What strategies enabled this company to make recent progress and which promise future gains as they continue to be implemented? An integrated approach between manufacturing and purchasing and supply management was one aspect. The pursuit of just in time (JIT) and total quality management (TQM), as the main philosophies for the reduction of waste, was seen as a task that could only be accomplished effectively if it was undertaken both in ETM's factories and also by suppliers in the external supply chain.

An improvement in materials flow was partly accomplished by altering factory layouts. Main stores are about to be closed down, lowering levels of inventory and saving space, and a policy of having parts delivered to near the point of use is being put into effect. Materials handling requirements are being reduced gradually, as more items are switched to a 'direct to line' arrangement. However, suppliers have had to develop capabilities to deliver more frequently and to demonstrate reliability in both quality and schedule adherence, as the system becomes less tolerant of defects and delays. Improved planning and control systems and the adoption of electronic data interchange (EDI) techniques have speeded up communication of more accurate demand data. The adoption of bar-coding has assisted with part identification and the monitoring of progress. Design teams have adopted the principle of ease of manufacture and have started to reduce the proliferation of part numbers, through standardisation of materials and parts. Further gains have been made by moving to two and three shift working.

Buyers have had to develop commodity strategies to guide the introduction of the JIT/TQM programme for key items. They have helped to bring about the necessary improvements in supplier performance by identifying areas for improvement and by adopting joint problem-solving approaches. These tasks are being carried out within the framework of long-term relationships. Multi-year contracts have provided stability for suppliers to make the investments in changes that were necessary. Suppliers are also expected to work at bringing about year-by-year cost reductions, and the benefits of these are being shared by the customer.

TASKS

1 *Analyse the meanings of the terms JIT and TQM and identify the main elements encompassed by these improvement programmes. Discuss whether they have any common elements.*

2 *Identify the benefits which the ETM company hoped to derive from its strategic changes.*

CASE 2: BANKCO PLC

TOPICS

1 Changing role of purchasing and supply in a service industry
2 Technological change
3 Staffing issues

This case concerns a well-known leading high street clearing bank in the United Kingdom, though it also has extensive operations on a global scale. It is placed in an industry that has undergone a major technological revolution as a result of the application of computer systems. The introduction of automated teller machines is but one example of how systems of dispensing and transmitting money have become less reliant on human intervention. As a result, the cost profile of banking operations has changed significantly. The level of labour costs as a proportion of total costs has fallen, in line with a fall in the level of labour intensity. A corollary of this is that the profile of purchasing and supply activities has become more prominent. The tasks of acquiring and providing equipment and supplies to support the new modes of operation are seen to play a crucial part in the effective provision of services to customers. The bank has made a strategic appraisal of the role of purchasing and supply management and has now recognised its strategic value to the business.

As part of the new corporate strategy, the purchasing and supply management function has undergone a major reorganisation. The head of the function has been appointed at a high level in the organisational structure and already a strategy to strengthen the role of the function and to manage the supply process more effectively and efficiently is being implemented. A recruitment programme has been put in place to attract people of a high calibre to take responsibility for developing small teams to manage key commodity areas, such as IT equipment and supplies, stationery and property services. Graduate qualifications, a good track record and membership of the Chartered Institute of Purchasing and Supply are seen to be credentials that people should have in order to take on these more demanding roles.

The teams have been given responsibility for developing sourcing plans that integrate all relevant elements of the supply chain. These can include, for example, the logistical arrangements for the supply of goods to each branch location, as well as the purchasing details of contracts with suppliers. Total cost of supply is a criterion of performance that is being applied. Personnel in the teams are required to have good communication skills to establish a close rapport with both suppliers and internal customers, who are the immediate recipients of the purchasing and supply service. Where appropriate, partnership arrangements are being fostered with preferred suppliers and opportunities for the implementation of improvement programmes are being identified.

Thus, the purchasing and supply function is being transformed from what was a fragmented clerical operation in which the placing of orders was regarded as a routine, administrative task. For example, a high percentage of print orders went previously to the same supplier. This was not a carefully thought out strategy, nor was the relationship one of a progressive partnership, focused on the search for innovations. It was more a case of purchasing inertia, in which the adoption of a quick solution was all that seemed to matter. Concern for value for money had not been a driving force. There had been no attempt to differentiate between different types of print order, nor had the varying capabilities of different printers been assessed. Thus, the different print requirements had not been matched with the corresponding skills and capabilities of different print companies. As a result high prices were being paid for much of the work, for which the original printer's facilities were unsuited.

A new set of values, both in the bank in general and in the purchasing and supply management function in particular, is helping to change the image of purchasing and supply. Its potential for contributing to the profitability of the business and to the level of service which the bank can offer its customers is now clearly recognised. Professional management of the function is reinforcing a stronger commercial and strategic perception of what can be achieved.

TASKS

1 *Comment on why purchasing and supply activities have become more important in recent years in many service industries.*
2 *Assess the nature of the difficulties which might be expected to arise when a programme, which is designed to enhance the role and position of purchasing and supply, is introduced into an organisation and suggest how they might be overcome.*

CASE 3: B & Q

TOPICS

1 Environmental or 'green' issues in purchasing and supply strategies
2 Supplier environmental audit

The DIY retail chain, B & Q, a member of the Kingfisher Group, is at the forefront of developments with regard to the formation and implementation of 'green' purchasing and supply strategies in relation to environmental issues. At first sight, it might seem strange that a retailer should show such concern for environmental problems. There is a tendency to focus attention on manufacturing firms, such as the petro-chemical companies, when thinking about environmental problems. The control of the emission of pollutants that might affect air and water and the safe disposal of waste products are subjects that receive much attention. However, an important aspect of B & Q's environmental strategy is concerned with the purchasing and supply of many of the products displayed and sold in its retail outlets.

Increasingly, firms are coming under pressure to consciously think out what might be called a 'from cradle to grave' approach in assessing the environmental impact of products. This covers stages of obtaining natural raw materials, manufacturing processes, retailing of products, products in use and disposal of products at the end of their life. Government legislation, such as the 1990 Environmental Protection Act, and European Community initiatives for 'eco-labels' and 'eco-audit regulations' are providing pressure for firms to do so. In addition, customer influence and public concern for products that are environmentally friendly are forces that firms cannot afford to ignore. While controversy over the value of being assessed by third parties in relation to the standard for quality management systems (BS 5750, ISO 9000, EN 29000), a new standard, BS 7750, has emerged. This operates in the same way for environmental management systems. Other European partners have made faster progress than the United Kingdom in some areas. Germany, for instance, has introduced regulations to increase the recycling of materials ahead of European Community legislation.

B & Q, however, took the initiative itself and decided actively to develop an environmental policy as a long-term strategy, even though it did not expect an immediate short-term payback. A corporate responsibility for the environment has implications for its purchasing and supply activities. When considering the potential impact of products on the environment, it became clear to B & Q that a number of key raw materials embodied in its product range had significant environmental implications. Timber is one particular case that can be examined in more detail. The purchasing strategies adopted to minimise the environmental impact can then be investigated.

As regards timber, most publicity has tended to focus on the destruction of tropical rainforests, as the result of indiscriminate felling of hardwood trees, and on the failure to make good use of the areas that have been cleared. Destruction of the environment seems to be the long-term consequence of the pursuit of short-term profit. However, from B & Q's point of view, softwood timber products from the temperate forest zones are more important. Doors, cut timber and garden furniture are typical products sold by B & Q. Is it possible to supply such products to satisfy the demands of customers and still protect the environment? This is the fundamental environmental question that confronts a firm like B & Q.

In 1991, the board of B & Q decided to adopt the 1995 target of the World Wide Fund for Nature (WWF), and buy timber from sources that were well managed and where a policy of sustainable production was pursued. Providing a continuous yield is one aspect of sustainable production, but, in addition, good management should also take into account the need both to maintain the balance of plant and animal life and to provide benefits to local populations. This policy means that B & Q has to be able to trace its timber supplies back to their original sources, and then ensure that these sources are being managed in a proper manner.

To achieve the first objective of traceability, B & Q has introduced a supplier environmental audit questionnaire, which timber suppliers have to complete. These suppliers can extend the analysis to their suppliers as well. Visits to suppliers and to the forest areas, as well as seminars, helped to increase general understanding of the problems. Experimental projects are being funded to study the viability of sustainable timber production. The idea of independent certification is being discussed as a way of proving that satisfactory forest management standards are being maintained by sources.

Similar approaches are being applied by B & Q to other product areas and the audit procedure has been used with over 200 suppliers. Packaging is another area that receives close attention, in order to look for ways of reducing the amount of packaging needed and to increase the amount of material that can be recycled. Buyers are becoming more aware of the environmental issues associated with the products for which they have responsibility. Environmental criteria are being included in the assessment and selection of suppliers.

TASKS

1 *What reasons might be used to justify the introduction of 'green' strategies in purchasing and supply arrangements?*

2 *Select a company and make an assessment of the potential of its operations to cause 'environmental harm'. Do the same for both its major 'upstream' suppliers and its 'downstream' customers.*

CASE 4: ARMOURED VEHICLE COMPANY

TOPICS

1 Changing market environment
2 Rationalisation of the supplier base
3 Quality improvement

The market for defence equipment had seen a number of major changes. The ending of the cold war, caused by the fragmentation of the former USSR and symbolised by the collapse of the Berlin wall, had led to a reappraisal of defence strategies and a cut-back of expenditures on equipment by many governments. The international market had thus become more competitive, as suppliers fought to obtain contracts in the face of falling demand. Efforts to strengthen the competitive nature of defence procurement in the United Kingdom had also added further pressure on suppliers. The Armoured Vehicle Company had taken stock of the changed environment and had developed strategies in an attempt to cope with these new conditions.

To remain a viable international supplier of defence vehicles and to maintain its position in the United Kingdom, the Armoured Vehicle Company saw that performance needed to improve. It wished to remain committed to goals of excellent quality and service, but it realised that customer perceptions of what constituted excellence were changing. In order to retain the image it wanted to project, therefore, standards had to be raised. Design and development capability is influential in winning contracts, but customers were also becoming more demanding in terms of cost, 'no defects' and 'on time delivery'. Both manufacturing and purchasing and supply strategies were involved in pursuing these goals.

The company took the decision to invest in new manufacturing facilities and these were purpose built and a significant improvement on its previous set-up. The opportunity was taken to introduce a different approach with regard to employment practices. A strategy of team-based manufacture was adopted, with a view to releasing untapped talent and to pursuing continuous improvement policies. Gains in flexibility from having multi-skilled teams were also being sought by these changes. As part of the programme of reducing costs, it had also been decided to reduce the levels of inventory by bringing the flow of supplies more into line with rates of usage. This meant reducing batch sizes of parts and subassemblies. While much could be accomplished by improving internal operations, it was recognised that performance overall was also dependent on the standards of the suppliers used by the company.

An overhaul of purchasing and supply strategies was also called for, therefore, as part of the corporate programme. A measure of the significance of the supply chain is indicated by the fact that 70 per cent of product cost was made up of the bought-out content. Past policies had been typical of western approaches. A large supply base had been maintained and sourcing had been conducted on an adversarial, competitive basis. Price had been the dominant concern. It might be summed up as a 'more the merrier approach'. The consequences, however, had been seen in terms of quality problems, late deliveries and a need to rely on a policy of goods inward inspection to screen out defective supplies.

A major plank in the revised purchasing and supply strategy was the goal of rationalising the supply base in order to improve the quality of supplier performance. Quality in this context was to include not only product quality in the technical sense, but also wider aspects of quality, with reference to service and ability to manage costs. It was decided that a switch to partnership sourcing with a smaller number of suppliers would be the best way of resolving all the problems. The first task, therefore, was to assess the performance and capabilities of existing suppliers and to identify the poor performers. Past performance data were analysed and supplier quality audit (SQA) teams visited suppliers to provide a fuller picture of capabilities. Those that were rated poor and who showed no signs of being able or willing to change were then dropped at the first opportunity and efforts were focused on building up partnerships with the remainder.

Arrangements were made with suppliers to operate with stricter quality standards and to place the main onus of responsibility for managing quality on their shoulders. Training and support was offered where necessary. The aim was to work with approximately 200 'A'-grade suppliers and to rely on receiving goods without applying quality checks as they are delivered to the factory. Fast moving items are being delivered directly to the point of use. While the company does not have the same volume of output as the motor vehicle industry generally, it was believed, nevertheless, that many aspects of JIT and TQM policies could be put into practice.

Additional benefits of the supply strategy, in working with better committed suppliers within the framework of stable, long-term relationships, can be identified. Ongoing cost reduction programmes, which concentrate on aspects such as design, quality, productivity and logistics improvements, are producing savings, to the benefit of both the suppliers and the customer. Better planning and scheduling has improved delivery performance and there is now less exposure to problems of shortages. Buyers are expected to have more time to work effectively with and manage the reduced number of suppliers.

TASKS

1 *What factors induced the Armoured Vehicle Company firm to introduce strategic changes?*

2 *Compare the old with the new policies for managing quality in this company.*

CASE 5: OEM MANUFACTURER

TOPICS

1 Strategic 'make or buy' questions
2 Sourcing strategies

One of the main strategic decisions of a machinery manufacturer, such as the OEM Manufacturer Company (OEMC), concerns the question of what steps in the manufacturing sequence it wishes to own and manage directly and which should be left to independent subcontractors to operate. In the case of OEMC, the nature of its products was changing as a result of product innovation and customer requirements. The switch was towards more sophisticated products as a result of the addition of a wider range of accessory features. This meant that the number of components needed to build the end products was increasing. Should the firm invest in both the development and the manufacture of these components, or should it rely on external sourcing? In the past OEMC had operated its own machine shops to make components that were assembled subsequently into the final products. There was nothing remarkable about this kind of work and any competent engineering firm could handle it. There was also a question, therefore, of whether this work should be retained in-house, or whether it should be outsourced.

OEMC realised that these strategic issues had to be confronted and that they should not be treated in an *ad hoc* way from a short-term point of view. The company was confident that it had a sound position in the various segments of the market in which it operated. Its products enjoyed a world-wide reputation in terms of functional performance and reliability. However, it foresaw the need for continual product innovation in order to sustain this position and new firms were establishing footholds in a growing global market. It was also believed that there were limits to how much customers would be prepared to pay for OEMC's better quality products. Management of costs to ensure that the firm could set prices in the market and still make a profit was seen to be important.

It was clear, therefore, that OEMC needed to identify where its strengths were and to concentrate on building on these. At the same time, it was necessary to look at supply markets both for standard machined components and for the accessory items that were now being called for. Small task forces in research and development, production and purchasing and supply functions were set up to carry out investigations as a first stage. Then a top management group met to assess the total picture and to develop the strategic plan for the company. All three of these functions were represented in this top group.

The main points to emerge from the analysis of the total situation, once the information had been pooled from the separate task forces, were as follows:

1 The R & D department did not have sufficient resources in terms of quantity or relevant expertise to become involved in the design and development

325

of the new accessory components that would be needed in the future. Specialist independent firms had already established themselves in particular areas and had already built up considerable expertise. OEMC did not have sufficient demand for these items to justify the level of investment, which would be needed both in R & D and in the required manufacturing facilities and labour resources. OEMC would have to market these components on its own, as well, in order to build up output sufficiently to be able to operate at an economical level. The purchasing task force had assessed that these independent suppliers were well managed companies and they were establishing sound reputations for using their technological expertise to bring innovations to the market-place at a rapid rate. Already economies of scope were being enjoyed and there were downward trends in the prices being charged.

2 It became clear that the main internal advantages, as far as R & D was concerned, which OEMC enjoyed, lay in two areas. The R & D department had built up expertise in co-ordinating the overall design of the finished products and in managing developments of a range of subassemblies, which were important functional elements in the final products.

3 Similarly, the production function had developed sound capabilities in the making of these key subassemblies. The production capabilities of OEMC were also strong with regard to the assembly of the finished products. The firm was already operating on a cellular basis, with each cell making a different 'family' of products. In recent years, investment had been made in modernising these facilities.

4 The situation with regard to the machine shops was found to be quite different. The present layout was based on the functional or process principle, and much of the equipment was now old-fashioned. It had become increasingly hard to maintain it in effective working order. The machine shops illustrated many of the typical problems of the process layout approach. High work in progress stocks, materials handling difficulties, as batches of parts were moved around the different centres, and space taken up by parts waiting to be moved are just some of these problems. Production scheduling was difficult to manage as varying mixes of work, with different routes through the plant, had to be handled. While individual batch cycle times on particular processes were not long, total throughput times for completed components were very high and work had to be started on the basis of forecast usage, well ahead of actual customer orders for the finished product.

5 Purchasing reported that many competent external suppliers had the ability to carry out this general type of machining work at lower cost. Some had modernised their facilities to be able to give a fast, flexible service. They would be more able to absorb some of the fluctuations in OEMC's demand level, by balancing the work with that of other customers.

The outcome of the analysis was a decision to outsource both types of component. It was felt that the adoption of a partnership philosophy would enable OEMC to keep in contact with product developments in relation to the accessory items. As regards general machining work, a more competitive posture seemed to be feasible. Suppliers would be manufacturing to OEMC's specifications and there was little to differentiate the capabilities of a number of them. External suppliers, therefore, appeared to offer the prospect of enhancing the added value of the finished products made by OEMC at lower cost, than if the company tried to manage these activities directly itself.

The R & D and manufacturing strategies that emerged from the planning group were to concentrate on those activities in which it was believed a competitive advantage could be sustained. Investments could be focused in these areas to support the continuing development of capabilities in them.

TASKS

1 *Discuss why 'make or buy' questions should play an important part in the development of both business and purchasing and supply chain strategies.*
2 *What criteria should be used to determine which goods and services should be outsourced?*

CASE 6: FENSTER SYSTEME GMBH

TOPICS

1 JIT delivery
2 Quality
3 Tiers in the supply chain

Fenster Systeme GMBH (FS) was a German firm, which had built up a sound position in Germany in supplying a range of components for the automotive industry, with its main factory in Coburg. It wished to develop a base in the United Kingdom as part of a strategy of expansion within Europe, which was deemed to be necessary to meet the requirements of several automotive assembly firms. Lower labour costs, and a more peaceful industrial relations climate in the United Kingdom than previously, were some of the factors determining the choice of country.

The purchase of a company in Coventry, Dryden Engineering, was the route adopted to implement the strategy. This company already had an established position in the automotive industry, making similar products, such as window regulators. However, it lacked the financial resources for either product development or the re-equipment of its factory with more modern computer-controlled machinery. FS could see that it would be able to supply existing customers in the United Kingdom, but it would also be relatively easy to transport goods to mainland Europe.

Ford was an important customer of FS in Germany and the Coventry plant was to be brought on stream to supply both UK and German plants. The plan was to supply daily on an 'ex works' basis. A trailer was to be filled on a daily 'call-off' basis, with information transmitted via a computer link. Once in the Ford logistics system, delivery was the responsibility of the customer and the final destination would not necessarily be known. In order that the Coventry factory could be accepted for this JIT arrangement, some of the work stations had to be redesigned for the complete assembly of components and facilities had to undergo the rigorous Ford quality certification process. A training programme was also needed to prepare the workforce to work to more exacting standards of quality and service.

At this time, ideas about the design, manufacture and supply of car windows and winding mechanisms were being modified. In the traditional way, the car assembler bought all the necessary parts and components and took on the responsibility for the assembly work. This meant that the assembler also had to buy in and co-ordinate the supply of all these items. Taking into account the range of different types of windows and window regulators – electric or manual, arm and cable – this meant coping with many parts and suppliers. Car assembly companies decided that it would be advantageous to change from this approach and buy in complete window systems, which could then be easily fitted into the door panels. This change of approach had a number of implications for companies like FS.

FS had an opportunity to become a main system designer and manufacturer of the window subassembly. This meant expanding the design skills that it already possessed and developing the expertise to design and develop the complete system. The disciplined approach of Failure Mode and Effects Analysis had to be accepted as part of the arrangements as well. Similarly production had to build capacity to carry out all the steps in the assembly of the complete product. The responsibility of purchasing and controlling the supply of parts that were outside the manufacturing competence of FS also had to be taken on board.

The customer's purchasing policy with respect to this subassembly was seen to provide a number of benefits. Smaller specialist suppliers can build up expertise in the design and manufacture of the complete system. The efforts of the customer's own designers and production personnel will not have to be diluted and diverted from the main core areas. Purchasing is able to concentrate on working closely with just the system or subassembly provider. A close partnership can be established and the problem of co-ordination is made easier, compared with having to deal with a larger number of parts suppliers.

From a supply chain point of view, the transition to a policy of sourcing the complete window system changes the structure of the chain. FS becomes a main first-tier supplier to the car assembly firm. Other parts suppliers, which previously supplied direct to the car assembly company, now become second-tier suppliers and deliver parts to the first-tier supplier, like FS.

Firms like FS, in this type of change in the structure of the supply chain, have to decide whether they wish to become a first-tier supplier and take on the expanded role required of them. The alternative is to remain a parts supplier and fight to win contracts from those who do become the system designers and producers. There may be a risk that such contracts will not be won and firms will find it harder to build up any special competitive advantage.

TASKS

1 *Investigate the implications for purchasing and supply of looking to a supplier to take on the role of a provider of a complete 'system'.*
2 *Suggest reasons why a firm might want to adopt a strategy of buying 'ex works' from its suppliers.*

CASE 7: GENERAL MOTORS

TOPICS

1 Strategies for survival
2 Competitive sourcing and buyer-supplier co-operation
3 Centralisation of purchasing

At the height of its crisis, the North American operations of General Motors were losing nearly $9 million a day. In 1991 the company announced the biggest loss in corporate history – $4.5 billion. As an automotive company it had come to the point when it demonstrated most of the ills that bedevilled many western manufacturing firms. Among these might be mentioned the following points. It had a very wide product range, with little contact and co-operation between the various marques – Cadillac, Buick, Pontiac, Oldsmobile, Chevrolet and Saturn. Many of its models lacked strong market appeal and its models generally were not being replaced fast enough. Both Ford and Chrysler had gained share as a result. General Motors' market share in the North American market had fallen by over 13 per cent in recent years, from just around 46 per cent to about 33 per cent. However, the company was still carrying the high fixed costs of most of the plants that had supported the company in its earlier successful era.

Although the company had had the opportunity to learn from its joint operation with Toyota (NUMMI – operating in an old plant in California, which had been rejuvenated by the adoption of Japanese methods) it had been slow to pursue the adoption of lean manufacturing methods. Earlier attempts to buy its way out of trouble with new technology, but without carrying out any fundamental reorganisation, had failed for the most part. It also had a large, bureaucratic organisational structure, with a complicated network of committees, which made decision making a slow process. The company was more vertically integrated than its other US competitors, and many of its plants in the components group were both inefficient and provided a poor standard of service.

It had become clear that if General Motors was to stem this decline a massive reform programme was needed. The divisional structure has been replaced by a single unit, called North American Operations, with a single strategy board and a vastly reduced corporate staff. The model range has been reduced and the plan has been formed to operate in future with almost half the number of 'platforms' (the basic structure of the car from which several models can be built). Plant rationalisation (closures), JIT and inventory reduction programmes, as well as changes to team-based methods, are other moves that will help to reduce costs and decrease the number of man-hours needed to build a car.

However, while it was necessary to improve productivity in the assembly plants, the need to reduce costs and improve quality and service with regard to the supply of parts and materials was also apparent. These goals applied equally to both internal suppliers, within the Automotive Components Group, and independent external suppliers. For a time, Ignacio Lopez was the purchasing chief. He had won a reputation for having helped General Motors in Europe to rationalise its supplies policies and to reduce costs. He had recognised that it was no good concentrating on internal plant reforms alone. The importance of both cost and quality of supplier performance was too great to be ignored, because of the high bought-out content.

The approach adopted by Lopez in his short period in North America (before leaving to join Volkswagen), has been controversial, to say the least! Many suppliers, sometimes openly, but often on an unattributed basis, have let it be known via the media that they are less than happy. Other buyers in the purchasing profession, convinced of the efficacy of the long-term partnership policy, with regard to buyer-seller relationships, have expressed the view that the clock has been turned back 20 or 30 years. It is not yet clear what the long-term consequences of the Lopez policies will be.

To some, the new purchasing policies appeared to be paradoxical. On the one hand, they seemed to support the partnership approach. The PICOS (Purchased Input Concept Optimisation with Suppliers) programme set out a scheme to provide assistance to suppliers to help them to identify sources of waste. Suppliers are expected then to introduce appropriate changes in order to improve quality and to increase productivity. However, an aggressive pricing policy, which was put into immediate effect, was based on traditional adversarial, competitive bidding methods. In the short term, approximately $4 billion was reputed to have been saved, at a time when General Motors desperately needed to make some cost cuts.

As part of the changes, the purchasing structure was modified. A single purchasing entity was established to replace 27 separate, decentralised purchasing groups. The intention was to rationalise the supply base through a centrally co-ordinated approach and to gain maximum leverage with suppliers. It emulated a move adopted previously in the European operation. For the North American operations, sourcing decisions were to be taken by a multi-functional committee, comprising members from purchasing, engineering, manufacturing, quality control and finance. Units within the Automotive Components Group were to have to compete for business against outside suppliers.

It is worth looking in more detail at the pricing policy. Lopez sought price cuts of between 10 and 20 per cent or more, not just the more usual 2 to 3 per cent reductions. Multiple bids (as many as ten to twelve) were sought for each contract and several rounds were pursued. While the majority of suppliers retained their contracts, at reduced prices, perhaps as many as 20 per cent lost business. Among the latter were some who had been given 'Targets for Excellence' quality awards. Some felt bitter, especially if they had invested in developments to provide a dedicated service to General Motors, and they suggested that they would be unwilling to co-operate in the same way in the future.

On the other hand, the PICOS programme has already shown that the provision of help to suppliers can pay off in improving productivity and quality, through JIT, target costing and value engineering approaches. Suppliers have been able to cut levels of inventory, reduce leadtimes and save space as a result of modifications to their operations. The PICOS teams have also come across cases in which the specifications agreed by engineering had been overspecified, thus contributing to costs that were higher than necessary. In the future, early supplier involvement in the product development process was expected to stop this sort of problem from happening again.

'Long-term relationships, but on a competitive basis', seems to be the motto. General Motors appears to have sufficient buying power to have the best of both worlds, but will the long-term advantages of a less adversarial approach be lost? The answer to this question will perhaps unfold with the passage of time. Buyers in Ford and Chrysler, on the other hand, appear to be following the partnership model in its purer form.

TASKS

1 *Compare 'competitive' and 'collaborative' approaches with regard to buyer-seller relationships.*
2 *Assess the feasibility of trying to adopt both simultaneously.*

CASE 8: SAFECO

TOPICS

1 Buying power
2 Integrated logistics
3 Information technology
4 European buying alliances

The 1970s and 1980s witnessed a revolution in the world of retailing in the United Kingdom. Whereas power in supply chains for the distribution of consumer goods had previously been in the hands of the manufacturers, it has now been taken up by major retail chains. This is especially apparent in the field of grocery distribution, in which the five leading chains supply more than 60 per cent of the grocery products in the United Kingdom. Retail chains have also transformed the distribution and selling of 'brown' and 'white' consumer durable goods. A number of factors have contributed to this growth of retailer power, power which manifests itself in the purchasing and logistics policies of the retailers.

One of the early contributing factors to the changes that have so dramatically altered shopping patterns was the ending of resale price maintenance in 1976. Retailers could treat the selling price of goods as a variable in their corporate strategies and this legislation enabled a 'pile it high, sell it cheap' philosophy. High volume sales at a lower margin could provide a more than satisfactory return on capital. The popularity of self-service supermarkets and superstores allowed retailers vastly to increase their scale of operations and to provide locations which were more convenient for a more mobile population. As the general level of affluence of customers gradually rose, so quality and variety of product range became important considerations in the retailing strategies. Perhaps as a result of seeing the success of Marks & Spencer in adopting an 'own label' policy from its early days, grocery retailers have developed 'own label' products themselves, to a greater or lesser extent. They have attempted to build up customer appeal and loyalty for their products and at the same time reduce the influence of manufacturers. Nevertheless, some manufacturers have been able to continue to support strong market positions for their own brands, and, thus, no retailer, other than M & S, has approached a one brand policy.

The huge increase in the volume of goods purchased and the greater sourcing freedom, when buying own label products, are two factors that have contributed to the growth of buying power by the retailers. Safeco buyers are able to use the threat of 'de-listing' brands (taking them off the shelves), if a supplier is reluctant to meet demands. They also negotiate 'listing allowances' for new products and manufacturers may be asked to pay premiums for shelf positions. Own brand products represent about 35 per cent of the total product lines, but a higher percentage in terms of sales value. Suppliers of these lines, though, are not given any security of contract, however. In short, therefore, policies are short term and manufacturers' margins are continually being squeezed.

Safeco is an example of a grocery retailer that has fully exploited conditions in successfully building up a strong national retailing chain. It also provides an illustration of how purchasing and logistics strategies have contributed to the success of the firm in meeting both financial and customer goals. Customer tastes for an ever expanding range of goods, many of them exotic and from overseas, and for fresh quality goods, have increased the demands for the tight control of specifications, sources of supply and distribution arrangements. Competitive pricing conditions have also placed a requirement on the need to operate supply chains efficiently. These demands have meant that firms like Safeco have had to look carefully at their logistics arrangements.

The typical distribution pattern before the retail revolution, organised mainly by manufacturers, was for their lorries to deliver directly to individual stores. Now, retailers like Safeco have taken over control of the supply chain logistics from source through to the shopping bags of their customers. Selection of the right structural and infrastructural features of these logistics systems are vital in achieving the right standards of performance. Information technology has had a major part to play in the strategies which are currently in use.

Information technology has made it possible to give effect to 'customer pull' at the store level and to provide central co-ordination of stock replenishment policies. Thus, techniques, such as bar-coding, laser scanning and electronic data interchange (EDI), and the interdependent suite of computer software systems, which process and communicate the information, enable sales data to be collected and analysed several times a day, and reorders are automatically transmitted up the supply chain. Historical data allows adjustments to be made to forecasts to allow for special events, holidays and various celebrations distributed throughout the calendar. Information systems are, therefore, an integral part of the logistics strategies being implemented by the retail chains.

The pattern of physical distribution adopted by Safeco is as follows. Fifteen depots are located around the country and these receive deliveries of goods directly from their sources of supply. Consolidated loads of mixed goods are then formed for onward movement to each of the stores served by the depot. The scope of the total supply task is revealed by the following figures. More than 15,000 items comprise the product range, 250 stores are located around the country, and more than 1,000 major suppliers in the UK and Europe are hooked into the network. Approximately 8 million cases a week are moved by around 700 lorries.

In terms of ownership of the distribution chain, Safeco operates a mixed strategy. Most depot and fleet facilities are owned and operated by third parties and they provide a dedicated service for the retailer. Safeco directly owns and manages a small part of the network, in order to gain operating experience and to provide a check on the performance of the third parties. In order to remain competitive and to increase profit margins if possible, Safeco is working with its distributors to reduce stocks in the pipeline and yet retain high levels of service for the customer at the sales outlets. As much space as possible is used for selling in the retail stores and backroom stocks are being kept to a minimum.

While supermarket chains like Safeco have enjoyed success in recent years, a number of new challenges are having to be confronted. As a result of a period of recession and slow economic growth, prices of goods have gained greater prominence in the eyes of at least some shoppers. Thus, alternative forms of grocery retailing are threatening to dent the dominance of the big five or so firms. Low-cost, limited line, 'discount' stores, operated by both UK and continental firms, and the arrival of 'warehouse clubs' from America are examples of these alternatives.

The structure of the food manufacturing industry is undergoing change as pan-European strategies are put into effect by firms through takeovers. American manufacturers are also trying to cash in on the development of the single market in Europe. These changes affect especially those goods which are able to surmount individual national taste preferences. Thus, as firms become larger, they may be able to increase their negotiating strength.

There are still differences in retailing formats and in distribution systems, as well as variations in national markets, in different European countries. Nevertheless, more pan-European retailing is emerging, though it is not yet widespread. More popular has been the emergence of buying alliances. Safeco has entered into such an alliance with a view to gaining benefits from increased buying power and central contracts with brand manufacturers on a pan-European scale. A further objective is to explore the possibility of taking in certain 'own label' products from partners in the alliance.

TASKS

1 *How should a customer which has a 'dominant' position in its supply chain use its buying power in relation to its suppliers?*
2 *Assess the part information technology has played in the development of retail supply systems and identify the benefits for the final consumer.*

CASE 9: THE NATIONAL HEALTH SERVICE

TOPICS

1 Organisational structure
2 Purchaser/provider functions and the internal market
3 Purchasing and supply management as an agency service

(The content of this case relates mainly to purchasing and supply for the hospital sector in England. There are differences in the organisational arrangements in Wales, Scotland and Northern Ireland.)

The National Health Service was subjected to another round of reforms in 1991 as a result of government concern for the growing level of expenditure for the provision of health care. The service is faced with demands that are growing year by year. Demographic changes contribute to a rise in demands from the elderly and innovations in medical technology increase the scope and costs of the treatments that are available. From the government's point of view there are perhaps two fundamental questions. What level of expenditure should be granted to the health service? Is the current level of expenditure being used in the most effective and efficient way? Doubts about the way in which current expenditure was being managed and a desire to curb the rise in the total led to the reforms already referred to. Among the objectives of these reforms was that of obtaining greater value for money. In addition, quality of service and a stronger customer focus were further aspects to be taken up by the new organisation. The reforms carried implications for purchasing and supply and these will be identified shortly. However, the background picture of the revised approach for managing the provision of health care in the hospital sector needs to be painted first.

The main thrust of the reforms, designed to provide a better quality service to suit the needs of customers and at the same time to control costs, was to introduce a clearer division between the purchase of services on behalf of patients and those units that provide the service. Thus, the idea of purchasing units in the district health authorities, which purchase services from provider units through the 'internal market', has come into practice. Sources that could be awarded contracts by these purchasing units or directorates include the directly managed provider units of the district health authorities, recently formed 'trusts' and privately owned hospitals. The trusts are quasi-independent units within the health service to which greater powers of authority and responsibility to govern their own destiny have been devolved. Nevertheless, the trusts are dependent on winning contracts for their services and they have to compete for business within the internal market. Certain general practitioner practices, with devolved budgets, may also take on the role of purchasers for these services. Thus, a new role for purchasing has been created by these reforms, and development programmes are under way to establish appropriate skill and information bases to carry it out effectively. Contracting and negotiating skills are needed to obtain economic and effective services and to provide incentives for providers both to improve the level of service and to manage cost reduction processes.

Another manifestation of the purchaser/provider split can be seen in relation to the provision of supplies needed by the provider units. A National Health Service Supplies Authority (NHSSA) has been set up to organise the purchasing and supply operation to meet the requirements of the provider units. It functions as an 'agency service' and service contracts for this supply service are negotiated with the hospital units – the customers. A fee for the provision of the service is negotiated as part of the contract. The supplies function is intended to develop a customer focus through this contracting process. The NHSSA operates at three levels. There is a national headquarters unit, six supply divisions located around the country and local teams within the provider units. The latter may be on the payroll of either the provider unit or the NHSSA.

The hospitals in England require goods and services worth approximately £4 billion in order to function, ranging from drugs and medical supplies to the provision of requirements to support 'hotel' and 'office' activities and general hospital facilities. A large number of consumer points are located around the country at and within the different hospital locations. The sum of money involved is sufficient for a significant amount of waste and unwanted cost to be incurred if purchasing and supply processes are not properly managed. Many of the supplies can also be critical from the point of view of patient welfare. Patients' lives may be put at risk by supply failures.

It is evident, therefore, that the supply of goods and services needs to be tackled from a strategic point of view. The NHSSA should contribute to the general aim of the NHS to contribute to the delivery of health care services with increased efficiency and effectiveness. As far as supplies are concerned there are three main ways through which a contribution can be made. First, greater value for money can be obtained in buying goods and services from suppliers. Second, improvements can be made with regard to the logistical arrangements for delivering the supplies to the point of use – taking into account storage and transport and distribution activities. Finally, there is scope for increasing efficiency in the use of the supplies by the users.

The problem of how best to organise the provision of supplies to the hospital users is not a new one, of course. Before 1991, a more fragmented approach had been in operation and there was no uniform pattern across the country. Steps had been taken to introduce a more co-ordinated approach by building up 12 regional supply units and by reducing the large number of small stores within the districts. Some streamlining of the distribution system had taken place, therefore. The adoption of 'centres of responsibility' for the negotiation of national purchase agreements for commonly used items had also brought a degree of co-ordination of the purchasing spend between the autonomous regions. However, the report of the Audit Commission in 1991 developed some strategic guidelines for the supply service, which have influenced the design of the existing structure.

Thus, the six supply divisions are the outcome of the proposal to set up fewer, but stronger supplies organisations. Within the divisions, professional expertise is being developed so that an effective and efficient, integrated supply service can be provided to its customers. Strategic direction and supervision is provided by the headquarters unit and the national purchasing unit has responsibility for establishing national contracts with major suppliers of commodities where there is a high total spend. Steps have been taken to reorganise and improve the efficiency of materials management activities at the local unit level. More effective management of stocks and replenishment procedures at ward level or equivalent is being achieved within the hospitals.

The overall organisational problem can be seen as finding the right balance between central and local involvement in decision making and exercising control over supplies operations. Devolution of influence and control to the units at the local level might provide more direct contact with users and a closer understanding of their needs. However, too much devolution can sacrifice the benefits of a more centralised co-ordination of the spending power of the NHS and lose the economies of scale in relation to storage and distribution. The present arrangements are intended to encourage the operation of a more effective and efficient supplies service and to use service contracts as the mechanism to ensure that customers in the hospitals receive value for money. Trust units are not obliged to use the services of the NHSSA.

Approximately 85 per cent of the supplies are delivered directly to the user units. The remainder are channelled via the storage and distribution system of the NHSSA. One of the questions that arises is whether this distribution service should continue to be operated within the NHS. There are suggestions that both storage and transport operations, or at least transport operations, should be subcontracted to the private sector. The NHSSA is striving to improve performance to ensure that its 'oncosts' for these logistics activities are economical. It has even been suggested that the NHSSA as a whole should be privatised.

TASKS

1 *Define the tasks of 'purchasers' and 'providers' and assess the merits of the mechanism of 'internal markets'.*

2 *Analyse the potential advantages and disadvantages of operating one central purchasing and supply unit and closing down the separate supply divisions.*

FURTHER READING

Abernathy, R.C. and Kantrow, T. (1983). *The New Industrial Renaissance*, Harvard University Press.

Abernathy, W.J., Clark, K.B. and Kantrow, A.M. (1981). 'The New Industrial Competition', *Harvard Business Review*, September–October, pp. 68–81.

Adam Jnr., E.E. and Swamidass, P.M. (1992). 'Assessing Operations Management from a Strategic Perspective', in Voss, C.A. (ed.) *Manufacturing Strategy – Process and Content*, pp. 373–400, Chapman and Hall.

Adamson, J. (1980). 'Corporate Long-range Planning Must Include Procurement', *Journal of Purchasing and Materials Management*, Spring, pp. 25–32.

Adcock, D., Bradfield, R., Halborg, A. and Ross, C. (1995). *Marketing: Principles and Practice*, 2nd edn, Pitman Publishing.

Andersen Consulting, Cardiff Business School and University of Cambridge. (1993). *In Search of World Class Manufacturing Practice*.

Andersen Consulting. (1995). *Worldwide Manufacturing Competitiveness Study – The Second Lean Enterprise Report*.

Ansari, A. and Modaress, B. (1990). *Just-in-Time Purchasing*, The Free Press.

Ansoff, H.I. (1968). *Corporate Strategy*, Penguin Books.

Ansoff, H.I. (1987). *Corporate Strategy*, Revised edn, McGraw-Hill Inc.

Ansoff, H.I. and McDonnell, E.J. (1990). *Implanting Strategic Management*, 2nd edn, Prentice-Hall.

Argenti, J. (1974). *Systematic Corporate Planning*, Nelson.

Bacon, R. and Eltis, W. (1978). *Britain's Economic Problems: Too Few Producers*, 2nd edn, Macmillan.

Baily, P., Farmer, D., Jessop, D. and Jones, D. (1994). *Purchasing, Principles and Management*, 7th edn, Pitman Publishing.

Baker, M.J. (1992). *Marketing Strategy and Management*, Macmillan.

Bauer, F.L. (1977). 'Managerial Planning in Procurement', *Journal of Purchasing and Materials Management*, Vol. 13, Fall, pp. 3–8.

Belbin, R.M. (1981). *Management Teams – Why They Succeed or Fail*, Heinemann.

Bessant, J. (1991). *Managing Advanced Technology*, NCC Blackwell.

Best, M.H. (1990). *The New Competition: Institutions of Industrial Restructuring*, Polity Press.

Biggs, J.B. (1978). 'Individual and Group Differences in Study Processes', *British Journal of Educational Psychology*, 48, pp. 266–79.

Bloom, B.S. (ed.) (1956). *Taxonomy of Educational Objectives: Cognitive Domain*, David McKay.

Bowman, C. and Asch, D. (1987). *Strategic Management*, Macmillan.

Brand, G.T. (1972). *Industrial Buying Decisions*, Cassell.

British Deming Association, the. (1990). 'Single Sourcing', *Total Quality Management*, February, pp. 33–5.

Browning, J.M., Zabriskie, N.B. and Huellmantel, A.B. (1983). 'Strategic Purchasing Planning', *Journal of Purchasing and Materials Management*, Spring, pp. 19–24.

Burnes, B. and New, S. (1996). 'Understanding Supply Chain Improvement', *European Journal of Purchasing and Supply Management*, Vol. 2, No. 1, pp. 21–30.

Burns, T. and Stalker, G.M. (1961). *The Management of Innovation*, Tavistock Publications.

Burt, D.N. (1989). 'Managing Suppliers Up to Speed', *Harvard Business Review*, July–August, pp. 127–35.

Burt, D.N. and Doyle, M.F. (1993). *The American Keiretsu: A Strategic Weapon for Global Competitiveness*, Business One: Irwin.

Burt, D.N. and Soukup, W.R. (1985). 'Purchasing's Role in New Product Development', *Harvard Business Review*, September–October, pp. 90–7.

Business Week. (1993). 'Can Jack Smith Fix GM?', 1 November, pp. 60–5.

Buzzell, R.D. and Ortmeyer, G. (1995). 'Channel Partnerships Streamline Distribution', *Sloan Management Review*, Spring, pp. 85–97.

Calli, J.F. (1993). *TQM for Purchasing Management*, McGraw-Hill.

Cammish, R. and Keough, M. (1991). 'A Strategic Role For Purchasing', *The McKinsey Quarterly*, No. 3, pp. 22–39.

Campbell, N. (1985). 'An Interaction Approach to Organizational Buying Behaviour', *Journal of Business Research*, Vol. 13, pp. 35–48.

Carter, J. and Narasimham, R. (1995). *Purchasing and Supply Management: Future Directions and Trends*, CAPS Research Report.

Cartwright, S. (1992). 'People – The Most Fundamental Asset of an Organisation', *Business Studies*, October, pp. 14–17.

Caves, R.E. and Associates. (1968). *Britain's Economic Prospects*, George Allen and Unwin.

Cavinato, J.L. (1991). 'Identifying Interfirm Cost Advantages for Supply Chain Competitiveness', *International Journal of Purchasing and Materials Management*, Fall, pp. 10–15.

Chadwick, T. and Rajagopal, S. (1995). *Strategic Supply Management*, Butterworth/Heinemann.

Chandler, A.D. (1962). *Strategy and Structure*, MIT.

Chartered Institute of Purchasing and Supply and Anderson Consulting. (1993). *Managing Logistics: Survey Report*.

Christopher, M. (1992). *Logistics and Supply Management*, Financial Times/Pitman Publishing.

Christopher, M., Payne, A. and Ballantyne, D. (1993). *Relationship Marketing: Bringing Quality, Customer Service and Marketing Together*, Butterworth/Heinemann.

Clark, K.B. (1989). 'Project Scope and Project Performance: The Effect of Parts Strategy and Supplier Involvement on Product Development', *Management Science*, Vol. 35, No. 10, October, pp. 1247–63.

Clark, K.B. and Fujimoto, T. (1991). *Product Development: Strategy, Organization, and Management in the World Auto Industry*, Harvard Business School Press.

Confederation of British Industry. (1991). *Competing with the World's Best*. CBI.

Cousins, P. (1992a). 'Choosing the Right Partner', *Purchasing and Supply Management*, March, pp. 21–3.

Cousins, P. (1992b). 'Purchasing Partnerships: A Professional Approach', *Purchasing and Supply Management*, December, pp. 33–5.

Coyle, J.J., Bardi, E.J. and Langley Jr., C.J. (1992). *The Management of Business Logistics*, 5th edn, West Publishing Company.

Cox, A. (1996a). 'Relational Competence and Strategic Procurement Management', *European Journal of Purchasing and Supply Management*, Vol. 2, No. 1, pp. 57–70.

Cox, A. (ed.) (1996b). *Innovations in Procurement*, Earlsgate Press.

Cox, C., Hughes, J. and Ralf, M. (1995). 'Influencing the Strategic Agenda', *Purchasing and Supply Management*, September, pp. 36–41.

Cox, C., Hughes, J. and Ralf, M. (1995). 'Developing Purchasing Leadership: Competing on Competence', *Purchasing and Supply Management*, October, pp. 37–42.

Crosby, P.B. (1979). *Quality is Free*, Mentor.

Cusumano, M.A. (1994). 'The Limits of "Lean"', *Sloan Management Review*, Summer, pp. 27–32.

Cyert, R.M. and March, J.G. (1965). *A Behavioral Theory of the Firm*, Prentice-Hall.

Dale, B.G. and Plunkett, J.J. (eds.) (1990). *Managing Quality*, Philip Allan.

Dale, B. and Cooper, C. (1992). *Total Quality and Human Resources: An Executive Guide*, Blackwell.

Davies, O. (1985). 'Strategic Purchasing', in Farmer, D. (ed.) *Purchasing Management Handbook*, pp. 59–83, Gower.

Deming, W.E. (1986). *Out of the Crisis*, Massachusetts Institute of Technology.

Dobler, D.W., Burt, D.N. and Lee, L. (1990). *Purchasing and Materials Management*, 5th edn, McGraw-Hill.

Dobler, D.W. and Burt, D.N. (1996). *Purchasing and Supply Management*, 6th edn, McGraw-Hill.

Drucker, P. (1990a). *The New Realities*, Mandarin.

Drucker, P. (1990b). 'The Emerging Theory of Manufacturing', *Harvard Business Review*, May–June, pp. 94–102.

DTI. (1988). *Competitive Manufacturing – A Practical Approach to the Development of a Manufacturing Strategy*, IFS Kempston.

DTI. (1989). *Managing into the '90s*.

DTI. (1991). *Purchasing: A Competitive Business*.

DTI. (1991). *Building a Purchasing Strategy*.

DTI. (1991). *Logistics and Supply Chain Management*.

DTI. (1991). *Managing your Purchasing Operation*.

DTI. (1991). *Getting the Best from Your Suppliers*.

DTI. (1991). *Better Value for Money from Purchasing*.

DTI. (1991). *Aiming for World Class Manufacturing*, Department of Trade and Industry.

DTI. (1995). *Logistics and Supply Chain Management*.

DTI. (1995). *Supplying the Challenge*.

DTI. (1995). *Efficiency and Value in Purchasing and Supply*.

DTI. (1995). *Getting the Best from your Supply Partners*.

Dwyer, F.R., Schurr, P.H. and Oh, S. (1987). 'Developing Buyer-Seller Relationships', *Journal of Marketing*, Vol. 51, April, pp. 11–27.

Dyer, J.H. and Ouchi, W.G. (1993). 'Japanese-Style Partnerships: Giving Companies a Competitive Edge', *Sloan Management Review*, Fall, pp. 51–63.

Eisenhardt, K.M. and Zbaracki, M.J. (1992). 'Strategic Decision Making', *Strategic Management Journal*, Vol. 13, Winter Special, pp. 17–37.

Elliott-Shircore, T.I. and Steele, P.T. (1985). 'Procurement Positioning Overview', *Purchasing and Supply Management*, December, pp. 23–6.

Ellram, L.M. (1990). 'The Supplier Selection Decision in Strategic Partnerships', *Journal of Purchasing and Materials Management*, Fall, pp. 8–14.

Eltis, W. and Fraser, D. (1992). 'The Contribution of Japanese Success to Britain and to Europe', *National Westminster Quarterly Review*, November, pp. 2–19.

Erridge, A. (1993). 'Competitive and Partnership Models and Public Procurement', Conference Paper at Purchasing and Supply Education Research Group 2nd Conference.

Erridge, A. (1995). *Managing Purchasing*, Butterworth/Heinemann.

Farmer, D.H. (1972). 'Source Decision-Making in the Multi-National Company Environment', *Journal of Purchasing*, Vol. 8, February, pp. 5–17.

Farmer, D.H. (1972). 'The Impact of Supply Markets on Corporate Planning', *Long Range Planning*, March, pp. 10–16.

Farmer, D.H. (1974). 'Corporate Planning and Procurement in Multi-National Firms', *Journal of Purchasing and Materials Management*, Vol. 10, No. 2, pp. 55–67.

Farmer, D.H. (1976). 'The Role of Procurement in Corporate Planning', *Purchasing and Supply*, November, pp. 44–6.

Farmer, D.H. (1978). 'Developing Purchasing Strategies', *Journal of Purchasing and Materials Management*, Fall, pp. 6–11.

Farmer, D. (1984). 'Competitive Analysis – Its Role in Purchasing', *Long Range Planning*, Vol. 17, No. 3, pp. 72–4.

Farmer, D. (1985). 'Organising for Purchasing', in Farmer, D. (ed.) *Purchasing Management Handbook*, pp. 59–83, Gower.

Farmer, D.H. and Taylor, B. (editors). (1975). *Corporate Planning and Procurement*, Heinemann.

Farmer, D. and Van Amstel, R.P. (1991). *Effective Pipeline Management*, Gower.

Farmer, D. and Van Weele, A. (eds.) (1995). *The Gower Handbook of Purchasing Management*, Gower.

Farrington, B. and Walters, D.W.F. (1994). *Managing Purchasing*, Chapman and Hall.

Fawcett, P., McLeish, R.E. and Ogden, I.D. (1992). *Logistics Management*, M & E Handbooks, Pitman Publishing.

Fernie, J. (1994). 'Quick Response: An International Perspective', *International Journal of Physical Distribution and Logistics Management*, Vol. 24, No. 6, pp. 38–46.

Ford, D. (1980). 'The Development of Buyer-Seller Relationships in Industrial Markets', *European Journal of Marketing*, Vol. 14, No. 5–6, pp. 339–54.

Ford, D. (editor). (1990). *Understanding Business Markets: Interaction, Relationships and Networks*, Academic Press.

Ford, D., Cotton, B., Farmer, D., Gross, A. and Wilkinson, I. (1993). 'Make-Or-Buy Decisions and their Implications', *Industrial Marketing Management*, Vol. 22, pp. 207–14.

Ford, D. and Farmer, D. (1986). 'Make or Buy – A Key Strategic Issue', *Long Range Planning*, Vol. 19, No. 5, pp. 54–62.

Forrester, J.W. (1961). *Industrial Dynamics*, MIT Press.

Fox, H.W. and Rink, D.R. (1979). 'Effective Implementation of Purchasing Operations', *International Journal of Physical Distribution and Materials Management*, Vol. 9, No. 1, pp. 62–73.

Fox, H.W. and Rink, D.R. (1977). 'Guidelines for Developing A Purchasing Portfolio', *Purchasing and Supply*, October, pp. 42–6.

Francis, A. (1992). 'The Process of National Industrial Regeneration and Competitiveness', *Strategic Management Journal*, Vol. 13, pp. 61–78.

Freeman, V.T. and Cavinato, J.L. (1990). 'Fitting Purchasing to the Strategic Firm: Frameworks, Processes, and Values', *Journal of Purchasing and Materials Management*, Winter, pp. 6–10.

Furlong, P., Lamont, F. and Cox, A. (1993). 'Competition or Partnership: CCT and EC Public Procurement Rules in The Single Market', Conference Paper at PSERG 2nd Conference.

Gadde, L.E. and Hakansson, H. (1993). *Professional Purchasing*, Routledge.

Gadde, L.E. and Hakansson, H. (1994). 'The Changing Role of Purchasing: Reconsidering Three Strategic Issues', *European Journal of Purchasing and Supply Management*, Vol. 1, No. 1, pp. 27–35.

Glaister, K. and Thwaites, K. (1993). 'Managerial Perception and Organizational Strategy', *Journal of General Management*, Vol. 18, No. 3, Summer, pp. 15–33.

Gore, C., Murray, K. and Richardson, B. (1992). *Strategic Decision-Making*, Cassell.

Grant, R.M. (1991). *Contemporary Strategy Analysis: Concepts, Techniques, Applications*, Blackwell.

Griffiths, M. (1996). *Law for Purchasing and Supply*, 2nd edn, Pitman Publishing.

Gronroos, C. (1994) 'From Marketing Mix to Relationship Marketing', *Management Decision*, Vol. 32, No. 2, pp. 4–20.

Haas, E.A. (1987). 'Breakthrough Manufacturing', *Harvard Business Review*, March–April, pp. 75–81.

Hahn, D. (1993). 'Strategic Management – Tasks and Challenges in the 1990s', *Long Range Planning*, Vol. 24, No. 4, pp. 26–39.

Hakansson, H. (editor). (1982). *International Marketing and Purchasing of Industrial Goods. An Interaction Approach*, John Wiley.

Hall, R.W. (1986). *Zero Inventories*, Dow-Jones Irwin.

Hamel, G. and Prahalad, C.K. (1994). *Competing for the Future: Breakthrough Strategies for Seizing Control of your Industry and Creating the Markets of Tomorrow*, Harvard Business School Press.

Hammer, M. (1990). 'Reengineering Work: Don't Automate, Obliterate', *Harvard Business Review*, July–August, pp. 104–112.

Handy, C. (1992). *The Age of Unreason*, 2nd edn, Century Business.

Hanson, P. (1993). 'Measuring Up', *Manufacturing Engineer*, August, pp. 185–7.

Harrison, A. (1993). *Just-In-Time Manufacturing in Perspective*, Prentice-Hall.

Harrison, A. and Storey, J. (1996). 'New Wave Manufacturing Strategies: Operational, Organisational and Human Dimensions', *International Journal of Operations and Production Management*, Vol. 16, No. 2, pp. 63–76.

Harrison, M. (1990). *Advanced Manufacturing Technology Management*, Pitman Publishing.

Harrison, M. (1993). *Operations Management Strategy*, Pitman Publishing.

Hayes, R.H. and Clark, K.B. (1985). 'Explaining Observed Productivity Differentials Between Plants: Implications for Operations', *Interfaces*, Vol. 15, No. 6, pp. 3–14.

Hayes, R.H. and Wheelwright, S.C. (1984). *Restoring Our Competitive Edge: Competing Through Manufacturing*, Wiley.

Hayes, R.H., Wheelwright, S.C. and Clark, K.B. (1988). *Dynamic Manufacturing: Creating the Learning Organization*, The Free Press.

Hax, A.C. (1991). 'Redefining the Concept of Strategy and the Strategy Formation Process', *Engineering Management Review*, Spring, pp. 19–24.

Hax, A.C. and Majluf, N.S. (1988). 'The Concept of Strategy and the Strategy Process', *Interfaces*, Vol. 18, No. 3, May–June, pp. 99–109.

Heinritz, S., Farrell, P.V., Giunipero, L. and Kolchin, M. (1991). *Purchasing: Principles and Applications*, Prentice-Hall.

Hill, R.W. and Hillier, T.J. (1977) *Organisational Buying Behaviour*, Macmillan.

Hill, T. (1991). *Production/Operations Management*, 2nd Edition, Prentice-Hall.

Hill, T. (1993a). *Manufacturing Strategy*, 2nd Edition, Macmillan.

Hill, T. (1993b). *The Essence of Operations Management*, Prentice-Hall.

Hill, T. (1994). *Market Driven Manufacturing*, Financial Times/Pitman Publishing.

Hines, P. (1992a). 'Studies in the East', *Logistics* (Supplement to *Purchasing and Supply Management*), February, pp. 22–5.

Hines, P. (1992b). 'Lessons from the West', *Logistics* (Supplement to *Purchasing and Supply Management*), May, pp. 13–15.

Hines, P. (1994). *Creating World Class Suppliers: Unlocking Mutual Competitive Advantage*, Financial Times/Pitman Publishing.

Hoffmann, K. and Kaplinsky, R. (1984). *Driving Force*, Westview Press.

Houlihan, J. (1988). 'Exploiting the Industrial Supply Chain', in Mortimer, J. (ed.) *Logistics in Manufacturing*, IFS Publications.

Howell, R.A. and Sakurai, M. (1992). 'Management Accounting (and Other) Lessons from the Japanese', *Management Accounting (USA)*, December, pp. 28–34.

Hunter, L., Beaumont, P. and Sinclair, D. (1996). 'A Partnership Route to Human Resource Management', *Journal of Management Studies*, Vol. 32, No. 2, pp. 235–57.

Hutchins, G. (1992). *Purchasing Strategies for Total Quality*, Business One: Irwin.

Innes, J. and Falconer, M. (1991). 'Managing with Activity Based Costing', *Professional Engineering*, July–August, pp. 20–1.

Jessop, D. and Morrison, A. (1994). *Storage and Supply of Materials*, 6th edn, Pitman Publishing.

Johansson, H.J., McHugh, P., Pendlebury, W.A. and Wheeler III, W.A. (1993). *Business Process Reengineering*, Wiley.

Johnson, G. and Scholes, K. (1988). *Exploring Corporate Strategy: Text and Cases*, 2nd edn, Prentice-Hall.

Johnson, G. and Scholes, K. (1993). *Exploring Corporate Strategy: Text and Cases*, 3rd edn, Prentice-Hall.

Johnson, H.J. and Kaplan, R.S. (1987). *Relevance Lost: The Rise and Fall of Management Accounting*, Harvard Business School Press.

Jones, D. (1992). 'The Procurement Control Systems Matrix', *Purchasing and Supply Management*, December, pp. 35–7.

Jones, D.T. (1992). 'Beyond the Toyota Production System: the Era of Lean Production', in Voss, C.A. (ed.) *Manufacturing Strategy – Process and Content*, pp. 189–210, Chapman and Hall.

Judd, S. (1993). 'Quality – the Key To World Class Performance', *CBI NEWS*, September, p. vii of *Manufacturing Bulletin*.

Juran, J.M. (1988). (ed.) *Quality Control Handbook*, McGraw-Hill.

Kanter, R.M. (1989). *When Giants Learn to Dance*, Unwin Hyman.

Kanter, R.M. (1994). 'Collaborative Advantage', *Harvard Business Review*, July–August, pp. 96–108.

Kaplan, R.S. (1984). 'Yesterday's Accounting Undermines Production', *Harvard Business Review*, July–August, pp. 95–101.

Kaplan, R.S. (1988). 'One System Isn't Enough', *Harvard Business Review*, January–February, pp. 61–6.

Kay, J. (1993). *Foundations of Corporate Success*, Oxford University Press.

Keough, M. (1993). 'Buying Your Way to the Top', *The McKinsey Quarterly*, No. 3, pp. 41–62.

Kinnie, N. and Staughton, R. (1994). 'The Problem of Implementing Manufacturing Strategy', in Storey, J. (ed.) *New Wave Manufacturing Strategies*, Paul Chapman Publishing.

Kiser, G.E. (1976). 'Elements of Purchasing Strategy', *Journal of Purchasing and Materials Management*, Fall, pp. 3–7.

Kolb, D.A. (1984). *Experiential Learning*, Prentice-Hall.

Krafcik, J.F. (1988). 'Triumph of the Lean Production System', *Sloan Management Review*, Fall, pp. 41–52.

Krafcik, J.F. (1989). 'A New Diet For Manufacturing', *Technology Review*, Vol. 92, Part 1, pp. 28–36.

Kraljic, P. (1983). 'Purchasing Must Become Supply Management', *Harvard Business Review*, September–October, pp. 109–17.

Kuhn, T.S. (1970). *The Structure of Scientific Revolutions*, 2nd edn, University of Chicago Press.

Kumpe, T. and Bolwijn, P.T. (1988). 'Manufacturing: The New Case for Vertical Integration', *Harvard Business Review*, March–April, pp. 75–81.

Lamming, R. (1993). *Beyond Partnership: Strategies for Innovation and Lean Supply*, Prentice-Hall.

Lamming, R. (1994). *A Review of the Relationships Between Vehicle Manufacturers and Suppliers*, DTI.

Lamming, R. and Cox, A. (eds.) (1994). *Strategic Procurement in the 1990s: Concepts and Cases*, Earlsgate Press.

Leenders, M.R. and Blenkhorn, D.L. (1988). *Reverse Marketing*, Free Press.

Lessem, R. (1991). *Total Quality Learning: Building a Learning Organisation*, Basil Blackwell.

Lewin, K. (1951). *Field Theory in Social Sciences*, Harper & Row.

Lorenz, K. (1993). 'In the Fast Lane', *The Sunday Times*, 8 August, Section 3, p. 3.

Lyne, C. (1996). 'Strategic Procurement In The New Local Government', *European Journal of Purchasing and Supply Management*, Vol. 2, No. 1, pp. 1–6.

MacBeth, D., Ferguson, N., Neil, G.C. and Baxter, L.F. (1989). 'Not Purchasing but Supply Chain Management', *Purchasing and Supply Management*, November, pp. 30–2.

MacBeth, D., Baxter, L., Ferguson, N. and Neil, G. (1990). *The Customer-Supplier Relationship Audit*, IFS Ltd.

MacBeth, D.K., Murphy, M.D., Ferguson, N. and Neil, G.C. (1993). 'Partnering Relationships: Barriers to Progress', Conference Paper at the Purchasing and Supply Education Research Group 2nd Conference.

MacBeth, D.K. and Ferguson, N. (1994). *Partnership Sourcing: An Integrated Supply Chain Approach*, Financial Times/Pitman Publishing.

Machinery and Production Engineering. (1990). 'Sub-contract Trend Makes More Sense', *Machinery and Production Engineering*, 15 February, pp. 108–113.

Merli, G. (1991). *Co-Makership: The New Supply Strategy for Manufacturers*, Productivity Press.

Miller, J.G. and Vollman, T.E. (1985). 'The Hidden Factory', *Harvard Business Review*, September–October, pp. 142–50.

Mills, J., Platts, K. and Gregory, M. (1995). 'A Framework for the Design of Manufacturing Strategy Processes: A Contingency Approach', *International Journal of Operations and Production Management*, Vol. 15, No. 4, pp. 17–49.

Mintzberg, H. (1987). 'Crafting Strategy', *Harvard Business Review*, July–August, pp. 66–75.

Mintzberg, H. (1990) 'The Design School: Reconsidering The Basic Premises of Strategic Management', *Strategic Management Journal*, Vol. 11, pp. 171–95.

Monczka, R.M. and Morgan, J.P. (1992). 'Strategic Sourcing Management', *Purchasing*, Part 1 – 18 June, pp. 52–5, Part 2 – 16 July, pp. 64–7, and Part 3 – 13 August, pp. 70–2.

Monczka, R.M., Trent, R.J. and Callahan, T.J. (1993). 'Supply Base Strategies To Maximize Supplier Performance', *International Journal of Physical Distribution And Logistics Management*, Vol. 23, No. 4, pp. 42–54.

Monczka, R. and Trent, R. (1995). *Purchasing and Sourcing Strategy: Trends and Implications*, CAPS Research Report.

Moody, P.E. (1992). 'Customer Supplier Integration: Why Being an Excellent Customer Counts', *Business Horizons*, July–August, pp. 52–7.

Moody, P. (1993). *Breakthrough Partnering*, Oliver Wight.

Moore, J.I. (1992). *Writers on Strategy and Strategic Management*, Penguin Books.

Morgan, M. (1993). 'Is ABC really a need, not an option?', *Management Accounting (UK)*, September, pp. 26–7.

Morgan, J.P. (1989). 'Are You Aggressive Enough For The 1990s?', *Purchasing*, 6 April, pp. 50–7.

Morgan, J.P. and Cayer, S. (1992). 'True Believers?', *Purchasing*, 13 August, pp. 49–57.

Morris, J. and Imrie, R. (1992). *Transforming Buyer-Supplier Relations*, Macmillan.

Morris, M.H. and Calantone, R.J. (1991). 'Redefining the Purchasing Function: An Entrepreneurial Perspective', *International Journal of Purchasing and Materials Management*, Fall, pp. 2–9.

National Economic Development Council (NEDC). (1990). *Developing Suppliers in Engineering*, London.

National Economic Development Council (NEDC). (1991). *The Experience of Nissan Suppliers: Lessons for the United Kingdom Engineering Industry*, London.

Nevem Working Group. (1989). *Performance Indicators in Logistics*, IFS Publications, UK.

New, C. (1992). 'World-class Manufacturing versus Strategic Trade-offs', *International Journal of Operations and Production Management*, Vol. 12, No. 6, pp. 19–31.

New, S. and Mitropoulos, I. (1996). 'Strategic Networks: morphology, epistemology and praxis', *International Journal of Operations and Production Management*, Vol. 15, No. 11, pp. 52–61.

Nishiguchi, T. (1993). *Strategic Industrial Sourcing: The Japanese Advantage*, Oxford University Press.

Nix, A., McCarthy, P. and Dale, B.G. (1992). 'The key issues in the development and use of Total Cost of Ownership Model', *2nd Conference of the Purchasing and Education Research Group*.

Nolan, A. (1993a). 'Purchasing Needs High Level Support', *Procurement Weekly*, 27 August.

Nolan, A. (1993b). 'Firms Miss Out', *Procurement Weekly*, 17 September.

Normann, R. and Ramirez, R. (1993). 'From Value Chain to Value Constellation: Designing Interactive Strategy', *Harvard Business Review*, July–August, pp. 65–77.

Oakland, J.S. (1993). *Total Quality Management*, 2nd edn, Butterworth/Heinemann.

Oates, D. (1993). 'Flat Pyramids: The Wave of the Future', *The Sunday Times*, Section 5, 28 March, p. 2.

Oliver, N. and Wilkinson, B. (1992). *The Japanization of British Industry*, 2nd edn, Blackwell.

Parkinson, S.T. and Baker, M.J., with Moller, K. (1986). *Organizational Buying Behaviour*, Macmillan.

Partnership Sourcing Ltd. (1992). *Making Partnership Sourcing Happen*.

Pascale, R.T and Athos, A.G. (1982). *The Art of Japanese Management*, Penguin Books.

Pender, R. (1993). 'Partnering for Profit', *Total Quality Management*, October, pp. 13–16.

Peters, T.J. (1988). *Thriving on Chaos*, Macmillan.

Peters, T.J. and Waterman, R.H. (1982). *In Search of Excellence*, Harper & Row.

Platts, K.W. and Gregory, M.J. (1992). 'Manufacturing Audit in the Process of Strategy Formulation', *International Journal of Operations and Production Management*, Vol. 10, No. 9, pp. 5–26.

Porter, A.M. (1992). 'Audits Under Fire', *Purchasing*, 5 November, pp. 50–5.

Porter, M.E. (1980). *Competitive Strategy: Techniques for Analyzing Industries and Competitors*, The Free Press.

Porter, M.E. (1985). *Competitive Advantage: Creating and Sustaining Superior Performance*, The Free Press.

Porter, M.E. (1987a). 'From Competitive Advantage to Corporate Strategy', *Harvard Business Review*, May–June, pp. 43–59.

Porter, M.E. (1987b). 'Corporate Strategy', *The Economist*, 23 May, pp. 22–8.

Porter, M.E. (1990a). *The Competitive Advantage of Nations*, The Free Press.

Porter, M.E. (1990b). 'The Competitive Advantage of Nations', *Harvard Business Review*, March–April, pp. 73–93.

Porter, M.E. (1991). 'Towards a Dynamic Theory of Strategy', *Strategic Management Journal*, Vol. 12, pp. 95–117.

Prahalad, C.K. and Hamel, G. (1990). 'The Core Competence of the Corporation', *Harvard Business Review*, May–June, pp. 71–91.

Primrose, P. (1993). 'Is Anything Really Wrong With Cost Management?', *Logistics Supplement* of *Purchasing and Supply Management*, February, pp. 19–21.

Primrose, P. (1993). 'Is Anything Really Wrong with Cost Management', *Logistics Supplement* of *Purchasing and Supply Management*, June, pp. 21–3.

Purchasing and Supply Lead Body. (1991). *Information Pack No. 2*.

Quayle, M.R. (1993). *Logistics: An Integrated Approach*, Tudor Publishing.

Rainnie, A. (1991). 'Just-in-Time, Sub-Contracting And The Small Firm', *Work, Employment and Society*, Vol. 5, No. 3, pp. 351–75.

Ramsey, J. (1988). 'The Product Purchase Life Cycle', *Purchasing and Supply Management*, October, pp. 22–4.

Ramsey, J. (1988). 'Pricing, Sourcing and Power', *Purchasing and Supply Management*, November, pp. 34–6.

Ramsey, J. (1990). 'Selection of Sourcing Strategies', *Purchasing and Supply Management*, May, pp. 19–23.

Ramsey, J. and Wilson, I. (1990). 'Sourcing/Contracting Strategy Selection', *International Journal of Operations and Production Management*, Vol. 10, No. 8, pp. 19–28.

Reck, R.F. and Long, B.G. (1988). 'Purchasing: A Competitive Weapon', *Journal of Purchasing and Materials Management*, Fall, pp. 2–8.

Rhys, G. (1990). 'The Motor Industry and the Balance of Payments', *The Royal Bank of Scotland Review*, pp. 11–25.

Richardson, J. (1993). 'Parallel Sourcing and Supplier Performance in the Japanese Automobile Industry', *Strategic Management Journal*, Vol. 14, pp. 339–50.

Ring, P.S. and Van de Ven, A.H. (1992). 'Structuring Cooperative Relationships Between Organizations', *Strategic Management Journal*, Vol. 13, pp. 483–98.

Rink, D.R. (1978). 'The Product Life Cycle: Vehicle For Fashioning a Purchasing Strategy', *International Journal of Physical Distribution and Materials Management*, Vol. 8, No. 4, pp. 200–14.

Robinson, P.J. and Faris, C.W. (1967). *Industrial Buying and Creative Marketing*, Allyn and Bacon.

Sako, M. (1992). *Prices, Quality and Trust*, Cambridge University Press.

Saunders, M.J., Gore, M., Jones, C. and Salt, D. (1988). 'Strategic and Policy Considerations', *Purchasing and Supply Management*, April, pp. 34–5.

Schendel, D.E. and Hofer, C.W. (1979). *Strategic Management: A New View of Business Policy and Planning*, Little Brown & Co.

Schonberger, R.J. (1982). *Japanese Techniques: Nine Hidden Lessons in Simplicity*, Free Press.

Servan-Schreiber, J. (1969). *The American Challenge*, Pelican Books.

Simon, H.A. (1961). *Administrative Behavior*, Macmillan.

Simon, H.A. (1979). 'Rational Decision Making in Business Organizations', *American Economic Review*, Vol. 69, pp. 493–513.

Skinner, W. (1969). 'Manufacturing – Missing Link in Corporate Strategy', *Harvard Business Review*, May–June, pp. 136–45.

Skinner, W. (1992). *Missing the Links in Manufacturing Strategy*, in Voss, C.A. (ed.) *Manufacturing Strategy – Process and Content*, pp. 12–25, Chapman and Hall.

Slack, N., Chambers, S., Harland, C., Harrison, A. and Johnston, R. (1995). *Operations Management*, Pitman Publishing.

Southey, P. (1993). 'Pitfalls to Partnering in the UK', Conference Paper, at the Purchasing and Supply Education Research Group 2nd Conference.

Spekman, R.E. (1985). 'Competitive Procurement Strategies: Building Strength and Reducing Vulnerability', *Long Range Planning*, Vol. 18, No. 1, pp. 94–9.

Spekman, R.E. (1988). 'Strategic Supplier Selection: Understanding Long-Term Buyer Relationships', *Business Horizons*, July–August, pp. 75–81.

Stacey, R.D. (1996). *Strategic Management and Organisational Dynamics*, 6th edn, Pitman Publishing.

Stalk Jr., G.H. and Hout, T.M. (1990). *Competing Against Time: How Time Based Competition is Re-shaping Global Markets*, Free Press.

Stevens, G.C. (1989). 'Integrating the Supply Chain', *International Journal of Physical Distribution and Materials Management*, Vol. 19, No. 8, pp. 3–8.

Stevens, J. (1978). *Measuring Purchasing Performance*, Business Books.

Storey, J. (ed.) (1994). *New Wave Manufacturing Strategies*, Paul Chapman Publishing.

Stuart, F.I. and Mueller, P. (1994). 'Total Quality Management and Supplier Partnerships: A Case Study', *International Journal of Purchasing and Materials Management*, Winter, pp. 14–20.

Stuckey, J. and White, D. (1993). 'When and When Not to Vertically Integrate', *Sloan Management Review*, Spring, pp. 71–83.

Sweeney, M.T. (1991). 'Towards a Unified Theory of Strategic Manufacturing Management', *International Journal of Operations Management*, Vol. 11, No. 8, pp. 6–22.

Syson, R. (1989). 'The Revolution in Purchase', *Purchasing and Supply Management*, September, pp. 16–21.

Syson, R. (1992). *Improving Purchase Performance*, Pitman Publishing.

Taylor, B. (1986). 'Corporate Planning for the 1990s: New Frontiers', *Long Range Planning*, Vol. 19, No. 6, pp. 13–18.

Thoburn, J.T. and Takashima, M. (1993). 'Improving British Industrial Performance: Lessons from Japanese Subcontracting', *National Westminster Bank Quarterly Review*, February.

Thoburn, J.T. and Takashima, M. (1992). *Industrial Subcontracting in the UK and Japan*, Avebury.

Thomas, R. and Oliver, N. (1991). 'Component Supplier Patterns in the UK Motor Industry', *International Journal of Management Science*, Vol. 19, No. 6, pp. 609–16.

Thompson, J.L. (1993). *Strategic Management: Awareness and Change*, 2nd edn, Chapman and Hall.

Thomson, P. (1992). 'Public Sector Management in a Period of Radical Change: 1979–1992', *Public Money & Management*, July–September.

Towill, D.R. (1992). 'Supply Chain Dynamics – the Change Engineering Challenge of the Mid 1990s', *Proceedings of the Institution of Mechanical Engineers*, Vol. 206, pp. 233–45.

Towill, D. and Naim, M. (1993). 'Partnership Sourcing', *Purchasing and Supply Management*, July, pp. 38–42.

Trevor, T. and Christie, I. (1988). *Manufacturers and Suppliers in Britain & Japan*, Policy Studies Institute.

Tricker, R.I. (1989). 'The Management Accountant as Strategist', *Management Accounting*, December, pp. 26–9.

Tse, K.K. (1985). *Marks and Spencer*, Pergamon.

Turnbull, P. (1986). 'The Japanization of Production and Industrial Relations at Lucas Electrical', *Industrial Relations Journal*, Vol. 17, No. 3, pp. 193–206.

Turnbull, P.W. and Cunningham, M.T. (eds.) (1981). *International Marketing and Purchasing*, Macmillan.

Van Weele, A. (1994). *Purchasing Management: Analysis, Planning and Control*, Chapman and Hall.

Van Weele, A. and Rozemeijer, F. (1996). *Revolution in Purchasing*, Philips Electronics.

Venkatesan, R. (1992). 'Strategic Sourcing: To Make Or Not To Make', *Harvard Business Review*, November–December, pp. 98–107.

Venkatraman, N. (1994). 'IT-Enabled Business Transformation: From Automation to Business Scope Redefinition', *Sloan Management Review*, Winter, pp. 75–87.

Vollman, T.E., Berry, W.L. and Whybark, D.C. (1992). *Manufacturing Planning and Control Systems*, 3rd edn, Irwin.

Vollmann, T.E., Cordon, C. and Raabe, H. (1995). 'Supply Chain Management', *Financial Times*, Mastering Management Series, No. 8, 5 December, pp. 13–14.

Voss, C.A. (1988). 'Integration of JIT and MRP – The Japanese Experience', *Proceedings of the 23rd European Conference of Production and Inventory Control*, pp. 209–21. BPICS.

Voss, C.A. (1995). 'Alternative Paradigms for Manufacturing Strategy', *International Journal of Operations and Production Management*, Vol. 15, No. 4, pp. 5–16.

Voss, C. (ed.) (1987). *Just in Time Manufacture*, IFS Publications.

Walsh, K. (1995). *Public Services and Market Mechanisms: Competition, Contracting and The New Public Management*, Macmillan.

Watts, C.A., Kim, K.Y. and Hahn, C.K. (1992). 'Linking Purchasing to Corporate Competitive Strategy', *International Journal of Purchasing and Materials Management*, Fall, pp. 2–8.

Weber, C.A. and Ellram, L.M. (1992). 'Supplier Selection Using Multi-objective Programming: A Decision Support System Approach', *International Journal of Physical Distribution and Logistics Management*, Vol. 22, No. 2, pp. 3–14.

Webster, Jnr., F.E. and Wind, Y. (1972). *Organisational Buying Behaviour*, Prentice-Hall.

Wells, P. and Rawlinson, M. (1994) *The New European Automobile Industry*, St Martin's Press.

Wheatley, M. (1993). 'The Stamp Of World Class', *Management Today*, November, pp. 88–127.

Wheelwright, S.C. and Clark, K.B. (1992) 'Competing through Development Capability in a Manufacturing-based Organization', *Business Horizons*, July–August.

Wickens, P.D. (1993). 'Lean Production and Beyond: The System, its Critics and the Future', *Human Resource Management Journal*, Vol. 3, No. 4, pp. 75–89.

Wiener, M. (1981). *English Culture and the Decline of the Industrial Spirit*, Penguin.

Williamson, O.E. (1975). *Markets and Hierarchies*, Free Press.

Williamson, O.E. (1979). 'Transaction Cost Economics: The Governance of Contractual Relations', *Journal of Law and Economics*, Vol. 22, October, pp. 223–61.

Womack, J.P., Jones, D.T. and Roos, D. (1990). *The Machine that Changed the World: The Triumph of Lean Production*, Rawson Associates: Macmillan.

Womack, J.P. and Jones, D.T. (1994). 'From Lean Production to the Lean Enterprise', *Harvard Business Review*, March–April, pp. 93–103.

Womack, J.P. and Jones, D.T. (1996a). *Lean Thinking: Banish Waste and Create Wealth in Your Corporation*, Simon & Schuster.

Womack, J.P. and Jones, D.T. (1996b). 'Beyond Toyota: How to Root out Waste and Pursue Perfection', *Harvard Business Review*, September–October, pp. 148–58.

Wood, S. (ed.). (1989). *The Transformation of Work*, Unwin Hyman.

INDEX